Mens Rea in EU Antitrust Law

International Competition Law Series

VOLUME 85

Editor

In its series editor, Alastair Sutton, Kluwer is fortunate to engage and benefit from the experience and expertise of one of the world's outstanding authorities on European Union and international economic law.

Introduction

In their efforts to regulate competition in an increasingly complex business environment, competition authorities face a daunting task. The European Commission and Courts, as well as national courts and legislatures, policymakers, and regulators, are constantly proposing, enacting, reviewing, and enforcing new legal measures, often addressing novel situations. Every industry and service is affected.

Contents/Subjects

With many titles currently available and new ones appearing regularly, the series' coverage includes detailed analyses of relevant legislation and case law in major global trading jurisdictions, defences used in cases involving the digital network economy, state aid cases, enforcement methodologies and a great deal more.

Objective & Readership

The purpose of Kluwer's International Competition Law Series is to follow the ever-changing contours of this dynamic area of the law, keeping the practice in sharp focus so that practising lawyers (including in-house counsel) and academics can be assured of the most up-to-date guidance and sources, in the widest possible range of applications.

The titles published in this series are listed at the end of this volume.

Mens Rea in EU Antitrust Law

When Intentions Matter

Jan Blockx

Wolters Kluwer

Published by:
Kluwer Law International B.V.
PO Box 316
2400 AH Alphen aan den Rijn
The Netherlands
E-mail: international-sales@wolterskluwer.com
Website: lrus.wolterskluwer.com

Sold and distributed in North, Central and South America by:
Wolters Kluwer Legal & Regulatory U.S.
7201 McKinney Circle
Frederick, MD 21704
United States of America
Email: customer.service@wolterskluwer.com

Sold and distributed in all other countries by:
Air Business Subscriptions
Rockwood House
Haywards Heath
West Sussex
RH16 3DH
United Kingdom
Email: international-customerservice@wolterskluwer.com

ISBN 978-94-035-2353-8

e-Book: ISBN 978-94-035-2354-5
web-PDF: ISBN 978-94-035-2355-2

Table of Contents

List of Abbreviations

AG	Advocate General
CFI	Court of First Instance
CJEU	Court of Justice of the European Union (prior to the Treaty of Lisbon: European Court of Justice)
EC	Treaty Establishing the European Community
ECLI	European Case Law Identifier
ECHR	European Convention on Human Rights
ECR	European Court Reports
ECSC	European Coal and Steel Community
ECtHR	European Court of Human Rights
EEC	Treaty Establishing the European Economic Community
NCA	National Competition Authority
OJ	Official Journal of the European Union
TFEU	Treaty on the Functioning of the European Union

Acknowledgements

This book would not have been possible without the many professional and private chances its author received. Chief among these was the willingness of Anne-Marie Van den Bossche to accept a middle-aged lawyer as a researcher in her team at the Faculty of Law of the University of Antwerp in 2016. The trust she gave me at that time and throughout the writing process has given me the space and time to conceive this book.

I have also benefitted from the guidance of Gert Straetmans and, in particular, from his comments on advanced versions of the draft in 2019. Steven Dewulf provided a much-needed critical review of the criminal law sections of the text, where I was most out of my depth. Further reviews by Jacques Bourgeois, Nathan Cambien and Okeoghene Odudu have helped my own thinking and therefore the argumentation on various points. Finally, Henri Swennen has provided not only invaluable comments on earlier drafts but also welcome distractions on all sorts of academic and unacademic topics, often together with Stéphanie De Somer.

Too numerous to mention are the family members, friends and other acquaintances from within the field of European competition law and outside of it, whose company, understanding and support I have enjoyed while writing this book. However, I cannot fail to mention my wife, Sophia, who not merely improved this book but without whom it could simply not have been written.

Introduction

> Every individual ... intends only his own gain, and he is in this, as in many other cases, led by an invisible hand to promote an end which was no part of his intention.
>
> Smith, *The Wealth of Nations*, IV (II)

1 There are not many more famous and certainly influential words in economics than those of Adam Smith cited above. While the statement is made in the context of restrictions on imports, the 'invisible hand' is often interpreted in a broader sense by reference to another statement at the beginning of this masterpiece, namely that '[i]t is not from the benevolence of the butcher, the brewer, or the baker, that we expect our dinner, but from their regard to their own interest'.[1] The metaphor of the invisible hand then conveys the idea, so fundamental for market operation, that everyone's regard for their self-interest may contribute to the wealth of all market participants. The corollary of this is, of course, that to determine what is good for the community as a whole, one should make abstraction of the 'good' or 'bad' intentions of the market participants: the most egotistic intentions may well yield the best results. What matters for economic welfare then are the effects of conduct, not the intentions of economic actors.

2 Under an economic approach to competition law, it would thus appear that the intentions of the undertakings involved should play no role: what matters is the result, i.e. whether their conduct tended to restrict competition or not. The effects-based approach to European competition law that has been in vogue for the last two decades favours such a disinterested, objective assessment of conduct under the antitrust rules.

3 On the other hand, there is also a movement towards the moralization of competition law in Europe, with ever-increasing fines, increased criminalization (of course only at the Member State level) and stigmatization of offenders, in particular cartelists and dominant undertakings abusing their position. This raises a question which is at the heart of this treatise: how can such moralization of competition law take place while the tools for antitrust analysis are meant to become increasingly objectified?

1. A Smith, *An inquiry into the nature and causes of the wealth of nations*, Book I, Chapter II (first published 1776, Encyclopaedia Britannica 1952) 7.

4 At the same time, as an experienced practitioner, I have the impression that the allegedly objective effects-based and more economic approach to antitrust enforcement may be reaching its limits. It seems to be just as true for economists as for lawyers that if you get four of them in a room, you will get four different opinions. The increased use of economic analysis in competition cases means that all parties on all sides use more economists, but whether the outcome is therefore always better seems hard to say.

5 An alternative approach could draw inspiration from a traditional element of criminal offences, *mens rea*. The guilty mind or blameworthiness of persons breaking the law has for a long time been an important element in the determination of whether persons should be punished for criminal violations. What role does this element play in EU competition law and more specifically EU antitrust law?[2]

6 This question naturally breaks down along the is/ought divide.[3] First, what role does *mens rea* play in positive EU antitrust law, i.e. in EU antitrust law as it currently stands, with the current legislation and the case law up to now? This question is dealt with in Chapters 2-4. Second, what role should *mens rea* play in EU antitrust law, if we want to improve it? This is the question Chapter 5 attempts to answer.

7 In order to set the scene, Chapter 1 first describes in more detail what is meant by the notion of *mens rea* outside of the field of European antitrust law. It focuses on the role of *mens rea* in the criminal law in France, Germany and England and Wales, making occasional excursions to the criminal law of other jurisdictions, to (the limited scope of) European criminal law, to the European Convention on Human Rights (ECHR) and to civil law. In this way, the different types of *mens rea* (such as intent, recklessness and negligence) are clarified and the role which *mens rea* evidence plays become clear. Also, more specific topics are discussed such as *mens rea* in a corporate context and the relationship with ignorance of law. As part of this first chapter, the role of *mens rea* evidence in United States (US) antitrust law is analysed, under both section 1 and section 2 of the Sherman Act.

8 Chapter 2 analyses the role of *mens rea* evidence under the substantive law of Article 101 of the Treaty on the Functioning of the European Union (TFEU). It describes how the notion of the 'meeting of minds' is relevant to the determination of whether there is an agreement or concerted practice, and also how the intentions of undertakings are relevant in determining their participation in an infringement. Subsequently, the case law on the role of intentions in the determination of the object of an agreement or

2. With their notification procedure and *ex ante* control, the two other areas of European competition law, merger control and state aid, are less comparable to criminal procedures. That does not mean that *mens rea* elements do not play a role in the assessment of mergers and state aid. For mergers in particular, internal documents reflecting the strategy of the undertakings concerned are increasingly important in the EU (as they have been for many years in the US). The analysis of the role of *mens rea* under the EU Merger Regulation and in state aid cases is, however, beyond the scope of this treatise.
3. Or, as it is customary to say in some European jurisdictions: *de lege lata* and *de lege ferenda*.

concerted practice is discussed. The chapter concludes with some words on the role of *mens rea* evidence under Article 101(3) TFEU.

9 Chapter 3 analyses the role of *mens rea* evidence under the substantive law of Article 102 TFEU. After a brief discussion of the role of such evidence in the context of the determination of a dominant position, most of this chapter is devoted to describing the case law on the notion of abuse. The role of intentions is discussed in single market abuses, such as predatory pricing and exclusivity agreements and rebates, in multima-rket abuses such as tying, refusal to supply and margin squeeze, and in the abuse of regulatory process and non-exclusionary abuses.

10 Chapter 4 discusses the role of *mens rea* evidence in the enforcement of the EU antitrust rules. This involves discussing its role in the two notions common to Articles 101 and 102 TFEU, namely the notions of 'undertaking' and of 'effect on trade between the Member States'. However, most of this chapter is devoted to the role of *mens rea* in the determination of the fines for antitrust breaches and therefore whether intention or negligence are relevant here as well. A discussion on the role of ignorance and awareness of illegality concludes this chapter.

11 After the three descriptive Chapters 2-4, Chapter 5 evaluates the role of *mens rea* evidence from a normative perspective. Five arguments in the literature against the use of *mens rea* evidence are discussed as well as arguments for the use of such evidence both in determining whether an antitrust infringement took place and how it should be punished.

12 Note that the words intent and intention are used interchangeably throughout the text below.[4] Case law and decisions have been reviewed up to 1 March 2020.

4. As opposed to what is stated by PL Parcu and ML Stasi, 'The role of intent in the assessment of conduct under Article 102 TFEU' in PL Parcu, G Monti and M Botta (eds), *Abuse of dominance in EU competition law. Emerging trends* (Edward Elgar 2017) 12, 13, I do not think there is a significant difference between the two and this is also not borne out by *Black's Law Dictionary* which these authors refer to.

CHAPTER 1

The Concept of *Mens Rea*

Even a dog distinguishes between being stumbled over and being kicked

Holmes, *The Common Law*, Lecture I

§1.01 *MENS REA* IN EUROPEAN CRIMINAL LAW

13 Reading behaviour by reference to intentions comes natural to us (and, it seems, even to other mammals). It is therefore no surprise that the law frequently distinguishes between intentional and unintentional actions. Criminal law in particular is primarily concerned with actions done out of 'malice', as is reflected in the maxim *actus non facit reum nisi mens sit rea*, namely that an act can only be a cause for a (criminal) trial if the perpetrator also has a mindset which warrants such a trial.[5] The person committing an offence needs to have an 'evil' or at least a 'guilty' mind before she can be convicted of the offence. This principle is also formulated (in a somewhat narrower sense), in particular in the German literature where it is known as the *Schuldprinzip*,[6] as *nulla poena sine culpa* (no punishment without fault), along the lines of the Latin formulation of the principle of legality, i.e. *nulla poena sine lege* (no punishment without law).

5. *Actus non facit reum nisi mens sit rea* is often translated as 'There can be no crime without an evil mind.' However, the Latin word '*reus*' originally referred to a party to a trial and later to the accused or the debtor (the defendant in a trial) (*see* '*reus*' in CT Lewis and C Short, *A Latin Dictionary* (Clarendon Press 1879) <www.perseus.tufts.edu/hopper/text?doc=Perseus:text:1999.04.0059:entry=reus> accessed 25 October 2016; or '*reus*' in F Gaffiot, *Dictionnaire Illustré Latin-Français* (Hachette 1934) <micmap.org/dicfro/search/gaffiot/reus> accessed 25 October 2016). 'Guilty mind' or 'Evil mind' is therefore not a perfect translation of the original sense of *mens rea*, but it is nevertheless the translation that is common today and I will therefore use these terms here as well.
6. *See* C Roxin, *Strafrecht Algemeiner Teil* (Beck 2006) 91-92; T Weigend, 'Societas delinquere non potest? A German perspective' (2008) 6 Journal of International Criminal Justice 927, 939. *See also* § 46 of the German *Strafgesetzbuch*: '*Die Schuld des Täters ist Grundlage für die Zumessung der Strafe*' ['*The guilt of the offender is the basis for sentencing*'].

14 For example, murder is commonly defined as intentional killing, i.e. the killing of a person (*actus reus*) accompanied by a *mens rea* which consists in the intention to kill (*animus necandi*). The French *Code pénal*, for example, defines murder as 'willingly' killing a person.[7] The English draft Criminal Code[8] states that a person is guilty of murder 'if he causes the death of another (a) intending to cause death; or (b) intending to cause serious personal harm and being aware that he may cause death'.[9] While the definition of murder ('*Totschlag*' – § 212 of the *Strafgesetzbuch*) under German law does not explicitly include the intent to kill, § 15 of the German *Strafgesetzbuch* provides that, unless the law provides otherwise, only intentional conduct attracts criminal liability,[10] so this also applies to murder.[11]

15 Similarly, theft is commonly defined as the taking of someone else's property (*actus reus*) with the intention to deprive the owner of his property (*animus furandi*). The German *Strafgesetzbuch* requires 'the intention of unlawfully appropriating the object for himself or a third person'.[12] The English draft Criminal Code states that a person is guilty of theft 'if he dishonestly appropriates property belonging to another, intending to deprive the other permanently of it'.[13] While the definition of theft in the French *Code pénal* merely requires that someone else's property is taken 'fraudulently',[14] the case law requires that the perpetrator has 'the intention to behave – even if only momentarily – as the owner of the property belonging to someone else'.[15]

16 Other terms than *mens rea* have been used to refer to the mental element that is necessary for an offence. These include the Latin terms '*dolus*' and '*culpa*', although these are sometimes used to refer to different forms of *mens rea* (namely 'intention' and 'negligence' respectively – *see* further below). 'Culpability' is also often used in the

7. *See* Article 221-1 of the French *Code pénal* of 1994: '*Le fait de donner volontairement la mort à autrui constitue un meurtre.*' *See also* Article 295 of the French *Code pénal* of 1810: '*L'homicide commis volontairement est qualifié meurtre.*'
8. The draft Criminal Code was created by a Criminal Code team at the Law Commission and aimed to codify the common law and on some points also modernize it. *See* the introduction to this project on the Law Commission's website: <https://www.lawcom.gov.uk/project/legislating-the-criminal-code/> accessed 6 March 2018.
9. Clause 54(1) of the draft Criminal Code Bill of the Law Commission of 1989.
10. § 15 of the German *Strafgesetzbuch*: '*Strafbar ist nur vorsätzliches Handeln, wenn nicht das Gesetz fahrlässiges Handeln ausdrücklich mit Strafe bedroht.*'
11. Note that § 211 *Strafgesetzbuch* also defines the more serious crime of '*Mord*' if the murder is done out of certain base motives. *See* para. 72 below.
12. § 242 of the German *Strafgesetzbuch*: '*Wer eine fremde bewegliche Sache einem anderen in der Absicht wegnimmt, die Sache sich oder einem Dritten rechtswidrig zuzueignen, wird mit Freiheitsstrafe bis zu fünf Jahren oder mit Geldstrafe bestraft.*'
13. Clause 140 of the draft Criminal Code Bill of the Law Commission of 1989.
14. *See* Article 311-1 of the French *Code pénal* of 1994: '*Le vol est la soustraction frauduleuse de la chose d'autrui.*' *See also* Article 379 of the French *Code pénal* of 1810: '*Quiconque a soustrait frauduleusement une chose qui ne lui appartient pas, est coupable de vol.*'
15. F Desportes and F Le Gunehec, *Droit pénal général* (Economica 2009) 438: '*l'intention de se comporter – serait-ce de façon momentanée – comme le propriétaire de la chose appartenant à autrui*' with references to the case law.

US[16] and '*culpabilité*' in France,[17] both obviously derived from the Latin *culpa*. 'Fault' ('*faute*' in French) is also used (although that term may also have the narrower meaning of negligence).[18] In particular, in continental literature, the mental element is sometimes referred to as the 'subjective'[19] or 'intellectual'[20] element.

17 *Mens rea* should, however, be distinguished from criminal responsibility.[21] Indeed, the criminal law only applies to individuals to the extent that they are criminally responsible for their actions. If they are not so responsible, for example because of force majeure or insanity or their young age, their actions can simply not be attributed to them and they are therefore not criminally responsible. Even for strict liability offences (where there is no *mens rea* requirement), the defence that one is not criminally responsible is therefore available since the question of criminal responsibility logically precedes the question of *mens rea*.[22]

18 A number of EU legislative instruments and the case law of the Court of Justice of the European Union (CJEU) make reference to *mens rea* requirements (and, in particular, intention and negligence) and I will make reference to some of them below. The notion of *mens rea* under EU criminal law has been explored by other scholars in the past, including in an attempt to construct a *Corpus Juris*, a unified set of penal rules, applicable to fraud against the financial interests of the European Union.[23]

---

16. *See* section 2.02 of the Model Penal Code developed by the American Law Institute in 1962 to help US states to revise and codify their criminal law.
17. *See*, for example, R Garraud, *Traité théorique et pratique du droit pénal français* (Recueil Sirey 1913) 553ff.
18. *See* clause 18 of the draft Criminal Code Bill of the Law Commission of 1989; F Desportes and F Le Gunehec, *Droit pénal général* (Economica 2009) 423.
19. *See* J Blomsma, *Mens rea and defences in European criminal law* (Intersentia 2012) 43 which refers to Dutch and German law.
20. *See* F Desportes and F Le Gunehec, *Droit pénal général* (Economica 2009) 423. In French also '*élément moral*' is used (*see* R Garraud, *Traité théorique et pratique du droit pénal français* (Recueil Sirey 1913) 556; F Desportes and F Le Gunehec, *Droit pénal général* (Economica 2009) 423), but 'moral' in French does not only mean 'relating to morality' but also 'mental'. Viewing the subjective element as relating to morality is controversial in the literature. *See* J Blomsma, *Mens rea and defences in European criminal law* (Intersentia 2012), who on page 35 states that 'the different standards of *mens rea* reflect a different moral judgment on the defendant and his conduct' but at the same time asserts on page 75: 'The EU concept of *dolus* should have no moral connotations.' *See also* HLA Hart, 'Prolegomenon to the principles of punishment' in HLA Hart, *Punishment and responsibility: essays in the philosophy of law* (OUP 1970) 1, 14, although he seems to confuse *mens rea* with criminal responsibility in this text.
21. In French '*imputabilité*' (*see*, for example, J Pradel, *Droit pénal général* (Cujas 2016) 427-456); in German '*Verantwortlichkeit*', '*Ansprechbarkeit*' or '*Schuldfähigkeit*' (*see*, for example, C Roxin, *Strafrecht Algemeiner Teil* (Beck 2006) 847ff. A Ashworth, *Principles of criminal law* (OUP 2006) sees this as 'negative fault' (202-248), as distinguished from 'positive fault', by which he means *mens rea* (157-201).
22. J Pradel, *Droit pénal général* (Cujas 2016) therefore discusses '*imputabilité*' (427-456) before '*culpabilité*' (456-482). *See also* P Murphy (ed.), *Blackstone's Criminal Practice* (Blackstone 2001) 66.
23. M Delmas-Marty (ed.), *Corpus juris introducing penal provisions for the purpose of the financial interests of the European Union* (Economica 1997). *See*, for other discussions of *mens rea* in European criminal law, for example: J Blomsma, *Mens rea and defences in European criminal law* (Intersentia 2012) and A Klip, *European criminal law. An integrative approach* (Intersentia 2016) 218-224.

19 But EU criminal law is still fairly limited in scope. Indeed, only since the 2009 Treaty of Lisbon is there an explicit legal basis for the EU's legislative competence in criminal matters in Article 83 TFEU.[24] The basic notions and principles of EU criminal law largely depend on the criminal law traditions of the Member States. These traditions will therefore also guide this survey of the notion of *mens rea*. I will focus here on the criminal law of France, Germany and the United Kingdom (UK) (England and Wales) as the three largest Member States and those with the largest influence on the legal thinking concerning EU law.[25] US law will also be referred to because of its shared common law tradition with English law and its influence on EU law (and in particular EU competition law). The purpose of the discussion of the notion of *mens rea* in these jurisdictions is not to arrive at a full-fledged comparative analysis. Rather my aim is to identify some key principles which can then be used in the next four chapters to determine whether and how *mens rea* does and should play a role in EU antitrust law.

[A] The Degrees of *Mens Rea*

20 The literature on *mens rea* is vast. The human mind is still largely a mystery, and this perhaps explains the multiple attempts that have been made to categorize what a 'guilty mind' is.[26] The focus of most writings has been on the 'degrees' or 'types' of *mens rea*, i.e. the intensity of the mental state that creates liability for an offence. Distinguishing between the various possible relevant states is a somewhat scholastic exercise[27] to which I here only want to add a minor gloss by pointing to the three main dimensions along which the degrees of *mens rea* are usually understood: (i) willing, (ii) knowing and (iii) normativity. The different permutations of these three dimensions allow me to discuss the degrees of *mens rea* which are identified in England and Wales, France and Germany (which are not identical).

[1] Willing and/or Knowing

21 The first two of these dimensions, (i) willing and (ii) knowing, are the most important ones in classical legal thinking.

---

24. For the situation prior to the Treaty of Lisbon, *see* A Klip, *European criminal law. An integrative approach* (Intersentia 2016) 185-190.
25. As of 31 January 2020, the UK has withdrawn from the European Union (so-called Brexit), but its future relationship with the EU had not been determined yet when this text was finalized. The influence of English law on European law may well change in the future, but its past influence is undeniable.
26. *See* FB Sayre, 'Mens rea' (1931) 45 Harvard law review 974, 974: 'No problem of criminal law is of more fundamental importance or has proved more baffling through the centuries than the determination of the precise mental element or *mens rea* necessary for crime.' *See also* SH Kadish, 'The decline of innocence' (1968) 26 Cambridge Law Journal 273, 273: 'The term "*mens rea*" is rivalled only by the term "jurisdiction" for the varieties of senses in which it has been used and for the quantity of obfuscation it has created.'
27. The multiple manifestations of intention have led some writers to reject attempts at scholastic classification. *See* R Garraud, *Traité théorique et pratique du droit pénal français* (Recueil Sirey 1913) 575.

22 Willing in particular is key to the prototypical form of *mens rea*, intention (in the narrow sense), i.e. the situation where the perpetrator clearly wanted the conduct and/or the result which is constitutive of an offence. For example, if murder is defined as intentional killing, this is usually understood as meaning that the perpetrator wanted the death of the victim (and, of course, committed the relevant *actus reus*, such as pulling the trigger). This state of mind of 'intention' ('*Absicht*' in German) is sometimes referred to by the Latin *dolus directus* (in French: '*dol direct*').

23 It is often said that the *mens rea* of intention is fulfilled, even if the criminal intention was not the sole or even primary intention of the perpetrator.[28] And this makes sense since the perpetrator will inevitably have other motives and objectives which determine his actions. But it also raises the question of how much the perpetrator must really want to engage in the criminal conduct or to achieve the criminal result: if it does not need to be his sole or even primary motive, is it sufficient that the perpetrator accepts it as the mere means or consequence of his primary intention?

24 The answer is yes: the fact that the perpetrator *knew* that he conducted the criminal conduct or that the criminal result would arise is sufficient *mens rea*. In other words, it is not necessary to show that the perpetrator actually wanted to engage in the criminal conduct or to achieve the result: it is sufficient to show that he knew with a great deal of certainty that he was conducting himself in a specific way or that the specific result would arise, in order to hold him criminally liable. It will therefore be sufficient that the perpetrator knew that his actions would cause the death of another person to conclude that he had the requisite *mens rea* for murder.[29] This requirement of knowledge or awareness (terms which I use interchangeably here) is sometimes referred to as *dolus indirectus* ('*dol indirect*' in French)[30] or as *dolus directus* of the second degree.[31]

25 One could see 'willing' and 'knowing' in some sense as communicating vessels.[32] If the perpetrator clearly knows that he is engaging in criminal conduct or that the criminal result will arise, it does not matter that he does not really want this conduct or

28. *See* C Roxin, *Strafrecht Algemeiner Teil* (Beck 2006) 440; J Blomsma, *Mens rea and defences in European criminal law* (Intersentia 2012) 82. Since J Bentham, *An introduction to the principles of morals and legislation* (first published 1780, Dover 2016) chapter VIII, 84, this issue is usually discussed under the heading 'oblique intent' in English law (*see*, for example, A Ashworth, *Principles of criminal law* (OUP 2006) 176).
29. As we have seen, this is in some way reflected in the definition of murder as proposed by the Law Commission in 1989: also the situation where the perpetrator caused the death of another person 'intending to cause serious personal harm and being aware that he may cause death' is considered to be murder (Clause 54(1)(b) of the draft Criminal Code Bill of the Law Commission of 1989).
30. J Blomsma, *Mens rea and defences in European criminal law* (Intersentia 2012) 69; J Pradel, *Droit pénal général* (Cujas 2016) 458-459. The term *dolus indirectus* is meant to express the idea that the perpetrator accepted the criminal conduct or result as a means towards his main objective.
31. C Roxin, *Strafrecht Algemeiner Teil* (Beck 2006) 436. R Garraud, *Traité théorique et pratique du droit pénal français* (Recueil Sirey 1913) 592 also refers to this as '*dol direct*'.
32. J Blomsma, *Mens rea and defences in European criminal law* (Intersentia 2012) 67.

result: if he is certain that it will happen, he must at least accept it. Similarly, if the perpetrator clearly wants to engage in the criminal conduct or to attain the criminal result, it does not matter that he believes the chances of this occurring to be quite slim: if there is the intention to kill, shooting someone to death is murder, even if the shot is fired from far away and so has a low chance of killing the victim.[33]

26 Dogmatic and legal difficulties arise when the perpetrator did not clearly want to engage in the prohibited conduct or to attain the prohibited result or did not clearly know that he engaged in the prohibited conduct or that the prohibited result would arise.

Intensity of knowing

27 The most problematic issue is the question of the level of knowledge, namely how certain the perpetrator needs to be that the result will ensue (or that he engages in the criminal conduct or that certain circumstances are present).

28 Knowledge in the criminal sense (*dolus indirectus* or *dolus directus* of the second degree) in principle requires that the perpetrator believes that it is certain or at least that there is a high degree of probability[34] that the result will ensue (or that he engages in the criminal conduct or that certain circumstances are present).

29 If, on the contrary, the perpetrator believes that there is a substantial or considerable risk (but no certainty) that the criminal result will ensue (or that he engages in the criminal conduct or that certain circumstances are present), he may be accused of recklessness or *dolus eventualis*, which may or may not be a sufficient state of mind for a certain offence. In the English draft Criminal Code, for example, recklessness is not sufficient to establish a conviction for murder, but it does allow a conviction for (the lesser offence of) manslaughter.[35] In Germany, however, if the perpetrator is aware that there is a significant risk that death will ensue, he can be convicted for murder on the basis of the theory of conditional intent (*'bedingte Vorsatz'* or *dolus eventualis*).[36]

30 Recklessness (a common law notion) and *dolus eventualis* (a civil law notion) therefore do not have exactly the same denotation. *Dolus eventualis* can only be established if the perpetrator has accepted the risk (that the result would occur),

33. P Murphy (ed.), *Blackstone's Criminal Practice* (Blackstone 2001) 21 and C Roxin, *Strafrecht Algemeiner Teil* (Beck 2006) 437. *See also* HLA Hart, 'Intention and punishment' in HLA Hart, *Punishment and responsibility: essays in the philosophy of law* (OUP 1970) 113, 121 and J Blomsma, *Mens rea and defences in European criminal law* (Intersentia 2012) 51: 'intended consequences are never too remote'. For an example of willing and knowing as communicating vessels in European criminal law, *see* C-72/11 *Afrasiabi* ECLI:EU:C:2011:874, paras 66-67.
34. J Blomsma, *Mens rea and defences in European criminal law* (Intersentia 2012) 72. C Roxin, *Strafrecht Algemeiner Teil* (Beck 2006) 445 refers to the 'highest degree of probability' [*'höchste Grade der Wahrscheinlichkeit'*]. P Murphy (ed.), *Blackstone's Criminal Practice* (Blackstone 2001) 21, 22 and 28 states that the perpetrator needs to be 'virtually certain'.
35. *See* Clause 55(c)(2) of the draft Criminal Code Bill of the Law Commission of 1989.
36. *See* C Roxin, *Strafrecht Algemeiner Teil* (Beck 2006) 445. Under French law, *'dol éventuel'* is usually considered a (aggravated) form of negligence. *See* J Pradel, *Droit pénal général* (Cujas 2016) 462 and 468.

whereas for recklessness this is not necessary: the mere fact that the perpetrator believes that there is a substantial risk means that he is reckless. In case the perpetrator believes that there is a substantial risk but he believes he can prevent it from materializing (or even tries to do so), he is still guilty of recklessness if the risk materializes, whereas he cannot be said to have acted with *dolus eventualis* (under civil law he may be guilty of conscious negligence though: *see* paragraph 33 below). It has been argued that recklessness therefore merely requires awareness, while *dolus eventualis* in addition requires the volitional element of acceptance (which can also be fulfilled by the indifference of the perpetrator).[37]

31 If the perpetrator believes that there is no or a negligible risk that the criminal result will ensue (or that he engages in the criminal conduct or that certain circumstances are present), he can merely be found to have been (unconsciously) negligent. Unconscious negligence is usually not sufficient *mens rea* for criminal liability,[38] unless a normative approach is followed (*see* below paragraphs 36-40).

Intensity of willing

32 The intensity of willing is much less debated in the literature, probably because of the influence of cognitive theories on intent. These argue that intention exists if the perpetrator continued to act despite the fact that he foresaw the possible consequences.[39] Willing is in those cases deduced from knowing. However, cognitive theories of intent have difficulty dealing with cases where the perpetrator somehow foresaw the criminal results and took precautions to avoid them but they nevertheless arose. In other words, when the perpetrator did not want the criminal results and even tried to avoid them, but they nevertheless arose because he was not careful enough, can he be held liable?

33 Such a situation is commonly described as conscious negligence (to differentiate it from the unconscious negligence discussed above) and often a basis for criminal liability.[40] The common law notion of recklessness also encompasses these situations.

Summary of willing and knowing

34 On the basis of the above explanations, the degrees of *mens rea* can be summarized in the following table where the rows express decreasing levels of willing and the columns decreasing levels of awareness.

37. J Blomsma, *Mens rea and defences in European criminal law* (Intersentia 2012) 117 and 134.
38. Most EU criminal legislation requires intention to hold a person liable for an offence. *See* A Klip, *European criminal law. An integrative approach* (Intersentia 2016) 220. And also under EU law, intention in principle requires awareness, *see* C-367/09 *SGS Belgium and Others* ECLI:EU:C:2010:648, para. 57.
39. J Blomsma, *Mens rea and defences in European criminal law* (Intersentia 2012) 127.
40. *See*, for example, J Pradel, *Droit pénal général* (Cujas 2016) 473 who considers it more serious than unconscious negligence.

	Certain knowledge	Consciousness of risk	Unconscious
Wanting	Intention		Unconscious negligence
Accepting	*Dolus indirectus*	*Dolus eventualis* (recklessness)	
Hoping/trying to avoid	X[1]	Conscious negligence (recklessness)	

1. This situation cannot arise: if the perpetrator is certain that he engages in criminal conduct or that criminal results will ensue, there is no point in trying to avoid this.

35 The grey shading in the table indicates the gravity of the state of mind: the darker, the more malicious the state of mind is considered to be. Offences with significant penalties will often require a particularly 'dark' state of mind. The French *Code pénal* of 1994 is fairly explicit on this. Under French law, there are three types of offences, '*crimes*', '*délits*' and '*contraventions*' and, according to Article 121-3 of the *Code penal*, '*crimes*' can only be committed intentionally, '*délit*' only intentionally, unless the law provides that negligence suffices.[41] For '*contraventions*', no *mens rea* is normally required (many of these are strict liability offences – *see* paragraphs 41ff. below).[42]

[2] Normativity

36 The above categories do not take into account the third dimension of *mens rea*, namely the fact that in some cases the law does not merely look at the actual state of mind of the perpetrator but also at a certain standard state of mind.

37 This normativity is particularly important if criminal liability is attributed to the perpetrator acting with unconscious negligence, i.e. to the actor that does not know that what he does is criminal conduct or is likely to yield criminal results. Purely based on that actor's 'willing' and 'knowing', no criminal liability can be attributed to him. If society considers that, despite this, the actor *should* have known that he engages in criminal conduct or that criminal results are likely to ensue, the law uses a normative concept of *mens rea*. The perpetrator can then be found guilty because he failed to act like a 'reasonable person', i.e. failed to comply with his 'duty of care'.

38 In criminal law, negligence is often (explicitly or implicitly) understood as 'gross' or 'serious' negligence.[43] Everyone makes mistakes, even the reasonable person, and therefore only mistakes that are sufficiently serious will attract criminal liability. What counts as sufficiently serious is therefore also defined normatively, although personal circumstances can be taken into account so that the standard against which the actor's

41. The French *Code pénal* of 1810 contained specific requirements of *mens rea* in relation to specific offences but did not enunciate such a general principle.
42. F Desportes and F Le Gunehec, *Droit pénal général* (Economica 2009) 479-482.
43. Article 121-3 of the French *Code pénal* of 1994 states in its fourth paragraph that, in case the perpetrator of a '*délit*' only indirectly caused the criminal result, he can only be held liable in case of a '*faute qualifié*'. *See also* WR LaFave and AW Scott, *Criminal law* (West 1986) 230ff.

conduct is assessed may take different forms.[44] This may be to the perpetrator's advantage or disadvantage. Particularly in a professional context, a stricter standard (requiring a higher level of care) will normally be applied. The standard for the professional will not be the reasonable ordinary man but the reasonable professional.[45]

39 Normativity is particularly relevant to attribute criminal liability for unconscious negligence, but normative elements can also play a role in case the perpetrator is aware of a risk.[46] Indeed, the perpetrator's awareness of a risk does not yet say anything about the chances he attributes to that risk or the harm that may flow from it. We have seen that English and German law come to different conclusions on whether recklessness or '*bedingte Vorsatz*' (*dolus eventualis*) is sufficient for a conviction for murder. It has been argued that one of the reasons for this is that they have a different conception of what a substantial risk is: while they both recognize the subjective aspects of the risk (in other words the perpetrator needs to foresee the chance of the risk occurring), they nevertheless give a different normative colouring to the risk. While the German notion of '*bedingte Vorsatz*' takes into account the objective chance of the risk occurring, the English notion of recklessness takes into account the objective harm done if the risk occurs, but for the assessment of the chance that the risk occurs, English law only takes into account subjective factors.[47]

40 This example shows that normativity is in fact a short cut through *mens rea*: normative elements reduce the assessment of the actual state of mind of the perpetrator to the assessment of certain standards of behaviour (or of knowledge or foresight). Normativity negates the actual state of mind of the perpetrator and can therefore also be said to be a substitute for *mens rea* (at least to the extent that normativity is relevant since it is often combined with elements of actual subjective knowing and wanting).[48]

44. Article 132-76 of the French *Code pénal* of 1994 requires that the assessment of negligence 'takes into account the nature of the missions and functions [of the perpetrator], his skills as well as the power and means which he had at his disposal' ['*compte tenu, le cas échéant, de la nature de ses missions ou de ses fonctions, de ses compétences ainsi que du pouvoir et des moyens dont il disposait*']. *See also* the CJEU in case C-308/06 *Intertanko* ECLI:EU:C:2008:312, para. 77 which defined 'serious negligence' within the meaning of Article 4 of Directive 2005/35 'as entailing an unintentional act or omission by which the person responsible commits a patent breach of the duty of care which he should have and could have complied with in view of his attributes, knowledge, abilities and individual situation'. However, in C-47/07 P *Masdar (UK) v Commission* ECLI:EU:C:2008:726, para. 90, the CJEU (in Grand Chamber) used this as a definition of negligence.
45. J Blomsma, *Mens rea and defences in European criminal law* (Intersentia 2012) 183.
46. J Blomsma, *Mens rea and defences in European criminal law* (Intersentia 2012) 111-112, 130, 137 and 142-143.
47. At least at the moment: up to 2003, the risk was also assessed in an objective manner. *See* P Murphy (ed.), *Blackstone's Criminal Practice* (Blackstone 2001) 23-24 and J Blomsma, *Mens rea and defences in European criminal law* (Intersentia 2012) 139.
48. *See* P Murphy (ed.), *Blackstone's Criminal Practice* (Blackstone 2001) 29 who points out that 'Some would exclude negligence from a discussion of *mens rea* on semantic grounds, i.e. on the basis that mens rea is concerned with states of mind and negligence is not a state of mind but is rather a failure to comply with the standards of the reasonable man.' However, this point does apply not only to negligence but also to recklessness when this is defined normatively (so-called objective recklessness or Caldwell recklessness). *See also* WR LaFave and AW Scott, *Criminal law* (West 1986) 212.

In those circumstances, the infringement of the standard can be viewed as simply part of the objective definition of the offence, so as one of the material elements of the *actus reus*.[49]

[3] Strict Liability

41 If no *mens rea* needs to be demonstrated to establish an offence, it is termed a 'strict liability' offence. For those offences, the mere fulfilment of the objective offence definition is sufficient to establish liability of the perpetrator (although the defences discussed in paragraph 17 above are available for such offences).

42 Strict liability offences are similar to offences requiring (normatively defined) negligence: in both cases, the assessment of the behaviour of the perpetrator takes place without reference to his subjective intentions or knowledge and merely by reference to objective norms. The difference is that in the case of a strict liability offence, the mere infringement of the norm is sufficient to create liability, whereas in the case of negligence, the perpetrator's behaviour is furthermore compared to certain abstract and general standards (although the breach of other norms can be indicative that the standard has not been complied with).[50]

43 The similarities between strict liability and negligence become apparent when comparing different legislative frameworks. Under German criminal law, there are no strict liability offences, but this appears to be compensated by a higher number of offences that can be committed out of negligence.[51] In England and Wales, however, strict liability is common for minor offences, while there are few offences defined in terms of negligence.[52] Under French law, the close relationship between strict liability and negligence became clear when strict liability was abolished for '*délits*' (offences of medium severity with possible imprisonment of up to ten years) in 1994: this led the courts to more easily find negligence for such offences.[53]

44 The CJEU has held that strict liability offences are compatible with European law,[54] although the absence of *mens rea* needs to be taken into account in the penalty for the

49. This is the position taken by C Roxin, *Strafrecht Algemeiner Teil* (Beck 2006) 1063-1064 on offences committed out of negligence under German law.
50. And in those circumstances negligence liability seems to be reduced to strict liability. *See* J Blomsma, *Mens rea and defences in European criminal law* (Intersentia 2012) 178 and 196.
51. J Blomsma, *Mens rea and defences in European criminal law* (Intersentia 2012) 172.
52. P Murphy (ed.), *Blackstone's Criminal Practice* (Blackstone 2001) 29 and 31.
53. As is apparent from the treatment of the same case in first instance and on appeal: *see* J Pradel, *Droit pénal général* (Cujas 2016) 480-481.
54. *See* C-210/10 *Urbán* ECLI:EU:C:2012:64, para. 52. The CJEU itself and also the literature (*see*, for example, M Poelemans, *La sanction dans l'ordre juridique communautaire* (Bruylant 2004) 575) often refer to C-326/88 *Anklagemyndigheden v Hansen and Søn I/S* ECLI:EU:C:1990:291 for the proposition that strict liability is compatible with European law, but that case specifically concerns vicarious liability which raises specific issues (*see* para. 86 below). Somewhat critical of the CJEU's approach to strict liability are J Pradel and G Corstens, *Droit penal européen* (Dalloz 2002) 495, who however seem to confuse strict liability offences with offences for which there are no defences (such as force majeure or insanity).

infringement.[55] The case law of the European Court of Human Rights (ECtHR) suggests that, although the right to a fair trial protected by Article 6 ECHR is not dependent on a *mens rea* requirement for all material elements of an offence, the legality principle of Article 7 ECHR nevertheless implies some mental element on the part of the perpetrator to hold him liable.[56]

[B] The Rationale for the *Mens Rea* Requirement

45 It is fairly well established today that *mens rea* should be a condition for punishment at least in the core of the criminal law.[57] It has been argued, however, that *mens rea* is a recent invention, even in the criminal law. Sayre has argued that 'English law started from a basis bordering on absolute liability' and that a 'killer seems to have been held liable for every death which he causes, whether intentionally or accidentally'. This would have only changed in the 12th century, under the influence of the church.[58] LaFave similarly states that '[d]uring the early days of the development of common law crimes, the judges often declared conduct to be criminal which did not include any bad state of mind. But in more recent times (i.e., since about 1600), the judges have generally defined common law crimes in terms which require, in addition to prescribed action or omission, some prescribed bad state of mind'.[59]

46 It may well be that the *mens rea* requirement was not made explicit or systematized in common law jurisprudence until this was fairly well developed. However, there is ample evidence that criminal law has distinguished between intentional and negligent acts for a much longer time. Even the Hammurabi Code provides that, although in principle the talion principle (an eye for an eye) applies, if a member of a higher class hits another member of the same class and takes an oath that this was done unintentionally, he must only pay the costs of the doctor's treatment or, if the victim dies, 30 silver shekels.[60] Also, in other cultures the concept of culpability existed and seemed to have been relevant for liability, such that it is hard to avoid the conclusion that 'primitive societies, both ancient and extant, universally seem to recognize a moral difference between accidents and non-accidents'.[61]

55. In C-210/10 *Urbán* ECLI:EU:C:2012:64, the CJEU considered the fine disproportionate in light of the offence. *See also* already C-157/80 *Rinkau* ECLI:EU:C:1981:120, para. 15, where the Court distinguishes between intentionally committed offences which are more serious in nature and not intentionally committed offences (including 'the mere objective breach of a legal provision') which are generally less serious.
56. *See Sud Fondi SRL and others v Italy* App No 75909/01 (ECtHR 20 January 2009) and *G.I.E.M. S.R.L. and others v Italy* App No 1828/06 (ECtHR, 28 June 2018).
57. Although there are some scholars who argue that even in the core of the criminal law the mindset of the perpetrator of a crime should be of little relevance. For a discussion, *see* SH Kadish, 'The decline of innocence' (1968) 26 Cambridge Law Journal 273, in particular 285-290.
58. FB Sayre, 'Mens rea' (1931) 45 Harvard law review 974, 977 and 980.
59. WR LaFave and AW Scott, *Criminal law* (West, 1986) 229.
60. *See* B Winiger, *Responsibility, restoration and fault* (Intersentia 2018) 24-25.
61. FX Shen, MB Hoffman, OD Jones, JD Greene and R Marois, 'Sorting guilty minds' (2011) 86 New York University Law Review 1306, 1309. For a discussion of *mens rea* in Islamic jurisprudence, *see* F Ahadi, 'Re-visiting the concept of mens rea: challenging the common approaches employed under Islamic jurisprudence and statute law' (2016) 9 Journal of Politics and Law 1 who even

47 That we consider intentionally causing harm more worthy of punishment than accidentally causing harm seems to be somehow innate. Daniel Kahneman, winner of the Nobel Memorial Prize in Economic Sciences in 2002, referred to an experiment which demonstrates that the urge to ascribe intentions comes as natural to humans as the urge to see causality:

> Viewers see an aggressive large triangle bullying a smaller triangle, a terrified circle, the circle and the small triangle joining forces to defeat the bully ... The perception of intention and emotion is irresistible, only people afflicted by autism do not experience it. All this is entirely in your mind, of course. Your mind is ready and even eager to identify agents, assign them personality traits and specific intentions, and view their actions as expressing individual propensities. Here again, the evidence is that we are born prepared to make intentional attributions: infants under one year old identify bullies and victims, and expect a pursuer to follow the most direct path in attempting to catch whatever it is chasing.[62]

48 That this affects our views of deserved punishment is demonstrated by versions of the ultimatum game which differentiate between random acts and acts to which intentions of fairness or unfairness can be attributed. These experiments show that humans attach far greater significance to perceived fairness intentions than to fair outcomes.[63] Human beings are 'intuitive retributivists'[64] and this may explain why intentions matter to them.

49 Taking into account *mens rea* has also been defended based on the deterrent function of criminal law. Some have argued that *mens rea* is relevant because of the criminal law's objective of specific deterrence: a person that knowingly or willingly commits an offence, is more likely to commit an offence again.[65] There may be some truth in this: the fact that a person chooses to do something which she knows is prohibited by the criminal law or morality is a sign that that person's hierarchy of values may not coincide with that of the society around her.

50 There is furthermore a general deterrence aspect to *mens rea* which fits with our natural sentiments towards intentional harm discussed above.[66] If a person knowingly or willingly causes harm but is not punished for this, this diminishes the standing in which a community holds the criminal law. If a person chooses to do somethings which she knows the criminal law or morality prohibits and gets away with it, this will make

---

claims that '[t]he Islamic Law, though implicitly and through different concepts, has accentuated the necessity of the existence of the *mens rea* or criminal liability long before the European Law' (at 4).

62. D Kahneman, *Thinking, fast and slow* (Penguin 2012) 76-77.
63. *See* A Falk, E Fehr, U Fischbacher, 'Testing theories of fairness – intentions matter' (2008) 62 Games and Economic Behaviour 287.
64. CR Sunstein, 'On the psychology of punishment' (2004) 11 Supreme Court Economic Review 171, 175.
65. For a critical discussion of these theories, *see* U Stein, '§ 15 Vorsätzliches und fahrlässiges Handeln' in J Wolter (ed.), *Systematischer Kommentar zum Strafgesetzbuch* (Carl Heymanns 2017) 412, 423-424.
66. *See* U Stein, '§ 15 Vorsätzliches und fahrlässiges Handeln' in J Wolter (ed.), *Systematischer Kommentar zum Strafgesetzbuch* (Carl Heymanns 2017) 412, 424-426.

it attractive for other members of society to try the same thing and will erode their moral attachment to the norm in question.

[1] The Correspondence Principle

51 Related to this last rationale of the *mens rea* requirement is the important principle that the *mens rea* of an offence needs to relate to its *actus reus*.[67] Each offence of course contains its own *actus reus*, its own objective elements which together constitute its *actus reus*. But, for the understanding of the notion of *mens rea*, it is helpful to consider that these objective elements can fall in one or more of the following three categories: (i) conduct, (ii) results and (iii) circumstances.[68] For example, battery is a typical conduct offence: it consists in the application of unlawful force by one person upon another, regardless of the consequences and/or the circumstances in which it takes place. Murder is a typical result offence: it consists in conduct resulting in the death of a person. Other offences require both certain conduct and certain results, for example assault occasioning actual bodily harm.[69] Finally, the circumstances in which certain conduct takes place are relevant for many other offences: perjury, for example, is certain conduct (lying) in the context of judicial proceedings. Depending on the type of offence, its objective elements may therefore concern (i) a type of conduct, (ii) one or more results of that conduct and/or (iii) one or more circumstances in which the conduct takes place.

52 The principle *actus non facit reum nisi mens sit rea* is generally interpreted as requiring *mens rea* in relation to each of the objective elements of the offence.[70] This is called the correspondence principle (or, more narrowly, the 'referential principle').[71] For example, in the case of battery, in relation to the application of unlawful force on another person: did the perpetrator intend to hit the victim? In the case of a result offence, like murder, in relation to the result: did the perpetrator intend that the victim would die? In case of perjury, a conduct offence in which the circumstances are an objective element of the offence, in relation to both the conduct and the circumstances: did the witness know that what she said was untrue (or was she merely mistaken) and did she know that her testimony would be used in court?

---

67. A Ashworth, *Principles of criminal law* (OUP 2006) 197-201; J Blomsma, *Mens rea and defences in European criminal law* (Intersentia 2012) 206.
68. Section 1.13 (9) of the Model Penal Code. *See also* HLA Hart, 'Intention and punishment' in HLA Hart, *Punishment and responsibility: essays in the philosophy of law* (OUP 1970) 113, 119 and J Blomsma, *Mens rea and defences in European criminal law* (Intersentia 2012) 50.
69. For the difference between conduct offences and result offences, *see also* P Murphy (ed.), *Blackstone's Criminal Practice* (Blackstone 2001) 3.
70. *See* para. (1) of section 2.02 of the Model Penal Code which states that the mental state is required 'with respect to each material element of the offense'. *See also* J Blomsma, *Mens rea and defences in European criminal law* (Intersentia 2012) 206 and 208.
71. *See* A Ashworth, *Principles of criminal law* (OUP 2006) 197; J Blomsma, *Mens rea and defences in European criminal law* (Intersentia 2012) 208.

53 It is important to point out that different *mens rea* requirements can exist for different objective elements of an offence.[72] It is obvious, for example, that, in case the circumstances in which conduct takes place are relevant for the definition of an offence (as in the case of perjury), it does not make sense to say that the perpetrator 'intended' these circumstances. Intention in the narrow sense of *dolus directus* can therefore not be a relevant state of mind in relation to circumstances. However, the fact that the perpetrator 'was aware' of the circumstances can be a relevant *mens rea*. Furthermore, some offence definitions may require intention or knowledge for some material elements of the offence and not refer to any subjective elements at all in relation to other elements such that for the latter the mere infringement of the rule (under strict liability or, normatively, due to negligence) is sufficient.[73]

54 *Mens rea* has specific relevance for inchoate offences, where the offence has not been completed and *mens rea* is needed to reconstruct the incomplete part of the offence. In criminal attempt, for example, where 'the desired result is per definition absent ..., we are often left with only the perpetrator's intentions to determine what he actually set out to achieve and how'.[74] In those cases, the correspondence principle is particularly important since it is only if the intention was addressed at the particular result (or the perpetrator was aware that that result would likely arise)[75] that an attempt to achieve that result (and the corresponding offence) can be found. *Mens rea* in those cases clearly has an interpretative function.[76]

55 The correspondence principle is also relevant for the determination of the liability of accessories, i.e. persons who have not performed the *actus reus* themselves but nevertheless are held criminally liable in addition to and together with the actual perpetrator. A person can only be found to be an accessory to an offence, if she has the relevant *mens rea* for the offence. If the principal does something outside of the scope of what the accessory intended, knew or should have known, the latter cannot be held liable for this.[77]

56 The correspondence principle implies the principle of contemporaneity: the perpetrator must possess the *mens rea* when performing the *actus reus*. A man who one day accidentally runs over his wife whom he planned to murder the next day is generally

72. *See* section 2.02 of the Model Penal Code which makes a very clear distinction between the *mens rea* relevant for each of the three material elements of an offence: (i) conduct, (ii) results and (iii) circumstances. *See also* WR LaFave and AW Scott, *Criminal law* (West 1986) 215.
73. In relation to recklessness, P Murphy (ed.), *Blackstone's Criminal Practice* (Blackstone 2001) 19 refers to this as the 'range of application'. In relation to negligence and strict liability *see ibid.*, 30.
74. J Keiler and D Roef, 'Inchoate offences: attempt and preparation' in J Keiler and D Roef, *Comparative concepts of criminal law* (Intersentia 2019) 253, 272.
75. There are differences in national law as to whether a less intensive state of mind than *dolus indirectus* suffices for attempt. *See* J Blomsma, *Mens rea and defences in European criminal law* (Intersentia 2012) 161 and J Keiler and D Roef, 'Inchoate offences: attempt and preparation' in J Keiler and D Roef, *Comparative concepts of criminal law* (Intersentia 2019) 253, 272-274.
76. *See* more generally on this: W Chan and AP Simester, 'Four functions of mens rea' (2011) 70(2) Cambridge Law Journal 381, 384-388.
77. *See* P Murphy (ed.), *Blackstone's Criminal Practice* (Blackstone 2001) 32; J Pradel, *Droit pénal général* (Cujas 2016) 418-420.

not considered to be guilty of murder.[78] In case of interrupted or continuous offences, the principle of contemporaneity requires that the perpetrator had the *mens rea* before the interruption *casu quo* at some point during the continuous offence.[79]

57 The mental element which needs to be demonstrated to establish an offence is often distinguished from the (ulterior) motive of the perpetrator which is generally considered to be irrelevant for the offence.[80] The *mens rea* of murder is the intention to kill. The motive is what led the murderer to have this intention or what he intended to achieve with the killing. Motives may be personal or social and they may be laudable or not. The motive can, for example, be 'jealousy', say when the victim is the new lover of the murderer's (ex-)partner. Another motive may be to 'silence' the victim, say when the victim knew about an affair the murderer was having.

58 The correspondence principle is what distinguishes *mens rea* from motives, which are in principle not relevant to establish offences. Murder is murder, regardless of what led the murderer to commit it or what the murderer wanted to achieve with it. That does not mean, however, that ulterior motives or ulterior intentions are entirely irrelevant: sometimes the law takes into account a specific mental state or a specific objective when defining or punishing offences. For example, genocide is defined as committing violent crimes against a national, ethnical, racial or religious group 'with intent to destroy, in whole or in part', the group.[81] I would argue that, if such an ulterior motive is taken into account to define an offence, this in fact suggests that the offence is inchoate, i.e. that the ulterior intent corresponds to an (possibly unrealized) *actus reus* (in the case of genocide, the destruction of the group).

[2] General Versus Specific Intent

59 As an aside, it is worth mentioning here that, in particular in French doctrine, a distinction is often made between general intent (*dol général*) and specific intent (*dol spécial*). While there is some disagreement in the literature as to the precise meaning of these terms, general intent is often understood as the intention relating to the conduct element of the *actus reus*,[82] while specific intent relates to the results of the offence: it

78. P Murphy (ed.), *Blackstone's Criminal Practice* (Blackstone 2001) 4-5. *See also* A Ashworth, *Principles of criminal law* (OUP 2006) 161-163.
79. P Murphy (ed.), *Blackstone's Criminal Practice* (Blackstone 2001) 5.
80. R Garraud, *Traité théorique et pratique du droit pénal français* (Recueil Sirey 1913) 577: '*le motif n'entre pas dans les éléments essentiels du délit*'; J Pradel, *Droit pénal général* (Cujas 2016) 459: '*Le mobile n'est pas une condition de la responsabilité.*' *See also* F Desportes and F Le Gunehec, *Droit pénal général* (Economica 2009) 441 and J Blomsma, *Mens rea and defences in European criminal law* (Intersentia 2012) 81.
81. Article 2 of the 1948 UN Convention on the Prevention and Punishment of the Crime of Genocide.
82. R Merle and A Vitu, *Traité de droit criminal. Tome I: Problèmes généraux de la science criminelle. Droit pénal général* (Cujas 1997) 729 : '*volonté de commettre le délit tel qu'il est déterminé par la loi*'; J Pradel, *Droit pénal général* (Cujas 2016) 458: '*la volonté de l'agent de commettre le délit tel qu'il est défini par la loi*'.

is the intention to attain a certain result prohibited by the criminal law.[83] According to this view, in the case of pure conduct offences, merely general intent needs to be established. For example, in the case of battery, it merely needs to be established that the perpetrator intended to hit the victim. In offences which (also) have a result component in the *actus reus*, a specific intention to achieve that result needs to be established in addition. For example, in case unlawful physical contact leads to the death of the victim, the perpetrator can only be convicted for murder if he had the intention to kill. If such a 'specific intent' was absent, he can only be convicted for a lesser offence (battery or involuntary manslaughter).[84] This distinction therefore reflects the correspondence principle: general intent relates to the conduct element of an offence and specific intent relates to the result element of an offence.

60 However, the notions of general and specific intent entail more than merely the correspondence principle. According to French literature, general intent also comprises an awareness that one violates the criminal law[85] – an issue which I will discuss in more detail in paragraphs 73ff. below. Specific intent, on the other hand, is also sometimes understood to refer to the motive of the perpetrator, in particular in the case of inchoate offences.[86]

61 These different meanings of the terms may be due to the different contexts in which these terms are used but they of course lead to confusion.[87] I will therefore refrain from using this terminology going forward as I believe that the ideas expressed by these notions (i.e. that an intention corresponding to conduct is not the same as an intention corresponding to results, that awareness of illegality may be relevant and that motives may play a role in defining infringements) can be expressed in other ways.

83. F Desportes and F Le Gunehec, *Droit pénal général* (Economica 2009) 438: '*l'intention d'atteindre un certain résultat prohibé par la loi pénale*'; J Pradel, *Droit pénal général* (Cujas 2016) 461: '*la recherche d'un résultat déterminé*'.
84. *See* R Merle and A Vitu, *Traité de droit criminal. Tome I: Problèmes généraux de la science criminelle. Droit pénal général* (Cujas 1997) 750 and J Pradel, *Droit pénal général* (Cujas 2016) 461.
85. *See* J Pradel, *Droit pénal général* (Cujas 2016) 458 '*la conscience chez le coupable d'enfreindre les prohibition légales*'. F Desportes and F Le Gunehec, *Droit pénal général* (Economica 2009) 435 define general intent as '*la volonté de commettre un acte en ayant conscience de violer la loi pénale*'. As a consequence, even in the case of pure result offences (such as murder), French doctrine considers that there is a general intent, namely the intention to do something that is prohibited (which in addition resulted in the death of a person, a consequence which the perpetrator specifically intended). *See also* R Merle and A Vitu, *Traité de droit criminal. Tome I: Problèmes généraux de la science criminelle. Droit pénal général* (Cujas 1997) 731-740.
86. J-Y Maréchal, 'Art. 121-3 – Facs. 20 : élément moral de l'infraction' in *JurisClasseur pénal code* (LexisNexis 2019), paras 38-40.
87. Because the notion of general intent 'has been an abiding source of confusion and ambiguity in the penal law', the Model Penal Code has simply abandoned the distinction between general intent and specific intent. *See* WR LaFave and AW Scott, *Criminal law* (West 1986) 225, footnote 65 and reference there.

[3] **Mens Rea *Outside the Core of the Criminal Law***

62 The number of criminal offences has increased exponentially over the last decades, which has resulted in complaints of 'over-criminalisation'.[88] At the same time, many regulations have been created which are subject to administrative 'sanctions' enforced by administrative authorities. This phenomenon of increasing criminal and regulatory liability is a reflection of the increasing complexity of our societies.

63 In many instances, such (criminal or administrative) offences outside the core of the criminal law attract strict liability or liability merely based on negligence.[89] Under French administrative law, strict liability is the rule and the same is true for the minor criminal offences of '*contraventions*' (only punishable with a fine).[90] This heightened risk of liability is often justified as being what society asks in return for allowing its members to engage in risk-creating activities. Many traffic violations fall in this category: if you engage in the risk-creating activity of driving a car, you will have to bear the consequences of any traffic rules you violate, whether or not you intended to violate them or even tried everything possible to abide by these rules. Strict liability implies that any damage resulting from a breach of the rules remains in those circumstances with the person that created the risk. By 'pricing' violations of the rules in this way, careless drivers are priced out of their cars and only rule-abiding drivers will remain on the road.

64 However, many of the new criminal and regulatory offences that were created also contain *mens rea* requirements. For some of these, this is the consequence of them being modelled on core criminal offences, such as fraud. An obvious example under European law is fraud affecting the EU interests: both the 1995 Convention on the protection of the European Communities' financial interests and its successor, Directive 2017/1371 on the fight against fraud to the Union's financial interests by means of criminal law, only require Member States to criminalize fraud affecting the EU's interests when committed intentionally.[91] In other instances, the *mens rea* requirement is introduced in 'novel' infringements. For example, although much of the Market Abuse Regulation is written without reference to *mens rea*, certain disclosures in the press only amount to market manipulation if an advantage or profit is derived from the disclosure or if the disclosure is accompanied by 'the intention of misleading the market'.[92] The German Regulatory Offences Act (*Ordnungswidrigkeitengesetz*) even provides that regulatory offences in principle only cover intentional conduct, unless an

88. J Coffee, 'Paradigms lost: the blurring of the criminal and civil models – and what can be done about it' (1992) 101 Yale Law Journal 1875, 1880; SP Green, 'Moral ambiguity in white collar criminal law' (2004) 18 Notre Dame Journal of Law, Ethics & Public Policy 501, 507.
89. J Blomsma, *Mens rea and defences in European criminal law* (Intersentia 2012) 211.
90. H-M Crucis, 'Fasc. 108-40: sanctions administratives' in *JurisClasseur Administratif* (LexisNexis 2012) para. 61; J Pradel, *Droit pénal général* (Cujas 2016) 482.
91. *See* Article 1 of the Convention drawn up on the basis of Article K.3 of the Treaty on European Union, on the protection of the European Communities' financial interest [1995] OJ C316/49, and recital 11 and Articles 3(1), 4(2) and 4(3) of Directive 2017/1371 on the fight against fraud to the Union's financial interests by means of criminal law [2017] OJ L198/29.
92. *See* Article 21 of Regulation 596/2014 on market abuse [2014] OJ L173/1.

offence definition explicitly states that it can also be committed through negligence (which is in fact the case for most regulatory offences).[93]

65 *Mens rea* for these new criminal and regulatory offences can create confusion because these 'new' offences appear *mala prohibita,* merely illegal because they are prohibited by law, not illegal because immoral (*mala in se*).[94] In the case of *mala in se,* the intention to do the act makes the mind 'evil' because the act is immoral; in the case of *mala prohibita,* the act is 'innocent', i.e. not morally repulsive, so it is difficult to speak of an 'evil' intention to engage in that act. It has been argued, for example, that there is nothing 'immoral' about what is termed market 'abuse': engaging in transactions based on information is the very nature of market functioning and will naturally influence the market price.[95]

66 However, the distinction between *mala in se* and *mala prohibita* is not carved in stone. Although criminal law is meant to reflect the moral values of a society, this is by no means a one-way process. The prohibition of conduct also affects what society perceives as morally permissible or not: 'the public learns what is criminal from what is punished, not vice versa'.[96] What is prohibited also attaches moral stigma and may therefore become to be perceived as a *malum in se.* Legal prohibition and punishment therefore have an educational function.

67 What does this mean for the use of *mens rea* in criminal or regulatory offences? First of all, it implies that the creation of criminal or regulatory offences is meant to shape what society perceives as morally acceptable or not. Furthermore, in case the offence is related to certain risk-creating behaviour which a person can choose to engage in or not (e.g. a game or another professional or non-professional activity), that person can be expected to learn and adopt the objectives of the game: the intention or awareness to thwart these objectives can then be seen as *mens rea.* In those circumstances, *mens rea* will become close to awareness of illegality, which will be discussed in paragraphs 79-80 below.

68 Although it usually has a different name, *mens rea* can also play a role in the (core of the) civil law, even in its non-normative form of intention. An obvious example is in fraudulent misrepresentation prior to contract which is subject to more serious

93. § 10 of the German *Ordnungswidrigkeitengesetz*: '*Als Ordnungswidrigkeit kann nur vorsätzliches Handeln geahndet werden, ausser wenn das Gesetz fahrlässiges Handeln ausdrücklich mit Geldbusse bedroht.*' *See also* T Noak, 'Einführung ins Ordnungswidrigkeitenrecht – Teil 1 Ahndungsvoraussetzungen' (2012) (2) Zeitschrift für das Juristische Studium 175, 181.

94. *See* SP Green, 'Moral ambiguity in white collar criminal law' (2004) 18 Notre Dame Journal of Law, Ethics & Public Policy 501, 507; C Waldhoff, 'Vollstreckung und Sanktionen' in W Hoffmann-Reim, E Schmidt-Assmann and A Vosskuhl (eds), *Grundlagen des Verwaltungsrechts* (Beck 2009) 269, 383; J Pradel, *Droit pénal général* (Cujas 2016) 479-480.

95. *See* D Nelken, 'White-collar crime' in M Maguire, R Morgan and R Reiner, *The Oxford handbook of criminology* (OUP 1997) 891, 917-919 and H de Vauplane and J-P Bronet, *Droit des marchés financiers* (Litec 2001) 900-901.

96. J Coffee, 'Paradigms lost: the blurring of the criminal and civil models – and what can be done about it' (1992) 101 Yale Law Journal 1875, 1889. *See also,* in the area of antitrust, ME Stucke, 'Morality and antitrust' (2006) Columbia Business Law Review 443, 490.

sanctions than negligent misrepresentation or innocent misrepresentation.[97] While the justification for this seems to be comparable to that in the criminal law, I will refrain from discussing this (in itself vast) topic in more detail here.

[C] The Relevance of the Mental State for Punishment

69 Apart from being relevant in defining an offence, *mens rea* is also relevant in punishment.[98] Indeed, often the same *actus reus* may constitute different offences (with different punishment), depending on the accompanying *mens rea*. The French *Code pénal*, for example, distinguishes between intentional killing (Article 221-1), which it defines as '*meurtre*', and unintentional killing (Article 221-6), the former being punishable with thirty years of imprisonment, the latter with only three years (five years in case of the 'manifestly deliberate violation of a specific duty of care or security')[99] and a fine.

70 Under German law as well, the killing of another person ('*Totschlag*', § 212 of the *Strafgesetzbuch*), which *per* § 15 of the *Strafgesetzbuch* is an intentional offence, is punished more severely than the negligent killing of a person ('*Fahrlässige Tötung*', § 222 of the *Strafgesetzbuch*), the former with *at least* five years of imprisonment (and according to § 212, second paragraph, 'in especially serious cases' with lifelong imprisonment), the latter with imprisonment of *no more than* five years *or* a fine. More generally, the German *Ordnungswidrigkeitengesetz* provides that the maximum fine for a negligent infringement may not be more than half the fine of an intentional infringement.[100]

71 In the context of punishment, it is worth mentioning the specific aggravating factor of premeditation, defined under French law as the design or plan formed before the act.[101] Premeditation could be viewed as an even more intense form of *mens rea* than (merely) intention: it implies that the perpetrator took time to weigh up contrasting

97. *See* HG Beale, 'Misrepresentation' in HG Beale (ed.), *Chitty on contracts* (Thomson Reuters 2018) 649, 680-714: damages are not possible for innocent misrepresentation, sometimes for negligent representation and always for fraudulent misrepresentation. In French law, a distinction is made between '*dol*' (fraud - Articles 1137-1139 of the French *Code civil*) and '*erreur*' (error - Articles 1132-1136 of the French *Code civil*), the former containing an intentional element and always allowing for nullity of the contract and giving rise to damages, whereas in the case of the latter, nullity depends on whether the error is excusable and damages can only be obtained by erring party A from party B if the latter has committed a fault; if, however, party A invokes the error but itself committed the fault, party B may obtain damages from party A (*see also* F Terré, P Simler and Y Lequette (eds), *Droit Civil. Les Obligations* (Dalloz 2005) 215-245). Under German law, compare § 119 (concerning '*Irrtum*', i.e. error) and § 123 (concerning '*Täuschung oder Drohung*', i.e. fraud or duress) of the *Bürgerliches Gesetzbuch* and note that § 122 is only applicable to error, not to fraud.
98. *See also* HLA Hart, 'Intention and punishment' in HLA Hart, *Punishment and responsibility: essays in the philosophy of law* (OUP 1970) 113, 115.
99. '*violation manifestement délibérée d'une obligation particulière de prudence ou de sécurité*'.
100. § 17 (2) of the German *Ordnungswidrigkeitengesetz*.
101. Article 132-72 of the French *Code pénal* of 1994: '*le dessein formé avant l'action*'.

courses of action and increasingly directed the events towards the unlawful conduct or result. This is indicative of a particularly high degree of knowing and willing.[102]

72 Punishment is also often differentiated depending on the motive (as in ulterior intentions or motivations – *see* paragraphs 57-58 above) underpinning the offence. This may be explicitly foreseen in the law: for example, under German law, where intentional killing is committed out of certain base motives,[103] it qualifies as '*Mord*' (§ 211 of the *Strafgesetzbuch*), which is punishable with lifelong imprisonment (instead of at least five years of imprisonment for '*Totschlag*', § 212 of the *Strafgesetzbuch*). It could be argued that motives play an even more important role in determining punishment *in practice* (in particular in jury cases).[104] However, unless such a motive is an ulterior intent which corresponds to an (uncompleted) *actus reus*, I would argue this is not *mens rea* properly speaking.

[D] Ignorance and Awareness of Fact and Law

73 On the flip side of the requirement of *mens rea* is the treatment of mistakes of fact and law. Mistakes of fact will usually lead to the absence of *mens rea*. For example, if someone mistakenly believes that he is shooting a scarecrow, he cannot be guilty of murder if the target turns out to be an actual person.[105] In line with the correspondence principle, mistakes of fact can relate to (i) the conduct which is constitutive of an offence, (ii) its results and (iii) the circumstances in which it takes place.

74 A more controversial issue is to what extent mistakes of law can preclude (or otherwise affect) *mens rea*. What if a person is aware of the nature of her conduct, the results of her conduct and the circumstances in which it is undertaken, but is unaware that any of these are prohibited by the law? This issue does not arise so often in the case of so-called *mala in se*, such as murder. But in the case of *mala prohibita*, behaviour which is only prohibited as a result of societal convention, the question of mistakes of law is acute.

75 Based on the fiction that *nemo censetur ignorare legem*, the general principle in Western European criminal law is that ignorance of the law is no excuse (*ignorantia legis non excusat*) and that errors of law are therefore to the detriment of those that commit them (*error iuris nocet*).[106] Under English law, no doctrine of avoidable

---

102. J Blomsma, *Mens rea and defences in European criminal law* (Intersentia 2012) 45.
103. Namely 'for pleasure, for sexual gratification, out of greed or otherwise base motives, by stealth or cruelly or by means that pose a danger to the public or in order to facilitate or to cover up another offence' ['*aus Mordlust, zur Befriedigung des Geschlechtstriebs, aus Habgier oder sonst aus niedrigen Beweggründen, heimtückisch oder grausam oder mit gemeingefährlichen Mitteln oder um eine andere Straftat zu ermöglichen oder zu verdecken*'].
104. *See* J Pradel, *Droit pénal général* (Cujas 2016) 460.
105. P Murphy (ed.), *Blackstone's Criminal Practice* (Blackstone 2001) 35. A similar example is provided by J Pradel, *Droit pénal général* (Cujas 2016) 452.
106. *See* the explanatory note to section 2.02 (9) of the Model Penal Code. *See also* J Blomsma, *Mens rea and defences in European criminal law* (Intersentia 2012) 87; J Pradel, *Droit pénal général* (Cujas 2016) 452.

mistakes of law exists: errors of (criminal) law are never an excuse (but errors of civil law can be).[107]

76 Similarly, prior to the new *Code pénal*, the French Cour de Cassation did not accept that an error of law, even if it were unavoidable, could reduce liability for an offence. However, the *Code pénal* currently provides that unavoidable errors do absolve from criminal liability, although the scope of this exception is limited.[108]

77 In German doctrine, there has been a long debate between proponents of the so-called *Vorsatztheorie*, who considered that intentional offences imply awareness of illegality (and therefore that mistakes of law would prevent a finding of an intentional offence), and those of the so-called *Schuldtheorie*, who considered that perpetrators of an offence could be found to have acted intentionally despite an error of law.[109] § 17 of the *Strafgesetzbuch* currently remains close to the *Schuldtheorie* but still provides that unavoidable mistakes exclude guilt.[110] The *Ordnungswidrigkeitengesetz* goes further by pointing out that a perpetrator's understanding of wrongfulness may be absent 'because he is ignorant of the existence or applicability of a legal provision'.[111] This fits in with the argument that outside of the core of the criminal law, the *Vorsatztheorie* makes more sense.[112]

78 The writers of the *Corpus Juris* for fraud against the EU's financial interests made explicit reference to the French and German examples when they foresaw a form of excusable mistake of law.[113]

---

107. P Murphy (ed.), *Blackstone's Criminal Practice* (Blackstone 2001) 39-40.
108. Article 122-3 of the French *Code pénal* of 1994: '*N'est pas pénalement responsable la personne qui justifie avoir cru, par une erreur sur le droit qu'elle n'était pas en mesure d'éviter, pouvoir légitimement accomplir l'acte.*' For a discussion, *see* J Pradel, *Droit pénal général* (Cujas 2016) 454-456.
109. *See* C Roxin, *Strafrecht Algemeiner Teil* (Beck 2006) 927-932; K Rogall, '§ 17 Verbotsirrtum' in J Wolter (ed.), *Systematischer Kommentar zum Strafgesetzbuch* (Carl Heymanns 2017) 511, 514ff.
110. § 17 of the German *Strafgesetzbuch*: '*Fehlt dem Täter bei Begehung der Tat die Einsicht, Unrecht zu tun, so handelt er ohne Schuld, wenn er diesen Irrtum nicht vermeiden konnte. Konnte der Täter den Irrtum vermeiden, so kann die Strafe nach § 49 Abs. 1 gemildert werden*' ['If at the time of the commission of the offence the offender lacks the awareness that he is acting unlawfully, he shall be deemed to have acted without guilt if the mistake was unavoidable. If the mistake was avoidable, the sentence may be mitigated pursuant to section 49(1)']. *See also* § 11(2) of the *Ordnungswidrigkeitengesetz*.
111. § 11(2) of the *Gesetz über Ordnungswidrigkeiten (OWiG)* provides: '*Fehlt dem Täter bei Begehung der Handlung die Einsicht, etwas Unerlaubtes zu tun, namentlich weil er das Bestehen oder die Anwendbarkeit einer Rechtsvorschrift nicht kennt, so handelt er nicht vorwerfbar, wenn er diesen Irrtum nicht vermeiden konnte*' ['If the perpetrator, at the time the act is committed, is incapable of understanding its wrongfulness *because he is ignorant of the existence or applicability of a legal provision*, he shall not be deemed to have acted reprehensibly if he could not avoid this error'].
112. C Roxin, *Strafrecht Algemeiner Teil* (Beck 2006) 931.
113. Its Article 11(2) provides: 'Mistake about the existence of a legal prohibition or its interpretation excludes liability if it would have inevitably have been committed by a careful and sensible person. If the mistake was avoidable, the penalty will be reduced, which means that the judge may not impose the maximum penalty.' *See* M Delmas-Marty (ed.), *Corpus juris introducing penal provisions for the purpose of the financial interests of the European Union* (Economica 1997) 66 and 154.

79 What about the reverse situation, i.e. where the perpetrator is acutely aware of the illegality of his conduct? Although it is rare that awareness of the illegal nature of the conduct is part of the offence,[114] such awareness can nevertheless be indicative of *mens rea* in respect of the constitute elements of the *actus reus*. Obviously, great care should be taken here: it is not because a person believes that what she is doing is illegal, that it is also illegal. As a consequence, the fact that a person believes that what she is doing is illegal does not mean that she is also actually doing what amounts to an offence. *A fortiori*, the mere secrecy surrounding a particular act, does not suffice to conclude that that act amounts to an offence: the actor may not want to conceal its conduct from the law but may have other reasons to act secretly.

80 Nevertheless, as noted in paragraph 50 above, much of the logic of taking into account *mens rea* in the definition or punishment of offences is that the willing or knowing disregard of the basic rules of society is what warrants punishment. This logic implies that awareness of illegality is indicative of guilt. It seems that this idea is also expressed in the (otherwise confusing) notion of 'general intent' under French law which seems to entail an awareness of illegality (*see* paragraph 60 and footnote 85 above).

81 The relationship between *mens rea* and awareness/ignorance of the law can be summarized as follows:

	Ignorance of illegality	Awareness of illegality
Awareness of relevant facts (i.e. conduct, results or circumstances)	Intentionality	Intentionality
Ignorance of relevant facts (i.e. conduct, results or circumstances)	(Unconscious) Negligence[1]	[2]

[1]. This of course assumes that there was a duty of care in respect of the knowledge of the relevant facts, otherwise there would be strict liability.

[2]. In the (rare) case of conscious negligence, there may be awareness of illegality in addition to ignorance of relevant facts. In those circumstances, the main question will be what the actor did to avoid an infringement.

[E] Proof of the State of Mind

82 A particularly difficult issue when discussing mental states is evidence. Indeed, it may appear hard to assess at least the subjective *mens rea* elements (willing and knowing) of the perpetrator: the only person that has direct access to his state of mind is the accused himself. This would appear to give him an easy way out of liability, by denying that he had the relevant state of mind. Declarations of the accused are

114. *See* section 2.02 (9) of the Model Penal Code and J Blomsma, *Mens rea and defences in European criminal law* (Intersentia 2012) 85.

nevertheless obviously relevant to establish whether he had the relevant *mens rea* or not: not only the declarations he makes at trial but also declarations he made (orally or in writing) during or prior to the *actus reus*.[115] I will call intention evidenced in this way 'subjective intention' (as is done in most of the antitrust literature on this topic – *see* paragraph 317 below).

83 But other evidence can also be used. Under the common law, for example, it is well established that, in result offences, if the criminal result is the natural and probable result of the accused's conduct, this could (absent any other indications) lead to the conclusion that the accused probably knew that this result would arise.[116] Under French law as well, for some offences, the intentional element is deduced from the material facts of the offence,[117] and, more generally, 'general intent' is often established by simple proof of the material elements of the infringement, whereas for 'specific intent' this depends on whether the behaviour is ambiguous or not.[118] And the intentional nature of fraud against the EU's financial interests 'may be inferred from objective, factual circumstances'.[119]

84 However, there is a risk that by deducing intentions from the *actus reus*, it collapses into negligence. There is not much difference between stating that someone must have known the consequences of his actions (sometimes termed 'objective intention') and that he should have known the consequences of its actions (negligence) – although the former may be punished more severely than the latter. I will discuss the circumstances when objective intentions can be deduced legitimately without reducing it to negligence in more detail in Chapter 5.

[F] Corporate *Mens Rea*

85 A final, general remark to be made on the notion of *mens rea* concerns corporate defendants. The role of corporations in our societies continues to increase and with it also comes the question of the criminal liability of these corporations for offences.

115. Although it relates to motive, Article 132-76 of the French *Code pénal* of 1994 makes this quite explicit for the aggravating circumstance of racism, antisemitism or xenophobia: '*lorsque l'infraction est précédée, accompagnée ou suivie de propos, écrits, images, objets ou actes de toute nature portant atteinte à l'honneur ou à la considération de la victime ou d'un groupe de personnes dont fait partie la victime à raison de leur appartenance ou de leur non-appartenance, vraie ou supposée, à une ethnie, une nation, une race ou une religion déterminée.*'
116. *See* P Murphy (ed.), *Blackstone's Criminal Practice* (Blackstone 2001) 33. *See also* WR LaFave and AW Scott, *Criminal law* (West 1986) 225 and the explanation of the Australian High Court in *R. v Vallance*, 108 CLR (1961) 56, para. 82, quoted in RB Baker, 'Customary international law in the 21st century: old challenges and new debates' (2010) 21 European Journal of International Law 173, 193: 'A jury must consider the whole of the evidence relevant to it as a fact in issue. If an accused gives evidence of what his intentions were, the jury must weigh his testimony along with whatever inference as to his intentions can be drawn from his conduct or from other relevant facts.'
117. J Pradel, *Droit pénal général* (Cujas 2016) 464. *See also* the presumptions under French law discussed in F Desportes and F Le Gunehec, *Droit pénal général* (Economica 2009) 431-432.
118. *See* F Desportes and F Le Gunehec, *Droit pénal général* (Economica 2009) 433 and 440.
119. *See* recital 11 of Directive 2017/1371 on the fight against fraud to the Union's financial interests by means of criminal law [2017] OJ L198/29.

Since they are a legal fiction and have no physical presence nor mind of their own, there are many hurdles to imposing criminal liability on corporations.

86 One way to avoid these hurdles is to use a system of so-called vicarious liability, i.e. where the company is strictly liable for the criminal offences of its employees, based on the theory of agency. For minor regulatory offences, vicarious liability of the corporation often accompanies strict liability for the employee, and this is even foreseen by some EU legislation where the CJEU has found it compatible with the principles of European law.[120]

87 Nevertheless, for more serious offences, some form of *mens rea* is usually required. The question then arises how *mens rea* needs to be assessed for companies: in particular when it comes to the 'subjective' elements of *mens rea*, willing and knowing: in which circumstances can these be said to arise in entities that do not have a mind?

88 In England and Wales, corporate criminal liability developed through the case law of the courts, and these hold that acts and states of mind of senior employees and officers of the company can be identified with those of the company itself (this is the so-called identification theory which was mainly developed around the middle of the 20th century).[121] In other words, in order to prove that the company has the requisite mental state for the offence, it is sufficient to prove that senior employees and officers of the company have that mental state. Even though 'senior employee' was interpreted in a relatively broad way, in particular if management functions are delegated,[122] criminal liability could not arise because of the acts and mental states of any employee (contrary to 'vicarious' corporate liability). The identification theory poses difficulties, however, when it is not possible to identify the senior employee(s) at fault for an offence. The Corporate Manslaughter and Corporate Homicide Act 2007 therefore used a different theory of attribution, namely a form of the 'aggregation theory', which takes into account deficiencies in the way a company is organized and, in that sense, the 'collective knowledge' of the company.[123]

89 In France, criminal liability for most legal entities was introduced by the *Code pénal* of 1994 which provides that legal entities are liable for 'offences committed by their bodies and representatives'.[124] As in England and Wales, states of minds of ordinary employees can therefore not create criminal liability for their corporate employers, although the law does accept liability as a result of delegation of powers.[125] At some

---

120. *See* case C-326/88 *Anklagemyndigheden v Hansen and Søn I/S* ECLI:EU:C:1990:291, paras 11ff and subsequent case law such as C-501/14 *EL-EM-2001* ECLI:EU:C:2016:777, para. 31.
121. P Murphy (ed.), *Blackstone's Criminal Practice* (Blackstone 2001) 83ff; N Cavanagh, 'Corporate criminal liability: an assessment of the models of fault' (2011) Journal of Criminal Law 414, 416.
122. P Murphy (ed.), *Blackstone's Criminal Practice* (Blackstone 2001) 84.
123. *See* N Cavanagh, 'Corporate criminal liability: an assessment of the models of fault' (2011) Journal of Criminal Law 414, 421 and 425.
124. Article 121-2 of the French *Code pénal* of 1994: '*des infractions commises, pour leur compte, par leurs organes ou représentants.*'
125. Note that the case law does appear to accept that a material act of an ordinary employee creates liability if the moral element of the offence (also) resides with the organ or representative. *See*

point, the French Supreme Court also accepted that liability could be the consequence of a certain commercial policy of a company, but recent case law appears to require that the actual organ or representative that committed the offence be identified.[126]

90 Since corporate criminal liability is a particularly controversial issue in the German literature, corporate liability for criminal (and regulatory) offences is dealt with outside of the *Strafgesetzbuch*, in the *Ordnungswidrigkeitengesetz*. § 30 of the latter provides that a legal person such as a corporation can be fined for criminal or regulatory offences committed by its representatives if as a result of such an offence 'duties incumbent on the legal person ... have been violated, or where the legal person ... has been enriched or was intended to be enriched'.[127] In order to attract liability, the representative needs to be an organ, a representative or a person with control functions, although that person does not need to be identified.[128] As a step towards the aggregation theory discussed above, German law includes a separate offence of insufficient supervision, for which a corporation can also be liable.[129]

91 Under the *Corpus Juris* for fraud against the EU's financial interests, corporations could be liable for an offence 'provided the offence is committed for the benefit of the organisation by some organ or representative of the organisation, or any person acting in its name and having power, whether by law or merely in fact, to make decisions'.[130]

92 In all jurisdictions then, corporate criminal liability (often as opposed to civil liability) does not arise from the acts and states of minds of any employee: at the very least the *mens rea* of the offence needs to be demonstrated in respect of the (senior) management of the company. In some cases, national jurisdictions also appear to accept that the liability of a company is the result of its organization or policy, instead of requiring a personal fault by its management.

[G] Conclusion

93 The maxim *actus non facit reum nisi mens sit rea* expresses the idea that someone who committed an act prohibited by the criminal law can generally only be punished

---

B de Lamy and M Segonds, 'Facs. 7: responsabilité pénale des personnes morales' in *JurisClasseur pénal des affaires* (LexisNexis 2018), paras 30-31 and 35.

126. *See* B de Lamy and M Segonds, 'Facs. 7: responsabilité pénale des personnes morales' in *JurisClasseur pénal des affaires* (LexisNexis 2018), paras 44-46 and J-Y Maréchal, 'Facs. 20 : responsabilité pénale des personnes morales' in *JurisClasseur pénal code* (LexisNexis 2018), paras 91-98. *See also*, for a historical view: F Desportes and F Le Gunehec, *Droit pénal général* (Economica 2009) 578-579.
127. § 30, first paragraph of the *Ordnungswidrigkeitengesetz*.
128. As '*Generalbevollmächtigter*' or '*in leitender Stellung als Prokurist oder Handlungsbevollmächtigter*' or '*als sonstige Person, die für die Leitung des Betriebs oder Unternehmens einer juristischen Person ... verantwortlich handelt*'. *See* § 30, first paragraph of the *Ordnungswidrigkeitengesetz*. *See also* T Weigend, 'Societas delinquere non potest? A German perspective' (2008) 6 Journal of International Criminal Justice 927, 931.
129. § 130 of the *Ordnungswidrigkeitengesetz*. *See also* T Weigend, 'Societas delinquere non potest? A German perspective' (2008) 6 Journal of International Criminal Justice 927, 931.
130. Article 14(1). *See* M Delmas-Marty (ed.), *Corpus juris introducing penal provisions for the purpose of the financial interests of the European Union* (Economica 1997) 70 and 156.

if he or she did so with a specific state of mind. How intense that state of mind must be depends on the offence and, to some extent, also on the legal system.

94 The most serious offences are generally considered those that involve an *intention* to conduct oneself unlawfully or to cause an unlawful result. However, usually the *knowledge* of the material elements of the offence (i.e. that one engages in specific conduct, that one causes specific results or that specific circumstances are present) is equated with intention. In order to protect some of the most important values of a legal system, also the *consciously taking of a substantial risk*, that certain results will arise may sometimes attract criminal liability. Although awareness of illegality is not required to establish intention or knowledge, it is indicative of it.

95 This is the sense in which I will use *mens rea* in the remainder of this treatise: as the (at least) awareness of the type of conduct one engages in, of the (likely) results of that conduct and/or of the relevant circumstances. An intention to engage in certain conduct or to achieve certain results entails such an awareness that one engages in that conduct or that certain results will likely follow. When investigating the relevance of *mens rea* in European antitrust law, I will therefore focus on whether 'intentions' are relevant for the establishment of antitrust offences (*see* in particular Chapters 2-3). I will distinguish between 'objective' and 'subjective' intentions, i.e. those that are deduced from external factors such as conduct and those that are evidenced by statements (*see* paragraphs 82-84 above).

96 A number of offences in the criminal law do not require evidence of the perpetrator's mental state, or at least not for all elements of the offence. In those cases, only the perpetrator's conduct, the consequences of his actions and the circumstances in which they take place will be assessed, possibly taking into account certain standards of conduct which are normatively prescribed. These are *strict liability* or *negligence* offences and I believe that even the latter do not in fact have a *mens rea* requirement. Chapters 2-3 will also discuss whether infringements of European antitrust law fall in this category.

97 Even for strict liability and negligent offences, however, the perpetrator's mental state may nevertheless be relevant as an aggravating or attenuating circumstance to be taken into account when meting out punishment. In other words, even if an offence may be committed unintentionally, the intentional offence will nevertheless generally be punished more severely. In this context, the awareness of illegality also plays a role since it implies intention. The relevance of intentions in the punishment of EU antitrust infringements will be discussed in Chapter 4.

98 In the case of corporations, *mens rea* for criminal law purposes is normally identified by reference to senior management. However, a company's organization or policy may in some circumstances be indicative of guilt as well. Chapter 4 will also discuss whether the same principles apply under EU antitrust law.

§1.02 *MENS REA* IN US ANTITRUST LAW

99 A detailed discussion of the role of *mens rea* in US antitrust law goes beyond the scope of this treatise. Nevertheless, after discussing the notion of *mens rea* in the criminal law in Europe, it makes sense to at least briefly touch upon the role this concept plays in US antitrust law. There are significant differences between antitrust law in the EU and the US, not least of all that US antitrust law also entails criminal offences in the classical sense (punishable with imprisonment). But US antitrust law nevertheless had an important influence on competition law in Europe, not only at its inception (when the introduction of an antitrust policy was very much encouraged by the US after the Second World War)[131] but also in subsequent decades, as I will highlight a number of times in the following chapters.[132]

100 Because of this influence, antitrust law in Europe has often developed in dialogue with US antitrust case law and doctrine. To understand what role *mens rea* can, does or should play in EU antitrust law, it is therefore useful to understand what role it plays in US antitrust law.

101 After a brief discussion of the origins of US antitrust law (section [A]), I will focus on three specific aspects of US antitrust law where the *mens rea* requirement seems to have played a role, namely: in section [B], the notion of agreement in section 1 of the Sherman Act; in section [C], the notion of restraint of trade in section 1 of the Sherman Act; and, finally, in section [D], the notion of monopolization in section 2 of the Sherman Act.

[A] The Origins of US Antitrust Law

102 Despite a number of precursors, antitrust law as we know it only really took off on 2 July 1890 when the US's Congress passed the *Act to protect trade and commerce against unlawful restraints and monopolies*[133] which in subsequent years became known as the *Anti-trust Act* and since 1976 is formally known as the *Sherman Act*,[134] after John Sherman, the senator who introduced the bill that led to it.

103 The industrialization of the US in the 18th and 19th century resulted in the concentration of the means of production in corporations and in wider combinations in order to both achieve the scale needed for ever bigger investments and shield industries

131. The Potsdam Agreement concluded between the USSR, the US and the UK in 1945 already provided in its clause 12: 'At the earliest practicable date, the German economy shall be decentralized for the purpose of eliminating the present excessive concentration of economic power as exemplified in particular by cartels, syndicates, trusts and other monopolistic arrangements.' *See* The Berlin (Potsdam) Conference, July 17-August 2, 1945 (a) Protocol of the Proceedings, August 1, 1945 <http://avalon.law.yale.edu/20th_century/decade17.asp> accessed 18 July 2018.
132. *See*, for example, for the influence on cartel enforcement, para. 180 below, for the influence on predatory pricing, paras 329ff., for the influence on abuse of regulatory process, paras 418ff.
133. 26 Stat. 209, 15 U.S.C. 1.
134. Per section 305(a) of the Hart–Scott–Rodino Antitrust Improvements Act of 1976, 90 Stat. 1383.

from ruinous competition. Several US states liberalized corporate law towards the end of the 19th century in order to convince large businesses to base themselves there,[135] but the businesses themselves also sought for legal solutions to manage the large industrial organizations they had become. The common law concept of the 'trust' was the inspiration for some of these businesses, most famously Standard Oil which became a trust in 1882.

104 The concentration of economic power during the Gilded Age became a widespread public concern in the US in the 1880s when the concentration of businesses was associated with social inequality, unemployment and the ills resulting therefrom. Although the 'trust' model was only used by a small number of businesses to consolidate their organization, nevertheless, 'the trust became a symbol of the new order'.[136]

105 The opposition against economic concentration came from many corners of society and was inspired by a number of concerns, including not only consumer welfare but also the willingness to protect small businesses.[137] Indeed, it has been argued that the latter concern was the dominant driving force behind the Sherman Act but that in any event a multitude of interest groups lobbied John Sherman at the time of the creation of the act.[138]

106 Whatever its objectives, the text which was enacted in 1890 contained two principal sections which provided:

> Sec. 1. Every contract, combination in the form of trust or otherwise, or conspiracy, in restraint of trade or commerce among the several States, or with foreign nations, is hereby declared to be illegal. Every person who shall make any such contract or engage in any such combination or conspiracy, shall be deemed guilty of a misdemeanor, and, on conviction thereof, shall be punished by a fine not exceeding five thousand dollars, or by imprisonment not exceeding one year, or by both said punishments, in the discretion of the court.
>
> Sec. 2. Every person who shall monopolize, or attempt to monopolize, or combine or conspire with any other person or persons, to monopolize any part of the trade or commerce among the several States, or with foreign nations, shall be deemed guilty of a misdemeanor, and, on conviction thereof, shall be punished by a fine not exceeding five thousand dollars, or by imprisonment not exceeding one year, or by both said punishments, in the discretion of the court.[139]

135. EM Fox, LA Sullivan and RJR Peritz, *Cases and materials on U.S. antitrust in global context* (Thomson West 2004) 27.
136. EM Fox, LA Sullivan and RJR Peritz, *Cases and materials on U.S. antitrust in global context* (Thomson West 2004) 6.
137. R Bork, 'The role of the courts in applying economics' (1985) 54 Antitrust Law Journal 21, 24. *See also* MJ Sklar, 'Sherman Antitrust Act jurisprudence and federal policy-making in the formative period, 1890-1914' (1990) 35 New York Law School Law Review 791, 822.
138. *See* W Troesken, 'The letters of John Sherman and the origins of antitrust' (2002) 15 The Review of Austrian Economics 275.
139. The text has been amended a few times since 1890 but has substantially stayed the same. The penalties have increased, however. The Tunney Act of 1974, 88 Stat. 1708, requalified the violation of the statute from a misdemeanour to a felony. Since the Antitrust Criminal Penalty

107 The ambiguity of the concepts used in the Sherman Act and even of its objectives meant that a lot of room was left for judicial interpretation.[140]

[B] The Notion of Agreement in Section 1

108 In order to be declared illegal under section 1 of the Sherman Act, there must be (i) a 'contract, combination ..., or conspiracy' which (ii) is 'in restraint of trade'. The first of these conditions is discussed in this section, the second in the next.[141]

109 The notions of 'contract', 'combination' and 'conspiracy' are usually used interchangeably:[142] While the notion of contract is fairly uncontroversial, this is not the case for the words 'combination' and 'conspiracy'. The notion of 'combination' appears to have been very common at the time of the enactment of the Sherman Act to refer to combinations of businesses in the form of the infamous trusts. This is also apparent from the addition 'in the form of trust or otherwise'. Finally, the notion of 'conspiracy' has its origin in a criminal offence under the common law: a conspiracy is an agreement between two or more persons to do an unlawful act, or to do a lawful act by unlawful means.[143] Since the agreement is sufficient (even if the unlawful act is never accomplished or the unlawful means never used) to establish the offence, it is an inchoate offence.[144] In any event, the crucial question to answer for this criterion of section 1 of the Sherman Act is whether the conduct of the firms in question 'stemmed from independent decision or from an agreement, tacit or express'.[145]

110 The Supreme Court has ruled in *American Tobacco* that '[w]here the circumstances are such as to warrant a jury in finding that the conspirators had a unity of purpose or a common design and understanding, or a meeting of minds in an unlawful arrangement, the conclusion that a conspiracy is established is justified'.[146] Similarly,

---

Enhancement and Reform Act of 2004, 118 Stat. 665, the maximum fine has been increased to USD 100 million and the maximum term of imprisonment to 10 years.

140. Initially the Sherman Act was mostly used to target combinations of workers (labour unions), but section 6 of the Clayton Antitrust Act of 1914 (38 Stat. 730) exempted these from its application, so this case law is of little relevance today and I will therefore not discuss it further.
141. I will not discuss here the requirement that there is an effect on interstate commerce or foreign commerce, which is the consequence of the limited jurisdiction of the US Congress (as distinguished from the jurisdiction of the states) pursuant to Article I, section 8, clause 3 of the US Constitution.
142. *Bogosian v Gulf Oil Corp*, 561 F.2d 434, 445 (3d Cir. 1977), cert. denied, 434 U.S. 1086 (1978). *See also* PE Areeda and H Hovenkamp, *Antitrust law – An analysis of antitrust principles and their application* (Wolters Kluwer 1978, Supp May 2018) ¶ 1403.
143. P Murphy (ed.), *Blackstone's Criminal Practice* (Blackstone 2001) 88. *See also* X, 'The nature of a Sherman Act conspiracy' (1954) Columbia Law Review 1108, 1108.
144. It is sometimes said that the notion under the Sherman Act has a somewhat different meaning than under criminal law in that the object of the conspiracy in antitrust law (e.g. setting the price at a certain level) is not independently unlawful, but only because of the conspiracy, whereas the object of a conspiracy in the criminal law is something unlawful (it is a conspiracy *to commit an offence*). *See* PE Areeda and H Hovenkamp, *Antitrust law – An analysis of antitrust principles and their application* (Wolters Kluwer 1978, Supp May 2018) ¶ 1402a.
145. *Theatre Enterprises v Paramount Film Distribution Corp*, 346 U.S. 537, 540 (1954).
146. *American Tobacco Co. v United States*, 328 U.S. 781, 810 (1946).

in *Monsanto*, it held that section 1 of the Sherman Act required evidence that parties 'had a conscious commitment to a common scheme designed to achieve an unlawful objective'.[147] The Court therefore clearly uses psychological language: should this be understood as a reference to actual mental states or is it based on more objective elements?

111 Beyond the obvious case of express agreements, the case law seems to take into account whether there is interdependence between the parties to the alleged agreement. In those circumstances, they may have an objective motive to forego their immediate self-interest (to compete to gain business) and instead cooperate for their joint longer-term interest of market stability. A good example is *Interstate Circuit*, where the eponymous cinema chain wrote identical letters to eight of its movie suppliers asking that they ensure a minimum charge for movies displayed in other cinemas. In order to establish horizontal (hub-and-spoke) collusion between the movie suppliers, the Supreme Court pointed out that the letter of Interstate Circuit 'named on its face as addressees the eight local representatives of the distributors, and so from the beginning each of the distributors knew that the proposals were under consideration by the others. Each was aware that all were in active competition and that without substantially unanimous action with respect to the restrictions for any given territory there was a risk of a substantial loss of the business and good will of the [competing cinemas], but that with it there was the prospect of increased profits. There was, therefore, strong motive for concerted action'.[148]

112 However, the case law also makes clear that interdependence alone cannot be sufficient to establish collusion in the sense of section 1 of the Sherman Act. Although it may be an objective motive for collusion, there is always going to be a high degree of interdependence between the players in a market, in particular in an oligopoly, such that parallelism in their conduct may arise absent any collusion.[149] While parallel behaviour may therefore point towards interdependence, a 'contract, combination ..., or conspiracy' can only be established if something more is present. The Third Circuit has in this context referred to 'plus factors' which suggest that the parallel conduct cannot be explained by interdependence alone. The 'most important evidence [of such plus factors] will generally be non-economic evidence "that there was an actual, manifest agreement not to compete" [...]. That evidence may involve "customary indications of traditional conspiracy," or "proof that the defendants got together and exchanged assurances of common action or otherwise adopted a common plan even though no meetings, conversations, or exchanged documents are shown"'.[150]

147. *Monsanto Co. v Spray-Rite Svc. Corp.*, 465 U.S. 752, 768 (1984).
148. *Interstate Circuit v United States*, 306 U.S. 208, 222 (1939).
149. *Bell Atlantic Corp v Twombly*, 550 U.S. 544, 557 (2007). *See* already *Bogosian v Gulf Oil Corp*, 561 F.2d 434, 446 (3d Cir. 1977), cert. denied, 434 U.S. 1086 (1978) and *Flat Glass Antitrust Litigation*, 385 F.3d 350, 359 (3d Cir. 2004).
150. *Flat Glass Antitrust Litigation*, 385 F.3d 350, 361 (3d Cir. 2004).

113 Unfortunately this explanation is somewhat circular and vague.[151] It has even been suggested that, in the event of litigation, courts may prefer to leave the question of whether there is a 'contract, combination ..., or conspiracy' unanswered as long as possible and focus instead on whether there is a restraint of trade.[152] If it can be excluded that there is such a restraint, then there is no need to rule on this first requirement for the application of section 1.

114 With this lack of a systematic answer, the case law has instead developed a practice of focusing on other objective elements which turn mere interdependence into an agreement in the sense of section 1. The main objective element is the existence of certain types of communications by and between the parties to an alleged agreement.[153]

115 It seems therefore – similar to what I will conclude in relation to Article 101 TFEU in the EU (*see* Chapter 2) – that, despite the psychological language of the 'meeting of minds', the notion of agreement in section 1 of the Sherman Act should be established by reference to objective factors.

[C] The Notion of Restraint of Trade in Section 1

116 The second key concept in section 1 that needed elucidation was the notion of 'restraint of trade'. In *Trans-Missouri*, the US Supreme Court considered this notion for the first time. Justice Peckham who wrote the majority opinion of the strongly divided Court (voting five-to-four) concluded that *any* restraint of trade was unlawful. While the railroad companies which were the subject of the case argued that the common law only prohibited 'unreasonable' restraints on trade and not 'reasonable' restraints, Peckham stated that the Court could not accept this argument: 'the plain and ordinary'[154] meaning of the Sherman Act showed that it also covered 'contracts which are not in unreasonable restraint of trade'.[155] Peckham concluded that:

> For these reasons, the suit of the Government can be maintained without proof of the allegation that the agreement was entered into for the purpose of restraining trade or commerce, or for maintaining rates above what was reasonable. The necessary effect of the agreement is to restrain trade or commerce, no matter what the intent was on the part of those who signed it.[156]

151. *See also* WH Page, 'Tacit agreement under section 1 of the Sherman Act' (2017) 81(2) Antitrust Law Journal 593, in particular 603.
152. PE Areeda and H Hovenkamp, *Antitrust law – An analysis of antitrust principles and their application* (Wolters Kluwer 1978, Supp May 2018) ¶ 1406g.
153. *See* in particular WH Page, 'Tacit agreement under section 1 of the Sherman Act' (2017) 81(2) Antitrust Law Journal 593 and PE Areeda and H Hovenkamp, *Antitrust law – An analysis of antitrust principles and their application* (Wolters Kluwer 1978, Supp May 2018) ¶ 1416-1427.
154. *United States v Trans-Missouri Freight Association*, 166 U.S. 290, 328 (1897).
155. *United States v Trans-Missouri Freight Association*, 166 U.S. 290, 340 (1897).
156. *United States v Trans-Missouri Freight Association*, 166 U.S. 290, 342 (1897).

117 The strict prohibition of any restraint of trade as enunciated by the majority opinion in *Trans-Missouri* was viewed by many as overly inclusive: any contract concluded by a business will in one way or another restrain its ability to do business. Based on *Trans-Missouri*, atomistic competition based on a war of all against all seemed to be the only lawful way in which businesses could conduct themselves.[157]

118 The overinclusive rule of *Trans-Missouri* was somewhat attenuated in subsequent judgments, in particular at the instigation of the lower courts. In its *Addyston Pipe* judgment, the US Court of Appeals for the Sixth Circuit in particular (subsequently confirmed by the Supreme Court) distinguished between restraints of trade which were ancillary to the main, lawful objectives of an agreement (such as a sale or a partnership) and restraints which were not (i.e. which were the sole object of the agreement) and therefore unlawful.[158]

119 However, it was only when the composition of the Supreme Court had sufficiently changed and Justice White who wrote a dissenting opinion in *Trans-Missouri*, had become Chief Justice, that *Trans-Missouri* was reversed. This happened in *Standard Oil* where the Court held that in order to determine whether agreements amount to an unlawful restraint of trade, they need to be assessed in light of a 'rule of reason'.[159] This interpretation in line with the common law meant that a contract could put an unreasonable restraint upon a business 'where the nature and the character of the dealing was such as to engender the presumption of intent to bring about at least one of the injuries which it was deemed would result from monopoly, that is an undue enhancement of price'.[160] The Court then determined that in *Standard Oil* the creation of the trust 'necessarily involved the intent to drive others from the field and to exclude them from their right to trade and thus accomplish the mastery which was the end in view'.[161]

120 The reversal of the case law operated in *Standard Oil* seemed to have provided closure to the heated debates over the 'trust question' around the turn of the century. With the adoption shortly afterwards in 1914 of the Clayton Act and the Federal Trade Commission Act, and the more pressing issue of the First World War, the trust question suddenly receded from the centre of national politics in the US.[162]

121 One important qualification to the rule of reason which was introduced by the Supreme Court later on was the identification in *Socony-Vacuum* of a category of

---

157. *See* the dissenting opinion of Justice Holmes in *Northern Securities Co. v United States*, 193 U.S. 197, 411 (1904): 'an interpretation of the law which in my opinion would make eternal the bellum omnium contra omnes and disintegrate society so far as it could into individual atoms'.
158. *See United States v Addyston Pipe & Steel Co.*, 85 F. 271, in particular 282-283 (6th Cir. 1898), modified and affirmed by the Supreme Court in *United States v Addyston Pipe & Steel Co.*, 175 U.S. 211 (1899).
159. *Standard Oil Co. of New Jersey v United States*, 221 U.S. 1 (1911).
160. *Standard Oil Co. of New Jersey v United States*, 221 U.S. 1, 54 (1911).
161. *Standard Oil Co. of New Jersey v United States*, 221 U.S. 1, 76 (1911).
162. MJ Sklar, 'Sherman Antitrust Act jurisprudence and federal policy-making in the formative period, 1890-1914' (1990) 35 New York Law School Law Review 791, 824.

agreements (in particular direct price-fixing) which were illegal per se and to which the 'rule of reason' therefore did not need to be applied.[163]

122 As is evident from the quotes above, much of the discussion on what was a reasonable or unreasonable restraint of trade was couched in terms of the intent of the parties to the agreement. This stress on 'intent' and indeed the creation of a rule of reason in *Standard Oil* has been criticized as leaving too much space to judicial discretion and therefore causing legal uncertainty.[164]

123 Nevertheless, in civil cases adjudicated under the rule of reason, the courts have continued to rely on evidence of intent. The Supreme Court has even held that restraints in agreements that fall under the rule of reason can be judged unreasonable if 'a restraint otherwise reasonable is accompanied with a specific intent to accomplish a forbidden restraint'.[165] However, in most cases, the Court seems to follow the principle that intent is not the final word on whether a restraint of trade is reasonable or not. Intentions are merely an interpretative tool: according to the Supreme Court in *Chicago Board of Trade*, they are relevant 'not because a good intention will save an otherwise objectionable regulation or the reverse; but because knowledge of intent may help the court to interpret facts and to predict consequences'.[166] The Fifth Circuit explained in *Lehrman* that:

> The circumstances surrounding the use of a particular business practice give strong clues as to what those who employ the practice hope to accomplish by it, and what those individuals hope to accomplish may shed light on whether the practice does in fact have the hoped-for, but anti-competitive, effect. In short, when a firm displays an anti-competitive animus in the operation of an otherwise ambiguous business practice, what the firm seeks to accomplish provides as sure an indicator of the actual effect of the practice on competition as can be found in the shifting sands of antitrust litigation.[167]

124 This is still the position taken by the US agencies in their guidance on collaborations between competitors.[168]

125 In criminal cases, the *mens rea* requirement is stricter. In *Gypsum*, the Supreme Court held that 'the existence of a *mens rea* is the rule of, rather than the exception to, the principles of Anglo-American criminal jurisprudence'[169] and that therefore it was

163. *United States v Socony-Vacuum Oil Co.*, 310 U.S. 150, in particular 218 and 213 (1950).
164. *See* EM Fox, LA Sullivan and RJR Peritz, *Cases and materials on U.S. antitrust in global context* (Thomson West 2004), 48.
165. *United States v Columbia Steel Co.*, 334 U.S. 495, 522 (1948).
166. *Board of Trade of the city of Chicago v United States*, 246 U.S. 231, 231 (1918).
167. *Lehrman v Gulf Oil Corp*, 464 F.2d 26, 38 n. 9 (5th Cir. 1972).
168. *See* footnote 35 to the Federal Trade Commission and US Department of Justice, Antitrust guidelines for collaborations among competitors (2000): 'Anticompetitive intent alone does not establish an antitrust violation, and procompetitive intent does not preclude a violation. *See, e.g.*, Chicago Bd. of Trade, 246 U.S. at 238. But extrinsic evidence of intent may aid in evaluating market power, the likelihood of anticompetitive harm, and claimed procompetitive justifications where an agreement's effects are otherwise ambiguous.'
169. *United States v United States Gypsum Co.*, 438 U.S. 422, 436 (1978).

'unwilling to construe the Sherman Act as mandating a regime of strict liability criminal offences'.[170]

126 *Gypsum* concerned the exchange of information between competitors, conduct that was not viewed as per se illegal, and the Court noted that the Sherman Act 'does not, in clear and categorical terms, precisely identify the conduct which it proscribes'.[171] The Court therefore found that, although the 'indeterminacy of the Sherman Act's standards did not constitute a fatal constitutional objection to their criminal enforcement',[172] 'the same basic concerns which are manifested in our general requirement of *mens rea* in criminal statutes ... are at least equally salient in the antitrust context'.[173] It is useful to quote the Court in full on this point:

> With certain exceptions for conduct regarded as per se illegal because of its unquestionably anticompetitive effects, ..., the behaviour proscribed by the Act is often difficult to distinguish from the grey zone of socially acceptable and economically justifiable business conduct. Indeed, the type of conduct charged in the indictment in this case – the exchange of price information among competitors – is illustrative in this regard. The imposition of criminal liability on a corporate official, or for that matter on a corporation directly, for engaging in such conduct which only after the fact is determined to violate the statute because of anticompetitive effects, without inquiring into the intent with which it was undertaken, holds out the distinct possibility of overdeterrence; salutary and procompetitive conduct lying close to the borderline of impermissible conduct might be shunned by businessmen who chose to be excessively cautious in the face of uncertainty regarding possible exposure to criminal punishment for even a good faith error of judgment. ... The criminal sanctions would be used not to punish conscious and calculated wrongdoing at odds with statutory proscriptions, but instead simply to regulate business practices regardless of the intent with which they were undertaken. While, in certain cases, we have imputed a regulatory purpose to Congress in choosing to employ criminal sanctions, ... the availability of a range of nonpenal alternatives to the criminal sanctions of the Sherman Act negates the imputation of any such purpose to Congress in the instant context. For these reasons, we conclude that the criminal offenses defined by the Sherman Act should be construed as including intent as an element.[174]

127 To find such an offence, the prosecution therefore needed to prove that the perpetrators had the relevant *mens rea*.

128 The next question the US Supreme Court faced in *Gypsum* was what type of *mens rea* needed to be established for antitrust offences. When discussing this, the Court referred to the Model Penal Code developed by the American Law Institute in 1962 which distinguishes between four possible levels of *mens rea*: purpose, knowledge, recklessness and negligence. The Court's position was that '[i]n dealing with the kinds of business decisions upon which the antitrust laws focus, the concepts of recklessness

170. *United States v United States Gypsum Co.*, 438 U.S. 422, 436 (1978).
171. *United States v United States Gypsum Co.*, 438 U.S. 422, 438 (1978).
172. *United States v United States Gypsum Co.*, 438 U.S. 422, 439 (1978).
173. *United States v United States Gypsum Co.*, 438 U.S. 422, 440 (1978).
174. *United States v United States Gypsum Co.*, 438 U.S. 422, 440-443 (1978).

and negligence have no place'[175] and also that it is not necessary to show that the disputed conduct was undertaken with the 'conscious object'[176] to produce anticompetitive effects. According to the Court, 'action undertaken with knowledge of its probable consequences and having the requisite anticompetitive effects can be sufficient predicate for a finding of criminal liability under the antitrust laws'.[177] Or in other words: 'Where carefully planned and calculated conduct is being scrutinized in the context of a criminal prosecution, the perpetrator's knowledge of the anticipated consequences is a sufficient predicate for a finding of criminal intent.'[178]

129 *Gypsum* was a case involving indirect price-fixing, which is assessed under the rule of reason. Subsequent appellate judgments have held that, in case of per se violations such as direct price-fixing, no evidence is required of the defendant's intent to restrain trade: it is sufficient to prove that the defendant knowingly entered into the alleged agreement or conspiracy.[179] Per se restraints of trade are in principle prosecuted criminally by the Department of Justice but, faithful to *Gypsum*, it has stated that, in case 'there is clear evidence that the subjects of the investigation were not aware of, or did not appreciate, the consequences of their action', criminal investigation and prosecution may not be appropriate.[180] The state of mind of the perpetrator will therefore already be relevant at the prosecution stage.

[D] The Notion of Monopolization in Section 2

130 Holding a monopoly is as such not an offence under section 2 of the Sherman Act: it makes a great deal of difference whether monopoly is 'thrust upon' a firm or whether the firm actively pursues it.[181] What is illegal is to 'monopolize, or attempt to monopolize, or combine or conspire ... to monopolize'. Although these were construed as three distinct notions in the early case law, monopolization and attempt to monopolize have now almost merged into one concept, and conspiracy to monopolize is interpreted strongly in line with section 1 of the Sherman Act.[182]

131 In order to establish monopolization or an attempt to monopolize, it is necessary to identify conduct which is commonly referred to as 'exclusionary' or 'predatory'.[183] Much like in Europe, however, there remains a lot of disagreement as to what

175. *United States v United States Gypsum Co.*, 438 U.S. 422, 444 (1978).
176. *United States v United States Gypsum Co.*, 438 U.S. 422, 444 (1978).
177. *United States v United States Gypsum Co.*, 438 U.S. 422, 444 (1978).
178. *United States v United States Gypsum Co.*, 438 U.S. 422, 446 (1978).
179. ME Stucke, 'Is intent relevant?' (2012) 8 Journal of Law, Economics & Policy 801, 811. *See also* American Bar Association, *Criminal Antitrust Litigation Handbook* (American Bar Association 2006) 302-303 and case law cited there.
180. Department of Justice, *Antitrust Division Manual* (5th edition, 2015) III-12.
181. *United States v Alcoa*, 148 F.2d 416, 429 (2d Cir. 1945).
182. *See* EM Fox, LA Sullivan and RJR Peritz, *Cases and materials on U.S. antitrust in global context* (Thomson West 2004) 207. *See also* PE Areeda and H Hovenkamp, *Antitrust law – An analysis of antitrust principles and their application* (Wolters Kluwer 1978, Supp May 2018) ¶ 804 and 809.
183. The terms are used interchangeably: *see Taylor Publishing Co v Jostens, Inc*, 216 F.3d 465, 475 n. 2 (5th Cir. 2000).

behaviour falls into this category.[184] Instead of coming up with a unitary standard, the case law instead developed a classification of different types of monopolizing behaviour, each with their own criteria.[185] Possibly to overcome the uncertainty that surrounds the concept of monopolization, the case law regularly refers to the intention of the firm in question. Already in *Standard Oil*, the Supreme Court stated that the eponymous firm's creation 'gives rise, in and of itself, in the absence of countervailing circumstances, to say the least, to the prima facie presumption of intent and purpose to maintain the dominancy over the oil industry, not as a result of normal methods of industrial development, but by new means of combination which were resorted to in order that greater power might be added than would otherwise have arisen had normal methods been followed'.[186] In later case law, this has been summarized as requiring, beyond the possession of monopoly power, the 'wilful acquisition or maintenance of that power as distinguished from growth or development as a consequence of a superior product, business acumen, or historic accident'.[187]

132 Specifically for the notion of 'attempt to monopolize', the early case law referred to the meaning of attempt in the criminal law. In *Swift*, the Supreme Court held: 'Where acts are not sufficient in themselves to produce a result which the law seeks to prevent – for instance, the monopoly – but require further acts in addition to the mere forces of nature to bring that result to pass, an intent to bring it to pass is necessary in order to produce a dangerous probability that it will happen.'[188] In *Alcoa*, this was termed a 'specific intent' to monopolize.[189]

133 However, if such intent is understood in an objective way, as in *Standard Oil* and many other cases,[190] i.e. deduced from the conduct of the undertaking itself, it is of dubious use. As the First Circuit noted in *Barry Wright*: if intent 'is meant to refer to a set of objective economic conditions that allow the court to "infer" improper intent, ..., then, using Occam's razor, we can slice "intent" away'.[191] Positing such improper intent is superfluous,[192] unless it is used, in a circular manner, to reconfirm that the conduct was improper.[193]

184. PE Areeda, L Kaplow and A Edlin, *Antitrust analysis. Problems, text, and cases* (Aspen 2004) 368; M Lao, 'Reclaiming a role for intent evidence in monopolization analysis' (2004) 54 American University Law Review 151, 155.
185. M Lao, 'Reclaiming a role for intent evidence in monopolization analysis' (2004) 54 American University Law Review 151, 161.
186. *Standard Oil Co of New Jersey v United States*, 221 U.S. 1, 75 (1911).
187. *United States v Grinnell*, 384 U.S. 563, 570-571 (1966).
188. *Swift & Co v United States*, 196 U.S. 375, 396 (1905).
189. *United States v Alcoa*, 148 F.2d 416, 432 (2d Cir. 1945). As the Court explains and as discussed in paras 59ff. above, the notion of 'specific intent' refers to 'an intent which goes beyond the mere intent to do the act'. *See also* RA Cass and KN Hylton, 'Antitrust intent' (2001) 74 Southern California Law Review 657 who discuss the monopolization case law in terms of general and specific intent.
190. *See*, for example, *Aspen Skiing Co v Aspen Highlands Skiing Corp*, 472 U.S. 585 (1985) and *Eastman Kodak Co v Image Technical Services*, 504 U.S. 451 (1992).
191. *Barry Wright Corp v ITT Grinnell Corp*, 724 F.2d 227, 232 (1st Cir. 1983).
192. *See* PE Areeda and H Hovenkamp, *Antitrust law – An analysis of antitrust principles and their application* (Wolters Kluwer 1978, Supp May 2018) ¶ 805b. Compare also *United States v Alcoa*, 148 F.2d 416, 432 (2d Cir. 1945).
193. *See* more generally on this issue, paras 656ff. below.

134 The case law, in particular in predatory pricing cases, has nevertheless also considered intent in a subjective sense, i.e. by reference to internal documents. While some of the case law relies merely on objective factors (in particular pricing below a certain cost variable and, since *Brooke*,[194] evidence of a prospect of recoupment), other courts also consider, in addition to these objective factors, evidence of subjective intent. The Eleventh Circuit pointed out in *McGahee* that, in its view, 'the test for predatory pricing must consider subjective evidence'.[195]

135 To what extent a court or an author accepts or requires evidence of subjective intent may depend on whether it considers certain conduct to be ambiguous. A court which is strongly convinced of the qualification of a certain practice, may not find intent evidence helpful. This was the case for the Seventh Circuit in *A.A. Poultry Farms*, which considered that recoupment of the allegedly predatory prices in that case was impossible and dismissed evidence of intent as it 'does not help to separate competition from attempted monopolisation'.[196]

136 However, when a court considers that it is not obvious to qualify a certain practice, it can rely on the Supreme Court's ruling in *Chicago Board of Trade* that evidence of subjective intent can be a useful interpretative tool. In relation to section 2, the Fifth Circuit did so in *Taylor Publishing*, pointing out that intent 'retains its customary role as an aid in characterizing ambiguous conduct'.[197] Also in *Microsoft*, the district court and the DC Circuit performed a detailed analysis of the internal documents of Microsoft and documents provided to its customers to assess whether it engaged in monopolization.[198]

137 Also in monopolization cases, evidence of *mens rea* has therefore often played a role.

[E] Conclusion

138 *Mens rea* considerations have played a role in some of the case law under the Sherman Act. References to a 'meeting of minds' have informed the notion of 'agreement' under section 1 of the Sherman Act, although it seems that the existence of such an agreement still needs to be established in an objective manner. For criminal prosecutions under section 1 of the Sherman Act, an intention to restrain trade needs to be established according to the Supreme Court. In monopolization cases, evidence of subjective intentions has been used to disambiguate conduct.

139 The relevance of *mens rea* in the establishment of antitrust infringements is the subject of much debate in the US. Since some of the issues are quite similar to those in Europe (which I will describe in the next three chapters), it is useful to be aware of this US case law. In Chapter 5, I will discuss the debate in the literature in more detail, with reference to American scholarship as well.

---

194. *Brooke Group Ltd v Brown & Williamson Tobacco Corp*, 509 U.S. 209 (1993).
195. *McGahee v Northern Propane Gas Co*, 858 F.23d 1487, 1496 (11th Cir. 1988).
196. *A.A. Poultry Farms v Rose Acre Farms*, 881 F.2d 1396, 1402 (7th Cir. 1989).
197. *Taylor Publishing Co v Jostens, Inc*, 216 F.3d 465, 475 n. 2 (5th Cir. 2000).
198. *United States v Microsoft*, 253 F.3d 54 (D.C. Cir. 2001).

CHAPTER 2

Mens Rea in Article 101 TFEU

Quid non mortalia pectora cogis,
auri sacra fames?

Virgil, *Aeneid*, III, 56-57

140 Article 101(1) TFEU prohibits 'all agreements between undertakings, decisions by associations of undertakings and concerted practices which may affect trade between Member States and which have as their object or effect the prevention, restriction or distortion of competition within the internal market'.

141 This prohibition is commonly viewed as containing the following cumulative elements:

(a) an agreement, concerted practice or (in the case of associations) a decision;
(b) between undertakings or (for decisions) of an association of undertakings;
(c) which has as its object or effect the restriction (or prevention or distortion) of competition;
(d) which may affect trade between Member States.

142 Each of these elements can be viewed as a material element of the infringement of Article 101(1) TFEU. The question that is being investigated here is to what extent any or all of these four elements require or imply a mental state, a *mens rea*. For the avoidance of doubt, based on the correspondence principle, the mental state of the perpetrator can be related to all the material elements of an offence: a gardener who takes the tools of his client is not a thief, even if he knows that the tools belong to his client. If he takes them for a lawful purpose (e.g. to do work in his client's garden), he does not commit an offence. But, although his awareness that the tools belong to his client is not sufficient to conclude he is a thief, it is a necessary condition: if the gardener mistakenly believes that the spade he takes home after he finishes is his, even though it is actually his client's, he cannot be accused of theft.

143 In the context of Article 101(1) TFEU, we therefore need to assess whether such a mental state is required in relation to each of these four elements, even though the third element (the restriction of competition) is probably the key element in the definition of the infringement of Article 101(1) TFEU. The restriction of competition is the defining characteristic of the infringement described in Article 101(1) TFEU, but the presence of each of the other three elements is nevertheless required to establish that infringement. For example, a restriction of competition which is not the result of an agreement or concerted practice or decision of an association of undertakings will not fall foul of Article 101(1) TFEU. For each of these four elements, we therefore need to determine whether they entail a mental element.

144 I will not discuss here the notions of 'undertaking' and 'association of undertakings' as these concern first and foremost the perpetrator of the infringement as opposed to the infringement itself. However, I will discuss the notion of undertaking when analysing the case law on corporate liability in Chapter 4 (*see* paragraphs 464ff. below).

145 Since the criterion of the effect on trade between Member States is a jurisdictional criterion which is common between Article 101 and 102 TFEU, this will also be discussed in Chapter 4 (*see* paragraphs 453ff.).

146 The other two elements will be discussed in detail in this chapter. Section §2.01 discusses the notion of agreement and concerted practices. I will explain that, although this notion presupposes the mental state of human beings, best exemplified in the notions 'concurrence of wills' and 'meeting of minds', obviously only material manifestations of these 'wills' and 'minds' can be used to determine their existence. More importantly for the question of the role of *mens rea*, the existence of an agreement or concerted practice is not premised on the private manifestations of the 'wills' and 'minds' of the undertakings in question: the existence of an agreement or concerted practice is assessed by reference to the communications exchanged *between the undertakings*.

147 However, the attribution of liability to an individual undertaking for participation in an infringement is couched in terms that are more reminiscent of *mens rea*: what matters is whether they 'intended to contribute' to the infringement and 'were aware' or 'could reasonably have foreseen' the conduct of other participants. In practice, a number of presumptions that imply participation limit the evidentiary burden of the Commission to establish this.

148 Section §2.02 discusses the relevance of mental elements in the establishment of a restriction of competition. I will explain that an undertaking's intention to restrict competition or its awareness that an agreement or concerted practice restricts competition is neither necessary nor sufficient to find such a restriction. The restriction is assessed in an objective manner. However, evidence of an undertaking's intentions and knowledge of the consequences of its actions is relevant in making that objective assessment.

149 Article 101 TFEU also contains a third paragraph, which provides for an exception to the prohibition of Article 101(1) TFEU. In particular, that prohibition may be declared inapplicable (and in fact is declared inapplicable pursuant to Article 1(2) of Regulation 1/2003)[199] in case an agreement or concerted practice between undertakings (or decision of an association of undertakings):

> [a] contributes to improving the production or distribution of goods or to promoting technical or economic progress, while [b] allowing consumers a fair share of the resulting benefit, and ... does not;
> [c] impose on the undertakings concerned restrictions which are not indispensable to the attainment of these objectives;
> [d] afford such undertakings the possibility of eliminating competition in respect of a substantial part of the products in question.

150 In §2.03, I will say a few words about the relevance of *mens rea* in the assessment under Article 101(3) TFEU.

§2.01 AGREEMENT, CONCERTED PRACTICE AND DECISION OF AN ASSOCIATION

151 As already hinted at above, the language of EU competition law is anthropomorphic,[200] even though its main subjects are undertakings, which usually are not individuals. There are few areas of EU competition law where this is as apparent as in the notion of 'agreement' or 'concerted practice'.

152 I will not discuss in detail the notion of a 'decision' of an association of undertakings in the sense of Article 101 TFEU. This notion is not much more than an enforcement tool to hold associations of undertakings liable for infringements to that Article.[201] In most, if not all cases, the decision of an association of undertakings will reflect an agreement by its members which are undertakings and could therefore also be pursued on that basis. Especially in the case of associations with a large number of members (e.g. in the liberal professions), it is simply easier from an enforcement perspective to sanction the association rather than all its individual members.

153 The notions of 'agreement' and 'concerted practice', however, are much more fundamental to Article 101 TFEU: purely unilateral conduct is not caught by Article 101

199. Regulation 1/2003 on the implementation of the rules on competition laid down in Articles 81 and 82 of the Treaty [2003] OJ L1/1.
200. *See also* A Ezrachi and ME Stucke, 'Artificial intelligence & collusion: when computers inhibit competition' (2015) <https://www.law.ox.ac.uk/sites/files/oxlaw/cclpl40.pdf> accessed 31 August 2017, 7; A Ezrachi and ME Stucke, *Virtual competition: the promise and perils of the algorithm-driven economy* (Harvard University Press 2016) 42 and SK Mehra, 'Antitrust and the robo-seller: competition in the time of algorithms' (2016) 100 University of Minnesota Law Review 1323, 1329. The language of the law in general is probably anthropocentric: *see* Y Bathaee, 'The artificial intelligence black box and the failure of intent and causation' (2018) Harvard Journal of Law & Technology 890, 890-891.
201. *See* J Faull, L Kjølbye, H Leupold and A Nikpay, 'Article 101' in J Faull and A Nikpay (eds), *The EU law of competition* (Oxford University Press 2014) 183, 218 and A Jones and B Sufrin, *EC competition law* (Oxford University Press 2008) 171. *See also* case T-111/08 *MasterCard and Others v Commission* ECLI:EU:T:2012:260, para. 243 and the opinion of AG Léger in C-309/99 *Wouters and Others* ECLI:EU:C:2001:390, para. 62.

TFEU[202] and it is therefore essential to understand what 'agreement' and 'concerted practice' means.

154 It seems to be stating the obvious to say that there is a mental element to the notion of 'agreement' and 'concertation' (as in 'concerted practices'). EU competition law is not unique in this: the notion of 'agreement' is also fundamental to contract law in many jurisdictions and has there often also been defined as a 'meeting of minds'.[203] In contract law, this 'mental' or 'moral' phraseology has been criticized as a source of confusion,[204] and, as I will discuss below, in my view this phraseology is also questionable in EU competition law. This is not only for the obvious reason that mental states cannot be observed and the existence of an agreement can therefore only be deduced from any manifestations (or 'expressions') of the mental state of (employees or officers of) undertakings. More fundamentally, an agreement or concerted practice in EU competition law can only be established in case there is a communication (or the expression of the mental state) *between the parties* to the agreement or concerted practice. Thoughts expressed in private are not determinative.

155 Before delving into the case law on the notions of agreement and concerted practice as such, it is worthwhile recalling that these are not opposed notions but should rather be situated on a continuum, with the notion of concerted practice denoting a practice which is (even) less explicitly coordinated than if it were agreed. According to the CJEU, '[a] comparison between [the] definition of agreement and the definition of a concerted practice ... shows that, from the subjective point of view, they are intended to catch forms of collusion having the same nature and are only distinguishable from each other by their intensity and the forms in which they manifest themselves'.[205]

156 The notions of agreement and concerted practice are not identical, however, and there is a distinct line of case law concerning each notion, so that I will discuss them under separate headings below.

---

202. C-107/82 *AEG v Commission* ECLI:EU:C:1983:293, para. 38; joined cases C-25/84 and 26/84 *Ford and Ford Europe v Commission* ECLI:EU:C:1985:340, para. 21; T-43/92 *Dunlop Slazenger v Commission* ECLI:EU:T:1994:79, para. 56; T-41/96 *Bayer v Commission* ECLI:EU:T:2000:242, para. 66.
203. Although under contract law it is (also) often understood in an objective sense. *See*, for example, for English law: R Stone, *The modern law of contract* (Routledge-Cavendish 2009) 38-40 and S Whittaker, 'Introductory' in HG Beale (ed.), *Chitty on contracts* (Thomson Reuter 2015) 3, 16. Under French law, reference is often made to '*L'accord des volontés*' (*see* F Terré, P Simler and Y Lequette (eds), *Droit Civil. Les Obligations* (Dalloz 2005) 107). The German *Bürgerliches Gesetzbuch* mostly refers to the 'expression of will' (*Willenserklärung*) and in § 116 even explicitly states that mental reservations that are not expressed are usually not an obstacle to a contract.
204. *See* already OW Holmes, 'The path of the law' (1897) 110 Harvard Law Review 991, 996.
205. C-49/92 P *Commission v Anic Partecipazioni* ECLI:EU:C:1999:356, para. 131.

[A] The *Mens Rea* of Agreements

157 References to mental states are all over the notion of 'agreement' as defined in the case law of the European Courts. This is already true in earlier cases, such as *ACF Chemiefarma*, where the CJEU held that a document which 'amounted to the faithful expression of the joint intention of the parties' should be qualified as an agreement in the sense of Article 101 TFEU.[206]

158 The classical definition of an agreement as a 'concurrence of wills' was developed in the case law of the (then) Court of First Instance (CFI) in 2000. Although the notion is already present in the *Cimenteries* judgment,[207] it is the formulation from the *Bayer* judgment that is most often quoted: the Court held there that 'the concept of an agreement within the meaning of Article 85(1) of the Treaty, as interpreted by the case-law, centres around the existence of a concurrence of wills between at least two parties, the form in which it is manifested being unimportant so long as it constitutes the faithful expression of the parties' intention'.[208] The CJEU has subsequently endorsed this definition[209] and seems to also accept the idea that this can be viewed as a 'meeting of minds'.[210]

159 Does this mean that an agreement in the sense of Article 101 TFEU is a purely mental state? The fact that the *Bayer* judgment states that 'the form in which [the concurrence of wills] is manifested' is 'unimportant' suggests that form is irrelevant.[211] That could imply that an agreement is a purely mental state and that the manifestation of that mental state is only necessary for evidentiary purposes.

160 But this is an incorrect reading of the case law. The case law requires that the agreement is somehow communicated between the parties, be it in writing or orally, although the consent of some of the parties to the agreement can be deduced from their conduct (which brings us closer to the field of concerted practices). What is more, in the case of explicit agreements, the communication between the parties is *sufficient* to establish an agreement in the sense of Article 101 TFEU. It is therefore no defence that that manifestation was not accompanied by a concurrence of wills in the mental sense: uncommunicated reservations of one or both of the parties to the agreement do not negate that agreement. In those circumstances, the *actus reus* (the conclusion of an explicit agreement) makes an undertaking liable, regardless of whether it also had the relevant *mens rea*.

206. C-41/69 *Chemiefarma v Commission* ECLI:EU:C:1970:71, para. 112.
207. Joined cases T-25, 26, 30 to 32, 34 to 39, 42 to 46, 48, 50 to 65, 68 to 71, 87, 88, 103 and 104/95 *Cimenteries CBR v Commission* ECLI:EU:T:2000:77, para. 1498.
208. T-41/96 *Bayer v Commission* ECLI:EU:T:2000:242, para. 69.
209. At first in the appeals against the *Cimenteries* judgment of the CFI: *see*, for example, joined cases C-204, 205, 211, 213, 217 and 219/00 P *Aalborg Portland v Commission* ECLI:EU:C:2004:6, paras 244, 249, 252, 323.
210. Joined cases C-2/01 and 3/01 *BAI v Bayer and Commission* ECLI:EU:C:2004:2, para. 123.
211. *See also* J Faull, L Kjølbye, H Leupold and A Nikpay, 'Article 101' in J Faull and A Nikpay (eds), *The EU law of competition* (Oxford University Press 2014) 183, 204.

161 To determine whether an agreement has been concluded, the European Courts have often analysed whether there was an 'expression' of a joint intention or concurrence of wills.[212] If such an expression is present, it does not matter that the conduct of one or several of the parties was not in compliance with the agreement. In fact, even if one of the parties had tacit reservations about the agreement, that party will still be viewed as having concluded the agreement, if it did not communicate those reservations.[213]

162 Already in the early days of EU antitrust enforcement, undertakings have argued that the parties to written agreements did not actually consent to them and that therefore no concurrence of wills took place. In *BMW Belgium*, for example, which concerned export prohibitions imposed by BMW Belgium on its dealers, the car manufacturer invoked the fact that some of the dealers continued exporting as evidence that no agreement with the dealers on an export ban existed. The CJEU did not consider this argument relevant apparently because of the limited instances of successful exports.[214]

163 The issue came up again a few years later in *CRAM*, in which CRAM tried to stop its Belgian customer Schiltz from reimporting its products into Germany (where prices were higher than in Belgium). CRAM conditioned the sale of certain volumes to Schiltz on the commitment from Schiltz that it would export these outside the EU (to Egypt in particular) but Schiltz nevertheless continued selling these products into Germany. CRAM argued before the CJEU that Schiltz 'never intended to observe the agreement'.[215] While the existence of the agreement was never explicitly in dispute, in the context of the question of whether the agreement was restrictive of competition, the CJEU held that 'it is not necessary ... to verify that the parties had a common intent at the time when the agreement was concluded'.[216]

164 The principle that the *expression* of agreement *between the parties* is sufficient to conclude to an agreement in the sense of Article 101 TFEU can also be found in *Bayer*, although some authors seem to argue the opposite.[217] When rejecting the Commission's argument in that case, the CFI pointed out that the Commission had not shown

212. *See* already C-41/69 *Chemiefarma v Commission* ECLI:EU:C:1970:71, para. 112 and T-7/89 *Hercules Chemicals v Commission* ECLI:EU:T:1991:75, para. 256. In the non-cartel context, *see* joined cases C-209 to 215 and 218/78 *Van Landewyck v Commission* ECLI:EU:C:1980:248, para. 86.
213. The reverse is obviously not true: if there is uncommunicated evidence that an undertaking concluded an agreement, this may suffice to demonstrate that that undertaking actually concluded that agreement. Indirect proof may be a sufficient proof; this is merely a question of evidence. *See* joined cases C-40 to 48, 50, 54 to 56, 111, 113 and 114/73 *Suiker Unie and Others v Commission* ECLI:EU:C:1975:174, paras 126-166.
214. *See* joined cases C-32 and 36 to 82/78 *BMW Belgium v Commission* ECLI:EU:C:1979:191, para. 27.
215. Joined cases C-29 and 30/83 *CRAM v Commission* ECLI:EU:C:1984:130, at [1984] ECR 1695.
216. Joined cases C-29 and 30/83 *CRAM v Commission* ECLI:EU:C:1984:130, para. 26.
217. O Odudu, *The boundaries of EC competition law. The scope of Article 81* (Oxford University Press 2006) 60 argues that 'common intention [is] sufficient for agreement within the meaning of Article 81 EC'. O Black, 'Agreement: concurrence of wills, or offer and acceptance' (2008) 4 European Competition Journal 103, 118-119 also points out that Odudu is unclear on this.

that the distributors (through their conduct) 'wished to pursue Bayer's objectives or wished to make Bayer believe that they did'.[218] *A contrario*, this suggests that if the distributors had tried to make Bayer believe that they pursued its objectives, an agreement may have arisen.

165 The irrelevance of uncommunicated reservations has been the basis for a significant amount of litigation in the context of cartel enforcement. The Commission has several times rejected arguments of cartel participants that they did not actually adhere to the agreements they signed. In *Roofing Felt*, some of the undertakings which were not members of the Belasco trade association argued this and the Commission rejected their arguments as follows:

> The non-members also argued that if there had been agreements, they had had no intention of observing them. However, neither the state of mind of the non-members when they entered into such agreements as to their intention of abiding by them, nor the fact that the non-members did not in fact observe the agreements (as some evidence suggests) would affect the Commission's finding that the agreements were made and that the non-members were parties to them.[219]

166 But also absent an explicit agreement, the CJEU has required a manifestation of the agreement. This has in particular been an issue in vertical situations, where the Commission and the European Courts have rarely applied the notion of concerted practice[220] and therefore much more turns on whether the Commission can establish the existence of an agreement. In particular, suppliers imposing absolute territorial protection and resale price maintenance have argued that their distributors did not consent to these policies and that these could therefore not constitute an agreement, thereby excluding the application of Article 101 TFEU. The European Courts have in those circumstances required evidence of at least 'tacit acquiescence' on the part of the distributor with such a policy.[221]

167 I will discuss the issue of acquiescence in section [C] below. However, at this stage, it should already be noted that there has been an evolution in the case law on what the tacit acquiescence must be related to. In the 1985 *Ford* judgment in particular (and arguably already in the 1984 *AEG* judgment), the CJEU seems to have considered

218. T-41/96 *Bayer v Commission* ECLI:EU:T:2000:242, para. 156.
219. Commission decision of 10 July 1986 in case 31.371 *Roofing Felt*, recital 86.
220. But *see* M Paschke, 'Vereinbarungen (Verträge, Beschlüsse, aufeinander abgestimmte Verhaltensweisen) im Sinne des Kartellrechts' in J Bornkamm, F Montag and FJ Säcker (eds), *Münchener Kommentar Europäisches und Deutsches Wettbewerbsrecht, Band 1 Europäiches Wettbewerbsrecht* (Beck 2015) 692, 715 and J Faull, L Kjølbye, H Leupold and A Nikpay, 'Article 101' in J Faull and A Nikpay (eds), *The EU law of competition* (Oxford University Press 2014) 183, 223.
221. T-41/96 *Bayer v Commission* ECLI:EU:T:2000:242, para. 71. This has been viewed as offer and acceptance: *see* O Black, 'Agreement: concurrence of wills, or offer and acceptance' (2008) 4 European Competition Journal 103 and also X, 'Les ententes' in R Bout *et al.* (eds), *Le Lamy droit économique édition 2017* (Wolters Kluwer 2016) 555, 559; O Odudu, *The boundaries of EC competition law. The scope of Article 81* (Oxford University Press 2006) 61ff. *See also* the opinion of AG Tizzano in joined cases C-2/01 and 3/01 *BAI v Bayer and Commission* ECLI:EU:C:2003:299, paras 60 and 94.

that the dealership agreement implied acquiescence of the dealer to any policy unilaterally adopted by its supplier, even if this happened after the conclusion of the dealership agreement. In the 2000s, the CFI (supported by the CJEU) overturned this principle and required that the Commission prove acquiescence *after* the policy had been communicated to the dealer. In my view, this evolution was informed by the need to ensure that tacit acquiescence is only established in the face of an explicit statement by the supplier.

168 The first case in which the CJEU enunciated the idea that dealership agreements implied acceptance of policies adopted unilaterally by the supplier is *AEG*. This case concerned a selective distribution system for AEG's consumer electronics which AEG had notified to the Commission under Regulation 17/62[222] and which the Commission had approved. The system was based on qualitative criteria for the selection of distributors, such as the presence of qualified staff and suitable premises, but in practice AEG refused to accept dealers which, although fulfilling all the qualitative criteria, did not adhere to the minimum resale prices imposed by AEG. AEG claimed that this was its unilateral policy and that there was no evidence of an agreement with the dealers. However, the CJEU held that this policy 'forms part of the contractual relations between the undertaking and resellers' and that the admission of a distributor was 'based on the acceptance, tacit or express, by the contracting parties of the policy pursued by AEG'.[223] The statement of the CJEU is clearly in very broad terms which were not justified by the facts of the case (since there was ample evidence that AEG discussed the resale prices with its dealers)[224] but which nevertheless became the basis for the subsequent case law, in particular *Ford*.

169 In *Ford*, the car manufacturer in question had informed its German dealers that it would no longer supply them with right-hand drive cars which these German distributors used to export to the UK, where prices were higher. The Court followed the *AEG* precedent and held that the dealers had implicitly agreed to this policy because 'admission to the Ford AG dealer network implies acceptance by the contracting parties of the policy pursued by Ford with regard to the models to be delivered to the German market'.[225] A number of other judgments in subsequent years followed this same principle.[226]

170 The Fourth Chamber of the (then) CFI still adopted a similar position in its June 2000 judgment in *Volkswagen I*. This case concerned a number of measures, including

222. Regulation 17/62: first regulation implementing Articles 85 and 86 of the Treaty [1962] OJ 13/204.
223. C-107/82 *AEG v Commission* ECLI:EU:C:1983:293, para. 38.
224. And it is therefore difficult to see why AEG's policy would need to be inferred from its conduct as is argued by O Odudu, *The boundaries of EC competition law. The scope of Article 81* (Oxford University Press 2006) 65.
225. Joined cases C-25/84 and 26/84 *Ford and Ford Europe v Commission* ECLI:EU:C:1985:340, para. 21.
226. *See* C-277/87 *Sandoz Prototti Farmaceutici v Commission* ECLI:EU:C:1990:6 and C-279/87 *Tipp-Ex v Commission* ECLI:EU:C:1990:57 although only abstracts of these judgments have been published.

supply quotas and bonus restrictions, used by Volkswagen's Italian subsidiary to discourage Italian dealers from exporting Volkswagen vehicles following the devaluation of the Italian lira in 1992 and 1993. The Commission had found these to constitute agreements and/or concerted practices in the sense of Article 101(1) TFEU. When Volkswagen contested the qualification of agreement, in particular of the supply quotas, which the dealers had not agreed to, the CFI performed a very brief analysis and held, relying on *Ford* and *BMW Belgium*,[227] that '[i]t is settled law that a call by a motor vehicle manufacturer to its authorised dealers is not a unilateral act which falls outside the scope of Article 85(1) of the Treaty but is an agreement within the meaning of that provision if it forms part of a set of continuous business relations governed by a general agreement drawn up in advance'.[228]

171 The CJEU upheld the CFI's decision in *Volkswagen I* in 2003 reiterating the principle deduced by the CFI from the *Ford* and *BMW Belgium* case law and argued that Volkswagen did 'not deny that the dealership contract provided for the possibility of limiting supplies to Italian dealers and does not dispute the finding of the Court of First Instance that this limitation was imposed with the express aim of blocking re-exportation from Italy of the vehicles delivered to those dealers'.[229]

172 But only a few months after the CFI's judgment in *Volkswagen I*, the case law changed tack. In October 2000, the Fifth Chamber, Extended Composition of the CFI, in the *Bayer* judgment, annulled a Commission decision finding an agreement between a supplier and dealer, due to lack of consent by the dealer. This case concerned the decision of Bayer to reduce supplies to the French and Spanish distributors of its Adalat drug to prevent them from exporting to the UK, where prices were higher. Bayer did not inform the French and Spanish distributors that the volume reductions were due to concerns about parallel trade (it cited 'stock shortages'), but the distributors nevertheless guessed the real motives of Bayer and reduced their orders, while at the same time increasing purchases through other wholesalers, in order to continue exporting. Against the Commission's position, the CFI agreed with Bayer that there was no evidence of 'tacit acquiescence'[230] by the French and Spanish distributors with the policy of Bayer; on the contrary, the fact that they sought alternative sources of Adalat for export showed that they did not agree with the export restrictions. The CFI concluded that the Commission had not shown that the distributors 'wished to pursue Bayer's objectives or wished to make Bayer believe that they did'.[231]

173 The CFI also went to great lengths to distinguish its ruling from the previous case law. Most of its discussion was devoted to *Sandoz* and *Tipp-Ex*: the CFI pointed out in

227. Joined cases C-32 and 36 to 82/78 *BMW Belgium v Commission* ECLI:EU:C:1979:191. It should be noted that *BMW Belgium* is hardly a precedent for this proposition since in that case the BMW Dealers' Advisory Committee, comprising eight BMW dealers, had explicitly agreed to the policy introduced by BMW Belgium and several other dealers had signed the circular sent by BMW Belgium.
228. T-62/98 *Volkswagen v Commission* ECLI:EU:T:2000:180, para. 236.
229. C-338/00 P *Volkswagen v Commission* ECLI:EU:C:2003:473, para. 64.
230. T-41/96 *Bayer v Commission* ECLI:EU:T:2000:242, para. 71.
231. T-41/96 *Bayer v Commission* ECLI:EU:T:2000:242, para. 156.

particular that in those two cases, there was evidence that the suppliers informed their distributor of their concern (over parallel trade and resale prices respectively) and that the distributors acted according to the suppliers' wishes (in *Tipp-Ex* ensured through checks by the supplier). Neither of these features was present in *Bayer*. The Court also distinguished *Bayer* from *BMW Belgium* and *AEG* although its reasoning is brief.

174 While *Bayer* concerned the very specific market of pharmaceuticals where regulated prices pose specific parallel trade concerns,[232] the CFI pursued the *Bayer* principle in subsequent cases, even after the CJEU's confirmation of the CFI's approach in *Volkswagen I* (and before the CJEU could rule on the *Bayer* judgment of the CFI). This is already apparent in *General Motors*, where the CFI rejected the Commission's finding of an agreement (in the sense of Article 101 TFEU) to restrict supplies to Dutch dealers which exported Opel cars on the basis that there was no proof that the policy of the car manufacturer had been communicated to its dealers.[233] But even more clear is *Volkswagen II*, in which that car manufacturer sent letters to its German dealers requesting them to limit discounts on the sales of the VW Passat model. The CFI distinguished the facts of this case from the *Volkswagen I*[234] and *Ford*[235] case law and followed the stricter *Bayer* requirements. It held that the fact that the dealers had signed a dealership agreement, which only foresaw that Volkswagen could issue non-binding price recommendations, did not imply that Volkswagen's subsequent unlawful request to limit discounts would have been accepted in advance by the dealers as well: 'acquiescence in the unlawful contractual variation can occur only after the dealer has become aware of the variation desired by the manufacturer'.[236] The CFI considered that the Commission had not examined whether such acquiescence *post-factum* had taken place.[237]

175 The CJEU upheld the judgments of the CFI in *Bayer* and *Volkswagen II*. In the appeal against the *Bayer* judgment, the CJEU, sitting in Full Court, found that the Commission had failed to establish that 'there was a declared intention on the part of the wholesalers to join in with the intention of Bayer to prevent parallel imports'[238] –

232. *See also* U Wickihalder, 'The distinction between an "agreement" within the meaning of Article 81(1) of the EC treaty and unilateral conduct' (2006) 2 European Competition Journal 87, 111ff and references there.
233. T-368/00 *General Motors Nederland and Opel Nederland v Commission* ECLI:EU:T:2003:275, para. 81. However, the CFI did accept that new bonus conditions introduced by the car manufacturer 'became an integral part of the dealship contracts' (para. 98, with reference to *AEG* and *Ford*). The appeal before the CJEU in C-551/03 P *General Motors v Commission* ECLI:EU:C:2006:229 did not deal with the notion of agreement.
234. This is not entirely convincing: while there was evidence in *Volkswagen I* that the dealers had reduced exports, that does not mean that the supply quotas implemented by Volkswagen's Italian subsidiary could also be seen as agreed by the dealers.
235. The CFI argued that *Ford* did not so much concern the question of whether Ford had concluded an agreement with its dealers as whether that agreement could be exempted under Article 101(3) TFEU. The distinction is again not convincing: *see also* U Wickihalder, 'The distinction between an "agreement" within the meaning of Article 81(1) of the EC treaty and unilateral conduct' (2006) 2 European Competition Journal 87, 110 and references there.
236. T-208/01 *Volkswagen v Commission* ECLI:EU:T:2003:326, para. 45.
237. Confirmed in C-74/04 P *Commission v Volkswagen* ECLI:EU:C:2006:460.
238. Joined cases C-2/01 and 3/01 *BAI v Bayer and Commission* ECLI:EU:C:2004:2, para. 122.

which would have amounted to an explicit agreement.[239] Nor was there acquiescence on the part of the dealers with Bayer's policy which 'could be carried out without the cooperation of the wholesalers'[240] and therefore could not be viewed as 'the manifestation of the wish of one of the contracting parties to achieve an anti-competitive goal constitut[ing] an invitation to the other party, whether express or implied, to fulfil that goal jointly'.[241]

176 In *Volkswagen II*, the CJEU also reiterated that what counts is whether an act or conduct is 'the expression of the concurrence of wills'[242] and this formulation has been repeated by the CJEU since.[243]

177 In light of the case law discussed above, it is submitted that whether or not there is an agreement in the sense of Article 101 TFEU turns on whether there is an *expressed* agreement *between the parties*, in the sense of a verbal or written communication from either all of the parties or an invitation from one party to another with the receiver tacitly acquiescing to it. Concurrence of wills is therefore not a question of *mens rea*.

[B] The *Mens Rea* of Concerted Practices

178 A large share of the case law and literature suggests that the notion of concerted practices is very similar or even identical to the notion of agreement under Article 101 TFEU but with a lower evidentiary burden. Proving collusion is difficult because the parties to it will often be aware that what they are doing is illegal and will therefore try to avoid leaving evidence of any agreement. Some of the leading cases on concerted practices, such as *Dystuffs* and *Wood Pulp II*, have also involved undertakings which were not based in the EU and for which it was therefore more difficult for the Commission to obtain evidence.

179 It is then not surprising that the Commission has stated that '[t]he importance of the concept of a concerted practice does not thus result so much from the distinction between it and an "agreement" as from the distinction between forms of collusion falling under Article 85 (1) and mere parallel behaviour with no element of concertation'.[244] As I pointed out earlier, the CJEU has also stated that the notions of agreement and concerted practice 'are intended to catch forms of collusion having the same nature and are only distinguishable from each other by their intensity and the forms in which they manifest themselves'.[245]

239. A similar situation arose in T-18/03 *CD-Contact Data v Commission* ECLI:EU:T:2009:132, paras 59-70, confirmed by C-260/09 P *Activision Blizzard Germany v Commission* ECLI:EU:C:2011:62, para. 80.
240. Joined cases C-2/01 and 3/01 *BAI v Bayer and Commission* ECLI:EU:C:2004:2, para. 110.
241. Joined cases C-2/01 and 3/01 *BAI v Bayer and Commission* ECLI:EU:C:2004:2, para. 102.
242. Confirmed in C-74/04 P *Commission v Volkswagen* ECLI:EU:C:2006:460, para. 37.
243. *See* C-194/14 P *AC-Treuhand v Commission* ECLI:EU:C:2015:717, para. 28.
244. Commission decision of 23 April 1986 in case 31.149 *Polypropylene*, recital 87.
245. C-49/92 P *Commission v Anic Partecipazioni* ECLI:EU:C:1999:356, para. 131.

180 This view of concerted practices has been informed by the restrictive interpretation which the Commission and the European Courts gave to the notion of 'agreement' in Article 101 TFEU in the early days of EU antitrust enforcement.[246] Also US antitrust rules, which allowed for the establishment of a conspiracy in the sense of section 1 of the Sherman Act in the absence of an agreement, have certainly played a role.[247] It is in this context that the CJEU has defined 'concerted practices' as 'a form of coordination between undertakings which, without having reached the stage where an agreement properly so-called has been concluded, knowingly substitutes practical cooperation between them for the risks of competition'.[248] The Court adds to this in *Dyestuffs*, '[b]y its very nature, then, a concerted practice does not have all the elements of a contract but may *inter alia* arise out of coordination which becomes apparent from the behaviour of the participants'.[249]

181 In this view, concerted practices are forms of collusion for which the evidentiary standards are lower than for agreements. Much of the case law has therefore concerned the question of the evidence of the concerted practice and in particular whether parallel conduct as such is sufficient to constitute proof of concertation/collusion. In the 1972 *Dyestuffs* judgment, the CJEU held that '[a]lthough parallel behaviour may not by itself be identified with a concerted practice, it may however amount to strong evidence of such a practice'.[250] In *Dyestuffs*, the Court found that the introduction by the producers of dyestuffs of public announcements of price increases within a very short period of time could only be explained by prior collusion – although it is worthwhile to point out that in that case, it was established that, at least prior to the last one of the price increases covered by the Commission decision (the one in 1967), all addressees of the Commission decision, except one, had held a meeting in which one of them announced its intention to increase prices.

182 The CJEU's statement in *Dyestuffs* that parallel conduct constituted 'strong evidence' of collusion was significantly qualified in *Wood Pulp II*, where the CJEU held that 'parallel conduct cannot be regarded as furnishing proof of concertation unless

246. *See* O Odudu, *The boundaries of EC competition law. The scope of Article 81* (Oxford University Press 2006) 71-75.
247. Although it is not clear what the impact of that comparison should be. AG Mayras in his opinion in C-48/69 *ICI v Commission* ECLI:EU:C:1972:32, at [1972] ECR I 669-670 suggests that EU and US antitrust law are different and that the American notion should therefore not necessarily guide the interpretation of Article 101 TFEU, whereas AG Darmon in his opinion in joined cases C-89, 104, 114, 116, 117 and 125 to 129/85 *Ahlström Osakeyhtiö and Others v Commission* ECLI:EU:C:1992:293, at [1994] ECR I 1482 simply states that the European notion was 'derived' from the US notion, without qualifying this in any way. *See* already W Van Gerven, *Principes du droit des ententes de la communauté économique européenne* (Bruylant 1966) 19. More generally on the influence of the common law notion of conspiracy, *see* JM Joshua and S Jordan, 'Combinations, concerted practices and cartels: adopting the concept of conspiracy in European community competition law' (2004) 24 Northwestern Journal of International Law & Business 647.
248. C-48/69 *ICI v Commission* ECLI:EU:C:1972:70, para. 64; joined cases C-40 to 48, 50, 54 to 56, 111, 113 and 114/73 *Suiker Unie and Others v Commission* ECLI:EU:C:1975:174, para. 26.
249. C-48/69 *ICI v Commission* ECLI:EU:C:1972:70, para. 65.
250. C-48/69 *ICI v Commission* ECLI:EU:C:1972:70, para. 66.

concertation constitutes the only plausible explanation for such conduct'.[251] With the help of experts, the Court found that much of the parallelism between wood pulp producers, such as the system of quarterly price announcements, could be explained by the very high degree of transparency of the market. Since Article 101 TFEU 'does not deprive economic operators of the right to adapt themselves intelligently to the existing and anticipated conduct of their competitors',[252] in those circumstances the Court could not find an infringement of that provision.

183 As indicated above, the case law of the CJEU has now accepted a much broader notion of agreement.[253] Does that mean that the notion of concerted practices has become redundant and that it merely refers to a lower evidentiary burden?

184 It is submitted that the case law does not support such a conclusion.[254] Indeed, there are substantive differences between the notion of agreement and concerted practice. First of all, in terms of the constituent elements: a concerted practice requires conduct (it is a 'practice'),[255] whereas in the case of an agreement, the fact that the agreement has not been implemented and therefore has no effects is not relevant.[256] Second but related to the previous point, the fact that there is another plausible explanation for parallel conduct excludes the qualification of concerted practice[257] but it is irrelevant in the presence of an agreement.[258] Although agreement and concerted practices are forms of collusion that are situated on a continuum, they therefore nevertheless constitute different phenomena. What is their defining difference?

185 It has been argued that agreements differ from concerted practices in that agreements express a specific common intention of the parties, whereas concerted practices merely reduce the uncertainty and risk which is inherent in the competitive process.[259] But this approach makes it hard to draw a clear line between agreements and concerted practices: agreements also reduce uncertainties and risks inherent in the

251. Joined cases C-89, 104, 114, 116, 117 and 125 to 129/85 *Ahlström Osakeyhtiö and Others v Commission* ECLI:EU:C:1993:120, para. 71.
252. Joined cases C-40 to 48, 50, 54 to 56, 111, 113 and 114/73 *Suiker Unie and Others v Commission* ECLI:EU:C:1975:174, para. 174; joined cases C-89, 104, 114, 116, 117 and 125 to 129/85 *Ahlström Osakeyhtiö and Others v Commission* ECLI:EU:C:1993:120, para. 71.
253. *See also* M Paschke, 'Vereinbarungen (Verträge, Beschlüsse, aufeinander abgestimmte Verhaltensweisen) im Sinne des Kartellrechts' in J Bornkamm, F Montag and FJ Säcker (eds), *Münchener Kommentar Europäisches und Deutsches Wettbewerbsrecht, Band 1 Europäiches Wettbewerbsrecht* (Beck 2015) 692, 695-697.
254. This is also the view of O Odudu, *The boundaries of EC competition law. The scope of Article 81* (Oxford University Press 2006) 80.
255. C-199/92 P *Hüls v Commission* ECLI:EU:C:1999:358, para. 165.
256. Joined cases C-56 and 58/64 *Consten and Grundig v Commission* ECLI:EU:C:1966:41, at [1966] ECR 342.
257. Joined cases C-89, 104, 114, 116, 117 and 125 to 129/85 *Ahlström Osakeyhtiö and Others v Commission* ECLI:EU:C:1993:120, para. 71.
258. Joined cases C-239, 489 and 498/11 P *Siemens v Commission* ECLI:EU:C:2013:866, para. 220; T-48/00 *Corus UK v Commission* ECLI:EU:T:2004:219, para. 72. Note, however, that alternative plausible explanations may nevertheless be relevant in terms of evidencing the very existence of an agreement, in particular if the latter has not been concluded in a written form.
259. *See* O Odudu, *The boundaries of EC competition law. The scope of Article 81* (Oxford University Press 2006) 81-83.

competitive process[260] so, in this view, they merely seem to be a specific form of concerted practice. Furthermore, this view seems to confound the notion of collusion with the notion of restriction of competition (the second material element of Article 101(1) TFEU) since, in the definition of concerted practice, the restriction of competition (in the sense of a reduction of uncertainty and risk) is already included. The case law has made it clear that these are two distinct criteria.[261]

186 It is submitted that the difference between agreements and concerted practices is that, for an agreement to arise, the communication from one party to another must take the form of an invitation (an 'offer' in contract law parlance)[262] which the other party either explicitly accepts or tacitly acquiesces to through its conduct. In the case of a concerted practice, the communication from the first party is not an invitation (or offer), but merely a communication of information. If the receipt of that information influences (or can influence) the recipient's market conduct, a concerted practice arises.[263]

187 As already indicated before, one of the differences between an agreement and a concerted practice is that the latter requires conduct on the market (it is a 'practice'), whereas an agreement does not. However, the case law has clarified that it is not necessary to show that the conduct on the market was concerted; it is sufficient that concertation took place and that subsequently the undertakings involved in the concertation were active on the market. In that case, a presumption applies that the undertakings used the information they obtained in the concertation for their conduct on the market.

188 This principle was developed by AG Vesterdorf in his 1991 opinion in the *Polypropylene* case before the CFI and subsequently confirmed by the CJEU in its 1999 judgment in *Anic Partecipazioni*.[264] It is therefore commonly known as the 'Anic presumption'.[265]

260. But without giving absolute certainty to the cartel participants. *See also* JM Joshua and S Jordan, 'Combinations, concerted practices and cartels: adopting the concept of conspiracy in European community competition law' (2004) 24 Northwestern Journal of International Law & Business 647, 669.
261. *See*, for example, C-238/05 *Asnef-Equifax* ECLI:EU:C:2006:734, paras 46-48 where the CJEU held that the information exchange in that case did not have as its object the restriction of competition and required the national judge to determine whether it had such a restriction as its effect.
262. *See* in particular joined cases C-2/01 and 3/01 *BAI v Bayer and Commission* ECLI:EU:C:2004:2, para. 102.
263. The difference is apparent from an example: if an undertaking communicates to a competitor the message: 'let's raise prices', this is an invitation to collude; if it merely states 'I'm raising prices,' this is not as such an invitation to collude but merely the transmission of (commercially sensitive) information. This example also shows why agreements and concerted practices are instances of collusion that form a continuum: while an invitation to collude is different from the mere transmission of information, also in the latter case, the result can be collusion.
264. C-49/92 P *Commission v Anic Partecipazioni* ECLI:EU:C:1999:356.
265. *See*, for example, the AG opinion in C-74/14 *Eturas and Others* ECLI:EU:C:2015:493, para. 33.

189 In his opinion, AG Vesterdorf tries to make sense of the statement of the CJEU in the *Suiker Unie* judgment that, while market operators can 'adapt themselves intelligently to the existing and anticipated conduct of their competitors', Article 101 TFEU prohibits 'any direct or indirect contact between such operators, the object or effect whereof is either to influence the conduct on the market of an actual or potential competitor or to disclose to such a competitor the course of conduct which they themselves have decided to adopt or contemplate adopting on the market'.[266]

190 Why would such direct or indirect contacts between competitors be prohibited, asks AG Vesterdorf? His answer is that undertakings which engage in such contacts 'will then necessarily, and normally unavoidably, act on the market in the light of the knowledge and on the basis of the discussions which have taken place in connection with the concertation'.[267]

191 The CFI endorsed this position and held that, 'in determining the policy which it intended to follow on the market', an undertaking which has received commercially sensitive information from a competitor 'could not fail to take account, directly or indirectly of the information obtained'.[268] On appeal, the CJEU clarified that 'there must be a presumption that the undertakings participating in concerting arrangements and remaining active on the market take account of the information exchanged with their competitors when determining their conduct on that market'.[269]

192 AG Vesterdorf already made it clear in his opinion that the presumption is rebuttable. Even if an undertaking (i) engages in concertation and (ii) remains active on the market, 'it remains at least theoretically possible to prove that the practice being pursued is not concerted in the sense that in some circumstances a party will be able to show that it has cast off the ties or bonds ensuing from the concertation and closed its mind to the knowledge gained from it'.[270] AG Vesterdorf gives the example of an undertaking which is taken over and gets new management unaware of the concertation. The CJEU endorsed this position, stating that the presumption is 'subject to proof to the contrary, which it is for the economic operators concerned to adduce'.[271]

193 The presumption of a causal connection between the concertation and the conduct of a market participant has been confirmed multiple times by the CJEU since.[272]

266. Joined cases C-40 to 48, 50, 54 to 56, 111, 113 and 114/73 *Suiker Unie and Others v Commission* ECLI:EU:C:1975:174, para. 174.
267. AG opinion in joined cases T-1/89 to T-4/89 and T-6/89 to T-15/89 *Rhône-Poulenc et al v Commission* ECLI:EU:T:1991:38, in particular at [1991] ECR II 941.
268. T-6/89 *Enichem Anic v Commission* ECLI:EU:T:1991:74, para. 201.
269. C-49/92 P *Commission v Anic Partecipazioni* ECLI:EU:C:1999:356, para. 121.
270. AG opinion in joined cases T-1/89 to T-4/89 and T-6/89 to T-15/89 *Rhône-Poulenc et al v Commission* ECLI:EU:T:1991:38, in particular at [1991] ECR II 943.
271. C-49/92 P *Commission v Anic Partecipazioni* ECLI:EU:C:1999:356, para. 121.
272. *See*, for example, C-8/08 *T-Mobile Netherlands and Others* ECLI:EU:C:2009:343, para. 51; C-74/14 *Eturas and Others* ECLI:EU:C:2016:42, para. 33.

[C] Participation: Acquiescence and Distancing

194 In terms of what counts as tacit acquiescence, the CJEU has consistently held that tacit acquiescence can arise if the business conduct of the recipient of the invitation to collude is influenced by that invitation[273] although obviously only if the conduct is changed in such a way as to amount to compliance with the invitation, not the rejection of it.[274]

195 The tacit acquiescence of the recipient of the communication implies that there is a form of reciprocity in the relation between them,[275] but this reciprocity is minimal. If an undertaking receives an invitation to collude (in the case of an agreement) or commercially sensitive information (in the case of a concerted practice), it will almost inevitably be found to have colluded with the sender of the invitation or the information: it will be difficult for the recipient not to be influenced by the invitation or the information in its business conduct.[276]

196 The same principle applies in the case of participation in meetings. In the *PVC II* judgment, the CJEU stated that:

> in the case of agreements reached at meetings of competing undertakings:
>
> - [Article 101 TFEU] is infringed where those meetings have such an aim and are thus intended to organise artificially the operation of the market;
> - the liability of a particular undertaking in respect of the infringement is properly established where it participated in those meetings with knowledge of their aim, even if it did not proceed to implement any of the measures agreed at those meetings.[277]

197 But the Court clarified that it was not necessary to show that the undertaking in question had knowledge of the anticompetitive aims of the meetings: that knowledge

273. C-338/00 P *Volkswagen v Commission* ECLI:EU:C:2003:473, para. 67; C-74/04 P *Commission v Volkswagen* ECLI:EU:C:2006:460, para. 39.
274. Joined cases C-2/01 and 3/01 *BAI v Bayer and Commission* ECLI:EU:C:2004:2, paras 129 and 155.
275. *See* the opinion of AG Szpunar in case C-74/14 *Eturas and Others* ECLI:EU:C:2015:493, paras 45-47. *See also* A Jones, 'Woodpulp: concerted practice and/or conscious parallelism?' (1993) 6 European Competition Law Review 273, 275-276 and G Van Gerven and E Navarro Varona, 'The Wood Pulp case and the future of concerted practices' (1994) 31 Common Market Law Review 575, 600 and the reference there to R Joliet, 'La notion de pratique concertée et l'arrêt I.C.I. dans une perspective comparative' (1974) 10 Cahiers de droit européen 251.
276. I therefore disagree with T Lettl, 'Abstimmung im Sinne von Art. 101 Abs. 1 AEUV, § 1 GWB' (2017) Wirtschaft und Wettbewerb 422, in particular 425-426, that it is always necessary to prove an intention of the recipient to collude. Such an intention may need to be established in case information is obtained in a non-suspicious setting (e.g. when it comes from a supplier or customer – *see* the discussion of hub-and-spoke infringements below), but when it comes directly from a competitor, alarm bells should go off with the recipient.
277. Joined cases C-238, 244, 245, 247, 250 to 252 and 254/99 P *Limburgse Vinyl Maatschappij v Commission* ECLI:EU:C:2002:582, para. 509.

'in fact resulted from its participation in the meetings'.[278] Participation in the meeting therefore implies acquiescence with what was agreed at the meeting.

198 In the case of an exchange of information, the question may arise whether the party whose acquiescence is alleged actually received the commercially sensitive information. The CJEU has recently held that, in the case of a message dispatched over an online platform, the addressees of that message can be presumed to be aware of the content of that message. It is for the addressees to demonstrate that they did not receive the message or did not look at it.[279]

199 This logic is similar to the principle that people are presumed to intend the natural and foreseeable consequences of their actions[280] and this analysis therefore seems to be based on the idea of 'objective intention' which I discussed in paragraph 84 of Chapter 1. Odudu has argued in this context that the presumption in the case law must be rebuttable[281] but the threshold will be high.

200 Often it will be immediately apparent which undertakings were party to an illicit agreement or concerted practice, for example if they are signatories to a written agreement. But in other instances it may not be so easy to identify the participants, in particular if the illegality of the agreement or concerted practice induces the participants to be secretive about the existence of the arrangement and their participation in it, as in the case of cartels.

201 Partially because they are secretive, cartels are usually complex infringements, comprising multiple agreements and concerted practices between several parties which restrict competition in multiple ways and often cover multiple products. In those circumstances, the question may arise what precisely a specific undertaking can be accused of. It may have been party to some agreements and concerted practices but not to others: what are the boundaries of its liability for the cartel as a whole?

202 In the 1980s and 1990s, the Commission developed a new legal concept, the 'single and continuous infringement', which was specifically meant to capture complex infringements. It has been said that the arrival of lawyers from common law traditions at the Commission after the accession of the UK and Ireland to the EU in 1973 facilitated

278. Joined cases C-238, 244, 245, 247, 250 to 252 and 254/99 P *Limburgse Vinyl Maatschappij v Commission* ECLI:EU:C:2002:582, para. 517.
279. C-74/14 *Eturas and Others* ECLI:EU:C:2016:42, paras 40-41.
280. *See* O Odudu, 'Interpreting Article 81(1): object as subjective intention' (2001) 26 European Law Review 60, 73 and O Odudu, 'Interpreting Article 81(1): the object requirement revisited' (2001) 26 European Law Review 379, 388. *See also* the opinion of AG Kokott in case C-209/07 *Beef Industry Development and Barry Brothers* ECLI:EU:C:2008:467, para. 45.
281. *See* O Odudu, 'Interpreting Article 81(1): the object requirement revisited' (2001) 26 European Law Review 379, 384, although the examples he gives of rebuttals (*Coditel* and *Erauw-Jacquery*) in fact concern instances where the European Courts accepted that the agreements had a different, procompetitive aim. In those circumstances, the agreements did not have the restriction of competition as their object and there simply cannot have been a presumption that the parties to those agreements had such an intention.

the development of this concept because of the common law offence of 'conspiracy'.[282] It may be true that these common law lawyers facilitated the understanding of the notion of conspiracy in the Sherman Act and thereby its parallel application in European competition law. However, the common law offence of 'conspiracy' has equivalents in continental European legal traditions[283] and it is therefore hard to believe that it was a direct import from English or Irish law.

203 What seems to be correct is that the European Commission developed the concept of a single and continuous infringement as a result of the information it gathered during inspections (dawn raids) conducted in October 1983 at the premises of petrochemical producers which participated in the Polypropylene cartel.[284] These inspections gave it an insight into the inner workings of a cartel and it is indeed in the judgments of the CFI and the CJEU in the appeals against the Commission decision in this case that the broad principles of the concept of a 'single and continuous infringement' were first enunciated. However, that does not mean that this case law is not relevant outside the sphere of cartels.[285]

204 I already discussed in paragraphs 188ff. above that in the case law of the CFI and CJEU in the appeals against the *Polypropylene* decision, the question of the constitutive elements of a concerted practice was elucidated and that in this context the so-called *Anic* presumption was developed. This presumption was affirmed in response to arguments from Anic's lawyers that the Commission should have demonstrated that its market conduct had been affected by the concertation.

205 Anic had contested the Commission's decision on several other grounds as well. It had in particular taken issue with the Commission's characterization of the infringement as a 'single continuing' agreement or concerted practice.[286] Indeed, the Commission had stated that the cartel had comprised a 'whole complex of schemes and arrangements decided in the context of a system of regular and institutionalized meetings'[287] whereby prices were fixed, volume quotas were set and information on the individual activities of the participants had been shared. Instances of individual

282. JM Joshua and S Jordan, 'Combinations, concerted practices and cartels: adopting the concept of conspiracy in European community competition law' (2004) 24 Northwestern Journal of International Law & Business 647, 648 and J Joshua, 'Single continuous infringement of article 81 EC: has the commission stretched the concept beyond the limit of its logic?' (2009) 5 European Competition Journal 451, 452.
283. For example, Article 265 of the French *Code pénal* of 1810 prohibited '*une association formée ou à une entente établie en vue de la préparation, concrétisée par un ou plusieurs faits matériels, d'un ou de plusieurs crimes contre les personnes ou les biens*' ['an association or collusion evidenced by one or more material facts which is formed in order to prepare one or more crimes against persons or good']. § 129 of the German *Strafgesetzbuch* similarly has banned the creation of and participation in criminal organizations since 1872.
284. *See* J Joshua, 'Single continuous infringement of article 81 EC: has the commission stretched the concept beyond the limit of its logic?' (2009) 5 European Competition Journal 451, 452.
285. J Faull, L Kjølbye, H Leupold and A Nikpay, 'Article 101' in J Faull and A Nikpay (eds), *The EU law of competition* (Oxford University Press 2014) 183, 211.
286. Commission decision of 23 April 1986 in case 31.149 *Polypropylene*, recital 81.
287. Commission decision of 23 April 1986 in case 31.149 *Polypropylene*, recital 81.

undertakings not attending certain meetings or cheating on the cartel had not prevented this single continuing agreement from arising, in the Commission's view.

206 The CFI agreed with the Commission that the various meetings, agreements and concerted practices could be viewed as constituting one infringement because they 'were part of a series of efforts made by the undertakings in question in pursuit of a single economic aim, namely to distort the normal movement of prices on the market of polypropylene. It would thus be artificial to split up such continuous conduct, characterized by a single purpose, by treating it as consisting of a number of separate infringements'.[288]

207 However, this raised the issue of the liability of the individual undertakings for their participation in that single infringement: could an undertaking be liable for the whole single continuing agreement if it participated in only a small part of it? How could this be reconciled with the personal nature of liability? The debate between the Commission and the undertakings fined was already alive before the CFI, and AG Vesterdorf in his opinion used the analogy of banknote forgery to explain that, also under criminal law, personal responsibility can attach to actions undertaken by others as part of the same offence: 'it would hardly be a crucial bar to the passing of sentence under the legal system of any Member State if it were not possible to prove who filled the printing press with ink and who operated the press when each party must be presumed to have been present and to have taken part'.[289]

208 The question of personal responsibility came particularly to the fore in the judgment of the CJEU which agreed with AG Vesterdorf's opinion before the CFI and ruled that 'the mere fact that each undertaking takes part in the infringement in ways particular to it does not suffice to exclude its responsibility for the entire infringement, including conduct put into effect by other participating undertakings but sharing the same anti-competitive object or effect'.[290] The CJEU reiterated that this was in line with the attribution of responsibility to several perpetrators who together participated in criminal offences under the law of EU Member States. In order to attribute to an undertaking responsibility for the entire cartel, 'the Commission must, in particular, show that the undertaking intended to contribute by its own conduct to the common objectives pursued by all the participants and that it was aware of the actual conduct planned or put into effect by other undertakings in pursuit of the same objectives or that it could reasonably have foreseen it and that it was prepared to take the risk'.[291]

---

288. T-6/89 *Enichem Anic v Commission* ECLI:EU:T:1991:74, para. 204. This also implied a different burden of proof for the Commission, which did not need to demonstrate that all the constituent elements of an agreement or concerted practice were present for each separate infringement. This evidentiary aspect of the single, continuous infringement doctrine has been often stressed (and criticized) in the literature. *See* D Riley, 'Revisiting the single and continuous infringement of Article 101: the significance of *Anic* in a new era of cartel detection and analysis' (2014) 3 World Competition 293, in particular 294-295.
289. AG opinion in joined cases T-1/89 to T-4/89 and T-6/89 to T-15/89 *Rhône-Poulenc et al v Commission* ECLI:EU:T:1991:38, in particular at [1991] ECR II 952.
290. C-49/92 P *Commission v Anic Partecipazioni* ECLI:EU:C:1999:356, para. 80.
291. C-49/92 P *Commission v Anic Partecipazioni* ECLI:EU:C:1999:356, para. 87.

209 This principle has been reiterated many times since then and can implicate not only the undertakings which are active in the cartelized market but also other undertakings which somehow facilitated the cartel or otherwise participated in it.[292] The logic of the CJEU is that 'a party which tacitly approves of an unlawful initiative, without publicly distancing itself from its content or reporting it to the administrative authorities, encourages the continuation of the infringement and compromises its discovery'.[293] The fact that the party did not have a direct interest in the functioning of (a particular aspect of) the cartel does not therefore mean that it should not be viewed as party to it.[294]

210 In this context wording that is clearly reminiscent of the *mens rea* for accessories (*see* paragraph 55 above) is being used. The CJEU states that an undertaking which contributed to a single continuing infringement can be held liable for that infringement as a whole if (i) it was aware of the illegal activities of the other undertakings or (ii) it could have reasonably foreseen those activities – and in both cases nevertheless went ahead (was prepared to take the risk). It is not surprising that this is said in a cartel context and that the question of participation is one that is particularly relevant for the liability of the undertakings involved for fines. Indeed, as I will discuss in more detail below, in order to be liable for a fine, Article 23 of Regulation 1/2003 requires that an undertaking has committed the infringement 'intentionally or negligently'. The awareness or reasonable foreseeability of the infringement that is enunciated in the *Anic* judgment is what allows for such a conclusion.

211 In practice, there is little need for the Commission to demonstrate this *mens rea* because of the rebuttable presumption, also established under the *Anic* case law, that the receipt of commercially sensitive information will influence the commercial behaviour of an undertaking active on the same market as the provider of the information. As a consequence of this, the burden of proof is shifted onto the undertaking in question. This gave rise in the case law coming out of the *Polypropylene* decision to a set of rules on how an undertaking can extricate itself from an infringement – whether agreement or concerted practice – which it may otherwise be (presumed to be) implicated in. This is the requirement of 'public distancing' which in the literature is often viewed as the flip side of the *Anic* presumption.[295]

212 In relation to a specific part of the cartel, the price initiative, Anic had argued that, although it attended certain meetings, 'it did not subscribe to the agreed price initiatives', as was demonstrated through its passive attitude during the meetings and

292. *See* C-194/14 P *AC-Treuhand v Commission* ECLI:EU:C:2015:717, para. 30; C-625/13 P *Villeroy & Boch v Commission* ECLI:EU:C:2017:52, paras 59-60.
293. *See* C-194/14 P *AC-Treuhand v Commission* ECLI:EU:C:2015:717, para. 31.
294. For an example of the same principle prior to the introduction of the concept of a single continuous infringement, *see* the role of ANSEAU in *IAZ* as discussed in paras 249-251 below.
295. *See*, for example, D Bailey, '"Publicly distancing" oneself from a cartel' (2008) 31 World Competition 177, in particular 200-202 and M Abenhaïm, 'Public distancing and liability in cartel cases: does distance lend enchantment' (2016) 39 World Competition 413.

its competitive behaviour on the market.[296] The CFI rejected this argument: Anic 'cannot assert that it did not support the price initiatives which were decided on, planned and monitored at those meetings, without providing any evidence to corroborate that assertion. In the absence of such evidence, there is no reason to believe that the applicant would not have supported those initiatives, unlike other participants at the meetings'.[297] The CJEU agreed that 'it was for Anic to adduce evidence that it had not subscribed to those initiatives' - which it failed to do.[298]

213 In another judgment on *Polypropylene*, the requirements for undertakings to escape liability for anticompetitive meetings they attend were enunciated more clearly. Hüls, like Anic one of the smaller participants in the cartel, argued that it had only participated in a limited number of meetings and that it had only done so because, as a smaller player, it could not afford to stay away. Hüls also argued that its strategy on the market showed that it did not agree with what was discussed at the meetings and that it had applied a strategy of disinformation and had mental reservations during the meetings.

214 The CFI did not accept these arguments. It held, in line with the principles on participation to an agreement which I outlined above, that 'since it is not disputed that the applicant took part in those meetings and it is established that their object was in particular to fix price and sale volume targets, the applicant at least gave its competitors the impression that it was participating in the meetings in the same spirit'.[299] The CFI continued that '[i]n those circumstances, it is for the applicant to adduce evidence to show that its participation in the meetings was without any anti-competitive intention by demonstrating that it had indicated to its competitors that it was participating in those meetings in a spirit which was different from theirs'.[300] The CJEU confirmed this principle[301] and a string of cases has discussed what an undertaking needs to do to indicate to its competitors that it distances itself from the anticompetitive content of a meeting.[302] The case law on distancing also has particular relevance for companies that wish to terminate their participation in an infringement.[303]

296. T-6/89 *Enichem Anic v Commission* ECLI:EU:T:1991:74, para. 111. It also argued that it took a passive attitude during the meetings but this was rejected on the facts by the General Court.
297. T-6/89 *Enichem Anic v Commission* ECLI:EU:T:1991:74, para. 110.
298. C-49/92 P *Commission v Anic Partecipazioni* ECLI:EU:C:1999:356, para. 96.
299. T-9/89 *Hüls v Commission* ECLI:EU:T:1992:31, para. 125.
300. T-9/89 *Hüls v Commission* ECLI:EU:T:1992:31, para. 126.
301. C-199/92 P *Hüls v Commission* ECLI:EU:C:1999:358, para. 155. It was afterwards also repeated in joined cases T-202, 204 and 207/98 *Tate & Lyle and Others v Commission* ECLI:EU:T:2001:185, para. 64; T-61/99 *Adriatica di Navigazione v Commission* ECLI:EU:T:2003:335, para. 135.
302. *See*, in addition to the cases discussed in the next point, joined cases C-204, 205, 211, 213, 217 and 219/00 P *Aalborg Portland v Commission* ECLI:EU:C:2004:6, paras 85 and 323; joined cases C-189, 202, 205 to 208 and 213/02 P *Dansk Rørindustri v Commission* ECLI:EU:C:2005:408, paras 144-146; joined cases C-403 and 405/04 P, *Sumitomo Metal Industries and Nippon Steel v Commission* ECLI:EU:C:2007:52, paras 49ff. M Abenhaïm, 'Public distancing and liability in cartel cases: does distance lend enchantment' (2016) 39 World Competition 413 lists more cases but does not seem to be complete (*Sumitomo* is not mentioned).
303. *See* D Bailey, '"Publicly distancing" oneself from a cartel' (2008) 31 World Competition 177, 187.

215 More recent case law has made it explicit that, in order to assess whether distancing took place, what is of 'critical importance', is 'the understanding which the other participants in a cartel have of the intention of the undertaking concerned'.[304] The perception which these other participants have of the distancing is therefore what matters, rather than the undertaking's own intentions in this respect. If other cartelists continue to consider that undertaking as part of the cartel (e.g. by including it in documents as a cartel member), the distancing will not have been effective. There are not many instances were undertakings have managed to convince the Commission or the European Courts that they distanced themselves from the anticompetitive content of a meeting.[305]

216 As indicated in paragraph 209 above, the principles of attribution also apply if an undertaking is not active on the market in which the infringement took place, but in that case the rebuttable presumption of the *Anic* case law does not apply. In those circumstances, the Commission actively needs to show that the undertaking (i) was aware of the illegal activities of the other undertakings or (ii) could reasonably have foreseen those activities. In its *Icap* judgment, the General Court provided a fairly detailed analysis of circumstances in which one of these conditions is and is not fulfilled: it held that an alleged facilitator could be said to be aware of a cartel in another market if one of the participants to the cartel informed the facilitator 'in unambiguous terms' of the agreement it had reached with a competitor.[306] Furthermore, if an alleged facilitator is aware of collusion which is meant to take place at a later stage, it must reasonably foresee that certain earlier information 'formed part of the preparation of the [later] collusion' of which it is aware.[307] In those circumstances, the alleged facilitator can be held liable for the cartel if there is a 'very high degree of complementarity' between its conduct and that of the cartel members, since this implies that it intended to contribute to the cartel.[308] However, in case there is 'ambiguity in the wording' of the information received by the alleged facilitator from a cartel participant, this is insufficient to prove awareness of the alleged facilitator, and the alleged facilitator will not be liable for the actions of the cartelists on this basis.[309]

217 This case law has found particular application in hub-and-spoke infringements, i.e. where information is communicated between competitors via a joint supplier or customer.[310]

---

304. C-510/06 P *Archer Daniels Midland v Commission* ECLI:EU:C:2009:166, para. 120; C-373/14 P *Toshiba Corporation v Commission* ECLI:EU:C:2016:26, para. 62; T-448/14 *Hitachi Metals v Commission* ECLI:EU:T:2018:442, para. 132.
305. But *see*, for example, the Commission decision of 1 October 2006 in case 39.181 *Candle waxes*, recital 604 and, since the public version of that decision is heavily redacted, case T-566/08 *Total Raffinage Marketing v Commission* ECLI:EU:T:2013:423, para. 387.
306. T-180/15 *Icap v Commission* ECLI:EU:T:2017:795, para. 130.
307. T-180/15 *Icap v Commission* ECLI:EU:T:2017:795, para. 163.
308. T-180/15 *Icap v Commission* ECLI:EU:T:2017:795, para. 180.
309. T-180/15 *Icap v Commission* ECLI:EU:T:2017:795, para. 143. The European Commission brought an appeal against this judgment, but not concerning this point: *see* C-39/18 P *Commission v Icap* ECLI:EU:C:2019:584.
310. *See Argos Limited and Littlewoods Limited v Office of Fair Trading and JJB Sports plc v Office of Fair Trading* [2006] EWCA Civ 1318 where the question of whether there was an intention of

[D] Conclusion

218 The concepts of 'agreement' and 'concertation' are infused with the terminology of the human mind. However, according to the case law of the CJEU, the external manifestation of that mental state also needs to be communicated between the parties to give rise to an agreement or concerted practice. The expression of an invitation or the communication of information can give rise to an agreement or concerted practice, respectively, if they are followed by tacit acquiescence.

219 Tacit acquiescence in turn is assumed if the invitation or information is received by a second undertaking. In this context, where often the question of participation of an undertaking in an infringement is posed, the presence of mental terminology is even more apparent, as it needs to be demonstrated that the recipient was aware of or could reasonably have foreseen the infringement. Nevertheless, because of the '*Anic* presumption', participation often depends on whether an undertaking distanced itself from an infringement, and this is in turn determined from the perspective of the other parties to the infringement. What matters is therefore not the intention of the undertaking as such but the perception thereof by the other parties.

§2.02 OBJECT OR EFFECT THE PREVENTION, RESTRICTION OR DISTORTION OF COMPETITION

220 Agreements and concerted practices will not be prohibited by Article 101 TFEU unless they 'have as their object or effect the prevention, restriction or distortion of competition within the internal market'.

221 The interpretation of this provision was at the heart of the landmark preliminary ruling of the CJEU in *Société Technique Minière* in 1966. In *Société Technique Minière*, the CJEU held that the '*or*' in this provision should indeed be understood as providing for alternatives: it is not necessary to prove that an agreement or concerted practice has both as its object *and* as its effect the prevention, restriction or distortion of competition; an anticompetitive object *or* effect suffices. The CJEU points out that, in a first step, the object of the agreement or concerted practice can be assessed, i.e. 'the precise purpose of the agreement, in the economic context in which it is to be applied'. According to *Société Technique Minière*, this needs to be done through an analysis 'of the clauses of the agreement itself'. When such an analysis does not show a restriction of competition, in a second step, 'the consequences of the agreement should then be considered [to] show that competition has in fact been prevented or restricted or distorted'.[311]

---

the retailers that the information they provided to their suppliers be passed on to other retailers was key to the assessment of the legality of the practices.

311. C-56/65 *Société Technique Minière v Maschinenbau Ulm* ECLI:EU:C:1966:38, at [1966] ECR 249. The disjunctive function of 'object or effect' has been confirmed in later case law (*see*, for example, C-8/08 *T-Mobile Netherlands and Others* ECLI:EU:C:2009:343, para. 28) and seems to be one of the few things all commentators agree on. *See* S King, *Agreements that restrict*

222 *Société Technique Minière* kicked off a polemic in the literature and in the case law which continues to this day, namely when are agreements and concerted practices restrictive by object and when are they not. This polemic goes to the fundamentals of Article 101 TFEU and in its scale, level of abstraction and almost fanatic reading of some judgments of the European Courts, it sometimes seems akin to theological debates about the nature of the Divine. I will touch upon some aspects of this controversy here but to trace the full extent of this debate goes beyond the scope of this treatise.

223 In what follows I will only discuss restrictions by object and the role *mens rea* plays in them. The reason for not discussing restrictions by effect is that there are simply too few decisions and judgments finding restrictions by effect. Prior to Regulation 1/2003 and the direct application of what is now Article 101(3) TFEU, the Commission often did not distinguish between restrictions by object and restrictions by effect.[312] And despite all the rhetoric about a more 'effects-based' analysis (*see also* paragraphs 710ff. below), after modernization only a handful of prohibition decisions were adopted by the Commission based on an alleged restriction of competition by effect.[313] The situation at National Competition Authority (NCA) level does not appear to be very different.[314]

[A] Restrictions by Object: Preliminary Observations

224 The notion of restriction by object is problematic because it has so many meanings. In the context of Article 101(1) TFEU, the notion of 'object' is obviously juxtaposed or even opposed to the notion of 'effect'. It implies, in the wording of the case law, an analysis of the agreement or concerted practice, without the need to take into account its concrete effects.[315] But the original meaning of the notion of 'object' in Article 101(1) TFEU is probably that of 'objective' in the sense of 'purpose', 'goal' or 'aim'. In French *objet* also has the meaning of '*but*', '*objectif*',[316] but the German

---

competition by object under Article 101(1) TFEU: past present and future, <http://etheses.lse.ac.uk/3068/1/King_Agreements_that_restrict_competition_by_object_under_Article_101.pdf> accessed 20 January 2017, 114-115.

312. *See*, for example, the Commission decision of 1 December 1976 in case 29.018 *Miller International Schallplatten GmbH*, recital 11 and the Commission decision of 19 December 1990 in case 33.133-B *Soda-ash – Solvay, CFK*, recital 12.
313. AC Witt, 'The enforcement of Article 101 TFEU: what has happened to the effects analysis?' (2018) 55 Common Market Law Review 417, 425-431 identified only one prohibition decision exclusively based on effects up to June 2017 and three (possibly four) decisions where an effects-analysis was added 'for the sake of completeness' to an object-analysis. In December 2017, one additional prohibition decision included a brief effects-analysis in addition to a full object-analysis (Commission decision of 8 December 2017 in case 40.208 *International Skating Union's Eligibility rules*).
314. *See* AC Witt, 'The enforcement of Article 101 TFEU: what has happened to the effects analysis?' (2018) 55 Common Market Law Review 417, 440-443.
315. Joined cases C-56 and 58/64 *Consten and Grundig v Commission* ECLI:EU:C:1966:41, at [1966] ECR 342.
316. Note that '*objet*' is also often used to denote the subject of a contract under French law. It is then juxtaposed to the notion of '*cause*', referring to the reason or objective of the contract,

language version of the treaty is even clearer, using the word '*Zweck*' (*goal*).[317] Determining the 'object' of an agreement then requires an a priori analysis as opposed to the *a posteriori* analysis required to assess its effects. The (English translation of the) early case law often refers to 'purpose' or 'aim' of an agreement in the context of object infringements.[318]

225 Identifying which agreements and concerted practices are restrictive by object is important, because such agreements and concerted practices are prohibited by Article 101 TFEU, regardless of whether any actual negative effects on competition are demonstrated.[319] If the Commission establishes that an agreement or concerted practice is restrictive by object, it therefore obtains a 'procedural economy',[320] since it does not need to analyse the actual effects of the agreement or practice. The flip side of this rule is that it should be possible to determine the restrictive object of an agreement or concerted practice without it being necessary to look at its effects.

226 How to determine whether an agreement or practice is restrictive by object is controversial but recent case law reiterates that regard must be had to (i) the content of the agreement or practice, (ii) its objectives and (iii) the economic and legal context of which it forms part.[321]

[1] Content

227 First of all, the content of an agreement can be indicative that an agreement has a restrictive object. This is particularly true if an agreement contains any of the

although there is a lot of doctrinal discussion about the two notions. *See*, for example, F Terré, P Simler and Y Lequette (eds), *Droit Civil. Les Obligations* (Dalloz 2005) 274-377.

317. If J Faull, L Kjølbye, H Leupold and A Nikpay, 'Article 101' in J Faull and A Nikpay (eds), *The EU law of competition* (Oxford University Press 2014) 183, 229 are correct that the rules on competition were introduced in the Treaty of Rome at the insistence of the German delegation, this could even be said to be the 'original' wording of the text. However, other authors have contested that Germany was at the origin of the competition provisions: *see* Y Karagiannis, 'The causes and consequences of the collegial implementation of European competition law' (2013) 19 European Law Journal 682, 702-703. *See also* the discussion in B Sufrin, 'The evolution of Article 81(3) of the EC treaty' (2006) 51(4) The Antitrust Bulletin 915, 921-922.
318. *See*, for example, C-56/65 *Société Technique Minière v Maschinenbau Ulm* ECLI:EU:C:1966:38, at [1966] ECR 249 referring to the 'specific purpose of the agreement'; joined cases C-96 to 102, 104, 105, 108 and 110/82 *IAZ v Commission* ECLI:EU:C:1983:310, para. 25 referring to 'the purpose of the Agreement'; joined cases C-29 and 30/83 *CRAM v Commission* ECLI:EU:C:1984:130, at [1984] ECR 1703, para. 26 which requires 'examining the aims pursued by the agreement'.
319. This is implicit in C-56/65 *Société Technique Minière v Maschinenbau Ulm* ECLI:EU:C:1966:38, at [1966] ECR 249 but more explicit in joined cases C-56 and 58/64 *Consten and Grundig v Commission* ECLI:EU:C:1966:41, at [1966] ECR 342 and a vast amount of case law since. *See*, more recently, for example, C-209/07 *Beef Industry Development and Barry Brothers* ECLI:EU:C:2008:643, para. 16; C-8/08 *T-Mobile Netherlands and Others* ECLI:EU:C:2009:343, para. 29; C-32/11 *Allianz Hungaria Biztosito* ECLI:EU:C:2013:160, para. 34.
320. Opinion of AG Wahl in C-67/13 P *Cartes Bancaires v Commission* ECLI:EU:C:2014:1958, para. 28.
321. *See* joined cases C-501, 513, 515 and 519/06 P *GlaxoSmithKline Services and Others v Commission and Others* ECLI:EU:C:2009:610, para. 58; C-32/11 *Allianz Hungaria Biztosito* ECLI:EU:C:2013:160, para. 36; C-67/13 P *Cartes Bancaires v Commission* ECLI:EU:C:2014:2204, para. 53; C-373/14 P *Toshiba Corporation v Commission* ECLI:EU:C:2016:26, para. 27.

provisions listed in points (a)-(e) of Article 101(1) TFEU, even though that list does not provide an exhaustive list of provisions that may be restrictive by object.[322]

228 The case law does not appear to be entirely consistent on whether the wording of the agreement needs to be on its face problematic in order to qualify as a restriction by object[323] or whether ambiguously worded agreements can also qualify as such.[324] Furthermore, some of the case law[325] and literature[326] indicates that certain (clauses in) agreements are, by their very nature, restrictive by object, without there being much need to take into account the legal and economic context in which these (clauses in) agreements were concluded. According to this view, certain (clauses in) agreements are by their very nature injurious to the proper functioning of normal competition. Such (clauses in) agreements can therefore be presumed to necessarily have a restrictive effect on competition without the need to actually show that effect.[327] The (clauses in) agreements which fall in this category would have been identified based on experience.[328]

229 The notification system which existed under Regulation 17/62 may have been one of the causes of this view of object restrictions. Since the Commission had the sole power to grant derogations from the prohibition of (the predecessors of) Article 101(1) TFEU under Article 101(3) TFEU, the Commission (supported by the CJEU) may initially have had the tendency to extend its jurisdiction over certain types of agreements.[329] Paradoxically, this point of view may have crystallized when the notification system was abolished in the Commission's 2004 *Guidelines on the application of Article*

322. C-209/07 *Beef Industry Development and Barry Brothers* ECLI:EU:C:2008:643, para. 23.
323. This seems to be the position in C-67/13 P *Cartes Bancaires v Commission* ECLI:EU:C:2014:2204, paras 65-69 where it is stated that a provision needs to exhibit a sufficient degree of harm in order to be qualified as a restriction by object.
324. As in the cases C-35/83 *BAT v Commission* ECLI:EU:C:1985:32 and C-32/11 *Allianz Hungaria Biztosito* ECLI:EU:C:2013:160.
325. Joined cases T-374, 375, 384 and 388/94 *European Night Services and others v Commission* ECLI:EU:T:1998:198 have been said to be the clearest embodiment of this approach. *See* S King, *Agreements that restrict competition by object under Article 101(1) TFEU: past present and future*, <http://etheses.lse.ac.uk/3068/1/King_Agreements_that_restrict_competition_by_object_under_Article_101.pdf> accessed 20 January 2017, 32. But *see also* C-243/83 *Binon v AMP* ECLI:EU:C:1985:284, para. 44, C-345/14 *Maxima Latvija* ECLI:EU:C:2015:784, para. 19.
326. In particular R Whish, *Competition law* (Oxford University Press 2008) 119-120.
327. *See* the Commission Guidelines on the application of Article 81(3) of the Treaty [2004] OJ C101/97, para. 21. AG Cruz Villalón also uses the word 'presumption' in this context in his opinion in C-32/11 *Allianz Hungaria Biztosito* ECLI:EU:C:2012:663, para. 64 but this has been criticized by AG Wathelet in his opinion in C-373/14 P *Toshiba Corporation v Commission* ECLI:EU:C:2015:427, para. 57.
328. C-67/13 P *Cartes Bancaires v Commission* ECLI:EU:C:2014:2204, para. 51; C-286/13 P *Dole Food and Dole Fresh Fruit Europe v Commission* ECLI:EU:C:2015:184, para. 115; C-345/14 *Maxima Latvija* ECLI:EU:C:2015:784, para. 19. *See also* the opinion of AG Wahl in C-67/13 P *Cartes Bancaires v Commission* ECLI:EU:C:2014:1958, para. 46 and the Commission Guidelines on the application of Article 81(3) of the Treaty [2004] OJ C101/97, para. 21. O Odudu, 'Interpreting Article 81(1): the object requirement revisited' (2001) 26 European Law Review 379, 381, however, claims that it is a 'fallacy that such a category has been developed inductively from analysis of actual effects'.
329. *See* A Jones, 'Left behind by modernisation? Restriction by object under Article 101(1)' (2010) 6 European Competition Journal 649, 651.

81(3) of the Treaty which list in their point 23 a number of object restrictions.[330] This view of the notion of restriction by object is still present in the case law of the CJEU today.[331]

[2] Context

230 Despite this, the case law, starting with *Société Technique Minière* (*see* paragraph 221 above) states clearly that, in order to determine whether a restriction by object exists, the economic context of the agreement should also be taken into account.[332] This context may indicate that what may appear as anticompetitive wording in an agreement is actually not a restriction by object,[333] or, conversely, that what may not appear problematic at first blush is, in the specific legal and economic context of the agreement, nevertheless a restriction by object.[334]

231 Much of the controversy is then about the extent to which the legal and economic context needs to be analysed to interpret the wording of the agreement. Requiring an analysis that is so detailed that it involves assessing the actual effects of the agreement or concerted practice risks blurring the object-effect distinction which is clearly established in the case law.[335]

[3] Objectives

232 Apart from the content and context of the agreement or concerted practice, the case law also requires an analysis of the objectives of the agreement or practice. As pointed out above, the notion 'object' in Article 101(1) TFEU may have originally been meant to refer to its 'objective' (as in the German '*Zweck*') and, in that sense, it could even be argued that the purpose of the analysis of the content and context of the agreement is merely to determine its objectives.

233 Specific difficulties arise because agreements often have more than one objective. Exclusive distribution agreements, for example, both aim at expanding the distribution network of a supplier and at protecting the new distributor from existing members of

330. Commission Guidelines on the application of Article 81(3) of the Treaty [2004] OJ C101/97.
331. *See* the case law references in footnote 328.
332. This is repeated also in the judgments mentioned in footnote 328.
333. *See*, for example, C-27/87 *SPRL Louis Erauw-Jacquery v La Hesbignonne SC* ECLI:EU:C1988: 183, para. 11.
334. *See* the cases referenced in footnote 324.
335. *See* X, 'Les ententes' in R Bout *et al.* (eds), *Le Lamy droit économique édition 2017* (Wolters Kluwer 2016) 555, 578; J Faull, L Kjølbye, H Leupold and A Nikpay, 'Article 101' in J Faull and A Nikpay (eds), *The EU law of competition* (Oxford University Press 2014) 183, 243; P Ibáñez Colomo and A Lamadrid de Pablo, 'On the notion of restriction of competition: what we know and what we don't know we know' in D Gerard, M Merola and B Meyring (eds), *The notion of restriction of competition: revisiting the foundations of antitrust enforcement in Europe* (Bruylant 2017) 333, 351ff. *See also* the opinion of AG Wahl in C-67/13 P *Cartes Bancaires v Commission* ECLI:EU:C:2014:1958, para. 46.

the supplier's network. Similarly, standard setting agreements allow for interoperability of devices but may also create barriers to entry. An obvious question is therefore whether the fact that an agreement has lawful or even procompetitive objectives means that it cannot have an anticompetitive object.

234 First of all, I am not talking here about cases where the parties claim the agreement has lawful objectives but the European Courts do not accept that they have the stated objectives[336] or do not view these objectives as lawful.[337] To discuss such cases to clarify the question of whether legitimate objectives are relevant in the assessment of object infringement obfuscates the analysis.

235 The case law is clear that an agreement may be regarded as having a restrictive object even if it does not have the restriction of competition as its sole aim but also pursues other legitimate objectives.[338] Multiple parallel aims can be pursued by one agreement; when it appears that one of these aims is the restriction of competition, the Commission and European Courts do not need to assess whether there is a plausible alternative explanation for the conduct at issue.[339]

236 But what if the restrictive objective of the agreement (e.g. the fact that it aims to grant a distributor territorial exclusivity) is merely a tool to ensure another legitimate or even procompetitive purpose (such as to set up a distribution network). Some of the case law suggests that such an ulterior purpose can only be taken into account in the assessment of Article 101(3) TFEU and is not relevant for the assessment of whether it has a restrictive object in the sense of Article 101(1) TFEU.[340]

237 The European Courts have in some circumstances nevertheless accepted, under the influence of US law,[341] that restrictions which are necessary and proportionate to achieve a legitimate objective may not be restrictive by object. This so-called doctrine of ancillary restraints[342] is most influential in the context of non-compete provisions in

---

336. *See*, for example, C-35/83 *BAT v Commission* ECLI:EU:C:1985:32, para. 38 where the Court held that 'that agreement served no other purpose' than to restrict competition (despite the fact that para. 33 suggests through the word 'also' that there were multiple objectives).
337. C-209/07 *Beef Industry Development and Barry Brothers* ECLI:EU:C:2008:643 is a case in point.
338. *See*, for example, in the early case law, joined cases C-96 to 102, 104, 105, 108 and 110/82 *IAZ v Commission* ECLI:EU:C:1983:310, para. 25 and, more recently, C-551/03 P *General Motors v Commission* ECLI:EU:C:2006:229, para. 64 and C-209/07 *Beef Industry Development and Barry Brothers* ECLI:EU:C:2008:643, para. 21.
339. Joined cases C-239, 489 and 498/11 P *Siemens v Commission* ECLI:EU:C:2013:866, para. 220. This is different in the case of concerted practices: joined cases C-89, 104, 114, 116, 117 and 125 to 129/85 *Ahlström Osakeyhtiö and Others v Commission* ECLI:EU:C:1993:120, para. 71. *See also* T-48/00 *Corus UK v Commission* ECLI:EU:T:2004:219, para. 72.
340. *See* C-243/83 *Binon v AMP* ECLI:EU:C:1985:284, para. 46, but also C-209/07 *Beef Industry Development and Barry Brothers* ECLI:EU:C:2008:643, para. 21 and C-382/12 P *MasterCard and Others v Commission* ECLI:EU:C:2014:2201, in particular para. 180.
341. X, 'Les ententes' in R Bout *et al.* (eds), *Le Lamy droit économique édition 2017* (Wolters Kluwer 2016) 555, 582. *See also* the discussion of US law in KH Jebelli, 'EU ancillary restraints: a reasoned approach to Article 101(1)' <https://papers.ssrn.com/sol3/Delivery.cfm/SSRN_ID 2900150_code1543611.pdf?abstractid=2166318&mirid=1> accessed 30 January 2017.
342. *See*, Commission Guidelines on the application of Article 81(3) of the Treaty [2004] OJ C101/97, paras 28-31 and, for a discussion of the case law, KH Jebelli, 'EU ancillary restraints:

corporate transactions[343] but has also been applied in many other contexts, including in relation to territorial exclusivity in distribution[344] and licensing agreements,[345] horizontal cooperation between competitors[346] and trade associations with non-economic objectives.[347]

238 However, it is not easy to discern clear rules in the case law as to what objectives are accepted as justifying provisions that could otherwise be viewed as restrictive. In the literature, it has been argued that if provisions are necessary and proportionate to an agreement that protects legitimate interests of the parties, they cannot be restrictive under Article 101(1) TFEU.[348] Others have argued that the mere fact that an agreement is a plausible source of efficiency gains means that its provisions cannot be restrictive by object.[349]

239 Furthermore, whether or not a restriction is necessary and proportionate to an alleged objective is a factual question which may be answered differently in different contexts.

240 While the notion of ancillary restraints is therefore an important element to make sense of the case law on restrictions by object, it is certainly not the final word on it. For the discussion on the relevance of *mens rea* below, this case law is, however, of utmost importance since the objectives of an agreement are often interpreted in the context of the intentions of the parties.

241 For the avoidance of doubt, it is sufficient that a provision restricts competition to fall foul of Article 101 TFEU: it does not need to prevent or distort it.[350]

---

a reasoned approach to Article 101(1)' <https://papers.ssrn.com/sol3/Delivery.cfm/SSRN_ID2900150_code1543611.pdf?abstractid=2166318&mirid=1> accessed 30 January 2017.

343. *See* C-42/84 *Remia v Commissioni* ECLI:EU:C:1985:327, paras 19-20. *See also* the Commission Notice on restrictions directly related and necessary to concentrations [2005] OJ C56/24.
344. *See*, for example, C-56/65 *Société Technique Minière v Maschinenbau Ulm* ECLI:EU:C:1966:38, at [1966] ECR 250; C-107/82 *AEG v Commission* ECLI:EU:C:1983:293, para. 33.
345. *See*, for example, C-262/81 *Coditel v Ciné-Vog Films* ECLI:EU:C:1982:334, para. 19; C-27/87 *SPRL Louis Erauw-Jacquery v La Hesbignonne SC* ECLI:EU:C1988:183, para. 11.
346. *See*, for example, C-382/12 P *MasterCard and Others v Commission* ECLI:EU:C:2014:2201, in particular para. 90.
347. *See*, for example, C-519/04 P *Meca-Medina and Majcen v Commission* ECLI:EU:C:2006:492, in particular para. 47; C-309/99 *Wouters and Others* ECLI:EU:C:2002:98, in particular paras 107-110.
348. KH Jebelli, 'EU ancillary restraints: a reasoned approach to Article 101(1)' <https://papers.ssrn.com/sol3/Delivery.cfm/SSRN_ID2900150_code1543611.pdf?abstractid=2166318&mirid=1> accessed 30 January 2017, 31.
349. P Ibáñez Colomo and A Lamadrid de Pablo, 'On the notion of restriction of competition: what we know and what we don't know we know' in D Gerard, M Merola and B Meyring (eds), *The notion of restriction of competition: revisiting the foundations of antitrust enforcement in Europe* (Bruylant 2017) 333, 353.
350. Joined cases C-40 to 48, 50, 54 to 56, 111, 113 and 114/73 *Suiker Unie and Others v Commission* ECLI:EU:C:1975:174, para. 291: 'in order to establish that there are concerted practices within the meaning of Article 85 of the Treaty, it is sufficient to show that competition has been restricted and it is unnecessary to prove that it has been prevented'. Even before this judgment, *see* W Van Gerven, *Principes du droit des ententes de la communauté économique européenne*

[B] The Relevance of Subjective Intentions for Restrictions by Object

242 There is a fair amount of confusion in the case law on the relevance of *mens rea* for the establishment of restrictions of competition by object. That confusion seems to find its origin in Article 15(2) of Regulation 17/62 which provides,[351] like Article 23(2) Regulation 1/2003 today,[352] that fines can be imposed on undertakings and associations of undertakings that 'intentionally or negligently' breach (what is now) Article 101 or 102 TFEU. Because of this provision, the question of the culpability of the undertakings needed to be discussed each time the Commission imposed a fine on an undertaking.

243 The question of whether a certain agreement or concerted practice restricts competition is clearly distinct from whether the undertakings which are party to it should be fined. But, nevertheless, as I will discuss below, the CJEU and its Advocates General have on several occasions discussed the question of culpability – according to the implementing regulations relevant for fines – when assessing the object of an agreement.

[1] Subjective Intentions Not Necessary

244 The CJEU was off on a good start in the 1978 *Miller* case, where the questions of the object of the agreement and the culpability for fining purposes were discussed separately.

245 *Miller* concerned a distribution contract granted by the eponymous supplier to Sopholet for the sale of Miller's products in Alsace-Lorraine. This contract provided that 'No Miller products shall as a rule be exported from Alsace-Lorraine to other countries.'[353] Miller argued that this provision was stipulated at the express request of Sopholet and that Miller itself did not seek to restrict competition so that the prohibition could not have as its object the restriction of competition – a 'blameworthy objective' in the words of the Court.[354] The Court rejected this argument:

> by its very nature, a clause prohibiting exports constitutes a restriction on competition, whether it is adopted at the instigation of the supplier or of the customer since the agreed purpose of the contracting parties is the endeavour to isolate a part of the market.
>
> ...

(Bruylant 1966) 56. *See also* the Guidelines on the applicability of Article 101 of the Treaty on the Functioning of the European Union to horizontal co-operation agreements [2011] OJ C11/1, footnote 5.

351. Regulation 17: First Regulation implementing Articles 85 and 86 of the Treaty [1962] OJ 13/204.
352. Regulation 1/2003 on the implementation of the rules on competition laid down in Articles 81 and 82 of the Treaty [2003] OJ L1/1.
353. C-19/77 *Miller International Schallplatten GmbH v Commission* ECLI:EU:C:1978:19, at [1978] ECR 133.
354. It is the Court that uses the term 'blameworthy' to summarize Miller's argument. *See* C-19/77 *Miller International Schallplatten GmbH v Commission* ECLI:EU:C:1978:19, para. 6.

> Consequently Miller's statement that the disputed prohibitions originated in the wishes of its co-contractors rather than its own unilateral and premeditated strategy, even if it is correct, cannot allow its behaviour to escape the prohibition contained in Article 85 (1) of the Treaty.[355]

246 Miller brought a separate plea on the level of the fine: it argued that it had not committed the infringement intentionally and that therefore its fine should be reduced. It referred in this context to the fact that it had obtained an opinion from a legal adviser when drafting the relevant agreement and that this opinion did not point out that the clause prohibiting exports might be incompatible with Article 101 TFEU. The CJEU rejected this argument and held:

> As is clear from the foregoing as a whole, the clauses in question were adopted or accepted by the applicant and the latter could not have been unaware that they had as their object the restriction of competition between its customers.
>
> Consequently, it is of little relevance to establish whether the applicant knew that it was infringing the prohibition contained in Article 85.[356]

247 I will discuss the relevance of *mens rea* for fining purposes in more detail in Chapter 4, but for current purposes, it is important to see that the CJEU clearly distinguished the question of the relevance of intentions for the purpose of determining the object of a restriction, on the one hand, and for the level of the fine, on the other.

248 The same very clear distinction was followed by the CJEU in the 1983 *IAZ* case – even though the parties in the case tried to confuse matters. *IAZ* is a judgment that is often misunderstood so it is useful to discuss it in some detail here. *IAZ* concerned a new system introduced by a number of trade associations to verify that domestic appliances were built in such a way that waste water from these appliances would not flow back into the drinking water pipelines. In the past, the trade associations had used lists of authorized products to help identify products which were in conformity with these requirements. Since the compilation and use of these lists was burdensome, the trade associations agreed to introduce a new system based on a conformity label, but this was only made available to manufacturers and sole importers of these appliances, not to parallel importers. The Commission considered that this was a restriction of competition by object and imposed fines on the trade associations.

249 One of the trade associations involved, ANSEAU, was the association of public bodies providing drinking water and, while it therefore had an interest in ensuring that the drinking water was not contaminated, the restrictions on parallel imports contained in the new rules were of no commercial interest to it or its members. In its fining decision in *IAZ*, the Commission considered that the other trade associations had

355. C-19/77 *Miller International Schallplatten GmbH v Commission* ECLI:EU:C:1978:19, para. 7.
356. C-19/77 *Miller International Schallplatten GmbH v Commission* ECLI:EU:C:1978:19, para. 18.

committed the infringement 'intentionally'[357] but ANSEAU was found to have committed it merely through 'gross negligence'.[358]

250 Using this distinction between 'intentional' and 'negligent' infringements in Regulation 17/62, ANSEAU argued that the introduction of the conformity label could not be said to be restrictive by object since the Commission had accepted that not all the parties to the system had an anticompetitive objective in mind. It argued that '[n]o such intention is apparent either from the provisions of the Agreement or from the circumstances surrounding its implementation or from the economic context in which it was concluded'.[359] On the contrary, ANSEAU argued, '[t]he real purpose of the Agreement is to reduce the financial and administrative costs of carrying out checks by delegating to manufacturers and sole importers the task of checking the conformity of models placed on the market'.[360] This was clearly one of the objectives of the new rules and probably the only objective as far as ANSEAU was interested.[361]

251 The Court analysed the new rules in some detail and concluded that the provisions of the agreement and the context in which it was concluded and implemented showed that the purpose of the agreement was to restrict competition. The Court added: 'That finding is not invalidated by the fact that it has not been established that it was the intention of all the parties to the Agreement to restrict competition.'[362] In other words, the fact that ANSEAU merely agreed to the new system because it wanted to reduce its administrative burden did not exclude that the system was restrictive by object.

252 The Court then turned to the separate question of the level of the fine imposed on the undertakings in question and their culpability, which I will discuss again in Chapter 4.

253 One year after the *IAZ* judgment, the question of the relevance of the intentions of the parties for the object of a restriction was raised again in the 1984 *CRAM* judgment. As discussed in paragraph 163 above, this case concerned the attempt by CRAM and Rheinzink, two German suppliers of rolled zinc, to stop their Belgian customer Schiltz from reimporting their zinc products into Germany (where prices were higher than in

357. In the *IAZ* judgment, it is said that they committed the infringement 'deliberately' but this is clearly the (too literal) translation of the term '*de propos délibéré*' in Regulation 17/62 (which is 'intentional' in the English language version).
358. Joined cases C-96 to 102, 104, 105, 108 and 110/82 *IAZ v Commission* ECLI:EU:C:1983:310, at [1983] ECR 3384.
359. Joined cases C-96 to 102, 104, 105, 108 and 110/82 *IAZ v Commission* ECLI:EU:C:1983:310, at [1983] ECR 3389.
360. Joined cases C-96 to 102, 104, 105, 108 and 110/82 *IAZ v Commission* ECLI:EU:C:1983:310, at [1983] ECR 3389.
361. And it is therefore difficult to say that, at least as far as ANSEAU was concerned, it was a '*sham*', as does O Odudu, 'Interpreting Article 81(1): object as subjective intention' (2001) 26 European Law Review 60, 66. For the other parties to it, it may have been a 'disguised' cartel (P Ibáñez Colomo and A Lamadrid de Pablo, 'On the notion of restriction of competition: what we know and what we don't know we know' in D Gerard, M Merola and B Meyring (eds), *The notion of restriction of competition: revisiting the foundations of antitrust enforcement in Europe* (Bruylant 2017) 333, 338) but ANSEAU did not care about this.
362. Joined cases C-96 to 102, 104, 105, 108 and 110/82 *IAZ v Commission* ECLI:EU:C:1983:310, para. 25.

Belgium). One of the infringements found by the Commission was that CRAM and Rheinzink conditioned the sale of certain volumes of rolled zinc to Schiltz on the commitment from Schiltz that it would export these outside the EU (to Egypt in particular). Despite this commitment, Schiltz nevertheless sold the rolled zinc to Germany. Before the CJEU, CRAM argued that Schiltz 'never intended to observe the agreement' and that therefore it could not have had as its object the restriction of competition.[363] Rheinzink argued that the condition regarding export to Egypt 'was inserted at the initiative of Schiltz, which thereby sought to obtain the goods at more favourable export prices'.[364]

254 It is apparent that the arguments of CRAM and Rheinzink are hard to reconcile: the latter argued that the initiative of the clause came from Schiltz, while the former said that Schiltz did not even agree with the clause (although it did not say so). Regardless, the Court rejected both arguments and held:

> In order to determine whether an agreement has as its object the restriction of competition, it is not necessary to inquire which of the two contracting parties took the initiative in inserting any particular clause or to verify that the parties had a common intent at the time when the agreement was concluded. It is rather a question of examining the aims pursued by the agreement as such, in the light of the economic context in which the agreement is to be applied.[365]

255 In all three cases discussed above, *Miller*, *IAZ* and *CRAM*, the CJEU therefore clearly rejected the pleas of the applicants that the agreements in question could not be restrictive by object because the undertakings' intentions were good. On the contrary, the Court held that the assessment of whether an agreement has a restrictive object needs to be made in an objective way and is not dependent on the subjective intentions of the parties.

256 Despite these clear statements, twenty years later, the same question arose again in the 2006 *General Motors* case.[366] But, this time it was the Commission, not the parties, that made reference to the intentions of the undertakings involved.

257 *General Motors* concerned a Commission decision which had found that the Dutch subsidiary of General Motors (Opel Nederland) had pursued a general strategy aimed at restricting export sales by its dealers and had implemented this through a number of measures, one of them being that export sales were excluded from retail bonus campaigns. When interpreting the exclusion of export sales from the retail bonus campaigns, the CFI had also made reference to the Commission's evidence (in the form of internal documents, in particular notes of a meeting) of Opel Nederland's general strategy to prevent exports. So, contrary to the *Miller*, *IAZ* and *CRAM* cases, where the undertakings concerned argued that their subjective intentions demonstrated that the agreement did not have a restrictive object, in *General Motors*, it was the CFI (and the

363. Joined cases C-29 and 30/83 *CRAM v Commission* ECLI:EU:C:1984:130, at [1984] ECR 1695.
364. Joined cases C-29 and 30/83 *CRAM v Commission* ECLI:EU:C:1984:130, para. 25.
365. Joined cases C-29 and 30/83 *CRAM v Commission* ECLI:EU:C:1984:130, para. 26.
366. I already briefly touched upon the CFI judgment in this case in para. 174 above.

Commission) that relied on the parties' subjective intentions to demonstrate that the agreement did have such a restrictive object. General Motors argued before the CJEU that this was not allowed: the object of the exclusion of exports from the retail bonus campaigns needed to 'be assessed objectively and not by reference to any subjective intentions of one of the parties'.[367]

258 In his opinion, AG Tizzano recommended that the CJEU reject the argument of General Motors. But when doing so, he referred to the discussion in *Miller* about the relevance of culpability in the determination of the fine (paragraph 18 of the judgment, quoted in paragraph 246 above).[368] The CJEU was much clearer and referred to the relevant paragraphs on object restrictions in the *Miller, CRAM* and *IAZ* judgments and held that:

> [as regards the CFI] basing its reasoning on the intention of Opel Nederland to restrict competition, it is true that proof of that intention is not a necessary factor in determining whether an agreement has such a restriction as its object.
>
> However, even if the intention of the parties does not constitute a necessary factor in determining the restrictive character of an agreement, there is nothing to prohibit the Commission or the Community courts from taking that intention into account.[369]

259 The wording in the last paragraph has been the standard answer to any question on the relevance of the intentions of the parties to determine the object of an agreement.[370] The CJEU hereby confirms the earlier rulings of *Miller, IAZ* and *CRAM* that a restriction of competition by object can be established despite any good intentions of the undertakings involved.

260 But what is meant by the second part of the CJEU's ruling? If they are not necessary, how can intentions be taken into account? I will turn to this now.

[2] Subjective Intentions Are Relevant

261 To understand what is meant by the possibility to take into account intentions, it is useful to return to the *IAZ* judgment, which is the only one of the older judgments that continues to be referenced in the recent case law on this point. As we have seen, in *IAZ*, the CJEU had found that the introduction of the conformity label in that case

367. C-551/03 P *General Motors v Commission* ECLI:EU:C:2006:229, para. 63.
368. AG opinion in C-551/03 P *General Motors v Commission* ECLI:EU:C:2005:639, para. 77.
369. C-551/03 P *General Motors v Commission* ECLI:EU:C:2006:229, paras 77-78.
370. *See* C-8/08 *T-Mobile Netherlands and Others* ECLI:EU:C:2009:343, para. 27; joined cases C-501, 513, 515 and 519/06 P *GlaxoSmithKline Services and Others v Commission and Others* ECLI:EU:C:2009:610, para. 58; C-32/11 *Allianz Hungaria Biztosito* ECLI:EU:C:2013:160, para. 37 and C-67/13 P *Cartes Bancaires v Commission* ECLI:EU:C:2014:2204, para. 54; T-472/13 *Lundbeck v Commission* ECLI:EU:T:2016:449, para. 344; T-691/14 *Servier and Others v Commission* ECLI:EU:T:2018:922, para. 222. *See also*, in the context of a concerted practice, C-286/13 P *Dole Food and Dole Fresh Fruit Europe v Commission* ECLI:EU:C:2015:184, para. 118.

was restrictive by object and that that finding 'is not invalidated by the fact that it has not been established that it was the intention of all the parties to the Agreement to restrict competition'.[371] However, to conclude that the agreement was restrictive by object, the CJEU *also* relied on the intentions of the other parties to the agreement.

262 Indeed, the Court states that the agreement 'clearly expresses the intention of treating parallel imports less favourably than official imports with a view of hindering the former'. To come to this conclusion, the Court refers to the content of the agreement itself but adds: 'That conclusion is also based on certain statements made by the CEG and by the FCAE [two of the trade associations involved] at the preliminary meetings. During those meetings, the CEG *stated that it wished* to obtain for its members *preferential treatment* as against non-members *and that it regarded* the proposed Agreements as a *"weapon" against* parallel imports. Moreover, the FCAE emphasized that the *disadvantage* of the system of listing authorized appliances was that parallel importers also benefited from the verification obtained by the official importer without having to share in its costs. Finally, the *intention of hindering parallel imports is also apparent* from the steps taken by the CEG and ANSEAU after the conclusion of the Agreement in order to put dealers and consumers on their guard against the sale and purchase respectively of appliance not bearing a conformity label.'[372]

263 While the CJEU does not deny that the object of an agreement needs to be determined in an objective way, it seems to say that the views of the authors of that agreement are helpful in understanding the object of the agreement. Who is better placed to assess the objectives of an agreement or a certain practice than the parties who drafted the agreement or engaged in the practice? Obviously, the parties may be wrong: they may think that they are doing something entirely innocuous but in fact restrict competition. But, ordinarily, the parties closest to the agreement or the practice are best placed to assess its objectives. This is in particular true in non-cartel cases where the anticompetitive object of the agreement/practice may not be immediately apparent.

264 Advocate General Saugmandsgaard Øe took a similar position in his recent opinion in *Hoffmann-La Roche v AGCM*. This case concerned concertation between Hoffmann-La Roche and Novartis to allegedly exaggerate the risks of using one medicinal product in order to increase demand for another product with equivalent effect. To establish that the misleading allegation of risks restricted competition by object, the Italian competition authority needed to analyse the content, objective and context in which these allegations took place. But AG Saugmandsgaard Øe considered that evidence of subjective intentions could also be taken into account:

371. Joined cases C-96 to 102, 104, 105, 108 and 110/82 *IAZ v Commission* ECLI:EU:C:1983:310, para. 25.
372. Joined cases C-96 to 102, 104, 105, 108 and 110/82 *IAZ v Commission* ECLI:EU:C:1983:310, paras 23-24 (emphasis added).

> The subjective intention of the applicants in the main proceedings, as suggested by the findings of the AGCM that are set out in the order for reference, if established, could corroborate the existence of an anticompetitive aim behind the collusive conduct at issue. According to the AGCM, the applicants in the main proceedings expressed in various documents the intention to 'generate and disseminate' unjustified concerns relating to the safety of Avastin with a view to steering demand towards Lucentis. Thus, they sought to exploit uncertainty regarding the comparative safety of the two products in a manner favourable to their own commercial interests, but harmful to competition.[373]

265 It is therefore not surprising that the Commission has often relied on evidence of the parties' objectives (their intentions) to interpret the agreements they concluded or the practices they engaged in. A recent example is *Lundbeck* where the Commission attached considerable importance to evidence of the strategy of Lundbeck to conclude that the patent settlements it concluded with various generic producers delayed the market entry of generic forms of Lundbeck's drug, citalopram.[374] The Commission's approach in *Lundbeck* has in the meantime been endorsed by the General Court which held that the Commission was entitled to interpret the settlements 'in their wider context [which] demonstrated that the applicants sought to delay the market entry of generics in order to find a suitable window for the launch of escitalopram (recitals 123 et seq. of the contested decision), by all possible means, whether lawful or unlawful'.[375]

266 Also in the subsequent *Fentanyl* and *Perindopril (Servier)* patent settlement cases, the Commission attached considerable importance to the strategies pursued by the undertakings concerned.[376] No application for annulment was brought against the *Fentanyl* decision. In its judgment on the application for annulment by Servier against the Commission's *Perindopril* decision, the General Court agreed with the Commission's assessment of the relevance of the intention of generics to enter a market in order to assess their capacity to do so.[377]

267 The CJEU still has to rule on the *Lundbeck* and *Perindopril (Servier)* cases at the time of writing but it has endorsed the role of intentions in its *Paroxetine* preliminary ruling. This case concerned a decision by the UK Competition and Markets Authority

373. AG opinion in C-179/16 *F. Hoffmann-La Roche and Others* ECLI:EU:C:2018:25, para. 172. The CJEU did not discuss the relevance of subjective intentions in its judgment: *see* C-179/16 *F. Hoffmann-La Roche and Others* ECLI:EU:C:2018:25, in particular paras 76-95.
374. Commission decision of 19 June 2013 in case 39.226 *Lundbeck*, in particular recitals 803-816; 858-866; 950-954; 1000-1005; 1075-1079; 1161-1166.
375. T-472/13 *Lundbeck v Commission* ECLI:EU:T:2016:449, *see* in particular paras 517-533. An appeal before the CJEU is still pending (case C-591/16 P *Lundbeck v Commission*).
376. Commission decision of 10 December 2013 in case 39.685 *Fentanyl*, in particular recitals 334-359. Commission decision of 9 July 2014 in case 39.612 *Perindopril (Servier)*, in particular recitals 103-242.
377. T-691/14 *Servier and Others v Commission* ECLI:EU:T:2018:922, in particular paras 382-384, with reference to case T-461/07 *Visa Europe and Visa International Service v Commission* ECLI:EU:T:2011:181, para. 169. Both the Commission and Servier have brought an appeal against this judgment in which the fine on Servier was reduced but the Commission decision was largely upheld (C-176/19 P *Commission v Servier and others* and C-201/19 P *Servier and other v Commission*).

finding a patent settlement agreement anticompetitive. The CJEU held that, in order to determine whether a generics manufacturer is a potential competitor, its intention and ability to enter the market needs to be established. This requires an assessment of not only the preparatory steps which the generics manufacturer has taken to enter the market but also 'the perception of the manufacturer of originator medicines of the risk' the generics manufacturer represents for its business is relevant.[378] This perception may be evidenced by the willingness of the originator to transfer value to the generics manufacturer in order to delay its entry (so by the content of the patent settlement agreement itself).

[3] Subjective Intentions Are Probably Not Sufficient

268 We have seen that the CJEU has held that evidence of the parties' intention is not necessary to conclude that an agreement is restrictive by object. But, since it is relevant, could evidence of the parties' anticompetitive intentions be *sufficient* to conclude that an agreement has a restrictive object?

269 Some authors have in the past defended this position;[379] it seems primarily for reasons of deterrence. Object infringements are, in a way, inchoate offences, it is argued: undertakings which aim to restrict competition should be punished for this, even if they fail in their efforts.

270 These authors support this interpretation by referring to how much the CJEU relies on the objectives of an agreement to determine whether it has a restriction of competition as its object. I believe that this is based on a misreading of the case law. While the case law clearly states that the objectives of an agreement are of prime importance to determine whether it has as its object the restriction of competition, these objectives are not defined in a subjective manner. The European Courts have sometimes attributed these objectives to the parties to an agreement, thereby using the terminology of intentions[380] but that does not mean that an agreement's objectives can be reduced to the parties' intentions.

271 This issue was explicitly raised in *Cartes Bancaires*, which the CJEU ruled on in 2014. This case concerned a modification of the rules of an association administrating a system of payment cards. The Commission had found that the new rules had as their

---

378. C-307/18 *Generics (UK) and Others* ECLI:EU:C:2020:52, para. 57.
379. *See* in particular O Odudu, 'Interpreting Article 81(1): object as subjective intention' (2001) 26 European Law Review 60. *See also* O Odudu, 'Interpreting Article 81(1): the object requirement revisited' (2001) 26 European Law Review 379 and support from other authors, such as in IF Wendt, *EU competition law and liberal professions: an uneasy relationship?* (Martinus Nijhoff 2012) 256-262. *See also* the AG opinion in C-209/07 *Beef Industry Development and Barry Brothers* ECLI:EU:C:2008:467, para. 46 and in joined cases T-1/89 to T-4/89 and T-6/89 to T-15/89 *Rhône-Poulenc et al v Commission* ECLI:EU:T:1991:38, in particular at [1991] ECR II 944-5.
380. *See*, for example, in joined cases C-56 and 58/64 *Consten and Grundig v Commission* ECLI:EU:C:1966:41, at [1966] ECR 342-3 where the CJEU states: 'The applicants thus *wished* to eliminate any possibility of competition at the wholesale level ...' (emphasis added).

object and effect the restriction of competition. For its analysis of the object of the rules, the Commission had relied on the wording of the new rules as well as the context in which they operated and had also referred to certain documents obtained during inspection visits. According to the Commission, these documents revealed the 'true objectives' of the new rules, namely to hinder entry, to protect the main members of the association and to avoid price erosion.[381] The General Court upheld the Commission's decision but, on appeal, the CJEU ruled that the General Court had not exercised sufficient judicial review of the Commission's decision.

272 As regards specifically the internal documents relied on by the Commission and the General Court, AG Wahl in his opinion in *Cartes Bancaires* held a passionate plea for 'a properly objective examination, irrespective of the will of the parties' to determine the object of an agreement.[382] He considered that 'any intentions expressed by the participants in a supposed restrictive agreement, decision or concerted practice, like any legitimate objectives pursued by them, are not directly relevant in examining whether the agreement, decision or practice has an anticompetitive "object"'.[383]

273 The CJEU was much less emphatic on this point. It focused its analysis on the judicial review carried out by the General Court of the Commission decision. It added to this:

> Since the intentions of the Grouping could not in themselves, ..., be sufficient to establish the existence of an anti-competitive object and the General Court moreover itself stated, in paragraphs 134, 136 and 267 of the judgment under appeal, that those intentions had been analysed as additional confirmation only, its findings in that regard, in particular, in paragraphs 251 to 266 of that judgment, cannot justify such a characterisation [namely that of a restriction by object] and there is no need to examine the arguments put forward by the appellant on that point.[384]

274 The CJEU's statement certainly does not have the scope of AG Wahl's opinion and, to the extent that it also relies on the General Court's view that the intentions were analysed 'as additional confirmation only', the CJEU's statement that the intentions alone are not sufficient could even be viewed as *obiter*. Nevertheless, this is the only answer the European Courts seem to have provided so far to the question of whether (subjective) intentions alone are sufficient to determine whether the object of an agreement is restrictive of competition: they are not.

[C] Conclusion

275 An agreement or concerted practice can be found to be restrictive of competition by object, even if the parties to the agreement or concerted practice did not intend to

381. Commission decision of 17 October 2007 in case 38.606 *Groupement des cartes bancaires 'CB'*, recitals 235ff.
382. C-67/13 P *Cartes Bancaires v Commission* ECLI:EU:C:2014:1958, para. 110.
383. C-67/13 P *Cartes Bancaires v Commission* ECLI:EU:C:2014:1958, para. 110.
384. C-67/13 P *Cartes Bancaires v Commission* ECLI:EU:C:2014:2204, para. 88.

restrict competition by it. The object of an agreement needs to be determined in light of the content, the economic context and the objectives of the agreement.

276 However, the intentions of parties to an agreement or concerted practice are highly relevant to determine whether that agreement or practice has a restrictive object. The authors of an agreement are of course very well placed to determine what its objectives are and any evidence that they intended to restrict competition or were aware that it restricted competition will therefore be useful to elucidate the agreement's objective. The same holds true for concerted practices in which undertakings engage.

277 However, any evidence of the intentions of the parties cannot be the last word on the object of an agreement or concerted practice. Evidence of intentions is often ambiguous, sometimes contradictory and necessarily incomplete; it can therefore not provide conclusive proof of the illicit or the innocuous character of an agreement or concerted practice. These and other limitations of evidence of intentions will be discussed at a more general level (beyond the case law) in Chapter 5.

§2.03 ARTICLE 101(3) TFEU

278 Article 101(3) TFEU contains an exception to the prohibition of Article 101(1) TFEU. Agreements and concerted practices which fulfil the conditions for this exception are not void,[385] nor subject to any other sanctions for breach of Article 101 TFEU. The four conditions for the exception of Article 101(3) TFEU are enumerated in paragraph 149 above.

279 Under Regulation 17/62, the Commission had the 'sole power to declare Article 85 (1) inapplicable pursuant to Article 85 (3) of the Treaty'.[386] In many of the decisions which the Commission adopted under Regulation 17/62, it considered the application of what is now Article 101(3) TFEU in quite some detail but few of these decisions were actually examined by the CJEU or (from 1989) the CFI.[387] Since the advent of Regulation 1/2003 and the abolition of the notification system, detailed analysis of Article 101(3) TFEU in Commission decisions has become even rarer and there is even less case law on this topic.[388] At the moment of the entry into force of Regulation 1/2003, the Commission did, however, publish guidelines containing its interpretation of what was then Article 81(3) EC:[389] these guidelines are informed by the Commission's experience applying this paragraph (and indeed also the first paragraph of Article 101 TFEU) and, since other sources are limited, continue to be very relevant.

385. Article 101(2) TFEU provides that any agreement or concerted practice which is prohibited under Article 101(1) TFEU 'shall be automatically void'.
386. Article 9(1) of Regulation 17 of 6 February 1962: First Regulation implementing Articles 85 and 86 of the Treaty [1962] OJ 13/204.
387. *See* B Sufrin, 'The evolution of Article 81(3) of the EC treaty' (2006) 51(4) The Antitrust Bulletin 915, 971.
388. *See* D Bailey, 'Reinvigorating the role of Article 101(3) under Regulation 1/2003' (2016) 81 Antitrust Law Journal 111, 120-123 and 129-130.
389. Commission Guidelines on the application of Article 81(3) of the Treaty [2004] OJ C101/97.

280 When assessing the relevance of *mens rea* in the context of Article 101(3) TFEU, it is important to consider that the case law has always viewed the burden of proof for the establishment of the conditions of this paragraph to be firmly on the shoulders of the parties claiming the benefit of the exception, i.e. the parties to the allegedly anticompetitive agreement or concerted practice.[390] This position is now also made explicit in Article 2 of Regulation 1/2003. As a consequence, the parties are required to put forward the evidence to meet the conditions of the exception, and the Commission (or under Regulation 1/2003 the NCAs or indeed private litigants) do not need to seek out evidence proving (or, at least initially, disproving) the undertakings' position. This more passive position implies that *mens rea* evidence will be less important: it will mostly play a role (like in the case of objective justifications under Article 102 TFEU – *see* Chapter 3) to disprove arguments initially presented by the undertakings.

281 Article 101(3) TFEU contains four cumulative conditions.[391] The first condition, which is arguably key,[392] is that the agreement or concerted practice 'contributes to improving the production or distribution of goods or to promoting technical or economic progress'. This condition is generally understood to mean that the agreement or concerted practice entails certain efficiencies which potentially outweigh the restriction of competition which it also brings about.[393]

282 In line with the case law,[394] the Commission states in the *Article 81(3) Guidelines* that, for the analysis of this condition, 'only objective benefits can be taken into account', meaning 'that efficiencies are not assessed from the subjective point of view

390. *See* already joined cases C-43 and 63/82 *VBVB and VBBB v Commission* ECLI:EU:C:1984:9, para. 52; joined cases C-204, 205, 211, 213, 217 and 219/00 P *Aalborg Portland v Commission* ECLI:EU:C:2004:6, para. 78. Note that in joined cases C-56 and 58/64 *Consten and Grundig v Commission* ECLI:EU:C:1966:41, at [1966] ECR 347, the CJEU still saw a greater role for the Commission in this respect 'may not confine itself to requiring from undertakings proof of the fulfilment of the requirements for the grant of the exemption but must, as a matter of good administration, play its part, using the means available to it, in ascertaining the relevant facts and circumstances'. *See also* joined cases C-501, 513, 515 and 519/06 P *GlaxoSmithKline Services and Others v Commission and Others* ECLI:EU:C:2009:610, paras 93, finding that it should be 'sufficient for the Commission, on the basis of the arguments and evidence in its possession, to arrive at the conviction that the occurrence of the appreciable objective advantage is sufficiently likely in order to presume that the agreement entails such an advantage' (although this appears to also concern the standard, rather than the burden, of proof).
391. That the conditions are cumulative was already stated by the CJEU in joined cases C-43 and 63/82 *VBVB and VBBB v Commission* ECLI:EU:C:1984:9, para. 61.
392. B Sufrin, 'The evolution of Article 81(3) of the EC treaty' (2006) 51(4) The Antitrust Bulletin 915, 933 even argues that the paragraph in fact only contains 'one substantive condition' (namely the first one) and that the '[t]he other three are limitations on, or requirements of, the first'.
393. *See* title 3.2 of the Commission Guidelines on the application of Article 81(3) of the Treaty [2004] OJ C101/97. *See also* B Sufrin, 'The evolution of Article 81(3) of the EC treaty' (2006) 51(4) The Antitrust Bulletin 915, 942-952; J Faull, L Kjølbye, H Leupold and A Nikpay, 'Article 101' in J Faull and A Nikpay (eds), *The EU law of competition* (Oxford University Press 2014) 183, 317-321.
394. *See* already joined cases C-56 and 58/64 *Consten and Grundig v Commission* ECLI:EU:C:1966:41, at [1966] ECR 348, and T-7/93 *Langnese-Iglo v Commission* ECLI:EU:T:1995:98, para. 180 and T-65/98 *Van den Bergh Foods v Commission* ECLI:EU:T:2003:281, para. 139.

of the parties'.[395] This position has been repeated many times since but what it exactly means is not clear. While some case law suggests that the fact that the agreement or concerted practice is beneficial for the parties, is not relevant,[396] that interpretation is untenable even in light of the *Article 81(3) Guidelines* themselves which include among possible efficiencies cost savings for the parties.[397]

283 What is true though is that 'the improvement, within the meaning of the first condition laid down in Article 81(3) EC, cannot be identified with all the advantages which the parties obtain from the agreement in their production or distribution activities'.[398] In other words, not any advantage the parties obtain for themselves is an efficiency in the sense of the first condition for Article 101(3) TFEU. This makes sense since restrictions of competition themselves are often advantageous to the parties, and it would make little sense for this to imply that the first condition of Article 101(3) TFEU was automatically met. But where the line should be drawn precisely is not fully clear.

284 The second condition in any event qualifies the efficiencies relevant for the Article 101(3) TFEU exception. Indeed, only if the agreement or concerted practice allows consumers a fair share of the benefit resulting from the efficiencies, can the exception apply. In the case law and the literature there is much debate about which consumers can be taken into account for this assessment but *mens rea* considerations do not appear explicitly relevant here.[399]

285 The third condition of the Article 101(3) TFEU exception, which is treated second by the Commission in its guidelines,[400] is that the restrictions imposed by the agreement are not indispensable to the attainment of the efficiencies. This is simply a 'less-restrictive means' test.[401]

286 The fourth condition, finally, is that competition is not eliminated in respect of a substantial part of the goods or services in questions. The *Article 81(3) Guidelines* clarify that if the restrictions also amount to an abuse of dominance, this condition cannot be met. However, the fact that this condition is met does not exclude that the restriction still constitutes such an abuse.[402]

---

395. Commission Guidelines on the application of Article 81(3) of the Treaty [2004] OJ C101/97, para. 49.
396. T-65/98 *Van den Bergh Foods v Commission* ECLI:EU:T:2003:281, para. 140.
397. *See* title 3.2.2.1 of the Commission Guidelines on the application of Article 81(3) of the Treaty [2004] OJ C101/97.
398. C-382/12 P *MasterCard and Others v Commission* ECLI:EU:C:2014:2201, para. 234. *See also* T-679/14 *Teva UK and Others v Commission* ECLI:EU:T:2018:919, para. 336; T-701/14 *Niche Generics v Commission* ECLI:EU:T:2018:921, para. 347.
399. *See*, for example, B Sufrin, 'The evolution of Article 81(3) of the EC treaty' (2006) 51(4) The Antitrust Bulletin 915, 934-936 and the discussion by AG Mengozzi in his opinion in case C-382/12 P *MasterCard and Others v European Commission* ECLI:EU:C:2014:42, paras 155-160.
400. *See* Commission Guidelines on the application of Article 81(3) of the Treaty [2004] OJ C101/97, paras 73-82.
401. *See* Van Bael & Bellis, 'Competition law of the European Community, Chapter 2: basic principles (chapter updated april 2018)' in Van Bael & Bellis (ed.), *Competition law of the European Community* (Kluwer 2010) 15.
402. Commission Guidelines on the application of Article 81(3) of the Treaty [2004] OJ C101/97, para. 106.

287 As indicated, the role of *mens rea* in all of this is limited, except in order to check certain claims made by the parties to the agreement or concerted practice. If internal documents are in line with these claims, then this will make them more credible. If, however, internal documents indicate, for example, that prices are likely to go up (so that consumers will not benefit from any efficiencies) or that alternative ways of achieving the efficiencies are possible (so that the restrictions are not indispensable for the efficiencies), this will discredit the parties' arguments.

288 An example of this can be seen in the *Cartes Bancaires* decision. In respect of the first condition of Article 101(3) TFEU, the Commission dismissed Cartes Bancaires' claim that the restrictions in its payment system were justified because of the investment cost involved which it estimated at EUR 4 billion. In support of this, the Commission referred to documents seized during the inspections it conducted which suggested much lower investment costs.[403]

289 Also the lack of contemporaneous documents can indicate that a certain intention was missing, as argued by the Commission in its *Servier* decision. In that case, Servier claimed that the settlement agreements allowed it to acquire certain patents which could be used to optimize its own processes. The Commission rejected this, pointing out that 'Servier was unable to provide any contemporaneous documents demonstrating expected savings from the use of these patent applications.'[404] The Commission also pointed to an oral explanation given by an employee of Servier during the inspection which indicated that similar contracts typically only take effect after a feasibility study has been conducted - but that no such study appears to have been made in this instance.[405]

290 In that same decision, the Commission also rejected a claim from Teva that the settlement agreement allowed it to enter the market earlier. One element the Commission relied on for this was a document from an employee of Teva which implied that the settlement entailed a 'delay to us in entering the market'.[406]

291 To conclude, the role of *mens rea* is limited in the determination of the conditions of Article 101(3) TFEU. Contemporaneous evidence (or the lack thereof) of an undertaking's understanding of the efficiencies which an agreement or concertation entails may mainly provide a first indication of the credibility of efficiencies claimed by an undertaking to benefit from the exception of Article 101(3) TFEU. For the other three conditions, *mens rea* evidence does not seem to play a role.

403. Commission decision of 17 October 2007 in case 38.606 *Groupement des cartes bancaires 'CB'*, recital 405.
404. Commission decision of 9 July 2014 in case 39.612 *Perindopril (Servier)*, recital 2080.
405. Commission decision of 9 July 2014 in case 39.612 *Perindopril (Servier)*, recitals 2080 and 288.
406. Commission decision of 9 July 2014 in case 39.612 *Perindopril (Servier)*, recitals 2119 and 714.

CHAPTER 3

Mens Rea in Article 102 TFEU

> Le temps assez souvent a rendu légitime
> Ce qui semblait d'abord ne se pouvoir sans crime.
>
> Corneille, *Le Cid*, V (VII), 1839-1840

292 Article 102 TFEU provides: 'Any abuse by one or more undertakings of a dominant position within the internal market or in a substantial part of it shall be prohibited as incompatible with the internal market in so far as it may affect trade between Member States.' The Article also lists a number of examples of such abuses.

293 In order for the prohibition to apply, four cumulative conditions must be fulfilled:

(1) an undertaking;
(2) which holds a dominant position;
(3) commits an abuse;
(4) which may affect trade between Member States.

294 For the reasons already enumerated in the chapter discussing Article 101 TFEU (*see* paragraphs 144 and 145), I will not here discuss the first and fourth condition and will instead focus in §3.01 on the relevance of *mens rea* in the establishment of a dominant position and in §3.02 on its relevance in the finding of abuse.

§3.01 DOMINANCE

295 The legal controversies concerning the interpretation of Article 102 TFEU mainly concern the existence of an abuse, and much less the existence of a dominant position.

The case law on what constitutes an abuse under Article 102 TFEU is therefore also much more extensive than the case law on the existence of a dominant position.[407]

296 In the triple division of objective elements of infringements (*see* paragraph 51 of Chapter 1 on the correspondence principle), the dominant position of an undertaking is a circumstance. As a consequence, the mental element pertaining to this element would be whether the undertaking in question was aware (or should have been aware) of the existence of that dominant position. There seems to be no instance where an undertaking has argued that it was not aware that it was in a dominant position and that therefore Article 102 TFEU should not be applicable to it. In the few instances in which the undertakings in question contested that they were aware of their market power,[408] they merely invoked this argument to attempt to escape the fine – a factor which I will discuss further in Chapter 4.

297 Although awareness of a dominant position may not be necessary to establish dominance, that does not mean that *mens rea* plays no role at all. Indeed, in the case law on *collective* dominance, the European Courts have referred to the existence of a joint intention of the undertakings involved to conduct themselves in a similar manner. This approach was followed in *Compagnie Maritime Belge*, which originated in a Commission decision of 1992 finding that Associated Central West Africa Lines (Cewal), a liner conference of which Compagnie Maritime Belge was a member, had infringed both the then Articles 85 and 86 of the Treaty Establishing the European Economic Community (EEC). The CFI accepted that the conference agreements between the members of Cewal and the practices engaged in by the conference 'reveal an intention to adopt together the same conduct on the market' and 'constituted aspects of an overall strategy which Cewal members pooled their forces in order to implement'.[409]

298 Furthermore, although awareness of dominance may not be necessary for a finding of dominance, the Commission seems to consider an undertaking's own perception of its ability to act independently of others relevant to support a finding of dominance. In *Microsoft*, for example, the Commission pointed to internal communication of Microsoft that showed that it was 'fully aware' that it 'can behave independently of its end-consumers'. The internal communication in question stated that 'there is huge switching cost to using a different operating system' instead of Microsoft's own

407. Eric Gippini-Fournier of the Commission's Legal Service has argued in a conference that this is because of 'applicants' unwillingness or ineffectiveness to challenge market definition and/or dominance in Court'. *See* A Lamadrid de Pablo, 'The elephant in the Courtroom: it's the dominance, stupid!' (*Chillin'Competition*, 8 June 2017) <https://chillingcompetition.com/2017/06/08/the-elephant-in-the-courtroom-its-the-dominance-stupid/> accessed 12 September 2018.

408. *See* C-27/76 *United Brands v Commission* ECLI:EU:C:1978:22, para. 298; C-85/76 *Hoffmann-La Roche v Commission* ECLI:EU:C:1979:36, para. 139; T-336/07 *Telefónica and Telefónica de España v Commission* ECLI:EU:T:2012:172, para. 325.

409. Joined cases T-24 to 26 and 28/93 *Compagnie Maritime Belge v Commission* ECLI:EU:T:1996:139, para. 65, approach confirmed in joined cases C-395 and 396/96 P *Compagnie Maritime Belge v Commission* ECLI:EU:C:2000:132.

Windows and that '[i]t is this huge switching cost that has given customers the patience to stick with Windows through all our mistakes'.[410]

299 Internal documents are also regularly taken into account by the Commission when defining relevant markets, a particularly important issue in dominance cases, where the market on which the dominant position exists must always be defined.[411] That this is a perilous task is evidenced by *Perindopril (Servier)*, where the Commission relied on internal strategy documents of Servier which suggested that Servier believed that perindopril was superior to other antihypertensive agents and could therefore be differentiated from it.[412] This evidence was used by the Commission, together with other materials, to conclude that perindopril was a separate product market. The General Court annulled the Commission's market definition, however, including because the Commission had wrongly relied on these internal documents. According to the Court, several internal documents on which the Commission relied had promotional purposes and it was therefore not surprising that they declared that perindopril was a superior product (promotional material of competitors in fact did the same thing for their products). Despite these promotional efforts, many doctors continued to view perindopril as substitutable with other antihypertensive agents.[413] Internal documents should therefore not always be taken at face value.[414]

300 In conclusion, the case law does not require that an undertaking is aware of its dominant position to establish the latter in accordance with Article 102 TFEU. However, the Commission has occasionally referred to internal documents which indicated such awareness in support of its conclusion that a dominant position existed. The CJEU has also found evidence of a joint intention or strategy of the undertakings involved to be a factor to determine the existence of collective dominance.

§3.02 ABUSE

301 While references to *mens rea* are extremely sparse in the case law on the existence of a dominant position, there is in contrast no other aspect of antitrust law where the relevance of *mens rea* has been discussed to such an extent as in relation to the abuse of that dominant position. The literature points out that evidence of exclusionary intentions in particular has often been used in the decisional practice of the Commission and the case law of the European Courts to distinguish lawful practices from

410. Commission decision of 21 April 2004 in case 37.792 *Microsoft*, recitals 463.
411. C-27/76 *United Brands v Commission* ECLI:EU:C:1978:22, para. 10; C-85/76 *Hoffmann-La Roche v Commission* ECLI:EU:C:1979:36, para. 21.
412. Commission decision of 9 July 2014 in case 39.612 *Perindopril (Servier)*, recitals 2219-2223.
413. T-691/14 *Servier and Others v Commission* ECLI:EU:T:2018:922, paras 1466-1472. The Commission has brought an appeal against this judgment (case C-176/19 P *Commission v Servier and others*).
414. That does not mean, however, that the perceptions of the parties involved are irrelevant to assess whether they are (potential) competitors. *See* the discussion of the *Paroxetine* judgment of the Court of Justice in para. 267 above.

unlawful ones.[415] However, much of the literature is very critical of the use of such evidence.[416]

302 In what follows, I will describe when and how the Commission and the European Courts have used evidence of abusive intentions and I will try to make sense of their approach. The discussion of whether or not evidence of intentions *should* play this role in the analysis of abusive practices (or whether it should play a different role) will take place in Chapter 5.

[A] General Observations

303 In order to better understand the role of *mens rea* in establishing an abuse of a dominant position, it is useful to consider how the European Courts have described the notion of abuse.

304 A first description that is recurrent in the case law is the principle, enunciated first in *Hoffmann-La Roche* that 'the concept of abuse is an objective concept'.[417] The CJEU's statement was made to respond to a certain interpretation of the notion of abuse by Hoffmann-La Roche. Indeed, the wording of Article 102 TFEU suggests that there needs to be a link between the dominant position and the abuse: the text refers to 'abuse by one or more undertakings *of* a dominant position', not to 'abuse by one or more undertakings *in* a dominant position'. The German language text of Article 102 TFEU in particular suggests that the dominant position needs to be the *instrument* through which the abuse takes place,[418] and it is therefore not surprising that this was

415. Fairly detailed discussions can be found in A Bavasso, 'The role of intent under Article 82 EC: from "flushing the turkeys" to "spotting lionesses in Regent's Park"' (2005) European Competition Law Review 616; MJ Melícias, 'The use and abuse of intent evidence in antitrust analysis' (2010) World Competition 569; P Akman, 'The role of intent in the EU case law on abuse of dominance' (2014) European Law Review 316; C O'Grady, 'The role of exclusionary intent in the enforcement of Article 102 TFEU' (2014) World Competition 459; and PL Parcu and ML Stasi, 'The role of intent in the assessment of conduct under Article 102 TFEU' in PL Parcu, G Monti and M Botta (Eds), *Abuse of dominance in EU competition law. Emerging trends* (Edward Elgar 2017) 12. R Nazzini, *The foundations of European Union competition law. The objectives and principles of Article 102* (OUP 2011) also points to the role of intent in the case law of the European Courts but, when referring to cases to support this, he often states that the Courts were wrong (*see*, for example, at 190, 192, 193, 194, 195, 199 and 218). *See also* P Actis Perinetto, 'Intent and competition law assessment: useless or useful tool in the question for legal certainty?' (2019) European Competition Journal 153.

416. The only truly positive evaluation of the role of evidence of intent can be found in the article by O'Grady mentioned in the previous footnote.

417. C-85/76 *Hoffmann-La Roche v Commission* ECLI:EU:C:1979:36, para. 91.

418. It refers to '... *die missbräuchliche Ausnutzung einer beherrschenden Stellung* ...'. Some German-speaking authors continued to defend the causation requirement between dominance and abuse in some form or other in more recent years: *see*, for example, T Eilmansberger and F Bien, 'Art. 102 AEUV Missbrauch einer marktbeherrschenden Stellung' in J Bornkamm, F Montag and FJ Säcker (eds), *Münchener Kommentar Europäisches und Deutsches Wettbewerbsrecht* (Beck 2015) 1519, 1568-1573; T Eilmansberger, 'How to distinguish good from bad competition under Article 82 EC: in search of clearer and more coherent standards for anti-competitive abuses' (2005) Common Market Law Review 129, in particular 140-146.

the position taken by AG Roemer in *Continental Can*.[419] However, the CJEU did not follow its Advocate General in that case and confirmed that a dominant undertaking can commit an abuse (in that case the acquisition of a competitor) if its behaviour strengthens its dominant position and that 'regardless of the means and procedure by which it is achieved'.[420]

305 Despite this earlier ruling, Hoffmann-La Roche again argued that an abuse in the sense of Article 102 TFEU (then Article 86 EEC) could only arise if 'the use of the economic power bestowed by a dominant position is the means whereby the abuse has been brought about'[421] which meant in particular that 'for Article 86 to apply, there must be a connexion between the dominant position and the conduct of the undertaking concerned; the conduct complained of must spring from the undertaking's strength and must only be possible by reason of its dominant position'.[422] Hoffmann-La Roche argued that such a connexion was missing in the case before the Court since it had 'never forced a customer to enter into an agreement or to agree to a particular clause'.[423] The Commission had responded to this that 'for the purpose of considering whether there is an abuse, there is no need to prove an improper act or some factor of a subjective nature or to substantiate immorality, since an abuse must be understood as being a practice the morality of which is immaterial but which is objectively unlawful'.[424]

306 The CJEU dismissed Hoffmann-La Roche's arguments by reference to the 'objective' concept of abuse relating to 'behaviour of an undertaking in a dominant position which is such as to influence the structure of a market where, as a result of the very presence of the undertaking in question, the degree of competition is weakened and which, through recourse to methods different from those which condition normal competition in products or services on the basis of the transactions of commercial operators, has the effect of hindering the maintenance of the degree of competition still existing in the market or the growth of that competition'.[425] Recourse to methods different from 'normal competition' is therefore sufficient to establish an abuse, even if the dominant position is not 'used' to 'force' other market parties.[426]

419. C-6/72 *Europemballange and Continental Can v Commission* ECLI:EU:C:1972:101, at [1973] ECR 254-257.
420. C-6/72 *Europemballange and Continental Can v Commission* ECLI:EU:C:1973:22, para. 27.
421. C-85/76 *Hoffmann-La Roche v Commission* ECLI:EU:C:1979:36, para. 91.
422. C-85/76 *Hoffmann-La Roche v Commission* ECLI:EU:C:1979:36, at [1979] ECR 497.
423. C-85/76 *Hoffmann-La Roche v Commission* ECLI:EU:C:1979:36, at [1979] ECR 498.
424. C-85/76 *Hoffmann-La Roche v Commission* ECLI:EU:C:1979:36, at [1979] ECR 499.
425. C-85/76 *Hoffmann-La Roche v Commission* ECLI:EU:C:1979:36, para. 91.
426. The debate lives on, however, in the context of multimarket abuses, where the case law has had to take position on what the link must be between the market on which there is a position of dominance, the market on which the abuse is committed and the market on which foreclosure effects arise. In C-333/94 P *Tetra Pak v Commission* ECLI:EU:C:1996:436, para. 27, the CJEU held that 'application of Article 86 presupposes a link between the dominant position and the alleged abusive conduct, which is normally not present where conduct on a market distinct from the dominated market produces effects on that distinct market' but that this may be the case if 'special circumstances' are present.

307 While the CJEU does not explicitly say so, the CFI in *British Plasterboard* added its own gloss to *Hoffmann-La Roche* by interpreting the 'objective concept' of abuse as meaning that 'the conduct of an undertaking in a dominant position may be regarded as abusive ... even in the absence of any fault'.[427] In other words, *mens rea* evidence is not required to establish an abuse. Although this case concerned an exclusivity obligation, the CFI went on to say that the argument that the dominant undertaking 'never had any intention to discourage or weaken [its competitor] has no bearing on the legal classification of the facts'.[428]

308 A similar position was taken by the CFI in *Aéroport de Paris*, where again the question of whether the owner of the Paris airports *used* its dominant position to commit the abuse (in that case discriminatory fees) was at stake. The CFI referred to the discussion on the 'objective concept' of abuse in *Hoffmann-La Roche* and to a somewhat obscure paragraph in *Continental Can*[429] to argue that a strengthening of a dominant position may be abusive 'irrespective of any fault' and that the concept of abuse 'implies no intention to cause harm'.[430] The 'objective concept' of abuse has consequently been interpreted as implying that *mens rea* plays no role in it.[431]

309 Another element from the case law which may appear relevant to understand the *mens rea* requirement in abuses is the recurrent idea that dominant undertakings have a 'special responsibility'.[432] To understand the meaning of this statement of the CJEU in *Michelin*, it is useful to see that it was a statement made in the context of the question of whether Michelin held a dominant position, not whether it abused that position. Indeed, the CJEU responded to Michelin's argument that it was being 'penalized for the quality of its products and services':[433] 'A finding that an undertaking has a dominant position is not in itself a recrimination but simply means that, irrespective of the reasons for which it has such a dominant position, the undertaking concerned has a special responsibility not to allow its conduct to impair genuine undistorted competition on the common market.'[434] Unfortunately, the judgment does not clarify what this special responsibility entails.

310 The subsequent case law seems to use this notion, like the idea that abuse is an objective concept, to counter the interpretation of dominance as the necessary instrument of abuse which I described above in paragraph 304. The 'special responsibility' then means that an abuse does not imply practices which can be only put into effect by a dominant company: even commercial practices, which are acceptable (and even

427. T-65/89 *BPB Industries and British Gypsum v Commission* ECLI:EU:T:1993:31, para. 70.
428. *Ibid.*
429. C-6/72 *Europemballange and Continental Can v Commission* ECLI:EU:C:1972:101, para. 29.
430. T-128/98 *Aéroports de Paris v Commission* ECLI:EU:T:2000:290, paras 170 and 173. *See also* T-321/05 *AstraZeneca v Commission* ECLI:EU:T:2010:266, paras 359 and 813.
431. *See* PL Parcu and ML Stasi, 'The role of intent in the assessment of conduct under Article 102 TFEU' in PL Parcu, G Monti and M Botta (eds), *Abuse of dominance in EU competition law. Emerging trends* (Edward Elgar 2017) 12, 15.
432. C-322/81 *Nederlandsche Banden-Industrie Michelin* ECLI:EU:C:1983:313, para. 57.
433. *Ibid.*
434. *Ibid.*

widespread) for non-dominant undertakings, may constitute an abuse by dominant companies – even if they use them in response to similar practices by their competitors.[435]

311 Further case law clarified that the 'special responsibility' of dominant undertakings implied that dominant companies may have to forego rights non-dominant companies have:[436] in certain circumstances, dominant undertakings may not be allowed to align their prices with those of competitors,[437] they may be required to waive contractual rights they have,[438] they may need to keep regulatory authorizations in place even if they do not need them anymore[439] or they may be prohibited from engaging in conduct which regulatory frameworks allow them to engage in.[440]

312 In the case law of the CFI, the idea of the 'special responsibility' also became linked to the principle formulated in *United Brands* that, while dominant companies have a right to protect their commercial interests, 'such behaviour cannot be countenanced if its actual purpose is to strengthen this dominant position and abuse it'.[441] But not much more was made of that, and in the recent case law of the Court of Justice, the 'special responsibility' is simply understood as excluding any behaviour which is not 'normal competition' or 'competition on the merits'[442] – terms which leave a lot to be desired in terms of clarity (*see also* paragraph 718 below). Some authors have therefore

435. *See* for example for exclusivity obligations: T-65/89 *BPB Industries and British Gypsum v Commission* ECLI:EU:T:1993:31, para. 67.
436. Wertheimer summarized this beautifully as '*Quod licet bovi non licet Iovi*': what is allowed for cows is not allowed for gods (a reversal of the traditional *quod licet Iovi non licet bovi*): *see* HW Wertheimer, 'Het adagium van artikel 86 E.E.G.-Verdrag: 'quod licet bovi non licet Jovi' in P verLoren van Themaat, *Europees kartelrecht anno 1980* (Kluwer 1981) 162. *See also* R Van den Bergh and P Camesasca, *European competition law and economics: a comparative perspective* (Sweet & Maxwell 2006) 48.
437. T-340/03 *France Télécom v Commission* ECLI:EU:T:2007:22, para. 189. Pleas on this point on appeal were held to be inadmissable: C-202/07 P *France Télécom v Commission* ECLI:EU:C:2009:214, paras 39-61. *See also* joined cases T-24 to 26 and 28/93 *Compagnie Maritime Belge v Commission* ECLI:EU:T:1996:139, paras 146-148.
438. Joined cases T-24 to 26 and 28/93 *Compagnie Maritime Belge v Commission* ECLI:EU:T:1996:139, para. 108, upheld in substance by joined cases C-395 and 396/96 P *Compagnie Maritime Belge v Commission* ECLI:EU:C:2000:132. *See also* T-111/96 *ITT Promedia v Commission* ECLI:EU:T:1998:183, paras 139-140.
439. C-226/84 *British Leyland v Commission* ECLI:EU:C:1986:421, para. 14.
440. T-271/03 *Deutsche Telekom v Commission* ECLI:EU:T:2008:101, para. 122, upheld by C-280/08 P *Deutsche Telekom v Commission* ECLI:EU:C:2010:603.
441. C-27/76 *United Brands v Commission* ECLI:EU:C:1978:22, para. 189. *See* for example T-65/89 *BPB Industries and British Gypsum v Commission* ECLI:EU:T:1993:31, para. 69; joined cases T-24 to 26 and 28/93 *Compagnie Maritime Belge v Commission* ECLI:EU:T:1996:139, paras 106-107; T-228/97 *Irish Sugar v Commission* ECLI:EU:T:1999:246, para. 112; T-219/99 *British Airways v Commission* ECLI:EU:T:2003:343, paras 242-243; T-203/01 *Michelin v Commission* ECLI:EU:T:2003:250, para. 55: T-155/06 *Tomra Systems and Others v Commission* ECLI:EU:T:2010:370, para. 207.
442. C-202/07 P *France Télécom v Commission* ECLI:EU:C:2009:214, paras 104-105; C-280/08 P *Deutsche Telekom v Commission* ECLI:EU:C:2010:603, paras 176-177; C-209/10 *Post Danmark* ECLI:EU:C:2012:172, paras 23-25; C-413/14 P *Intel v Commission* ECLI:EU:C:2017:632, paras 133-136.

argued that 'not too much should be read into the "special responsibility" requirement'.[443] I think it is correct that the 'special responsibility' merely means that dominant undertakings should not engage in abusive behaviour: it does not constitute an additional requirement.

[B] The Role of Intentions

313 While there are much fewer Commission decisions and CJEU judgments on Article 102 TFEU than on Article 101 TFEU, the topic of *mens rea*, in particular of exclusionary intentions, is much more present in the case law on abuse of dominance. As I will describe below, when discussing the different abusive practices identified in the case law, the presence (or absence) of such intentions plays a much more pivotal role for some abuses than for others. Yet, a few general observations can already be made here.

314 Although abuse is an objective concept, and despite the CFI's views on the role of intentions in *British Plasterboard* and *Aéroports de Paris*, the case law seems to require that the Commission determines what strategy the dominant undertaking was pursuing when it committed the alleged abuse. The point is made explicitly in *Tomra*, where the CJEU held that 'the Commission is necessarily required to assess the business strategy pursued by [the dominant] undertaking. For that purpose, it is clearly legitimate for the Commission to refer to subjective factors, namely the motives underlying the business strategy in question'.[444] Also in its Grand Chamber judgment in *Intel*, where the appellant had argued that the contested practices were not capable of excluding competitors, the CJEU held that the Commission needed in those circumstances to assess the market share of the dominant undertaking and the share of the market that was foreclosed by the practices as well as 'the possible existence of a *strategy* aiming to exclude competitors that are at least as efficient as the dominant undertaking from the market'.[445] In its *Paroxetine* judgment, the Court added to this that, in this context, 'any anticompetitive intent on the part of [the dominant undertaking] must be taken into consideration'.[446]

315 However, that does not mean that *mens rea* is also a necessary condition to find an (exclusionary) abuse. Again in *Tomra*, the CJEU held that 'the Commission is under no obligation to establish the existence of such intent on the part of the dominant undertaking in order to render Article 82 EC applicable'.[447] In the Grand Chamber

443. M de la Mano, R Nazzini and H Zenger, 'Article 102' in J Faull and A Nikpay (eds), *The EU law of competition* (OUP 2014) 329, 394.
444. C-549/10 P *Tomra and Others v Commission* ECLI:EU:C:2012:221, para. 19.
445. C-413/14 P *Intel v Commission* ECLI:EU:C:2017:632, para. 139 (emphasis added). The same wording is also repeated in C-525/16 *MEO – Serviços de Comunicações e Multimédia* ECLI:EU:C:2018:270, para. 31 although that case concerned price discrimination which was not purported to be exclusionary (*see* para. 35 of the judgment).
446. C-307/18 *Generics (UK) and Others* ECLI:EU:C:2020:52, para. 164.
447. C-549/10 P *Tomra and Others v Commission* ECLI:EU:C:2012:221, para. 21; C-307/18 *Generics (UK) and Others* ECLI:EU:C:2020:52, paras 162 and 164.

judgment in *Post Danmark I*, the CJEU also did not exclude that an abuse had been committed, although that case was premised on the condition that there was no evidence of an exclusionary intent.[448]

316 The existence of an exclusionary intention is therefore not a necessary condition to find a practice abusive, but it is a factor that may or even must be taken into account.[449] In its *Guidance Paper on Exclusionary Abuses*, the Commission also considers 'direct evidence of any exclusionary strategy' as one of the factors 'generally relevant' to determine whether 'allegedly abusive conduct is likely to lead to anti-competitive foreclosure'.[450] According to the Commission such evidence 'includes internal documents which contain direct evidence of a strategy to exclude competitors, such as a detailed plan to engage in certain conduct in order to exclude a competitor, to prevent entry or to pre-empt the emergence of a market, or evidence of concrete threats of exclusionary action. Such direct evidence may be helpful in interpreting the dominant undertaking's conduct'.[451]

317 In terms of the evidence of the intentions of the dominant undertaking, the case law refers to both objective and subjective intentions. As indicated in paragraphs 82-84 of Chapter 1, objective intentions are intentions that are apparent from the behaviour of the undertaking concerned (e.g. its prices, its margins or the fact that it engages in other exclusionary practices), whereas subjective intentions are those that are apparent from statements made by the individuals involved (e.g. in internal documents).[452] As explained in Chapter 1, there is a risk that objective intentions, being deduced directly from the *actus reus*, in fact amount merely to negligence. But objective intentions to exclude do play a particularly important role when assessing whether there is an objective justification for the practices concerned. Indeed, the European Courts and the European Commission have accepted that practices which may at first sight appear abusive may nevertheless not fall foul of Article 102 TFEU if they are

448. Because the order for reference stated that it could not be established that Post Danmark had deliberately sought to drive out its competitor. *See* C-209/10 *Post Danmark* ECLI:EU:C:2012:172, paras 13 and 29. *See also* again C-525/16 *MEO – Serviços de Comunicações e Multimédia* ECLI:EU:C:2018:270.

449. C-549/10 P *Tomra and Others v Commission* ECLI:EU:C:2012:221, para. 20.

450. Commission Guidance on the Commission's enforcement priorities in applying Article 82 of the EC Treaty to abusive exclusionary conduct by dominant undertakings [2009] OJ C45/7, para. 20.

451. Commission Guidance on the Commission's enforcement priorities in applying Article 82 of the EC Treaty to abusive exclusionary conduct by dominant undertakings [2009] OJ C45/7, para. 20.

452. M Lao, 'Reclaiming a role for intent evidence in monopolization analysis' (2004) American University Law Review 151, 158; MJ Melícias, 'The use and abuse of intent evidence in antitrust analysis' (2010) World Competition 569, 571; P Akman, 'The role of intent in the EU case law on abuse of dominance' (2014) European Law Review 316, 317-318. *See also* R Nazzini, *The foundations of European Union competition law. The objectives and principles of Article 102* (OUP 2011) 58, although he in practice often equates objective with subjective intent (*see*, for example, 209 where he states: 'The non economic sense test for prices below AVC is, therefore, a test of intent'). T Schrepel, *Predatory innovation in antitrust law* (Larcier 2018) 433 reverses the meaning of the two concepts.

objectively justified.[453] *Mens rea* evidence is often used here: if internal documents show that the dominant undertaking was not actually pursuing any procompetitive objectives, such objective justification is discredited and the Commission and the European Courts may conclude that only an anticompetitive objective explains its behaviour.[454] That does not mean, however, that the objective justification is entirely dependent on *mens rea* evidence. Indeed, the Court of Justice has held in *Paroxetine* that any efficiency gains of the practices that may amount to an objective justification 'cannot depend on the objectives that may be pursued by the party engaged in those practices and, therefore on whether those practices result from deliberate intention or, on the contrary, are only fortuitous or accidental'.[455]

[C] Specific Abuses

318 Article 102 TFEU lists four types of commercial practices which, according to the wording of that article, may constitute an abuse of dominance. The Commission and the CJEU have often attempted to fit abuses they identified in one or more of the examples listed in Article 102 TFEU, but from the beginning the CJEU has recognized that this list of abusive practices is not exhaustive.[456] In the literature, not much attention is paid anymore to the list of examples in Article 102 TFEU: practices that fit into these descriptions are sometimes considered abusive and sometimes not, and the descriptions are simply considered too vague to be applied.

319 The prime example of this is probably point c) of Article 102 TFEU: 'applying dissimilar conditions to equivalent transactions with other trading parties, thereby placing them at a competitive disadvantage'. There are so many factors (e.g. order volume, total volume, quality, mix, time, etc.) that may impact on the conditions for a transaction, that it is difficult to know when transactions should be considered equivalent for the purpose of this provision. What is more, many authors have argued that in some circumstances it is welfare-enhancing (even for dominant undertakings) to price discriminate in accordance with each purchaser's willingness to pay (so-called Ramsey pricing).[457]

320 The literature has instead developed a number of other typologies for abuses.[458] The main distinction that is often used is between exclusionary abuses and exploitative

453. *See* already C-27/76 *United Brands v Commission* ECLI:EU:C:1978:22, para. 184 and the Commission Guidance on the Commission's enforcement priorities in applying Article 82 of the EC Treaty to abusive exclusionary conduct by dominant undertakings [2009] OJ C45/7, paras 28-31.
454. *See* in particular paras 396, 398, 399 and 427 below.
455. C-307/18 *Generics (UK) and Others* ECLI:EU:C:2020:52, para. 168.
456. C-6/72 *Europemballange and Continental Can v Commission* ECLI:EU:C:1972:101, para. 26.
457. S Bishop and M Walker, *The economics of EC competition law* (Sweet & Maxwell 2010) 252-256; D Geradin and N Petit, 'Price discrimination under EC competition law: another antitrust doctrine in search of limiting principles' (2006) Journal of Competition Law & Economics 479, 483-486.
458. *See*, for example, the discussion in R Thomson, C Brown and N Gibson, 'Article 102' in V Rose and D Bailey (eds), *Bellamy & Child European Union law of competition* (OUP 2013) 751, 791-2;

abuses. Sometimes also a third category of (price) discrimination is distinguished. I distinguish below between exclusionary abuses and other kinds of abuses, the latter being a sort of rest category for practices that have been found problematic in the past but that do not aim at excluding a competitor. Most forms of price discrimination that have been found abusive in the past have an exclusionary objective and can be seen as exclusionary abuses.[459] I will categorize the few other instances where price discrimination has been found to be problematic together with abuses that have been termed 'exploitative' in the rest category.

321 Within the category of exclusionary abuses, I distinguish between single market abuses (where the clear rationale of the dominant undertaking is to strengthen its market power), multimarket abuses (where the rationale is more disputed in the literature) and abuse of regulatory process (where the abuse does not take place on the market as such).

322 The typology I will use below is as follows.

Typology	*Section Below*
A. Exclusionary abuses	
a. Single market exclusionary abuses	
- Predatory pricing	[1]
- Exclusionary price discrimination	[2]
- Exclusivity agreements	[3]
- Pricing practices conditional on exclusivity	[4]
b. Multimarket exclusionary abuses (leveraging)	
- Tying	[5]
- Refusal to supply	[6]
- Margin squeeze and other multimarket pricing abuses	[7]
c. Abuse of regulatory process	[8]
B. Non-exclusionary abuses	[9]

A Giraud, M de l'Estang, D Kupka, G Melot and S Petit, 'Les abus de position dominante' in M Chagny (ed.) *Le Lamy droit économique 2018* (Wolters Kluwer 2018) 334, 344-345 and the categorization in M de la Mano, R Nazzini and H Zenger, 'Article 102' in J Faull & A Nikpay (eds), *The EU law of competition* (OUP 2014) 329, 387-538.

459. *See also* D Geradin and N Petit, 'Price discrimination under EC competition law: another antitrust doctrine in search of limiting principles' (2006) Journal of Competition Law & Economics 479, in particular 499 and 501.

323 It will become apparent from the discussion below that evidence of (exclusionary) intentions has played a different role for different types of abuses. I will discuss below some explanations for this which are specific to the type of abuse in question. However, more generally, the amount of evidence of intentions available to the Commission and the European Courts of course also depends on the procedure leading up to the Commission decision or the judgment of the Court. In case a CJEU judgment is the result of a preliminary question coming from a national court dealing with private litigation in a country where discovery rules are strict, no internal documents of the dominant undertaking may be available to assess intent. On the other hand, when the Commission has conducted a dawn raid at the premises of the dominant undertaking, many such documents will have been assessed. In that sense, relying on evidence of intentions goes hand in hand with certain forms of procedure (*see also* the discussion in footnote 1054 below).

324 This does not mean, however, that reliance on intent is only dependent on procedure or that the availability of such evidence is a question of luck (*see* further below at paragraphs 675ff.). Indeed, it happens that evidence of (subjective) exclusionary intentions is available absent a dawn raid (e.g. in *Microsoft* – *see* paragraphs 399 and 408 below). Reversely, it is of course possible that dawn raids do not lead to evidence of exclusionary intentions: I suspect that in many such instances the case will simply be closed by the Commission or NCA conducting the raids.

[1] Predatory Pricing

325 It makes sense to start a discussion of the role of intentions in abuse of dominance with predatory pricing since much of the literature on this topic focuses on this type of abuse.[460] Indeed, the case law has stated that, in certain circumstances, evidence of an exclusionary intention plays a decisive role to determine whether a price is abusive or not. Evidence of an exclusionary strategy is in that case a necessary condition to establish predatory pricing.

326 The relevant principles were first established in European law by the 1991 *Akzo* judgment of the CJEU. For a good understanding of this judgment and why intentions play an important part in it, it is useful to look at the background of this case and the Commission decision which it concerned. The case originated in a complaint by a small British organic peroxide manufacturer ECS against Dutch producer Akzo. ECS had originally sold its organic peroxide only as a bleaching agent for flour (a niche market), but in 1979 it also started selling it to the plastic sector, where it can have several applications and which is the sector with the largest demand for organic peroxides. When it became aware of this, Akzo requested a meeting with ECS where it made

460. P Akman, 'The role of intent in the EU case law on abuse of dominance' (2014) European Law Review 316 and C O'Grady, 'The role of exclusionary intent in the enforcement of Article 102 TFEU' (2014) World Competition 459, for example, devote half of their discussion to predatory pricing.

threats that if ECS did not stop selling in the plastic sector, Akzo would retaliate against it in the flour sector.[461]

327 ECS applied for and obtained an injunction from the London High Court which continued until Akzo and ECS reached a settlement out of court in which Akzo agreed not to reduce its organic peroxide price 'with the intention of eliminating (ECS) as competitors'.[462] The idea that the intentions of Akzo were relevant to determine the lawfulness of its pricing practices was therefore already present before the case came to the European Commission. When ECS complained about further price cuts by Akzo, Akzo responded that it merely responded to price cuts by ECS and that ECS could not prove exclusionary intent.

328 In 1982, ECS brought a complaint to the European Commission which raided the offices of Akzo and in 1983 adopted an interim measures decision which required Akzo to return to the profit margins it had prior to its dispute with ECS, except in case Akzo's pricing was mere alignment to the prices of competitors.[463] At the end of 1985, the Commission adopted a final decision on Akzo's exclusionary practices in the flour sector in which it found a number of practices which it considered abusive, including 'unreasonably low prices designed to damage ECS's business viability in that ECS was obliged either to abandon the customer to AKZO Chemie BV or to match a loss-making price in order to retain the customer'.[464]

329 Already during the proceedings before the Commission, Akzo had argued that the lawfulness of its pricing practices should be assessed only by reference to its cost level. It referred to the seminal article published in 1975 by Harvard professors Areeda and Turner[465] to argue that there should be a per se test for predatory pricing: 'a price at or above marginal cost is presumed lawful and a price below marginal cost is presumed abusive'.[466] The Commission had dismissed this rule, saying that it was difficult to apply and too narrow, and that 'no such test would give sufficient weight to the strategic aspect of price cutting behaviour'.[467] The Commission did not deny, however, that '[a] detailed analysis of the alleged aggressor's costs may ... be of considerable importance in establishing the reasonableness or otherwise of its pricing conduct as well as the underlying purpose thereof'. It added that, nevertheless, 'where low pricing could be susceptible of several explanations, evidence of an intention to eliminate a competitor or restrict competition might also be required to prove an infringement'.[468]

330 Akzo again raised this argument before the Court of Justice. AG Lenz's opinion is of little relevance to analyse this question since he considered that the Commission had

461. Commission decision of 14 December 1985 in case 30.698 *ECS/AKZO*, recitals 1-26.
462. Wording of the settlement quoted in Commission decision of 14 December 1985 in case 30.698 *ECS/AKZO*, recital 27.
463. Commission decision of 29 July 1983 in case 30.698 *ECS/AKZO*.
464. Article 1 (ii) of the Commission decision of 14 December 1985 in case 30.698 *ECS/AKZO*.
465. P Areeda and DF Turner, 'Predatory pricing and related practices under Section 2 of the Sherman Act' (1975) Harvard Law Review 697.
466. Commission decision of 14 December 1985 in case 30.698 *ECS/AKZO*, recital 75.
467. Commission decision of 14 December 1985 in case 30.698 *ECS/AKZO*, recital 78.
468. Commission decision of 14 December 1985 in case 30.698 *ECS/AKZO*, recital 80.

not established that Akzo had been dominant on the relevant market.[469] When analysing the alleged abuse for the sake of completeness, AG Lenz opined that, because of the defective market analysis conducted by the Commission, 'it was impossible to determine what prices were economically justifiable or reasonable'.[470] The Advocate General nevertheless analysed whether Akzo had had the long-term purpose of damaging ECS and/or securing its withdrawal as a competitor. While he accepted that Akzo had this intention in 1979 when it first threatened ECS, he did not think there was sufficient evidence that such an intention continued after the intervention of the High Court. He considered that some of the later documents relied on by the Commission were inconclusive. While a document stating that it was necessary to 'continue to exert pressure' constituted evidence of that intention, it was not 'irrefutable final proof'. Another note of Akzo relied on by the Commission which showed that ECS was losing customers merely contained 'a description of the situation in the market, but not necessarily a description of the applicant's intention'.[471] The Advocate General pointed out that ECS had made inroads in Akzo's business with flour customers in 1980 and could even be viewed as having started a price war. Akzo's actions therefore 'can also be explained in the absence of the intention imputed to it by the Commission', namely as a response to ECS' pricing practices.[472]

331 The Court of Justice was more sympathetic to the Commission's arguments. It first of all dismissed Akzo's argument that only prices below average variable costs could be considered predatory and held:

> Prices below average variable costs (that is to say, those which vary depending on the quantities produced) by means of which a dominant undertaking seeks to eliminate a competitor must be regarded as abusive. A dominant undertaking has no interest in applying such prices except that of eliminating competitors ... .
>
> Moreover prices below average total costs, that is to say, fixed costs plus variable costs, but above average variable costs, must be regarded as abusive if they are determined as part of a plan for eliminating a competitor. Such prices can drive from the market undertakings which are perhaps as efficient as the dominant undertaking but which, because of their smaller financial resources, are incapable of withstanding the competition waged against them.[473]

332 One could say that the test enunciated by the Court refers to an exclusionary intention in both of its branches, even though it is more explicit in the second branch. Indeed, by pointing out that a dominant undertaking 'has no interest' to price below average variable cost, the CJEU follows one of the economic theories of abuse, the so-called sacrifice test which uses an objective notion of intention:[474] by pricing below

469. C-62/86 *Akzo v Commission* ECLI:EU:C:1989:154, para. 124.
470. C-62/86 *Akzo v Commission* ECLI:EU:C:1989:154, para. 148.
471. C-62/86 *Akzo v Commission* ECLI:EU:C:1989:154, paras 208-209.
472. C-62/86 *Akzo v Commission* ECLI:EU:C:1989:154, para. 215.
473. C-62/86 *Akzo v Commission* ECLI:EU:C:1991:286, paras 71-72.
474. *See* A Bavasso, 'The role of intent under Article 82 EC: from "flushing the turkeys" to "spotting lionesses in Regent's Park"' (2005) European Competition Law Review 616, 620. *See also* M Mandorff and J Sahl, 'The role of the "equally efficient competitor" in the assessment of abuse of dominance' (2013) Konkurrensverket Working Paper Series in Law and Economics 2013-1

average variable cost, an undertaking can only have intended to exclude a competitor. The 'eliminatory intent is implicit' in the price level.[475] This should then be contrasted to the second branch of the test, in case of pricing below average total cost, where (additional) evidence of a subjective intention becomes relevant.

333 In the *Akzo* judgment, the CJEU subsequently determined what Akzo's variable and fixed costs were based on arguments and calculations presented by the Commission and by Akzo. It concluded that some of Akzo's prices were below its average variable costs but that many others were between average variable and average total costs. While it had considered elements of Akzo's exclusionary strategy earlier on in the judgment, its determination that the instances of pricing between average variable and average total costs were part of a plan to eliminate ECS are sometimes curious. Indeed, contrary to what is claimed in the literature,[476] at this stage in the case law, the Court did not so much focus on the internal documents of the dominant undertaking (possibly because AG Lenz found these to be ambiguous?) but rather referred back to the pricing practices themselves to detect the intentions behind them.

334 For example, for the pricing to ECS customer Allied Mills, the Court refers to '[a] note prepared by one of AKZO's representatives [which] shows that AKZO established the prices offered to Allied Mills in January 1981 by calculating that they were well below those charged to Allied Mills by ECS'. Although this demonstrated that Akzo did not merely align itself to ECS' pricing to Allied Mills, the Court considered that it also showed 'that AKZO's intention was not solely to win the order which would have induced it to reduce its prices only to the extent necessary for this purpose'. The Court nevertheless observed that Akzo quoted to ECS customer Allied Mills the exact same price which ECS had quoted to Akzo customer Spillers: this had precisely allowed Akzo to argue that it was merely matching ECS' quotes.[477]

335 Also for the pricing to the group of customers known as the 'large independents', the Court's discussion of Akzo's plan to eliminate ECS is meagre: it states that 'the prices quoted by AKZO ... show that AKZO's aim was to damage ECS and not to restore its own profit margins. Those prices are well below what was necessary to compete with ECS, since, compared with the prices charged to this category of customers by ECS at that time, they show a difference of more than [UKP 60-100 for different types of

---

<http://www.konkurrensverket.se/globalassets/english/publications-and-decisions/the-role-of-the-equally-efficient-competitor-in-the-assessment-of-abuse-of-dominance.pdf> accessed 11 September 2017, 2-3; SS Markis, 'Applying normative theories in EU competition law: exploring article 102 TFEU' (2014) UCL Journal of Law and Jurisprudence 30, 54.

475. P Akman, 'The role of intent in the EU case law on abuse of dominance' (2014) European Law Review 316, 321. M de la Mano, R Nazzini and H Zenger, 'Article 102' in J Faull and A Nikpay (eds), *The EU law of competition* (Oxford University Press 2014) 329, 399 also point out: 'The "no economic sense" test for prices below average variable costs is, therefore, a test of intent.'
476. MJ Melícias, 'The use and abuse of intent evidence in antitrust analysis' (2010) World Competition 569, 582, argues that 'Both the European Commission's enforcement practice and the EU Courts' case law give clear preponderance to the dominant company's internal business documents.'
477. C-62/86 *Akzo v Commission* ECLI:EU:C:1991:286, para. 102.

products]'.[478] As evidence of the plan to eliminate ECS, the Court therefore again merely refers to the pricing level, rather than to any evidence external to it.

336 The principles of *Akzo* were confirmed by the European Courts in *Tetra Pak II*. In this case, the Commission had found that Tetra Pak had abused its dominant position in the markets for aseptic packaging (both machines and cartons) through a number of practices on that market and on the neighbouring markets of non-aseptic packaging (both machines and cartons). The Commission found predatory pricing in relation to two markets.

337 The Commission's decision refined the distinction between variable and total (fixed plus variable) costs from *Akzo* by also distinguishing between direct and indirect costs. 'Direct (fixed or variable) costs are those which may be entirely attributed to a given product. Indirect costs are those which, being, on the contrary, common to several products, cannot be allocated to them other than by the use of rates which, invariably, involve a degree of arbitrariness.'[479] Many variable costs are direct (e.g. raw materials, labour of staff working in production) but others are indirect (e.g. labour from sales staff) since, although they depend on the amount of products produced/sold, they are not directly correlated to it (sales representatives may sell a number of different products so it may be difficult to identify exactly which share of their salary depends on the sale of an individual product). This allowed for a slightly stricter test than in *Akzo*: namely whether prices are below average *direct* variable costs.

338 The Commission first of all identified predatory pricing on the market for non-aseptic cartons in Italy, where Tetra Pak had systematically sold its products not only below average total cost but also below average variable cost (but in one year, 1982, not below average *direct* variable cost).[480] Second, it found predatory pricing on the UK market for non-aseptic machines where Tetra Pak sold at a loss during four years, not even covering variable costs during three years.[481]

339 Tetra Pak argued before the CFI that, regardless of which cost benchmark is used, the Commission should establish predatory intent, but this was rejected by the Court. The latter held that the 'sale of Tetra Rex cartons constantly below not only their cost price but also their variable direct cost is sufficient evidence that the applicant pursued a policy of eviction'.[482] For 1982, where prices were above average variable direct cost, the Court held that '[a] whole series of important and convergent factors provides evidence of the existence of an eliminatory intent', in particular 'the duration, the continuity and the scale of the sales at a loss made throughout the period from 1976 to 1982'.[483] The Court also referred to the fact that the transfer prices used by Tetra Pak internally were lower than its external sales prices, to internal reports to Tetra Pak's

478. C-62/86 *Akzo v Commission* ECLI:EU:C:1991:286, para. 108.
479. Commission decision of 24 July 1991 in case 31.043 *Tetra Pak II*, footnote 29.
480. Commission decision of 24 July 1991 in case 31.043 *Tetra Pak II*, recital 149.
481. Commission decision of 24 July 1991 in case 31.043 *Tetra Pak II*, recital 157.
482. T-83/91 *Tetra Pak v Commission* ECLI:EU:T:1994:246, para. 150.
483. T-83/91 *Tetra Pak v Commission* ECLI:EU:T:1994:246, para. 151.

board from 1979 and 1980 'referring to the need to make major financial sacrifices in the area of prices and supply terms in order to fight competition', to the increase of the market share of Tetra Pak to the detriment of its competitors and the increasing divergence of Tetra Pak's prices and those of its competitors.[484]

340 In relation to the sales of non-aseptic machines in the UK, the CFI held that the fact that 'Tetra Pak regularly sold its non-aseptic machines below not only their cost price but also their variable direct cost' was 'sufficient evidence that the applicant pursued a policy of eviction during those years'.[485] For 1981, when prices were below average total cost but not below average variable direct cost, the Court again said that 'a whole series of important and convergent factors provides evidence of the existence of eliminatory intent', including 'the duration, the continuity and the scale – ... – of the losses made, and the deliberate nature of those losses, as expressly recognized by Tetra Pak, in the context of the policy of intensive pricing competition from 1981 to 1984, although the market was expanding'.[486] Finally, the Court also referred to the effects of the practices in the form of the increase of Tetra Pak's sales of non-aseptic machines in the UK, as compared to sales in other countries and those of its competitors.

341 Interestingly, while the CFI in this case did refer to evidence from internal reports and admissions by Tetra Pak, much of the evidence relied on is, like in *Akzo*, objective and even internal to the pricing practice itself (although changes in the market position and sales volumes are also used): this seems somewhat circular.[487] Perhaps the fact that Tetra Pak also engaged in other exclusionary practices (such as tying – *see* paragraph 397 below) was also relevant.[488]

342 In the appeal before the CJEU, the main question for the alleged predatory pricing was whether the Commission also needed to demonstrate that Tetra Pak would be able to recoup the losses it made through its pricing practices. This was a requirement under recent US case law[489] but had been denied by the CFI.[490] The CJEU agreed with the CFI and denied that such a requirement existed under EU law because it should be possible to stop predatory pricing which risks eliminating competitors without having to wait for such elimination to actually occur.[491] As regards the test for predatory pricing under EU law, the CJEU repeated the *Akzo* test, interestingly without reference to the distinction between direct and indirect costs, and held:

484. *Ibid.*
485. T-83/91 *Tetra Pak v Commission* ECLI:EU:T:1994:246, para. 189.
486. T-83/91 *Tetra Pak v Commission* ECLI:EU:T:1994:246, para. 190.
487. *See also* P Akman, 'The role of intent in the EU case law on abuse of dominance' (2014) European Law Review 316, 323.
488. *See* on this the speech of the Director General of DG Comp P Lowe, 'EU competition practice on predatory pricing: introductory address to the seminar 'Pros and cons of low prices' (5 December 2003) <http://ec.europa.eu/competition/speeches/text/sp2003_066_en.pdf> accessed 26 September 2018, 4.
489. *See* in particular *Brooke Group Ltd. v Brown & Williamson Tobacco Corp.*, 509 U.S. 209 (1993). For a discussion of the evolution of the US case law, *see* C Leslie, 'Predatory pricing and recoupment' (2013) Columbia Law Review 1695, 1700-1706.
490. T-83/91 *Tetra Pak v Commission* ECLI:EU:T:1994:246, para. 150.
491. C-333/94 P *Tetra Pak v Commission* ECLI:EU:C:1996:436, para. 44.

> For sales of non-aseptic cartons in Italy between 1976 and 1981, [the CFI] found that prices were considerably lower than average variable costs. Proof of intention to eliminate competitors was therefore not necessary. In 1982, prices for those cartons lay between average variable costs and average total costs. For that reason, in paragraph 151 of its judgment, the Court of First Instance was at pains to establish – ... – that Tetra Pak intended to eliminate a competitor.
>
> The Court of First Instance was also right, at paragraphs 189 to 191 of the judgment under appeal, to apply exactly the same reasoning to sales of non-aseptic machines in the United Kingdom between 1981 and 1984.[492]

343 In a third[493] predatory pricing case, *Wanadoo*, the Commission confirmed the principles set out in *Tetra Pak II*, but the evidence used to demonstrate intent became even more focused on internal business documents. *Wanadoo* is also interesting because it concerned high-speed Internet access for residential customers, at the time a rapidly expanding market. The Commission accepted that the assessment of cost-recovery in such a market needs to be done slightly differently than in markets which are fairly stable.[494] The Commission considered that a firm such as Wanadoo should 'seek to achieve a level of recovery of recurrent costs (network costs and production costs) which is sufficient to ensure that the margin between revenue and recurrent costs will, within a reasonable time, also cover the non-recurrent variable costs invested in the commercial development of the particular product, on items such as advertising, promotion, marketing, etc.'.[495] The time period taken into account by the Commission for the recovery of these non-recurrent variable costs was forty-eight months. The Commission concluded that from January 2001 to July 2001, Wanadoo did not cover the variable cost for providing the high-speed Internet service and from August 2001 to October 2002 not the full cost. At the same time, the Commission considered that there was evidence of a plan to eliminate competitors, in the form of an 'intention to preempt the high-speed market'[496] as evidenced by internal documents which also showed the sacrifice of profitability for the sake of market penetration and concerns over the lawfulness of the pricing practices.[497] The Commission further considered that other practices used by Wanadoo and its shareholder France Télécom attested to a strategy of exclusion.[498]

344 In its application for annulment before the CFI, Wanadoo contested the Commission findings in a number of ways. First of all, like Tetra Pak, it took issue with the lack of a requirement under EU law to demonstrate that losses could be recovered, but this

492. C-333/94 P *Tetra Pak v Commission* ECLI:EU:C:1996:436, paras 42-43.
493. Note that there is a fourth predatory pricing case in which the Commission adopted a decision prior to *Wanadoo*, namely by Commission decision of 20 March 2001 in case 35.141 *Deutsche Post*, but this decision was not challenged before the European Courts and will not be discussed further here, also because it was entirely built around the price levels used by Deutsche Post, without any consideration for *mens rea*.
494. A point also stressed in MJ Melícias, 'The use and abuse of intent evidence in antitrust analysis' (2010) World Competition 569, 583.
495. Commission decision of 16 July 2003 in case 38.233 *Wanadoo Interactive*, recital 76.
496. Commission decision of 16 July 2003 in case 38.233 *Wanadoo Interactive*, title G2.
497. Commission decision of 16 July 2003 in case 38.233 *Wanadoo Interactive*, title G3.
498. Commission decision of 16 July 2003 in case 38.233 *Wanadoo Interactive*, title G4.

was rejected by the Court.[499] Wanadoo also tried the meeting-competition-defence: it argued that it had the right to align its prices with those of its competitors. But the CFI held that a dominant company did not have an absolute right to align its prices with those of its competitors: '[e]ven if alignment of prices by a dominant undertaking on those of its competitors is not in itself abusive or objectionable, it might become so where it is aimed not only at protecting its interest but also at strengthening and abusing its dominant position'.[500]

345 As regards specifically the evidence used by the Commission to establish the exclusionary intention of Wanadoo, the Court held that, if variable costs are not recovered, predatory intent is 'presumed' but that, for the period for which only full costs were not recovered, the Commission had to prove a strategy of 'pre-emption'.[501] While Wanadoo argued that the internal documents referred to be the Commission as evidence of this strategy were 'informal and spontaneous', the Court contested this by pointing out that 'those words come from management-level staff within the undertaking and ... some of them were expressed in the context of formal presentations for the purpose of taking a decision or of a very detailed framework letter'[502] and, following a fairly detailed review,[503] accepted the evidence relied on by the Commission.

346 On appeal, the CJEU rejected a number of Wanadoo's arguments, including its arguments on its alleged right to align its prices with those of its competitors, on procedural grounds.[504] Diverging from the opinion of AG Mazák,[505] the CJEU also rejected Wanadoo's plea that the Commission should demonstrate the possibility of recoupment of losses – although it did not exclude that such a demonstration could be relevant to assess the abuse.[506]

347 Specifically of interest for current purposes is that the CJEU also briefly commented on the evidence used by the Commission and accepted by the CFI to show a plan of predation. Wanadoo argued that the alleged plan of predation had been established 'solely on the basis of subjective factors, while [Article 102 TFEU] requires proof of an objectively identifiable plan to eliminate competition based on objective indications, such as, *inter alia*, threats to competitors or selective price cuts in respect of competitors' customers'.[507] In response, the Commission contended that 'the element of intention in abuse of dominant position is necessarily subjective'.[508] The

499. T-340/03 *France Télécom v Commission* ECLI:EU:T:2007:22, paras 219-228.
500. T-340/03 *France Télécom v Commission* ECLI:EU:T:2007:22, para. 189.
501. T-340/03 *France Télécom v Commission* ECLI:EU:T:2007:22, paras 197-198.
502. T-340/03 *France Télécom v Commission* ECLI:EU:T:2007:22, para. 202.
503. MJ Melícias, 'The use and abuse of intent evidence in antitrust analysis' (2010) World Competition 569, 583 even argues that 'the major focus of the GC's analysis was on the accuracy of the Commission's interpretation of the expressions contained in Wanadoo's internal business documents'.
504. C-202/07 P *France Télécom v Commission* ECLI:EU:C:2009:214, paras 39-61.
505. C-202/07 P *France Télécom v Commission* ECLI:EU:C:2008:520, paras 65-77.
506. C-202/07 P *France Télécom v Commission* ECLI:EU:C:2009:214, paras 100-119.
507. C-202/07 P *France Télécom v Commission* ECLI:EU:C:2009:214, para. 95.
508. C-202/07 P *France Télécom v Commission* ECLI:EU:C:2009:214, para. 96.

CJEU held that Wanadoo was 'wrong to maintain that the Court of First Instance, in order to establish that a plan of predation existed, relied solely on subjective factors' since it 'deduced this from objective factors such as that undertaking's internal documents'.[509] This statement is certainly paradoxical but it seems to accept the use of (objective) evidence of subjective intentions.[510]

348 The CJEU furthermore reiterated the CFI's statement that in the case of pricing below average variable cost, the dominant undertaking 'is presumed to pursue no other economic objective save that of eliminating its competitors'.[511] In some of the literature, this has been interpreted as implying that the presumption can be rebutted, even in case of pricing below average variable cost.[512]

349 In conclusion, it can be said that, in case a dominant undertaking prices below average total costs but above average variable costs, this may constitute an abuse of dominant position under the case law of the European Courts if there is also evidence of an intention or strategy to eliminate competitors. To establish such an intention, the European Courts have, in particular in more recent case law, accepted reliance on internal documents, but in earlier decisions also took account of other circumstances, such as the duration and continuity of the loss-making prices and the scale of the losses, and the discrepancy between the dominant undertaking's allegedly abusive prices on the one hand and the prices used by the dominant undertaking internally and in (non-suspect) other markets or by the undertaking's competitors in the same market. Recent case law therefore refers more to evidence of subjective intent (internal documents), whereas older case law relies more on objective intention (deduced from conduct).

350 Already before the CJEU judgment in *France Télécom*, the Commission incorporated much of the above referenced case law in its *Guidance Paper on Exclusionary Abuses*, while slightly adjusting the relevant cost benchmarks (replacing average variable cost with average avoidable cost, and average total cost with long-run average incremental costs). As regards the relevance of subjective intentions, the Commission considered that '[i]n some cases it will be possible to rely upon direct evidence consisting of documents from the dominant undertaking which clearly show a predatory strategy, such as a detailed plan to sacrifice in order to exclude a competitor, to prevent entry or to pre-empt the emergence of a market, or evidence of concrete threats of predatory action'.[513]

---

509. C-202/07 P *France Télécom v Commission* ECLI:EU:C:2009:214, paras 97-98.
510. *See also* P Akman, 'The role of intent in the EU case law on abuse of dominance' (2014) European Law Review 316, 326.
511. C-202/07 P *France Télécom v Commission* ECLI:EU:C:2009:214, para. 109.
512. *See* M de la Mano, R Nazzini and H Zenger, 'Article 102' in J Faull and A Nikpay (eds), *The EU law of competition* (Oxford University Press 2014) 329, 399.
513. Commission Guidance on the Commission's enforcement priorities in applying Article 82 of the EC Treaty to abusive exclusionary conduct by dominant undertakings [2009] OJ C45/7, para. 66.

351 However, the Commission did not exclude that it could also establish an exclusionary strategy from objective factors: '[i]n order to show a predatory strategy, the Commission may also investigate whether the allegedly predatory conduct led in the short term to net revenues lower than could have been expected from a reasonable alternative conduct, that is to say, whether the dominant undertaking incurred a loss that it could have avoided'.[514] Such an analysis brings in uncertainty as to when pricing below average total costs can be abusive. However, as I will discuss next, the case law on selective price cuts is even less restrictive, sometimes considering pricing above average total costs to be abusive.

[2] Exclusionary Price Discrimination

352 A pricing practice which is often considered related to predatory pricing[515] is the use of selective price cuts. This practice can also be subsumed under the broader concept of price discrimination referred to in Article 102(c) TFEU. That, and under which circumstances, selective price cuts or price discrimination would be a problematic commercial practice is controversial in the literature. Indeed, as a general proposition and as pointed out in paragraph 319 above, most of the recent literature rejects the idea that undertakings, including dominant undertakings, would somehow need to apply identical prices to all customers in all circumstances. Nevertheless, in certain circumstances, the Commission and the European Courts have found that selective price cuts can be exclusionary, as I will discuss below.

353 In this section, I only discuss exclusionary price discrimination, not instances where rebates, discounts or other advantageous prices are conditional on (quasi) exclusivity. The latter, which are more akin to exclusivity agreements, will be discussed in paragraphs 379-390 below.

354 The case law seems to take into account a number of factors to determine whether a selective price cut can amount to an abuse, including whether the undertaking applying the price is superdominant instead of simply dominant[516] and whether the price cut not only affects competition but also restricts parallel trade.[517] What is of interest here is of course to what extent evidence of exclusionary intentions and strategies is a (necessary, relevant, sufficient) factor to establish that selective price cuts are an abuse.

355 To start, let us return to *Akzo*, since, as I indicated earlier (*see* paragraph 328 above), the Commission had found in its decision in that case a number of commercial

514. Commission Guidance on the Commission's enforcement priorities in applying Article 82 of the EC Treaty to abusive exclusionary conduct by dominant undertakings [2009] OJ C45/7, para. 65.
515. M de la Mano, R Nazzini and H Zenger, 'Article 102' in J Faull and A Nikpay (eds), *The EU law of competition* (Oxford University Press 2014) 329, 402.
516. Joined cases C-395 and 396/96 P *Compagnie Maritime Belge v Commission* ECLI:EU:C:1998:518, para. 119; T-228/97 *Irish Sugar v Commission* ECLI:EU:T:1999:246, para. 186.
517. T-228/97 *Irish Sugar v Commission* ECLI:EU:T:1999:246, para. 185.

practices that were abusive. Apart from the unreasonably low prices, the Commission also found it problematic that Akzo was 'making such quotations selectively to ECS customers for flour additives while maintaining substantially (up to 60 %) higher prices to comparable buyers which were already its own regular customers'.[518]

356 Akzo considered that such behaviour was not problematic: it had simply offered lower prices to customers which had received competing quotes (from ECS) than to those which had not received competing quotes (its own loyal customers). One could add that this is simply how competition works: if customers do not shop around, they risk paying higher prices. The CJEU did not accept Akzo's argument, however.[519] It simply considered that Akzo was able to finance low prices to ECS customers by maintaining high prices to its own customers and that '[t]his behaviour shows that AKZO's intention was not to pursue a general policy of favourable prices, but to adopt a strategy that could damage ECS'.[520]

357 This black-or-white manner in which the CJEU presents 'AKZO's intention' is certainly contestable.[521] Of specific interest for current purposes is, however, that the CJEU seems to say that Akzo's intentions can be deduced from its behaviour, in particular from the fact that prices for some customers were low and prices for others were not. However, I think this may be a lapsus:[522] was not the Court rather pointing to the fact that, in light of other evidence of Akzo's intention to exclude ECS, the differentiated prices were suspect as well?

358 This reading seems to fit better with subsequent cases. In particular, in *Compagnie Maritime Belge*, the CFI condemned the selective price cuts because of evidence of the intention of the (jointly dominant) undertakings concerned to exclude their only competitor (G&C) in this way. As indicated above in paragraph 297, the Commission had found in this case that liner conference Cewal had abused its dominant position, in particular on the trade between Northern Europe and Zaire. The practices which the Commission found problematic included the conclusion of exclusivity contracts with customers and actions to induce the Congolese government to keep Cewal's competitor out of the trade. The Commission also found that Cewal had used the technique of so-called fighting ships, whereby its members agreed on lower rates than the normal

518. Article 1 (iii) of the Commission decision of 14 December 1985 in case 30.698 *ECS/AKZO*.
519. For completeness, note that the CJEU did accept the argument that prices between two groups of customers needed to be comparable for there to be selective price cuts and that this was not the case for all the instances found problematic by the Commission. *See* C-62/86 *Akzo v Commission* ECLI:EU:C:1989:154, paras 116-121.
520. C-62/86 *Akzo v Commission* ECLI:EU:C:1989:154, para. 115.
521. There are not many companies that pursue a 'general policy of favourable prices' (whatever that means) but that does not mean they pursue an exclusionary strategy. What companies are interested in, according to classical economics, are not 'favourable prices' but 'profitable prices' or even 'the most profitable prices'. Differentiated pricing can be part of such a strategy.
522. *See also* the opinion of AG Mengozzi in C-209/10 *Post Danmark* ECLI:EU:C:2011:342, paras 87 and 121. However, the Advocate General did not seem to take into account that, also as regards predatory pricing, the *Akzo* judgment was based on objective intentions, whereas there clearly was an evolution in the case law (*Tetra Pak* and *France Télécom*) on predatory pricing to focus much more on subjective intentions.

tariff when ships were sailing at or close to the date on which G&C intended to sail. Cewal argued that its rates never went below cost but the Commission considered this irrelevant: the rates of the fighting ships 'were determined not according to economic criteria (i.e. on the basis of costs) but solely in order for them to be the same or lower than the prices advertised by G&C'.[523] The Commission considered that, according to CJEU case law, 'the multilateral and intentional character demonstrates the abusive nature of conduct that consists in establishing a concerted exceptional price with the aim of removing a competitor'.[524] The evidence which the Commission relied on included the use, in Cewal's internal documents, of references to the 'fighting ships' practices and the creation of a 'Special Fighting Committee' within Cewal.

359 The CFI followed the Commission's reasoning. It pointed out that, although a dominant company can defend its commercial interests, e.g. by matching the rates of a competitor, this may nevertheless be problematic in certain circumstances. The CFI accepted that on the basis of the minutes of the Special Fighting Committee of Cewal, in particular those 'which refer to "getting rid" of the independent shipping operation' the Commission could conclude that the practice was abusive, and that the Commission could also rely on Cewal's own use of the notion of 'fighting ships' in this respect.[525] This showed that Cewal's rate drop was not a simple reaction to the rate level of its competitor.

360 In his opinion on Compagnie Maritime Belge's appeal before the CJEU, AG Fennelly discussed in some detail the relationship between selective price cuts and predatory pricing. He considered that costs could not be an 'absolute yardstick against which all possible abusive and exclusionary pricing practices' can be assessed.[526] He considered that a number of elements needed to be taken into account to determine whether price cuts were abusive, including the fact that Cewal did not merely have a dominant position but that this was a case of 'superdominance', and also the 'exclusionary intention' behind the fighting ships practices.[527] In its judgment, the CJEU indeed took these two factors into account: it considered that it did not need to rule on the question of whether selective price cuts were in all circumstances problematic, because in this case Cewal had a market share of over 90% and only one competitor, and Compagnie Maritime Belge had not contested 'that the purpose of the conduct complained of was to eliminate G & C from the market'.[528]

523. Commission decision of 23 December 1992 in cases 32.448 and 32.450 *Cewal, Cowac and Ukwal* and 32.448 and 32.450 *Cewal*, recital 73.
524. Commission decision of 23 December 1992 in cases 32.448 and 32.450 *Cewal, Cowac and Ukwal* and 32.448 and 32.450 *Cewal*, recital 80.
525. Joined cases T-24 to 26 and 28/93 *Compagnie Maritime Belge v Commission* ECLI:EU:T:1996:139, para. 147.
526. Joined cases C-395 and 396/96 P *Compagnie Maritime Belge v Commission* ECLI:EU:C:1998:518, para. 131.
527. Joined cases C-395 and 396/96 P *Compagnie Maritime Belge v Commission* ECLI:EU:C:1998:518, paras 137 and 119 respectively.
528. Joined cases C-395 and 396/96 P *Compagnie Maritime Belge v Commission* ECLI:EU:C:2000:132, para. 119.

361 Price discrimination was also a concern in *Irish Sugar*, where the Commission established a number of abuses by Irish Sugar aimed at protecting the Irish market from competition from other Member States and at preventing others from repacking industrial sugar for resale as retail sugar. The abuses included exclusivity arrangements with customers and suppliers, and fidelity and target rebates but also four types of selective pricing: (i) lower prices to potential customers of importer ASI, (ii) lower prices for sugar aimed at export, (iii) lower prices to customers in border areas (where there was more competition from imports) and (iv) higher prices to customers which bought industrial sugar to repackage it for retail.[529] The first of these was dismissed by the CFI on the facts and the legal issues discussed in the second mostly concerned the extent to which rebates for exports were required by Irish and EU legislation so I will not discuss these further here.[530]

362 The fourth type of price discrimination will be discussed in paragraph 412 below, but of specific interest here is the third type, where Irish Sugar granted rebates to customers located in border areas where competition from neighbouring Northern Ireland was greatest. The Commission considered that these rebates were 'intended to and did deter imports of sugar from Northern Ireland' and formed 'part of a policy of dividing markets and excluding competitors'.[531] Irish Sugar argued that the Commission had not found a similar practice of rebates to meet competition to be problematic in its decision in *British Plasterboard*. The CFI dismissed this argument on the basis that Irish Sugar itself doubted the legality of the practice: '[i]t is, moreover, clear from the documents cited in points 57 to 59 of the contested decision that the applicant not only deliberately chose to offer a special rebate selectively to certain retailers but suspected that such a practice was illegal'.[532] The appeal against the CFI's judgment was rejected on procedural grounds.[533]

363 A discussion of the case law on selective price cuts would not be complete without the judgment in *Post Danmark I*. This Grand Chamber judgment arose as a result of a preliminary reference from the Danish Supreme Court in a case originally brought by the Danish competition authority against postal incumbent Post Danmark. The authority had accused this dominant undertaking of abusing its position by offering lower prices to customers of its competitor Forbruger-Kontakt for the delivery of unaddressed mail. The authority took into account that these prices charged by Post Danmark were not sufficient to cover its average total costs, although they did suffice to cover its average incremental costs (which was understood to comprise not only the costs directly related to the delivery of unaddressed mail but also a part of the costs of Post

529. Commission decision of 14 May 1997 in case 34.621 and 35.059 *Irish Sugar*.
530. T-228/97 *Irish Sugar v Commission* ECLI:EU:T:1999:246, paras 117-124 and 125-149.
531. Commission decision of 14 May 1997 in case 34.621 and 35.059 *Irish Sugar*, recital 129.
532. T-228/97 *Irish Sugar v Commission* ECLI:EU:T:1999:246, para. 183. Other possible differences with the Commission's decision of 5 December 1988 in case 31.900 *BPB Industries plc* include that in the latter the Commission also considered that the price cuts were largely justified by actual and expected cost savings and that they were not part of 'any scheme of systematic alignment' (para. 133).
533. C-497/99 P *Irish Sugar v Commission* ECLI:EU:C:2001:393.

Danmark's network which was used to deliver addressed mail, a market on which it had a legal monopoly).

364 The judgment's importance lies in its apparent rejection of price discrimination as an abuse of dominance. Indeed, the CJEU states that the practice of '"price discrimination", that is to say, charging different customers or different classes of customers different prices for goods or services whose costs are the same or, conversely, charging a single price to customers for whom supply costs differ, cannot of itself suggest that there exists an exclusionary abuse'.[534] The Court rather aligned itself with an assessment of the exclusionary character of price conduct by reference to the dominant undertaking's costs. It held that the mere fact that pricing was below average total cost (but above average incremental cost) was not sufficient to establish an exclusionary abuse because it would be 'possible for a competitor as efficient as that undertaking to compete with those prices without suffering losses that are unsustainable in the long term'.[535]

365 Of specific importance for our purposes is that the reference of the Danish Supreme Court and therefore the judgment of the CJEU was based on the premise that 'it could not be established that Post Danmark had intentionally sought to eliminate competition'.[536] It was precisely because of this that Post Danmark could not be accused of predatory pricing in the sense of the *Akzo* case law. The absence of an exclusionary intention also clearly distinguishes *Post Danmark I* from the earlier case law on selective price cuts (*Akzo*, *Compagnie Maritime Belge*, *Irish Sugar* and, in combination with tying, *Hilti*) where such intention was evident from internal documents and also from the existence of other exclusionary practices.

366 While some have viewed the CJEU's *Post Danmark I* ruling as vindicating the approach to pricing conduct in the *Akzo* judgment,[537] the fact that the Court did not simply reject the possibility of an abuse in case of prices above average incremental cost without evidence of an exclusionary intent suggests that *Akzo* is not the final word on this. Nevertheless, the *Post Danmark I* judgment does suggest that, in the absence of evidence of exclusionary intentions, it will be very difficult to demonstrate that prices are exclusionary. Although the CJEU did not follow its Advocate General's proposal to assess the legality of the pricing practice in light of the possibility for the monopolist to practise cross-subsidization, it is consistent with his suggestion that, in the absence of evidence of an exclusionary intention, it will be necessary to look much more at the effects of the practice.[538]

---

534. C-209/10 *Post Danmark* ECLI:EU:C:2012:172, para. 30.
535. C-209/10 *Post Danmark* ECLI:EU:C:2012:172, para. 38.
536. C-209/10 *Post Danmark* ECLI:EU:C:2012:172, para. 13. *See also* para. 29.
537. *See*, for example, F Bien and M Krah, 'The ruling of the CJEU in Post Danmark: putting an end to selective price cuts as an abuse under Article 102 TFEU and turning towards a more economic approach' (2012) European Competition Law Review 482.
538. C-209/10 *Post Danmark* ECLI:EU:C:2011:342, para. 89. This paragraph also confirms, however, that it is not always necessary to demonstrate the effects of a practice and that some practices are, by their object, abusive.

[3] Exclusivity Agreements

367 What is in a name? That exclusivity agreements are exclusionary appears obvious. Taking the *mens rea* perspective, one could say that in explicit exclusivity agreements, the intention to exclude is incorporated in the agreement itself. It is unclear how it would be possible to demonstrate that a dominant undertaking did not have exclusionary intentions when it concluded an explicit exclusivity agreement.

368 This probably explains why in its early case law, the Court of Justice without hesitation condemned explicit exclusive agreements concluded by dominant undertakings. This is already apparent in the first case in which it assessed the lawfulness of explicit exclusivity clauses in agreements, *Hoffmann-La Roche*.[539] In this case, the Commission had found that Hoffmann-La Roche had abused its dominant position in a number of vitamin markets by including explicit exclusivity clauses, quasi-exclusivity clauses and various types of rebates in agreements with its customers. Much of the attention of the CJEU in the appeal against the Commission decision was focused on clauses that did not explicitly provide for exclusivity, because if exclusivity was explicit, there could be little doubt as to the illegality of the clause. As the CJEU said: 'where exclusivity has been formally accepted the granting or not of a rebate is in the final analysis irrelevant'.[540] Formal exclusivity is by its very nature exclusionary.

369 There are remarkably few judgments of the European Courts that concern explicit exclusivity. One rare example is *Van den Bergh Foods* but that is also a very peculiar case, where the dominant supplier of ice cream products offered retail outlets freezer cabinets to store and display ice cream products on the condition that the cabinets could only be used for the dominant undertaking's products and not for those of competitors.[541]

370 However, that which we call an exclusivity clause is also known by other names. Indeed, rather than explicitly imposing exclusivity, a supplier can also require that a customer purchases all its requirements of a certain product from it. This may not explicitly exclude others but logically it certainly does. A very similar effect to exclusivity can be achieved by quasi-exclusivity, whereby a customer commits to purchase a high percentage (say 90%) of its requirements from the dominant company. It is for this reason that the CJEU in *Hoffmann-La Roche* did not merely condemn explicit exclusivity clauses. It held that '[a]n undertaking which is in a dominant position on a market and ties purchasers – ... – by an obligation or promise on their part to obtain all *or most* of their requirements exclusively from the said undertaking abuses

539. Although the Court was confronted in joined cases C-40 to 48, 50, 54 to 56, 111, 113 and 114/73 *Suiker Unie and Others v Commission* ECLI:EU:C:1975:174, paras 474-489, with exclusivity contracts as well, it considered that these escaped the prohibition of (what is now) Article 102 TFEU since they were concluded between the dominant undertaking and its agents. The CJEU did find some quantity rebates to be disguised loyalty rebates though (*see* further in para. 379 below).
540. C-85/76 *Hoffmann-La Roche v Commission* ECLI:EU:C:1979:36, para. 95. *See also* para. 120.
541. T-65/98 *Van den Bergh Foods v Commission* ECLI:EU:T:2003:281.

its dominant position ... '.[542] The Court considered that such clauses, even if they were not explicitly exclusive, were 'designed to deprive the purchaser of or restrict his possible choices of sources of supply and to deny other producers access to the market'.[543] One could again say that their exclusionary intention is apparent from the clauses themselves, without any need to prove subjective intention separately. But this is a slippery slope. What percentage of total requirements needs to be locked in to equate a clause with exclusivity?[544]

371 And the case law went further. Rather than explicitly (or *de jure*) linking sales volumes to the requirements of a customer, a supplier can also *de facto* achieve this through quantity commitments which happen to be identical or close to the factual requirements of a customer. In those circumstances, the exclusionary effect is not apparent from the clause itself: one needs to know what the actual requirements are of the customer in order to determine this. The exclusionary *intention* of the supplier is therefore less apparent from the clauses themselves: the dominant undertaking could argue that the correlation between the factual requirements of the customer and the quantity commitment is merely accidental. Indeed, in *Tomra*, the dominant supplier of reverse vending machines argued that it was unaware of the actual requirements of its customers and also unable to estimate them, so that it could not be faulted for including quantity commitments in its contracts which happened to coincide with the actual requirements of its customers. The General Court dismissed this argument, thereby implicitly confirming the Commission's condemnation of quantity commitments close to the total requirements of a customer.[545]

372 But the slippery slope remains: it is hard to determine precisely when a lawful quantity commitment becomes an unlawful exclusivity obligation. The problem is exacerbated because often contracts do not merely include a quantity commitment by the customer but also compensation for this commitment from the side of the dominant supplier, mostly in the form of a reduced purchase price (often through discounts or rebates). In this way, the quantity commitment does not merely impose a burden on the customer, but also contains a boon for it (*see* on this further paragraphs 379-390 below).

373 The case law on exclusivity was much criticized (*see* the discussion in paragraph 384 below) and during the 2000s the Commission started doubting whether exclusivity

542. C-85/76 *Hoffmann-La Roche v Commission* ECLI:EU:C:1979:36, para. 89 (emphasis added).
543. C-85/76 *Hoffmann-La Roche v Commission* ECLI:EU:C:1979:36, para. 90.
544. In the Commission Guidelines on vertical restraints [2010] OJ C130/1, para. 129, the Commission states that 'single branding' (whereby a buyer is required to exclusively purchase from one seller) also covers 'an obligation or incentive scheme which makes the buyer purchase more than 80% of its requirements on a particular market from only one supplier'. This interpretation is not a statement of the law, however, and may not be identical with 'exclusivity' under Article 102 TFEU where the CJEU has not established a strict threshold.
545. T-155/06 *Tomra Systems and Others v Commission* ECLI:EU:T:2010:370, in particular paras 68-87. The point was not raised on appeal to the CJEU in case C-549/10 P *Tomra and Others v Commission* ECLI:EU:C:2012:221. The same argument failed in joined cases C-40 to 48, 50, 54 to 56, 111, 113 and 114/73 *Suiker Unie and Others v Commission* ECLI:EU:C:1975:174, para. 520.

obligations (which came to include even simple quantity commitments) should always be considered unlawful. The Commission finally abandoned its per se approach in its 2009 *Guidance Paper on Exclusionary Abuses*. Much of the discussion on exclusivity obligations in this policy document is focused on the level of compensation which the dominant company grants its customer for the exclusivity. As I will discuss in more detail below, the Commission there proposes to look at whether the price at which the dominant undertaking sells the products in question is at any point below its costs because this would prevent an as-efficient-competitor from competing for these sales. The approach to plain exclusivity clauses (so without a rebate or other identifiable compensation) is based on the same principle but then applied to the whole contract: 'If competitors can compete on equal terms for each individual customer's entire demand, exclusive purchasing obligations are generally unlikely to hamper effective competition ... However, if the dominant undertaking is an unavoidable trading partner for all or most customers, even an exclusive purchasing obligation of short duration can lead to anti-competitive foreclosure.'[546]

374 According to some commentators, the CJEU has recently capitulated to the approach of the *Guidance Paper*.[547] Indeed, in *Intel*, which concerned exclusivity rebates, the Grand Chamber of the CJEU stated that the *Hoffmann-La Roche* case law needed to be 'further clarified in the case where the undertaking concerned submits, during the administrative procedure, on the basis of supporting evidence, that its conduct was not capable of restricting competition and, in particular, of producing the alleged foreclosure effects':

> In that case, the Commission is not only required to analyse, first, the extent of the undertaking's dominant position on the relevant market and, secondly, the share of the market covered by the challenged practice, as well as the conditions and arrangements for granting the rebates in question, their duration and their amount; it is also required to assess *the possible existence of a strategy aiming to exclude competitors that are at least as efficient as the dominant undertaking from the market*.[548]

375 Some have viewed this as a victory for the more economic approach to competition law and its focus on the quantitative analysis of business practices (efficiency).[549] I do not think the CJEU seeks to limit competition law to a mere quantitative exercise: it does not state that the Commission needs to assess whether the practice can exclude as-efficient-competitors (which would only require a comparison of price and cost) but whether there is 'a strategy aiming to exclude' as-efficient-competitors. In my reading

546. Commission Guidance on the Commission's enforcement priorities in applying Article 82 of the EC Treaty to abusive exclusionary conduct by dominant undertakings [2009] OJ C45/7, para. 36.
547. *See*, for example, R De Coninck, 'The as-efficient competitor test: some practical considerations following the ECJ Intel judgment' (2018) Competition Law & Policy Debate 73, 73.
548. C-413/14 P *Intel v Commission* ECLI:EU:C:2017:632, paras 138-139 (emphasis added).
549. Freshfields Bruckhaus Deringer, 'Intel in the Court of Justice. A more economic approach to exclusivity rebates' (7 September 2017) <http://knowledge.freshfields.com/h/Global/r/3581/intel_in_the_court_of_justice> accessed 11 September 2018; K Coates, 'The Court of Justice and *Intel*: an overdue ruling that was still over-hasty?' (2018) 32(2) Antitrust 57, 58.

of the judgment, this means that the CJEU clarified the requirements of the *mens rea* evidence which the Commission needs to adduce in cases such as this one: it is not sufficient for the Commission to merely show that the dominant undertaking wanted to defeat its competitors (in a competitive environment this is what any undertaking would want to do): the Commission needs to show that the dominant undertaking also intended to do so by unlawful means (which are here defined as pricing below cost).

376 Be that as it may, I do think that the Commission's approach to exclusivity obligations in the *Guidance Paper on Exclusionary Abuses* is problematic. This is already apparent from the assumption the Commission starts from in paragraph 36 of its *Guidance Paper*, namely that dominant undertakings are usually not unavoidable trading partners for all or most of their customers. There may well be situations where dominant undertakings are not unavoidable trading partners, but I would submit that in most cases they are. In *British Airways*, the CJEU similarly pointed out that '[b]y reason of its significantly higher market share, the undertaking in a dominant position generally constitutes an unavoidable business partner in the market'.[550] In many cases, including in *Hoffmann-La Roche* and *Intel*, the Commission and the European Court have found dominant undertakings practising exclusive dealing to be unavoidable trading partners.[551]

377 In addition, and more relevant to current purposes, I do not think the approach gives enough credence to the *mens rea* of the dominant undertaking in case of *explicit* exclusivity obligations. Indeed, the most obvious motive for a dominant undertaking to include an exclusivity provision in its contracts is an exclusionary intent. Such a provision has the explicit objective of preventing the customer from buying from competitors, thereby excluding those customers from the part of the market that can be serviced by competitors.

378 To be clear: I do not exclude that the dominant undertaking's exclusionary intent may be objectively justified in certain circumstances. For example, there may be a hold-up problem whereby a dominant undertaking is only willing to make relationship-specific investment for a customer if it can avoid freeriding on these investments by competitors.[552] However, sometimes non-relationship-specific investments are also invoked as justification for an exclusivity clause,[553] but I believe this can only justify quantity commitments (so not explicit exclusivity).

550. C-95/04 P *British Airways v Commission* ECLI:EU:C:2007:166, para. 75.
551. *See* C-85/76 *Hoffmann-La Roche v Commission* ECLI:EU:C:1979:36, para. 41 and T-286/09 *Intel v Commission* ECLI:EU:T:2014:547, para. 91. *See also*, for example, joined cases C-40 to 48, 50, 54 to 56, 111, 113 and 114/73 *Suiker Unie and Others v Commission* ECLI:EU:C:1975:174, para. 505 and C-322/81 *Nederlandsche Banden-Industrie Michelin* ECLI:EU:C:1983:313, paras 55-56.
552. Commission Guidance on the Commission's enforcement priorities in applying Article 82 of the EC Treaty to abusive exclusionary conduct by dominant undertakings [2009] OJ C45/7, para. 46. *See also* J Gual, M Hellwig *et al.* 'An economic approach to Article 82' (Report by the Economic Advisory Group on Competition Policy) (July 2005) <http://ec.europa.eu/dgs/competition/economist/eagcp_july_21_05.pdf> accessed 5 March 2018, 48. *Van den Bergh Foods* may be an example in this category although neither the Commission nor the CFI accepted this.
553. For example, when the supplier invests in its own factory.

[4] Pricing Practices Conditional on Exclusivity

379 Most of the cases in which exclusivity is discussed do not concern plain exclusivity clauses, but rather rebates linked to exclusivity or to certain quantity commitments. In fact, even before it pronounced itself in *Hoffmann-La Roche* on the lawfulness of plain exclusivity clauses, the CJEU had already taken issue with loyalty rebates in *Suiker Unie*. In that case, one of the sugar producers, Südzucker, had included in its bills of lading and sales contracts the sentence 'If you cover your annual requirements exclusively from the factories of our members, you will be granted at the end of the marketing year (30 June) an annual quantity discount on the contract price of DM 0-30 per 100 kg.'[554] Despite the explicit wording, Südzucker argued before the CJEU that this was merely a quantity rebate. The CJEU disagreed and considered that it had 'rightly been classified by the Commission as a "loyalty" rebate designed, through the grant of a financial advantage, to prevent customers obtaining their supplies from competing producers'.[555] As we have seen, the CJEU also stated in *Hoffmann-La Roche* that if the rebate is explicitly linked to exclusivity, it is in any event problematic.[556]

380 The European Courts have adopted the same position for other payments than rebates which are explicitly linked to exclusivity. In *British Plasterboard*, for example, the plasterboard producer granted (secret) payments to some of its dealers for advertising and promotional expenses. The CFI agreed with the Commission that internal documents of British Plasterboard and letters exchanged with the dealers showed that the payments were conditional on the dealer purchasing exclusively from British Plasterboard. The CFI concluded that the said payments 'are strictly conditional upon exclusive loyalty to [British Plasterboard] and are therefore abusive'.[557] The fact that British Plasterboard also pursued other objectives (such as promoting plaster products in general) was not relevant, according to the Court. For price arrangements which are explicitly linked to exclusivity, the principle should be simple enough: like in the case of explicit exclusivity agreements, explicit fidelity rebates reveal an intention to exclude, and they are therefore unlawful.

381 More complicated are situations where rebates (or other payments) are not explicitly linked to exclusivity. The CJEU held in *Hoffmann-La Roche* and *Michelin I* that, even if rebates were not explicitly linked to exclusivity, they could still *de iure* or *de facto* achieve the same loyalty-enhancing effect. In *Hoffmann-La Roche*, after saying that (quasi-)exclusivity obligations constitute an abuse of dominance (*see* paragraph 370 above), the CJEU continued: 'The same applies if the said undertaking, without tying the purchasers by a formal obligation, applies, either under the terms of agreements concluded with these purchasers or unilaterally, a system of fidelity rebates, that is to say discounts conditional on the customer's obtaining all or most of

554. Commission decision of 2 January 1972 in case 26.918 *European Sugar Industry* at [1973] OJ L140/29.
555. Joined cases C-40 to 48, 50, 54 to 56, 111, 113 and 114/73 *Suiker Unie and Others v Commission* ECLI:EU:C:1975:174, para. 518.
556. C-85/76 *Hoffmann-La Roche v Commission* ECLI:EU:C:1979:36, para. 95.
557. T-65/89 *BPB Industries and British Gypsum v Commission* ECLI:EU:T:1993:31, para. 71.

its requirements – whether the quantity of its purchases be large or small – from the undertaking in a dominant position.'[558] According to the Court, the quantity rebates were in fact fidelity rebates. This was demonstrated by the fact that they were not applicable in the same way to all possible purchasers but different for each customer.[559] This was evidenced by the fact that they were determined not by reference to absolute quantities but according to the requirements (or a proportion of the requirements) of the purchaser.[560] The Commission reiterates in its *Guidance Paper on Exclusionary Abuses* that individualized rebates linked to the requirements of individual customers are more likely to be problematic than standardized rebates based on absolute quantities.[561]

382 In *Michelin I*, the CJEU was confronted with a rebate scheme that did not explicitly make reference to the requirements of the customers but was nevertheless based on individualized targets which were determined according to the distributor's turnover of the dominant supplier's product in the previous year. The CJEU considered that this was problematic for a number of reasons, including because 'one last order, even a small one, affected the dealer's margin of profit on the whole year's sales of Michelin heavy-vehicle tyres'.[562] This provided the basis for a second criterion to distinguish lawful from unlawful rebates, namely whether the rebate was incremental or retroactive, i.e. whether it applies only to purchases in excess of the target or to all purchases so also those which preceded the achieving of the target (but obviously only on the condition that the target was met). In *Michelin I*, the CJEU pointed out that in the case of retroactive rebates, the dealers faced 'considerable pressure, especially towards the end of a year, to attain Michelin NV's sales targets if they did not wish to run the risk of losses' and the rebates in that case were therefore problematic.[563] In its *Guidance Paper on Exclusionary Abuses*, the Commission continues to point out that '[i]n general terms, retroactive rebates may foreclose the market significantly'.[564]

383 The criteria to distinguish lawful from unlawful rebates became increasingly complex. The apex of this evolution was the CFI judgment in *Michelin II*. This case concerned a rebate scheme used by Michelin in France almost two decades after the Commission had taken issue with its target rebates in the Netherlands in *Michelin I*. The behaviour which the Commission found to be abusive had many aspects but the one that interests us here was a standardized quantity rebate which contained

558. C-85/76 *Hoffmann-La Roche v Commission* ECLI:EU:C:1979:36, para. 89.
559. C-85/76 *Hoffmann-La Roche v Commission* ECLI:EU:C:1979:36, para. 100.
560. C-85/76 *Hoffmann-La Roche v Commission* ECLI:EU:C:1979:36, para. 95. *See also* C-95/04 P *British Airways v Commission* ECLI:EU:C:2007:166, para. 71.
561. Commission Guidance on the Commission's enforcement priorities in applying Article 82 of the EC Treaty to abusive exclusionary conduct by dominant undertakings [2009] OJ C45/7, para. 45.
562. C-322/81 *Nederlandsche Banden-Industrie Michelin* ECLI:EU:C:1983:313, paras 83 and 81.
563. C-322/81 *Nederlandsche Banden-Industrie Michelin* ECLI:EU:C:1983:313, paras 84. *See also* C-95/04 P *British Airways v Commission* ECLI:EU:C:2007:166, para. 73.
564. Commission Guidance on the Commission's enforcement priorities in applying Article 82 of the EC Treaty to abusive exclusionary conduct by dominant undertakings [2009] OJ C45/7, para. 40.

gradually increasing discounts depending on the quantities purchased by a dealer. Although the CFI referred to the position in the earlier case law that quantity rebates generally do not have a foreclosure effect, it nevertheless considered that in the instant case the rebate was abusive. Its reasoning seems to be based on the fact that the rebate was retroactive over a period of one year and that there was a significant variation between the level of the discount for small and large purchases.[565] Despite Michelin's arguments that quantity rebates are viewed as reflective of cost savings, the CFI considered that Michelin had to substantiate in the instant case what economies of scale they reflected - and had failed to do so.[566]

384 *Michelin II* was much criticized in the literature,[567] not only for its apparent condemnation of quantity rebate schemes but also for what some viewed as the enshrining of the formalistic approach to abuses (i.e. without consideration for the effects of conduct).[568] Together with the CFI judgment in *British Airways* a few months later,[569] this approach created a significant backlash and caused the Commission to rethink its approach to rebates in the context of the broader revision of exclusionary abuses. This led to the mostly quantitative approach to rebates in the 2009 *Guidance Paper on Exclusionary Abuses*.

385 Indeed, while the Commission in this guidance refers to qualitative elements as well, like for all price-based exclusionary conduct, the Commission states that it 'will examine economic data relating to cost and sales prices, and in particular whether the dominant undertaking is engaging in below-cost pricing'.[570] Along these lines, rebates are analysed as a special form of predatory pricing where 'the Commission will estimate what price a competitor would have to offer in order to compensate the customer for the loss of the conditional rebate if the latter would switch part of its

565. *See* in particular T-203/01 *Michelin v Commission* ECLI:EU:T:2003:250, para. 95.
566. *See* in particular T-203/01 *Michelin v Commission* ECLI:EU:T:2003:250, paras 107-109.
567. *See*, for example, J Kallaugher and B Sher, 'Rebates revisited: anticompetitive effects and exclusionary abuse under Article 82' (2004) European Competition Law Review 263; D Waelbroeck, '*Michelin II*: a per se rule against rebates by dominant companies?' (2005) Journal of Competition Law & Economics 149; C Ahlborn and D Bailey, 'Discounts, rebates and selective pricing by dominant firms: a trans-Atlantic comparison' (2006) European Competition Journal 101.
568. Mainly due to the statement in T-203/01 *Michelin v Commission* ECLI:EU:T:2003:250, para. 239 that it is not necessary to establish 'the actual effect of the abusive conduct complained of. For the purposes of establishing an infringement of Article 82 EC, it is sufficient to show that the abusive conduct of the undertaking in a dominant position tends to restrict competition or, in other words, that the conduct is capable of having that effect'. *See also* T-219/99 *British Airways v Commission* ECLI:EU:T:2003:343, para. 293.
569. T-219/99 *British Airways v Commission* ECLI:EU:T:2003:343. On appeal, the CJEU dismissed most arguments from British Airways as to the lack of the CFI's analysis of the effects of the rebates as inadmissible: *see* C-95/04 P *British Airways v Commission* ECLI:EU:C:2007:166, in particular paras 78, 89 and 115. No appeal was brought against the *Michelin II* judgment of the CFI.
570. Commission Guidance on the Commission's enforcement priorities in applying Article 82 of the EC Treaty to abusive exclusionary conduct by dominant undertakings [2009] OJ C45/7, para. 25.

demand ("the relevant range") away from the dominant undertaking'.[571] The relevant range depends on the purchase volume on which the rebate is conditional and which the customer is willing or able to switch to a competitor.

386 Up to very recently, the CJEU seemed to have been hesitant to follow the Commission's approach. In *Tomra*, for example, the dominant undertaking argued that the General Court had failed to properly assess whether it had been pricing below cost but the CJEU rejected this argument: 'the invoicing of "negative prices", in other words prices below cost prices, to customers is not a prerequisite of a finding that a retroactive rebate scheme operated by a dominant undertaking is abusive'.[572] Similarly in *Post Danmark II*, although the CJEU recognized the importance of the as-efficient-competitor test in predatory pricing and selective rebates, it considered that 'it is not possible to infer from Article 82 EC or the case law of the Court that there is a legal obligation requiring a finding to the effect that a rebate scheme operated by a dominant undertaking is abusive to be based always on the as-efficient competitor test'.[573] According to the Court, in markets in which a dominant undertaking has a very large market share and where barriers to entry are high, also less efficient competitors are important sources of competition.[574] As indicated above, some have viewed *Intel* as the final capitulation of the CJEU to the approach in the *Guidance Paper on Exclusionary Abuses*. However, although the CJEU indeed underlines the importance of the as-efficient-competitor test there, it does not consider this to be the final word on the lawfulness of rebates.

387 What is then the role of *mens rea* in assessing rebates which are not explicitly linked to exclusivity? There are two aspects to be considered here: (i) are certain rebates sometimes viewed as evidence of an objective intention to exclude; and (ii) can evidence of an intention to exclude play a role in interpreting rebates? The issues here are similar to those that are raised in price discrimination cases but the most explicit response to both questions can be found in *Irish Sugar*.

388 Indeed, in that case, both the Commission and the CFI postulated an anticompetitive intention by the eponymous dominant company because it used certain rebates. The Commission held that '[t]he granting of discounts by a company in a dominant position, which are conditional on a company meeting particular targets that are higher than previous purchase amounts is an infringement of Article 86, because the practice is clearly aimed at tying customers closely to the dominant company and making it difficult for competitors to gain a foothold in the market'.[575] The CFI agreed and held that 'such a practice can only be intended to tie the customers to which it is granted and place competitors in an unfavourable competition position'.[576]

---

571. Commission Guidance on the Commission's enforcement priorities in applying Article 82 of the EC Treaty to abusive exclusionary conduct by dominant undertakings [2009] OJ C45/7, para. 41.
572. C-549/10 P *Tomra and Others v Commission* ECLI:EU:C:2012:221, para. 73.
573. C-23/14 *Post Danmark* ECLI:EU:C:2015:651, para. 57.
574. C-23/14 *Post Danmark* ECLI:EU:C:2015:651, paras 59-61.
575. Commission decision of 14 May 1997 in case 34.621 and 35.059 *Irish Sugar*, recital 152.
576. T-228/97 *Irish Sugar v Commission* ECLI:EU:T:1999:246, para. 213.

389 The positing of such an objective intention is based on the idea that a commercial operator like any rational person can be expected to intend the normal consequences of its actions. Hence, if rebates have an exclusionary effect, one can assume that this is what the undertaking using them intended. However, this is based on the assumption that the rebates actually had an exclusionary effect – which is often what is disputed. In those circumstances, the postulation of an exclusionary intention may amount to a *procès d'intention* aimed at cementing what is otherwise not waterproof. Through this fallacy, the Commission and the European Courts may then mask the lack of evidence of exclusionary effect. This is of course a very serious concern which I will discuss in more detail in paragraphs 656ff. below.

390 What about the other situation, i.e. where the Commission or the CJEU have relied on other evidence of intentions than the rebates themselves and have used this evidence to interpret the rebate? As pointed out, *Irish Sugar* also provides an example of this in that the Commission had found evidence of discussions between Irish Sugar and ADM, one of its wholesalers, which had started distributing sugar from a competitor. Irish Sugar had told ADM that it would 'bonus back' the sugar, i.e. give ADM a bonus which was dependent on it not selling sugar from other manufacturers. The Commission concluded from this that the advantageous price which ADM got 'was evidently not a normal quantity discount and represented a target or fidelity rebate that had the effect of tying a customer to the dominant supplier'.[577] The CFI agreed and also pointed to the fact that the rebate was granted 'in the context of a strategy devised ... to prevent the expansion of the [competing] Eurolux brand on the Irish retail market'. It added that the effect of the practice was also clear, namely that of 'recovering a customer which was inclined to switch to the competition'.[578] In those circumstances, the fallacy discussed in paragraph 389 above does not arise since the exclusionary intention is deduced from other circumstances than the conduct which is interpreted in light of that intention. Once again, this point will be discussed in more detail in paragraphs 656ff.

[5] Tying

391 I will now turn to multimarket abuses. A first form of multimarket abuse is tying (or bundling): this arises when a product or service is only made available to a customer if the latter also purchases another product or service. This can be done either through technical means or by contract. The idea is that a dominant undertaking can in this way leverage its dominant position in one market (where it may be an unavoidable trading partner) to another market (either to earn supra-competitive margins or to effectively become an unavoidable trading partner there as well).

392 A dominant undertaking can also leverage its market position in a softer way through so-called mixed bundling, i.e. where it offers the two products or services

577. Commission decision of 14 May 1997 in case 34.621 and 35.059 *Irish Sugar*, recital 127.
578. T-228/97 *Irish Sugar v Commission* ECLI:EU:T:1999:246, para. 198.

separately but grants additional discounts if they are purchased together. It is in fact in this form of bundled discounts that the CJEU was first confronted with tying in *Hoffmann-La Roche* (although its analysis of this abuse was very limited).[579]

393 Tying will not always be a profitable strategy for a dominant undertaking. Indeed, the single-monopoly-profit theory explains that a monopolist has no interest in tying complementary products to the product in which it is dominant: any supra-competitive margin which it could earn on the bundle, it could also earn in the monopolized market alone because any additional margin would effectively reduce demand for the monopolized product below the profit-maximizing level.[580] However, tying may be a profitable strategy for a dominant undertaking in some circumstances, in particular if it is not a monopolist but faces some residual amount of competition in the market in which it is dominant.[581] Under European antitrust law, tying can indeed be an abuse of dominance if it protects a dominant undertaking's position in the market in which it is dominant or strengthens its position in a neighbouring market in which it is not dominant.[582]

394 Often the main issue in tying cases is whether the tying and the tied product are actually in two separate product markets or whether they, to use the wording of Article 102(d) TFEU, 'by their nature or according to commercial usage' belong together. This was also one of the main issues in the first proper tying decision the Commission adopted in 1988 when it found that nail gun maker Hilti had abused its dominant position by tying the sales of its explosive cartridges (for which there were few independent suppliers) to the sale of its nails. The Commission devoted three of the twenty-five pages of the decision to explaining why nail guns, cartridge strips and nails should be viewed as three separate markets and not as 'one integral system' as Hilti argued.[583] This issue was also the subject of Hilti's first plea in its application for annulment before the CFI[584] and all of its seven pleas before the CJEU.[585] *Mens rea* considerations played no significant role in this assessment.

395 The abusive nature of tying was subject to a much briefer assessment by the Commission. It simply noted that '[m]aking the sale of patented cartridge strips conditional upon taking a corresponding complement of nails constitutes an abuse of

579. C-85/76 *Hoffmann-La Roche v Commission* ECLI:EU:C:1979:36, para. 111.
580. *See* R Bork, *The antitrust paradox. A policy at war with itself* (Basic Books 1978), 372-373. *See also* E Elhauge, 'Tying, bundled discounts, and the death of the single monopoly profit theory' (2009) Harvard Law Review 397, 403-404; S Bishop and M Walker, *The economics of EC competition law* (Sweet & Maxwell 2010) 282.
581. SA Sullivan, 'Post-Chicago economics: economists, lawyers, judges, and enforcement officials in a less determinate theoretical world' (1995) 63 Antitrust Law Journal 669, 672; E Elhauge, 'Tying, bundled discounts, and the death of the single monopoly profit theory' (2009) Harvard Law Review 397, 417-9.
582. For the former, *see* Commission decision of 22 December 1987 in cases 30.787 and 31.488 *Eurofix-Bauco v Hilti*, recital 74; for the latter, *see* C-333/94 P *Tetra Pak v Commission* ECLI:EU:C:1996:436, paras 25-31.
583. Commission decision of 22 December 1987 in cases 30.787 and 31.488 *Eurofix-Bauco v Hilti*, recitals 55-65.
584. T-30/89 *Hilti v Commission* ECLI:EU:T:1991:70, paras 48-78.
585. C-53/92 P *Hilti v Commission* ECLI:EU:C:1994:77.

a dominant position'.[586] The Commission devoted more attention to the bundled discounts used by Hilti, i.e. that it systematically offered lower discounts on cartridge only purchases, as compared to those which comprised both cartridges and nails. In this context, the Commission relied on several internal documents which clarified that this was a policy pursued by Hilti.[587] It considered furthermore that, although 'aggressive pricing rivalry is an essential competitive instrument', 'a selectively discriminatory pricing policy by a dominant firm designed purely to damage the business of, or deter market entry by, its competitors, whilst maintaining higher prices for the bulk of its other customers' is abusive – regardless of whether pricing was below cost.[588] Albeit with scant reasoning,[589] the CFI upheld this finding.[590]

396 Also interesting in *Hilti* is that Hilti argued that its tying practices (and the supporting practices) were merely 'motivated by a desire to ensure the safe and reliable operation of its products, and not by any commercial advantage it may have derived from such action'.[591] This argument was rejected on the facts by the Commission which pointed out that Hilti never complained to the relevant authorities nor to the manufacturers concerned about the risks posed by nails produced by competitors.[592] The Commission also pointed to an internal document of Hilti which 'recognized the weakness of its arguments relating to safety and considered that any justification for non-supply of cartridges without nails based on safety reasons would inevitably not be accepted by the Commission or the Court of Justice even if temporary protection could be afforded by such arguments'.[593] The CFI fully endorsed the Commission's views.[594]

397 Also in *Tetra Pak II*, the legal issues as regards the abuse of tying mostly concerned the question of market definition and what the commercial usage was concerning tied sales. Tetra Pak argued that its packing systems were 'complete and indivisible

586. Commission decision of 22 December 1987 in cases 30.787 and 31.488 *Eurofix-Bauco v Hilti*, recital 75.
587. Commission decision of 22 December 1987 in cases 30.787 and 31.488 *Eurofix-Bauco v Hilti*, recitals 33-34.
588. Commission decision of 22 December 1987 in cases 30.787 and 31.488 *Eurofix-Bauco v Hilti*, recital 81.
589. As also remarked by M de la Mano, R Nazzini and H Zenger, 'Article 102' in J Faull & A Nikpay (eds), *The EU law of competition* (OUP 2014) 329, 403.
590. T-30/89 *Hilti v Commission* ECLI:EU:T:1991:70, para. 100. The issue was not discussed on appeal, where the CJEU upheld the judgment of the CFI: *see* C-53/92 P *Hilti v Commission* ECLI:EU:C:1994:77.
591. Commission decision of 22 December 1987 in cases 30.787 and 31.488 *Eurofix-Bauco v Hilti*, para. 88.
592. Commission decision of 22 December 1987 in cases 30.787 and 31.488 *Eurofix-Bauco v Hilti*, para. 89.
593. Commission decision of 22 December 1987 in cases 30.787 and 31.488 *Eurofix-Bauco v Hilti*, recital 96. The Commission also pointed out in recital 89.4 that Hilti did not seek the most efficient way of informing its customers of the alleged risks: 'it was its express policy only to warn verbally and never put in writing its criticism of the complainants products'. This could also be indicative of concealment efforts (*see* §4.04 below).
594. T-30/89 *Hilti v Commission* ECLI:EU:T:1991:70, paras 102-119. The issue was not discussed on appeal, where the CJEU upheld the judgment of the CFI: *see* C-53/92 P *Hilti v Commission* ECLI:EU:C:1994:77.

systems, comprising the machine, the packing material, training and after-sale service'[595] and that 'the resulting system of tied sales was objectively justified in the light of commercial usage and the very "nature" of the products in question'.[596] The CFI disagreed, referring to its discussion of the market definition. Two of the three pleas of Tetra Pak about the tying abuse before the CJEU similarly concerned the market definition and the commercial usage of tying and similarly failed.[597] It also tried to turn the tables on the Commission by arguing that, if the markets were separate, the case law had not previously found conduct on one market to constitute an abuse of a dominant position on another market, but this similarly failed.[598]

398 In *Microsoft I* as well, the question of whether the two products in question (PC operating systems and media players) were distinct played an important role.[599] Microsoft even argued before the Commission that it had been bundling these products for a longer time in an (fruitless) effort to demonstrate that they were one single product.[600] However, the Commission also proceeded to a more detailed analysis of the foreclosure effect of the tying practice, something which 'in classic tying cases' it believed was not necessary.[601] In a related heading (although it classifies this under the possible justifications for the tying), the Commission analysed the alleged absence of incentives for Microsoft to foreclose. Such an analysis of incentives could be viewed as an analysis of objective intention.

399 In this case, no dawn raids were conducted, so there was fewer evidence from internal company documents. Nevertheless, some internal evidence was used to discredit certain arguments made by Microsoft about what was technically feasible[602] and, even more interestingly for our purposes, what it was trying to achieve when combining the operating system and the media player. The General Court referred to such a document which was not mentioned in the Commission decision but apparently brought forward by the Commission during the proceedings before the General Court:

> Microsoft's argument that the integration of Windows Media Player in the Windows operating system was dictated by technical reasons is scarcely credible in the light of the content of certain of its own internal communication. Thus it follows from Mr Bay's email of 3 January 1999 (...) that the integration of Windows Media Player in Windows was primarily designed to make Windows Media Player more competitive with RealPlayer by presenting it as a constituent part of Windows and not as application software that might be compared with RealPlayer.[603]

595. T-83/91 *Tetra Pak v Commission* ECLI:EU:T:1994:246, para. 125.
596. T-83/91 *Tetra Pak v Commission* ECLI:EU:T:1994:246, para. 136.
597. C-333/94 P *Tetra Pak v Commission* ECLI:EU:C:1996:436, paras 7-20 and 34-38.
598. C-333/94 P *Tetra Pak v Commission* ECLI:EU:C:1996:436, paras 21-33.
599. Commission decision of 21 April 2004 in case 37.792 *Microsoft*, recitals 800-825; T-201/04 *Microsoft v Commission* ECLI:EU:T:2007:289, paras 872-944.
600. Commission decision of 21 April 2004 in case 37.792 *Microsoft*, recital 814. *See also* T-201/04 *Microsoft v Commission* ECLI:EU:T:2007:289, para. 886.
601. Commission decision of 21 April 2004 in case 37.792 *Microsoft*, recital 841.
602. *See* T-201/04 *Microsoft v Commission* ECLI:EU:T:2007:289, para. 1136.
603. T-201/04 *Microsoft v Commission* ECLI:EU:T:2007:289, para. 937.

400 In tying cases, *mens rea* therefore plays a limited role in establishing the abuse but it can be more relevant in a negative way (as in *Hilti* and *Microsoft I*), namely when the absence of any procompetitive (or competitively neutral) intentions justifying the tying of different products points to an anticompetitive objective.[604] *Mens rea* then has a role akin to that under Article 101(3) TFEU (*see* paragraphs 287-291 above).

[6] Refusal to Supply

401 Evidence of *mens rea* has also played a limited role in refusal to supply cases.[605] Most of the case law is in fact concerned with the legal question of whether a refusal to supply can be illegal at all, in particular where – as in most of these cases – intellectual property protection or another legal monopoly has been conferred on the dominant undertaking. The question then is whether and in which circumstances the antitrust rules take precedence over the rules granting the monopoly or vice versa.

402 In its decision in *Zoja/CSC-ICI*, the Commission did mention the different circumstances that seemed to have led dominant undertaking Commercial Solvents to refuse to supply Zoja any longer with aminobutanol, the raw material required to produce the latter's pharmaceutical product ethambutol. These included the failed merger talks with Zoja[606] and the subsequent decision of Commercial Solvents to have its subsidiary ICI make ethambutol itself.[607] It therefore appeared obvious that Commercial Solvents intended to avoid that Zoja could procure aminobutanol and to eliminate it from the market of ethambutol.[608] The CJEU rejected Commercial Solvents argument that Zoja could procure aminobutanol from other sources and ruled that 'an undertaking which has a dominant position in the market in raw materials and which, with the object of reserving such raw material for manufacturing its own derivatives, refuses to supply a customer, which is itself a manufacturer of these derivatives, and therefore risks eliminating all competition on the part of this customer, is abusing its dominant position'.[609] The intention of Commercial Solvents to leverage its position in aminobutanol appeared obvious from the facts.

403 In *Télémarketing*, the intentions of the dominant company were put in opposition to the existence of an objective necessity to refuse the supply. In that case, RTL, the

604. Presumably the reverse is also true: documentary evidence of procompetitive (or competitively neutral) intentions points to the absence of an anticompetitive objective, although I am not aware of this being discussed in the case law (which may be because such cases would never reach the stage of a prohibition decision).
605. The discussion below concerns pure refusal to supply cases, not instances where the refusal to supply is a retaliatory measure by the dominant undertaking for non-compliance with other abusive contractual conditions (e.g. exclusivity or tying). *See* Commission Guidance on the Commission's enforcement priorities in applying Article 82 of the EC Treaty to abusive exclusionary conduct by dominant undertakings [2009] OJ C45/7, para. 77.
606. Commission decision of 14 December 1972 in case 26.911 *Zoja/CSC-ICI*, at [1972] OJ L299/53.
607. Commission decision of 14 December 1972 in case 26.911 *Zoja/CSC-ICI*, at [1972] OJ L299/52.
608. Commission decision of 14 December 1972 in case 26.911 *Zoja/CSC-ICI*, at [1972] OJ L299/54.
609. Joined cases C-6 and 7/73 *Commercial Solvents v Commission* ECLI:EU:C:1974:18, para. 25.

only commercial television station in French-speaking Belgium, refused to sell Télémarketing television time for the latter's telesales programmes (at least using a telephone number other than the one of a subsidiary of RTL). The CJEU held that '[i]f ... that refusal is not justified by technical or commercial requirements relating to the nature of the television, but is intended to reserve to the [dominant undertaking] any telemarketing operation broadcast by the said station, with the possibility of eliminating all competition from another undertaking, such conduct amounts to an abuse'.[610]

404 Shortly after this, the CJEU was confronted with a preliminary reference which seemed to strike at the heart of IP protection. The London High Court in fact wanted to know whether Volvo could be required under competition law to grant licences to the manufacturers of spare parts. The CJEU ruled that to do so would result in Volvo, as owner of the design rights to these parts, 'being deprived of the substance of his exclusive rights, and that a refusal to grant such a licence cannot in itself constitute an abuse of a dominant position'.[611] The CJEU at the same time made it clear that certain other actions, such as arbitrarily refusing to supply spare parts, could amount to an abuse. The issue then became where to strike the balance between the legal monopoly conferred by IP rights and the competition rules. Intentions could play no significant role in this since it was fairly obvious that the holder of the IP right was trying to exploit this right to the fullest – as was his right. The question merely was: how extensive was his right?

405 In *Magill*, the European Courts ruled to limit the rights of the copyright holders in that case, possibly also because of the somewhat unusual circumstances in which copyright was granted by national law. English and Irish law granted English and Irish television stations copyright over the programme listings and therefore a right to prohibit others from reproducing these. As a result, Magill could not publish a weekly TV guide containing all programmes shown on English and Irish stations. The CFI held that the television stations' refusal to allow Magill to publish the weekly listings was 'arbitrary in so far as it was not justified either by the specific needs of the broadcasting sector ... or by those peculiar to the activity of publishing television magazines'.[612] The CJEU confirmed the ruling of the CFI, finding that there were three exceptional circumstances which in this case meant that the exercise of the exclusive rights of the televisions stations involved abusive conduct: (i) the fact that Magill wanted to market a product which did not exist yet, (ii) the absence of justification for the refusal per the quote of the CFI above and (iii) the fact that the television stations 'reserved to themselves the secondary market of weekly television guides by excluding all competition on that market'.[613]

406 In *Oscar Bronner*, the refusal to supply did not concern a legal monopoly (based on IP or otherwise) but merely the daily home-delivery distribution network of newspapers developed by Mediaprint in Austria. In its preliminary ruling, the CJEU

610. C-311/84 *CBEM/CLT and IPB* ECLI:EU:C:1985:394, para. 26.
611. C-238/87 *Volvo v Veng* ECLI:EU:C:1988:477, para. 8.
612. T-69/89 *RTE v Commission* ECLI:EU:T:1991:39, para. 73.
613. Joined cases C-241 and 242/91 P *RTE and ITP v Commission* ECLI:EU:C:1995:98, para. 56.

held that access to that distribution network was not indispensable for Oscar Bronner to distribute its own newspaper and that it was not impossible for it to develop its own home-delivery network, if necessary in cooperation with other publishers.[614]

407 In its preliminary ruling in *IMS Health*, the CJEU largely accepted the premise of the referring court that the use of the eponymous undertaking's brick structure (protected by an IP right under national law) was indispensable to allow a competitor to enter the market in question. It held that refusal to allow competitors to use that brick structure could be abusive 'only where the undertaking which requested the licence does not intend to limit itself essentially to duplicating the goods or services already offered on the secondary market by the owner of the intellectual property right, but intends to produce new goods or services not offered by the owner of the right and for which there is potential consumer demand'.[615]

408 In *Microsoft I*, finally, when analysing Microsoft's refusal to supply interoperability information to Sun, the Commission briefly referred as an 'additional circumstance to consider' to a broader strategy of Microsoft.[616] But the bulk of the Commission's analysis concerned the incentives for Microsoft's refusal to supply, including from the perspective of the single-monopoly-profit theory discussed in paragraph 393 above.[617] In this context, the Commission made use of internal documents of Microsoft to explain the latter's incentives to pursue a leveraging strategy and to rebut the application of the single-monopoly-profit theory in the instant case.[618] In its judgment on the application for annulment of the Commission decision, the CFI was mostly occupied with an analysis of the (slightly amended) criteria from the case law on whether a refusal to supply constitutes an abuse of dominance.[619]

409 In conclusion, *mens rea* evidence has played a very limited role in refusal to supply cases.

[7] Margin Squeeze

410 Margin squeeze is often viewed as a constructive refusal to supply:[620] rather than simply refusing supplies, the dominant undertaking offers its products or services at a price which is too high to allow the customer to compete with the dominant undertaking on downstream markets. However, the CJEU has held that the conditions to establish a margin squeeze are not identical to those required for a refusal to

614. C-7/97 *Bronner* ECLI:EU:C:1998:569, in particular paras 43-44.
615. C-418/01 *IMS Health* ECLI:EU:C:2004:257, para. 49.
616. Commission decision of 21 April 2004 in case 37.792 *Microsoft*, recitals 573-577.
617. *See* in particular the Commission decision of 21 April 2004 in case 37.792 *Microsoft*, recitals 765ff.
618. *See*, in particular the Commission decision of 21 April 2004 in case 37.792 *Microsoft*, recitals 771-778.
619. T-201/04 *Microsoft v Commission* ECLI:EU:T:2007:289, paras 291-712.
620. Commission Guidance on the Commission's enforcement priorities in applying Article 82 of the EC Treaty to abusive exclusionary conduct by dominant undertakings [2009] OJ C45/7, paras 79-80.

supply,[621] possibly reflecting a slightly stricter approach to margin squeezes because these are most common in regulated industries such as telecoms, where natural and legal monopolies present additional hurdles to competition.

411 The earlier cases of margin squeezes did not concern telecoms though. One of the first cases in which the Commission identified this abuse – although without terming it 'margin squeeze' – was *Napier Brown*, in the sugar sector. The Commission found in its decision that British Sugar had cut its prices for retail sugar to such a level that its wholesale sugar price to Napier Brown left 'an insufficient margin for a packager and seller of retail sugar, as efficient as [British Sugar] itself in its packaging and selling operations, to survive in the long term'.[622] But the Commission's analysis was not merely based on a comparison of the wholesale and retail prices of British Sugar and the costs it ran to transform wholesale sugar into retail sugar and to sell it. The Commission started its decision by pointing to attempts by British Sugar to convince retail outlets to delist Napier Brown products: this demonstrated, according to the Commission, the 'underlying strategy' of British Sugar.[623] The Commission also established other abuses, such as a refusal to supply and the use of loyalty bonuses. The Commission's decision that the margin squeeze was abusive was therefore also 'taken in the context of the other abuses as outlined above, and of the fact that the intention or natural and foreseeable consequence of the maintenance of this pricing policy [i.e. the margin squeeze] by [British Sugar] would be the removal of [Napier Brown] from the British retail sugar market'.[624]

412 As already explained in paragraph 361 above, in *Irish Sugar*, the Commission and the CFI analysed several forms of price discrimination. One of these seemed to be akin to a margin squeeze in that Irish Sugar offered higher prices to customers which repackaged its industrial sugar for sale as retail sugar (in competition with Irish Sugar). To demonstrate this practice, the CFI attached particular importance to 'documents of the applicant indicating its change of attitude towards two of its customers, Gem Pack and Burcom, before and after they marketed their own brand of sugar on the retail market'.[625]

413 In subsequent cases, the analysis of the abuse is very much focused on the price cost and margin benchmark. This is already the case in *Industrie des Poudres-Sphériques*, where the CFI rejected a complaint about an alleged margin squeeze on the facts[626] and this focus continued in the telecom cases in the 2000s. In *Deutsche Telekom*, there was not much discussion on the pricing level as such (wholesale prices were higher than retail prices, so the margin was inevitably negative) but rather on whether the eponymous dominant telecom supplier had any liberty over its pricing,

621. C-52/09 *Konkurrensverket v TeliaSonera Sverige AB* ECLI:EU:C:2011:83, paras 55-56. *See also* T-336/07 *Telefónica and Telefónica de España v Commission* ECLI:EU:T:2012:172, para. 180.
622. Commission decision of 18 July 1988 in case 30.178 *Napier Brown – British Sugar*, recital 65.
623. Commission decision of 18 July 1988 in case 30.178 *Napier Brown – British Sugar*, recital 13.
624. Commission decision of 18 July 1988 in case 30.178 *Napier Brown – British Sugar*, recital 66.
625. T-228/97 *Irish Sugar v Commission* ECLI:EU:T:1999:246, para. 157.
626. T-5/97 *Industrie des Poudres-Sphériques v Commission* ECLI:EU:T:2000:278, in particular paras 178-186.

given that the wholesale prices were regulated. The Commission considered that a margin squeeze nevertheless took place because Deutsche Telekom was not required to set its retail prices at a level below its wholesale prices.[627] The CFI and the CJEU upheld this position.[628] A discussion of Deutsche Telekom's *mens rea* did not take place in this context (Deutsche Telekom did, however, allege a mistake of law in the context of its pleas against the fine imposed on it as discussed in Chapter 4 below).

414 In its 2011 preliminary ruling in *Teliasonera*, the CJEU provided a clarification as to why margin squeezing is an abusive practice by a dominant undertaking: 'in the absence of any other economic and objective justification, such conduct can be explained only by the dominant undertaking's intention to prevent the development of competition in the downstream market and to strengthen its position, or even to acquire a dominant position, in that market by using means other than reliance on its own merits'.[629] This is clearly reminiscent of the objective intention also described in *Akzo*.

415 Finally, in *Telefónica*, the Commission did not investigate the existence of an exclusionary strategy by the Spanish telecom operator. It merely compared its downstream retail prices with its costs (including the upstream wholesale prices it charged to competitors) to assess whether this allowed it to operate with positive margins.[630] Also before the CFI and the CJEU the question of *mens rea* was not discussed when it came to the existence of an infringement (but Telefónica did allege a mistake of law in the context of its challenge against the fine - *see* Chapter 4 below).[631]

416 In conclusion, despite the considerations of *mens rea* in the early sugar cases, this factor is not considered in much detail in recent margin squeeze cases which focus on a comparison between price and cost. Although the margin squeeze is seen as evidence of an objective exclusionary intention, evidence of subjective intentions to exclude is not highlighted. This is may be a consequence of a choice for blatant infringements (where wholesale pricing is below retail pricing) as opposed to cases where margins are squeezed but still positive (and strategic questions may be more relevant).

[8] Abuse of Regulatory Process

417 This category of abuses concerns instances where a dominant undertaking abuses a regulatory (including judicial) process to (attempt to) exclude competitors from the market. The idea is that, although a dominant undertaking can of course participate in regulatory and judicial processes, it must act according to the rules of these processes:

627. Commission decision of 21 May 2003 in cases 37.451, 37.578 and 37.579 *Deutsche Telekom AG*.
628. T-271/03 *Deutsche Telekom v Commission* ECLI:EU:T:2008:101 and C-280/08 P *Deutsche Telekom AG v Commission* ECLI:EU:C:2010:603.
629. C-52/09 *Konkurrensverket v TeliaSonera Sverige AB* ECLI:EU:C:2011:83, para. 88. *See also* T-336/07 *Telefónica and Telefónica de España v Commission* ECLI:EU:T:2012:172, para. 189.
630. Commission decision of 4 July 2007 in case 38.784 *Telefónica*.
631. T-336/07 *Telefónica and Telefónica de España v Commission* ECLI:EU:T:2012:172 and C-295/12 P *Telefónica and Telefónica de España v Commission* ECLI:EU:C:2014:2062.

if it provides false or misleading information to the regulatory or judicial authorities or performs other actions which can be described as abusive of the process, this may also constitute an abuse of a dominant position.

418 The US Supreme Court already in the 1960s developed a theory according to which in principle attempts by undertakings to use government processes to defend their interests were immune from antitrust scrutiny (the so-called Noerr-Pennington doctrine).[632] This was partially based on the right to petition included in the First Amendment to the US Constitution and also derived from the idea that any anticompetitive government decisions resulting from lobbying are attributable to the authorities, not to the lobbyists themselves.[633] However, the Supreme Court subsequently made it clear that such immunity only applied if the government processes were used in good faith to obtain a positive outcome and were not a '*mere sham*'.[634]

419 The European Courts hesitantly came to a similar conclusion in a string of cases. In fact, in *Compagnie Maritime Belge*, they still avoided the question. In that case, the liner conference Cewal had managed to conclude an agreement with the Zairese government which granted it the exclusive right to ship from North-Western Europe to Zaire. It invoked the Noerr-Pennington doctrine to claim that this agreement was immune from the competition provisions of the EC treaty. The CFI considered that it was not necessary to rule on this question because, even though Cewal had obtained the exclusive right to ship under the agreement with the Zairese government, it had the option to waive that right: evidence obtained by the Commission that Cewal actively tried to enforce its exclusive rights under the agreement therefore showed that Cewal abused its dominant position, without it being necessary to rule on whether Cewal lawfully obtained the exclusive rights.[635] Interestingly, the CFI pointed out that minutes of conference meetings showed that the approaches made by Cewal to the Zairese government to ensure that the latter adhered to the exclusivity 'formed part of a strategy designed to remove the independent shipping operation G & C'.[636] The CJEU followed the approach taken by the CFI.[637]

420 The question of the circumstances under which the use of a government process can constitute an abuse of dominance was addressed more clearly in *ITT Promedia*. In this case the Commission had rejected a complaint by the eponymous company against dominant undertaking Belgacom, including for allegedly frivolous lawsuits brought by the latter. In its decision, the Commission stated that 'in principle the bringing of an

632. Based on *Eastern Railroad Presidents Conference v Noerr Motor Freight, Inc.*, 365 U.S. 127, 135 (1961); *United Mine Workers v Pennington*, 381 U.S. 657, 670 (1965).
633. *See* PE Areeda and H Hovenkamp, *Antitrust law - An analysis of antitrust principles and their application* (Wolters Kluwer 1978, Supp May 2018) ¶ 201a.
634. *California Motor Transport v Trucking Unlimited*, 404 U.S. 508 (1972).
635. Joined cases T-24 to 26 and 28/93 *Compagnie Maritime Belge v Commission* ECLI:EU:T:1996:139, in particular paras 107-110.
636. Joined cases T-24 to 26 and 28/93 *Compagnie Maritime Belge v Commission* ECLI:EU:T:1996:139, para. 105.
637. Joined cases C-395 and 396/96 P *Compagnie Maritime Belge v Commission* ECLI:EU:C:2000:132, paras 61-88.

action, which is the expression of the fundamental right of access to a judge, cannot be characterised an abuse [unless] an undertaking in a dominant position brings an action (i) which cannot reasonably be considered as an attempt to establish its rights and can therefore only serve to harass the opposite party, and (ii) which is conceived in the framework of a plan whose goal is to eliminate competition'.[638] The first criterion is therefore an objective intent test (formulated in a negative way) and the second criterion is a subjective intent test.[639] In its application for annulment of the rejection of its complaint, ITT Promedia did not challenge the criteria used by the Commission as such but only the application of the criteria in the instant case, such that the CFI considered that 'there is no need for it to rule on the correctness of the criteria chosen by the Commission in the contested decision'.[640]

421 The leading case on abuse of regulatory process is *AstraZeneca*, where the Commission found that the eponymous dominant undertaking had abused its position by (i) providing misleading information to patent offices in an effort to obtain supplementary protection certificates which it was not entitled to or only entitled to for a shorter period and (ii) selectively deregistering marketing authorizations for one of its pharmaceutical products in order to prevent generics from relying on these market authorizations to launch their competing products.

422 Much of the legal analysis of the first abuse focused on whether the information provided by AstraZeneca was actually misleading. The General Court indeed ruled that the submission of such misleading information is 'a practice falling outside the scope of competition on the merits' and is therefore 'not in keeping with the special responsibility of an undertaking in a dominant position'.[641] According to the General Court, the misleading nature of the information 'must be assessed on the basis of objective factors and [...] proof of the deliberate nature of the conduct and of the bad faith of the undertaking in a dominant position is not required'.[642] The Court continued that 'intention none the less also constitutes a relevant factor which may, should the case arise, be taken into consideration by the Commission' because 'that intention can still be taken into account to support the conclusion that the undertaking concerned abused a dominant position'.[643]

638. Commission decision of 21 May 1996 in case 35.268 *ITT Promedia – Belgacom*, recital 11. The decision itself is not published but the wording is included in T-111/96 *ITT Promedia v Commission* ECLI:EU:T:1998:183, para. 30.
639. Note that two criteria are similar to the criteria used to determine whether a petition under the Noerr-Pennington doctrine was done in good faith. *See Professional Real Estate Investors, Inc. v Columbia Pictures Indus.*, 508 U.S. 49, 60-61 (1993): 'We now outline a two-part definition of "*sham*" litigation. First, the lawsuit must be objectively baseless in the sense that no reasonable litigant could realistically expect success on the merits. ... Only if challenged litigation is objectively meritless may a court examine the litigant's subjective motivation. Under this second part of our definition of sham, the court should focus on whether the baseless lawsuit conceals "an attempt to interfere directly with the business relationships of a competitor".'
640. T-111/96 *ITT Promedia v Commission* ECLI:EU:T:1998:183, para. 58.
641. T-321/05 *AstraZeneca v Commission* ECLI:EU:T:2010:266, para. 355.
642. T-321/05 *AstraZeneca v Commission* ECLI:EU:T:2010:266, para. 356.
643. T-321/05 *AstraZeneca v Commission* ECLI:EU:T:2010:266, para. 359.

423 When examining the evidence used by the Commission, the General Court found that AstraZeneca 'could not reasonably be unaware' that the information it submitted would be misinterpreted by the patent offices and that 'there was no need for the Commission to demonstrate [AstraZeneca]'s bad faith or positively fraudulent intent on its part',[644] although the undertaking's 'conduct over the long term suggests [...] that it was motivated by the intention of misleading the patent offices'.[645] The General Court then went on to describe the numerous pieces of evidence that demonstrated that AstraZeneca was 'aware' of the erroneous nature of the information that was being provided to the authorities[646] which illustrated its 'deliberate intention'[647] to mislead the authorities and to 'conceal' information.[648] All of this evidenced a broader 'strategy' to mislead the patent offices.[649]

424 The CJEU endorsed the position of the General Court, stressing in particular that AstraZeneca was 'conscious' that it withheld information from the patent offices and 'could not reasonably be unaware' that its failure to provide information would lead the patent offices in error.[650] It was also 'aware' that the patent offices therefore granted supplementary protection certificates on an incorrect basis and 'knowingly accepted' this.[651] The CJEU consequently did not need to rule explicitly on whether unintentional (negligent) errors in applications to the patent offices could also amount to abuses.

425 According to the Commission, the second abuse committed by AstraZeneca consisted of the selective deregistration of market authorizations it held so that generics could not rely on an abridged procedure to obtain their own market authorizations. In parallel to deregistering its pharmaceutical product, AstraZeneca introduced a new registration for a modified product (biosimilar but in tablets instead of capsules) which it started marketing. Although some of the internal documents from AstraZeneca showed that it was developing a strategy to protect its products from generics, the General Court and CJEU pointed out that such a strategy is not as such unlawful 'provided that the conduct envisaged does not depart from practices coming within the scope of competition on the merits, which is such as to benefit consumers'.[652]

426 AstraZeneca argued that the Commission had not shown that it acted with 'malevolent' intentions when deregistering the product but the General Court pointed out, not only that a finding of abuse 'does not require an intention to cause harm to be established' but also that AstraZeneca 'was aware of the utility that the deregistration

644. T-321/05 *AstraZeneca v Commission* ECLI:EU:T:2010:266, para. 493.
645. T-321/05 *AstraZeneca v Commission* ECLI:EU:T:2010:266, para. 495.
646. *See* T-321/05 *AstraZeneca v Commission* ECLI:EU:T:2010:266, paras 508, 530, 594.
647. T-321/05 *AstraZeneca v Commission* ECLI:EU:T:2010:266, paras 519. *See also* paras 553, 599.
648. T-321/05 *AstraZeneca v Commission* ECLI:EU:T:2010:266, paras 537.
649. T-321/05 *AstraZeneca v Commission* ECLI:EU:T:2010:266, paras 305, 499, 548.
650. C-457/10 P *AstraZeneca v Commission* ECLI:EU:C:2012:770, paras 79 and 81.
651. C-457/10 P *AstraZeneca v Commission* ECLI:EU:C:2012:770, paras 88 and 96.
652. T-321/05 *AstraZeneca v Commission* ECLI:EU:T:2010:266, para. 804 and C-457/10 P *AstraZeneca v Commission* ECLI:EU:C:2012:770, para. 129.

... might have for the purpose of raising barriers to entry of a regulatory nature'.[653] Evidence of *mens rea* was accordingly not required to establish an abuse but could be taken into account. When discussing the impact of the deregistration on parallel imports, the Court states more explicitly: 'although the intention of an undertaking in a dominant position to restrict competition by methods falling outside the scope of competition on the merits may be taken into consideration in the identification of an abuse of a dominant position, that identification must first and foremost be based on the objective finding of conduct which, in the context in which it is implemented, is such as to restrict competition'.[654]

427 AstraZeneca claimed before the General Court, as an objective justification for the deregistrations, that keeping the registrations would mean that certain obligations of pharmacovigilance would remain applicable to it even though it would no longer market the product in capsule form. The General Court rejected this argument on the facts: it was not a consideration mentioned in AstraZeneca's internal documents, had not been argued before the Commission and was inconsistent with the fact that AstraZeneca deregistered the product in some countries and not in others. Yet, the absence of this objective justification provided the hallmark of the abuse in the instant case since it also amounted to the objective intention criterion of ITT Promedia: the General Court indeed held that the deregistration 'was not based on the legitimate protection of an investment which was part of competition on the merits', but on the contrary had 'the sole object of making the abridged procedure [for the registration of generics] unavailable'.[655] It was not competition on the merits and consequently abusive. The CJEU agreed that 'the deregistration, without objective justification and after the expiry of the exclusive right to make use of the results of the pharmacological and toxicological tests and clinical trials ... by which AZ intended ... to hinder the introduction of generic products and parallel imports – does not come within the scope of competition on the merits'.[656]

428 The position of the CJEU on this second abuse in *AstraZeneca* is reminiscent of the position it took twenty-five years earlier in *British Leyland*. One of the abuses the Commission had found in that case was the decision by British Leyland not to renew national type approvals (NTA) for left-hand-drive cars in the UK (where most cars are right-hand-drive).[657] The CJEU pointed out that British Leyland 'was aware of the existence of [parallel] trade in re-imported vehicles because of the complaints it received from the dealers belonging to its selective distribution network who demanded that BL take steps to eliminate it' and that '[i]t is clear, *inter alia*, from the minutes of the dealer council meetings on 16 January and 4 November 1981 that BL promised to make every effort to limit re-importations, in particular by allowing the NTA-certificate for left-hand-drive Metros to expire'.[658] Even the non-action of a

653. T-321/05 *AstraZeneca v Commission* ECLI:EU:T:2010:266, paras 813-814.
654. T-321/05 *AstraZeneca v Commission* ECLI:EU:T:2010:266, para. 849.
655. T-321/05 *AstraZeneca v Commission* ECLI:EU:T:2010:266, paras 825 and 829.
656. C-457/10 P *AstraZeneca v Commission* ECLI:EU:C:2012:770, para. 130.
657. Article 1(ii) of Commission decision of 2 July 1984 in case 30.615 *British Leyland*.
658. C-226/84 *British Leyland v Commission* ECLI:EU:C:1986:421, para. 14.

dominant undertaking can therefore amount to an abuse if the relevant *mens rea* is present.

429 One question to ask in respect of cases of abuse of regulatory process is whether the *mens rea* here complies with the correspondence principle discussed in paragraphs 51-58 of Chapter 1. Even if there is evidence that the dominant undertaking intentionally breached the rules, does that also mean that it intended thereby to restrict competition? This may be evident in some cases, but I would argue that the mere fact that misleading information is provided by a dominant undertaking to a regulator does not *ipso facto* imply that the dominant undertaking also intended thereby to abuse its dominant position. In other words, there should also be an indication that the misleading information was provided with the intention of excluding a competitor. The views of the CJEU on this point in the *AstraZeneca* judgment are ambiguous. Indeed, while it does not take issue with the General Court's ruling on the first abuse that AstraZeneca had acquired supplementary protection certificates 'in a manner contrary to the regulatory framework establishing SPCs',[659] it does state in respect of the second abuse that 'the illegality of abusive conduct under Article 82 EC is unrelated to its compliance or non-compliance with other legal rules and, in the majority of cases, abuses of dominant positions consist of behaviour which is otherwise lawful under branches of law other than competition law'.[660]

430 In conclusion, evidence of *mens rea* plays a particularly important role in abuses of regulatory process: the fact that the undertaking intended to abuse the regulatory process (or, in other words, that it was aware that it infringed the regulatory rules) is an important indicator that it abused that process. It is not clear, however, whether this is also the relevant *mens rea* for an abuse of dominance. Indeed, the *actus reus* to which this *mens rea* corresponds is the infringement of regulatory rules and not, as such, the exclusion of a competitor. It is unclear, therefore, whether there must, in addition, be an intention or awareness that through the abuse of regulatory process competition on the market will be affected.

[9] Non-exclusionary Abuses

431 As far as I am aware, none of the literature so far discusses the relevance of *mens rea* in non-exclusionary abuses. This may be partially due to the focus of in particular the European Commission on exclusionary abuses in the last twenty years or so, and the more limited case law on non-exclusionary abuses resulting from this.

432 If it is hard to define what conduct should be viewed as exclusionary (as opposed to merely competition on the merits), it is even more difficult to define what conduct is exploitative. Indeed, any rational economic operator can be expected to use (i.e. exploit) the market power it has in order to extract as much profit from a market as it can. Rather than using the term 'exploitative' abuses, I therefore prefer to speak in this

659. C-457/10 P *AstraZeneca v Commission* ECLI:EU:C:2012:770, para. 68.
660. C-457/10 P *AstraZeneca v Commission* ECLI:EU:C:2012:770, para. 132.

section about non-exclusionary abuses: these are instances where the Commission and the European Courts have found conduct by a dominant undertaking abusive even though there was no indication of an exclusionary objective, in particular because the undertaking in question was not competing with the undertakings suffering from the conduct.

433 The most typical example of such behaviour is excessive pricing, although there are very few instances where the Commission has found prices to be excessive. The earliest case, *General Motors*, concerned the allegedly excessive prices charged by General Motors in Belgium for the inspection certificate for General Motors cars imported from other EU Member States.[661] The CJEU annulled the Commission decision because, although the price of the inspection certificate was excessive compared to its cost, this could be explained by the newness of the Belgian requirement to inspect cars which were imported through parallel trade from other Member States, and it took into account the fact that General Motors quickly lowered the price (even before the Commission intervened).[662] A year later, in *United Brands*, the Commission identified four abusive practices engaged in by a dominant banana importer. One of these practices was charging distributors/ripeners of bananas in some Member States unfair prices.[663] Again the CJEU annulled the Commission decision in so far as the excessive pricing charge was concerned.[664]

434 In both cases, *mens rea* considerations seemed to have played a very limited role in the assessment of the abusive character of these practices.

435 The Commission was more successful in *British Leyland* - and in this case evidence of *mens rea* played a role. The situation in this case is somewhat comparable to *General Motors*: British Leyland had initially refused to grant certificates of conformity to left-hand-drive vehicles reimported into the UK from lower price countries and later requested a fee for this which was, according to the Commission, excessive. The Commission took into account that, when refusing to grant the certificate, the relevant department within British Leyland 'is unlikely to have been unaware of the company's desire to impede reimports'.[665] As indicated above in paragraph 428, the CJEU also pointed out that there was evidence of dealer complaints and of British Leyland's intention to limit reimports. Although the CJEU's analysis of the excessive prices takes place later in the judgment, this may well have also influenced its decision to accept the Commission's view that the fee charged for the certificate of conformity of left-hand-drive vehicles was excessive when compared to the fee charged for right-hand-drive vehicles since the cost for both verifications was almost the same.[666] The Court further pointed out that the subsequent reduction of the fee for certificates of left-hand-drive vehicles while those for right-hand-drive vehicles remained constant but at a lower

661. Commission decision of 19 December 1974 in case 28.851 *General Motors Continental*.
662. C-26/75 *General Motors v Commission* ECLI:EU:C:1975:150, paras 16-22.
663. Article 1(c) of Commission decision of 17 December 1975 in case 26.699 *Chiquita*.
664. C-27/76 *United Brands v Commission* ECLI:EU:C:1978:22, paras 204-234.
665. Commission decision of 2 July 1984 in case 30.615 *British Leyland*, recital 27.
666. C-226/84 *British Leyland v Commission* ECLI:EU:C:1986:421, paras 27-28.

level 'also suggests that it was fixed solely with a view to making the re-importation of left-hand-drive vehicles less attractive'.[667]

436 The above-mentioned cases of excessive pricing also concerned restrictions to parallel trade: they are attempts at partitioning the EU's internal market in national markets in order to reduce intra-brand competition. In fact, many of these cases go hand in hand with (non-exclusionary) price discrimination claims, i.e. situations where prices charged to some customers are different from prices to other customers, without the dominant undertaking itself being active on the downstream market (also referred to in the literature as secondary-line price discrimination)[668] and where the discrimination takes place along national lines. Such forms of discrimination are not problematic under EU competition law because they are exclusionary but because they are opposed to the goal of market integration.

437 Indeed, in *United Brands*, the Commission found that the dominant undertaking had been charging some distributors/ripeners in some Member States dissimilar prices for equivalent transactions.[669] The CJEU upheld this position[670] as well as the Commission's view that the provision in Chiquita's contracts prohibiting distributors/ripeners in some Member States from reselling bananas while still green was also abusive.[671] It is precisely this latter provision that allowed Chiquita to charge different prices in different Member States (and therefore high prices in some Member States)[672] because price discrimination is not a viable strategy if there is a possibility of arbitrage (i.e. of lower price customers selling to higher price customers). That excessive pricing is mainly an issue in the context of differentiated prices between Member States is also apparent from other case law.[673]

667. C-226/84 *British Leyland v Commission* ECLI:EU:C:1986:421, para. 29.
668. *See*, for example, D Geradin and N Petit, 'Price discrimination under EC competition law: another antitrust doctrine in search of limiting principles' (2006) Journal of Competition Law & Economics 479, in particular 508-521; C Bergqvist, 'Final curtain or another around on Post Danmark?' (2013) 34(6) European Competition Law Review 287, 288. In the US, this is dealt with by the Robinson-Patman Act. *See* PE Areeda and H Hovenkamp, *Antitrust law - An analysis of antitrust principles and their application* (Wolters Kluwer 1978, Supp May 2018) ¶ 2320.
669. Article 1(b) of Commission decision of 17 December 1975 in case 26.699 *Chiquita*.
670. C-27/76 *United Brands v Commission* ECLI:EU:C:1978:22, paras 235-268.
671. Article 1(a) of Commission decision of 17 December 1975 in case 26.699 *Chiquita*. *See* C-27/76 *United Brands v Commission* ECLI:EU:C:1978:22, paras 130-162. The CJEU also upheld a fourth abuse found by the Commission, namely Chiquita's refusal to supply bananas to a distributor that had participated in a promotion campaign for a competing brand but this is clearly an exclusionary practice and will not be discussed further here. *See* Article 1(d) of Commission decision of 17 December 1975 in case 26.699 *Chiquita* and C-27/76 *United Brands v Commission* ECLI:EU:C:1978:22, paras 163-203.
672. It has been argued that because only the prohibition of reselling bananas when green allowed Chiquita to charge different prices, only this provision should have been viewed as an abuse. *See* D Geradin and N Petit, 'Price discrimination under EC competition law: another antitrust doctrine in search of limiting principles' (2006) Journal of Competition Law & Economics 479, 529.
673. *See* recently C-177/16 *Autortiesību un komunicēšanas konsultaciju aģentura v Latvijas Autoru apvienība Konkurences padome* ECLI:EU:C:2017:689. More generally on the link between excessive pricing and price discrimination between Member States, *see* J Temple Lang & R O'Donoghue, 'Defining legitimate competition: how to clarify pricing abuses under Article 82

438 Price discrimination on the basis of nationality has in particular been found to be problematic in the case of infrastructure monopolies with a strong public interest. In those cases, the public operator of the monopoly may be trying to promote the national interest. In *Corsica Ferries*, for example, where the pilots of the port of Genoa charged different rates for services provided only to ships flying the Italian flag, the question of the compatibility of the prices with what is now Article 106 TFEU was raised. The Court pointed out that the 'national authorities' were prohibited from 'inducing' undertakings with a legal monopoly to price discriminate on the basis of nationality.[674] While the question of *mens rea* was not raised in this case, subsequently in *Aéroport de Paris*, which also concerned price discrimination on the basis of nationality, the CFI, with reference to the objective concept of abuse, held that an abuse may be committed 'irrespective of any fault' and that the concept of abuse 'implies no intention to cause harm'.[675]

439 What about the situation when price discrimination is not related to nationality or national geography? While a dominant undertaking may want to price discriminate to extract the maximum amount of profit from its customers, it has no other reason to favour one customer over another. In the recent *MEO* judgment, the CJEU therefore pointed out that, absent activities in the downstream market, 'the undertaking in a dominant position, in principle has no interest in excluding one of its trading partners from the downstream market'.[676] Nevertheless, the CJEU left the door open for abusive interpretations of the price discrimination by the dominant undertaking: with reference to *Intel*, it held that 'the possible existence of a strategy aiming to exclude from the downstream market one of its trading partners which is at least as efficient as its competitors' should be taken into account to assess whether price discrimination can produce a competitive disadvantage in the sense of Article 102(c) TFEU.

440 Overall, the category of non-exclusionary abuses is a mixed bag and the same can be said for the use of *mens rea* evidence in it: some cases refer to it, others do not but it does not appear to play a major role in them.

[D] Conclusion

441 It is clear that evidence of *mens rea* is not always necessary to establish an abuse of dominance. The CJEU and in particular the CFI have on occasion made statements that even contest the relevance of *mens rea* to establish an abuse. But other judgments state that, in some circumstances, such evidence is at the very least relevant and

EC' (2002) Fordham International Law Journal 83, 87; M Botta & K Wiedemann, 'EU competition law enforcement vis-à-vis exploitative conducts in the data economy. Exploring the terra incognita' (2018) Max Planck Institute for Innovation and Competition Research Paper Series 18-08 <https://papers.ssrn.com/sol3/papers.cfm?abstract_id=3184119> accessed 13 July 2018, 12 and 16.

674. C-18/93 *Corsica Ferries v Corpo dei piloti del porto di Genova* ECLI:EU:C:1994:195, para. 45.

675. T-128/98 *Aéroports de Paris v Commission* ECLI:EU:T:2000:290, paras 170 and 173. *See also* T-321/05 *AstraZeneca v Commission* ECLI:EU:T:2010:266, paras 359 and 813.

676. C-525/16 *MEO - Serviços de Comunicações e Multimédia* ECLI:EU:C:2018:270, para. 35.

possibly even determinative to find an abuse. It is thus hard to deduce hard-and-fast rules from the case law.

442 In relation to specific types of abuses, intentions (in particular exclusionary intentions) have a larger role to play than in respect of others. As far as single market abuses are concerned, exclusionary intentions play a particularly decisive role in predatory pricing cases: while pricing below average variable cost is always abusive according to the case law, pricing between average total cost and average variable cost is (one could add: only and always) predatory if accompanied by an exclusionary intention. The early case law on predation mainly relies on an objective intention to exclude, but in the most recent case law in particular evidence of subjective intentions (in internal strategic documents) is relied upon.

443 The case law on exclusionary price discrimination is more confusing. *Akzo* and *Compagnie Maritime Belge* suggest that evidence of an exclusionary intention can make selective price cuts abusive, even if pricing is not below average total cost. In the case of *Akzo*, such an intention was deduced from objective factors, in *Compagnie Maritime Belge* from subjective factors. Furthermore, *Post Danmark I* does not exclude that pricing below average total cost but above average variable cost can be abusive even absent an exclusionary intention (so when it is not predatory in the sense of *Akzo*).

444 Evidence of subjective intentions plays no role in explicit exclusivity agreements or loyalty rebates, probably because these necessarily entail an intention to exclude so there is no need to demonstrate this separately. However, when the exclusivity is not explicit, evidence of an exclusionary intention or strategy may become relevant. Not only has the CJEU in *Irish Sugar* deduced an exclusionary intention from certain rebates and used evidence of a subjective exclusionary intention to interpret a rebate. In *Intel*, the CJEU furthermore pointed out that evidence of such a subjective intention is in particular relevant if the dominant undertaking contests the exclusionary nature of a rebate.

445 Evidence of exclusionary intentions plays a limited role in multimarket abuses. Tying cases have focused on the question of whether the products that are being tied belong together or not, and in this context exclusionary intentions obviously do not play a significant role. Refusal to supply cases mostly concern intellectual property rights and therefore raise the policy question of how much protection these rights should offer their owners. Exclusionary intentions cannot be a decisive factor in this since exclusivity is the hallmark of IP rights. And, although evidence of exclusionary intentions has been highlighted to understand the logic of margin squeezes, most of these cases focus on cost and margin benchmarks. Evidence of subjective intentions has been scrutinized, however, in the context of the objective justifications alleged by dominant undertakings involved in multimarket abuses: when internal documents contradict the alleged non-exclusionary intentions of the dominant undertakings, this discredits the objective justification they put forward.

446 Intentions have played a prominent role in cases where abuses of regulatory processes have been viewed as an abuse of dominance: the awareness that the undertaking breaks the rules of the regulatory process has been used as key evidence of the abuse of that process. However, it is not clear whether the intention that is referred to in these cases, in particular in *AstraZeneca*, is the intention to exclude or (merely) the intention to abuse the process. In light of the correspondence principle, the latter cannot count as such as *mens rea* of an abuse of dominance.

447 Finally, it is hard to draw a line on the use of evidence of intentions in non-exclusionary abuse cases.

CHAPTER 4

Mens Rea in the Enforcement of the Antitrust Rules

On ne corrige pas celui qu'on pend, on corrige les autres par lui.

Montaigne, *Essais*, III, 8: De l'art de conférer

448 After having discussed the role *mens rea* plays in the two substantive antitrust rules of the TFEU in the previous two chapters, this chapter describes the role *mens rea* plays in the enforcement of the antitrust rules under positive EU law.

449 The first section discusses the relevance of *mens rea* for the assessment of the effect on trade between Member States, the jurisdictional criterion contained in both Article 101 and Article 102 TFEU.

450 The second section describes the relevance of *mens rea* in that other key concept that is contained in both antitrust articles, namely the notion of undertaking. The focus is there on the question of corporate liability, i.e. on how the case law deals with the fact that a corporation is a fiction which does not have a 'mind' of its own which can be guilty. Subsequently, the step is made from the corporation to the undertaking as an economic entity often comprising several corporations.

451 The third section discusses the relevance of *mens rea* in the imposition of fines for antitrust infringements and in particular the conditions contained in Article 23 of Regulation 1/2003 that fines can only be imposed on undertakings that 'intentionally or negligently' infringe the antitrust rules.

452 The fourth and final section analyses the relevance of awareness or ignorance of illegality of certain conduct, a topic which, as will be explained in the third section, is closely related to the question of *mens rea*.

§4.01 EFFECT ON TRADE BETWEEN MEMBER STATES

453 Both Article 101 and 102 TFEU only concern conduct which 'may affect trade between Member States'. The CJEU very early on made it clear that this was a jurisdictional criterion that 'intended to ... define the boundary between the areas respectively covered by Community law and national law'.[677]

454 In order to determine whether trade 'may' be affected by an agreement, it must, according to the CJEU, 'be possible to foresee with a sufficient degree of probability on the basis of a set of objective factors of law or of fact that the agreement in question may have an influence, direct or indirect, actual or potential, on the trade between Member States'.[678] The same applies *mutatis mutandis* to unilateral conduct for the purpose of Article 102 TFEU.[679]

455 The fact that an 'indirect' and even 'potential' influence on trade between Member States is sufficient for the EU antitrust rules to apply shows that this criterion is interpreted in a very wide manner.[680] Even conduct that is limited to a single Member State has on many occasions been found to fulfil this criterion, since it may affect imports to and exports from that Member State from/to other Member States.[681] The CJEU has even stated in some judgments that a practice covering an entire Member State 'by its very nature' affects trade between the Member States,[682] although other judgments come to a different conclusion.[683] As a minimal requirement, however, the

677. Joined cases C-56 and 58/64 *Consten and Grundig v Commission* ECLI:EU:C:1966:41, at [1966] ECR 341.
678. C-56/65 *Société Technique Minière v Maschinenbau Ulm* ECLI:EU:C:1966:38, at [1966] ECR 249; C-5/69 *Völk v Vervaecke* ECLI:EU:C:1969:35, para. 5. *See also* C-61/80 *Coöperatieve Stremsel- en Kleurselfabriek v Commission* ECLI:EU:C:1981:75, para. 14; joined cases C-89, 104, 114, 116, 117 and 125 to 129/85 *Ahlström Osakeyhtiö and Others v Commission* ECLI:EU:C:1993:120, para. 143; C-219/95 *Ferriere Nord v Commission* ECLI:EU:C:1997:375, para. 20.
679. C-250/92 *Gøttrup-Klim and Others Grovvareforeninger v Dansk Landbrugs Grovvareselskab* ECLI:EU:C:1994:413, para. 54; joined cases T-24 to 26 and 28/93 *Compagnie Maritime Belge v Commission* ECLI:EU:T:1996:139, para. 201.
680. *See* R Burnley, 'Interstate trade revisited – the jurisdictional criterion for Articles 81 and 82 EC' (2002) European Competition Law Review 217, 219; V Korah, *An introductory guide to EC competition law and practice* (Hart Publishing 2004) 59 and 60; W-H Roth and T Ackermann, 'Grundfragen Art. 81 Abs.1 EG' in *Frankfurter Kommentar Frankfurter Kommentar zum Kartellrecht* (Otto Schmidt, 2012) 265; J Faull, L Kjølbye, H Leupold and A Nikpay, 'Article 101' in J Faull and A Nikpay, *The EU law of competition* (OUP 2014) 183, 292; W Kirchhoff, 'Beeinträchtigung des zwischenstaatlichen Handels' in J Bornkamm, F Montag and FJ Säcker (eds), *Münchener Kommentar Europäisches und Deutsches Wettbewerbsrecht* (Beck 2015) 853, 854. *See also* C-172/80 *Züchner v Bayerische Vereinsbank* ECLI:EU:C:1981:178, para. 18.
681. C-246/86 *Belasco and others v Commission* ECLI:EU:C:1989:301, para. 33.
682. C-8/72 *Vereeniging van Cementhandelaren v Commission* ECLI:EU:C:1972:84, para. 29; C-126/80 *Salonia v Poidomani e Giglio* ECLI:EU:C:1981:136, para. 14.
683. *See*, for example, C-73/74 *Papiers peints v Commission* ECLI:EU:C:1975:160, para. 29; joined cases C-215 and 216/96 *Bagnasco and others* ECLI:EU:C:1999:12, para. 53. *See* already the criticism directed by AG Mischo in C-246/86 *Belasco and others v Commission* ECLI:EU:C:1989:95, para. 3 at an automatic effect on intra-EU trade for agreements covering an entire Member State, as well as J Faull, 'Effect on trade between Member States and Community: Member State jurisdiction' (1990) Fordham Corporate Law Institute 485, 494.

effect on trade needs to be 'appreciable'[684] (as opposed to merely 'insignificant')[685] in order for Article 101 and 102 TFEU to be applicable.

456 That the probability of an effect on trade needs to be assessed on the basis of 'objective factors' has been interpreted by the Commission as implying that '[s]ubjective intent on the part of the undertakings concerned is not required'. However, at the same time, the Commission considers that, '[i]f ... there is evidence that undertakings have intended to affect trade between Member States, for example because they have sought to hinder exports to or imports from other Member States, this is a relevant factor to be taken into account'.[686]

457 It is possible to imagine cases where an undertaking was justifiably ignorant of the effect its conduct had on trade between the Member States. For example, an undertaking may be manufacturing products for a very localized market in a Member State and, after a thorough examination, believe that none of its customers exports its products to other Member States.[687] If one of those customers secretly does engage in exports, thereby triggering the effect on trade between the Member States, could the original producer be subject to Article 101 and 102 TFEU? As far as I am aware, there is no case law on such mistakes of fact and whether the consequent ignorance of effect on trade could exclude the application of the EU antitrust rules.

458 There is, however, some case law on the relevance of mistakes of law (as opposed to mistakes of fact) for the application of this criterion which is not surprising for a criterion which, as pointed out above, is mainly jurisdictional. These cases concern Austria where exceptions to the cartel prohibition in national legislation apparently encouraged some companies to enter into cartels, unaware that the European cartel prohibition contained in Article 101 TFEU might be applicable to them.

459 A first example is the Lombard Club, a cartel between Austrian banks which dated back to the era before Austrian accession to the European Union and which was instituted with the approval of the Austrian public authorities and was (at least partially) a matter of public knowledge. The banks unsuccessfully argued before the European Commission, the CFI and the CJEU that trade between Member States was not affected by these practices.[688] Many of the parties' arguments were based on

684. C-22/71 *Béguelin Import v G.L. Import Export* ECLI:EU:C:1971:113.
685. C-5/69 *Völk v Vervaecke* ECLI:EU:C:1969:35, para. 7; C-306/96 *Javico v Yves Saint Laurent Parfums* ECLI:EU:C:1998:173; C-238/05 *Asnef-Equifax* ECLI:EU:C:2006:734, para. 34.
686. Paragraph 25 of the Guidelines on the effect on trade concept contained in Articles 81 and 82 of the Treaty [2004] OJ C101/81.
687. This situation is different from that discussed in C-123/83 *BNIC v Clair* ECLI:EU:C:1985:33, where the anticompetitive agreement concerned a product in a very localized market (potable spirits used in Cognac), but producers could not deny that they knew that that the final product (Cognac) would be exported.
688. Commission decision of 11 June 2002 in case 36871 *Austrian Banks – 'Lombard Club'*, recitals 438-469; joined cases T-259 to 264 and 271/02 *Raiffeisen Zentralbank Österreich and Others v Commission* ECLI:EU:T:2006:396, paras 153-197; joined cases C-125, 133, 135 and 137/07 P *Erste Group Bank and Others v Commission* ECLI:EU:C:2009:576, paras 25-70.

alleged mistakes of law (*see* on this topic §4.04 below) or were not supported by the facts (e.g. the allegedly public nature of the cartel – *see* paragraph 621 below).

460 Of particular interest here is that one of the banks argued that its subsidiary had only participated in a part of the cartel that had 'no connection with cross-border operations'.[689] The CFI dismissed any suggestion that this had an impact on the application of (then) Article 81 EC by reference to the *Anic* case law, namely that, given the undertaking's participation in an important part of the cartel, the undertaking could not have been unaware of the other parts of the cartel, including those dealing with cross-border operations. The Court furthermore referred to the established case law that cartels limited to one Member States may affect trade between the Member States.[690] The argument that the undertaking could not be fined for the infringement was dismissed on the same grounds.[691]

461 A second example is the international freight forwarding cartel prosecuted in Austria after the entry into force of Regulation 1/2003 which led to the Grand Chamber judgment in *Schenker*.[692] In this case, a number of Austrian freight forwarders had entered into a conference, the *Spediteurs-Sammelladungs-Konferenz* (SSK) in the 1990s. The SSK agreed tariffs for combined consignment transport on the Austrian market. The SSK had initially sought approval for their conference from the Austrian Cartel Court: this had come to the provisional conclusion that the conference did not affect trade between the EU Member States but it had rejected the request for approval because it considered that the conference was not justified from the perspective of the national economy. Subsequently, the SSK requested the Austrian Cartel Court for a declaration that the conference was a minor cartel (*Bagatellkartell*) exempted from the application of the Austrian law on cartels: this declaration was granted.

462 In 2010, after the Commission had started investigating a cartel in international freight forwarding services, the Austrian competition prosecutor took the view that the SSK constituted an infringement of Article 101 TFEU. The prosecutor considered that, contrary to what the SSK claimed, the conference did affect trade between EU Member States, and the exemption of minor cartels under Austrian law therefore did not prevent the application of EU competition law. The preliminary reference on a possible defence of mistake of law (due to reliance on an erroneous opinion of a court and a lawyer) will also be discussed in §4.04 below (*see* paragraphs 571ff.).

463 Finally, I already want to point out here that awareness or ignorance of an effect on trade between Member States can play a role when it comes to the liability for fines for infringements. As discussed in more detail below at paragraph 598, the *Guidelines on the effect on trade concept* provide for a presumption that trade is not affected by

689. Joined cases T-259 to 264 and 271/02 *Raiffeisen Zentralbank Österreich and Others v Commission* ECLI:EU:T:2006:396, para. 188.
690. Joined cases T-259 to 264 and 271/02 *Raiffeisen Zentralbank Österreich and Others v Commission* ECLI:EU:T:2006:396, paras 189-197.
691. Joined cases T-259 to 264 and 271/02 *Raiffeisen Zentralbank Österreich and Others v Commission* ECLI:EU:T:2006:396, para. 210.
692. C-681/11 *Schenker & Co. and Others* ECLI:EU:C:2013:404.

agreements or practices to which the parties have a market share of not more than 5% and combined turnover in the EEA of not more than EUR 40 million. Even if, despite this presumption, the Commission would institute proceedings for such agreements or practices, the Commission has stated in the notice that it would not impose any fines '[w]here the undertakings assume in good faith that an agreement is covered by this negative presumption'.[693] In those circumstances, the subjective belief that trade is not affected by the agreement or practice (because of the negative presumption) precludes liability.

§4.02 CORPORATE LIABILITY

464 When the question of *mens rea* is brought up in the literature, much space is often devoted to the issue of corporate liability.[694] As indicated already in Chapter 1, in the absence of a corporate 'mind', it seems difficult to ascribe a guilty mind to a legal entity such as a corporation. However, the same can be said of the *conduct* of a corporation: it cannot act on its own but only through its representatives. This in turn raises the question of whether the actions of its representatives can always be ascribed to the corporation or whether certain conditions need to be fulfilled to do so. In the case of illegal conduct by employees, one such condition could be that the corporation is somehow blameworthy for allowing its employee to engage in unlawful conduct. As will be discussed in this section, the CJEU has sidestepped this problem through reliance on the notion of undertaking, such that little guilt on the part of the corporation needs to be demonstrated in order to hold it (and its parents) liable for the actions of its employees. Arguments on the absence of blameworthiness on the part of the undertaking have therefore generally been quickly dismissed.

465 In *Musique Diffusion Française* in the early 1980s, the Court of Justice for the first time was asked to consider in which circumstances undertakings should be liable for the conduct of their employees. This case concerned agreements between electronics manufacturer Pioneer and some of its European distributors granting absolute territorial protection to the French distributor of Pioneer which gave its name to the case. The German distributor of Pioneer, Melchers GmbH, argued before the Court of Justice that it did not consider itself bound by the agreements: on its side, they were concluded by two employees which did not have the power under German corporate law to sign on behalf of their employer, a *Kommandit* corporation. The Court of Justice rejected this argumentation and held that 'it is not necessary for there to have been action by, or even knowledge on the part of, the partners or principal managers of the undertaking

693. Paragraph 50 of the Guidelines on the effect on trade concept contained in Articles 81 and 82 of the Treaty [2004] OJ C101/81.

694. Most of H Engels, *Unternehmensvorsatz und Unternehmensfahrlässigkeit im Europäischen Kartellrecht* (Berlin Verlag Arno Spitz 2002), the only book ostensibly devoted to *mens rea* in EU antitrust law, is in fact devoted to the question of corporate liability. *See also* the discussion in paras 682ff. of Chapter 5 below and references there.

concerned; action by a person who is authorized to act on behalf of the undertaking suffices'.[695]

466 The logic of this principle was explained a few years ago in the judgment of the CJEU in *Slovak Banks*. One of the banks had argued that its employee, who participated in one of the cartel meetings, did not have a mandate to do so and that it had also not been shown that the authorized representative of the undertaking had assented to the outcome of the meeting. The Court of Justice ruled that this was irrelevant and pointed out that participation in cartels 'is more often than not clandestine and is not governed by any formal rules. It is rarely the case that an undertaking's representative attends a meeting with a mandate to commit an infringement'.[696] Along the same lines, the General Court ruled in *Villeroy & Boch* that an undertaking can be liable for the participation of an employee in cartel meetings even if that employee is not responsible for the products that are discussed at the meeting (in particular because the products were sold by another entity within the corporate group).[697] In *Dole Food* and *FSL*, the General Court similarly rejected arguments that the undertaking did not participate in the cartels in question because the employee engaging in anticompetitive contacts did not have the final say on prices.[698]

467 As a consequence of this case law, it is not necessary for the Commission to identify the persons who acted improperly and whose actions are attributable to the undertaking, nor the persons who were responsible for the defective organization of an undertaking which made the infringement possible.[699] According to the General Court, the fact that the senior management is not involved in an infringement is not even an attenuating circumstance when calculating the fine for the infringement.[700]

468 The factual situation may be more complex when a director or employee is not working for one undertaking only but also has a position in another undertaking or an association of undertakings. In *Finnboard*, the CFI ruled on the latter situation: it ruled that the president of an association which participated in an infringement also implicated the undertaking of which he was the general director in that infringement.[701] Similar situations can easily arise in the case of joint ventures.

695. Joined cases C-100 to 103/80 *Musique Diffusion Française v Commission* ECLI:EU:C:1983:158, para. 97.
696. C-68/12 *Slovenská sporiteľňa* ECLI:EU:C:2013:71, para. 26.
697. Joined cases T-373, 374, 382 and 402/10 *Villeroy & Boch et al. v Commission* ECLI:EU:T:2013:455, para. 243. Note that the Court of Justice considered in the appeal against this judgment that the argument of the applicant on this point was inadmissible and therefore did not validate the reasoning of the General Court (*see* C-642/13 P *Villeroy & Boch – Belgium v Commission* ECLI:EU:C:2017:58, paras 33-36). Interestingly, the General Court also referred to the *AC-Treuhand* case law (T-99/04 *AC-Treuhand v Commission* ECLI:EU:T:2008:256) although this case law concerns situations where the undertaking as a whole is not active on the market in question, while this was not disputed in *Villeroy & Boch*.
698. T-588/08 *Dole Food & Dole Germany v Commission* ECLI:EU:T:2013:130, para. 582 and case T-655/11 *FSL et al. v Commission* ECLI:EU:T:2015:383, para. 304.
699. C-338/00 P *Volkswagen v Commission* ECLI:EU:C:2003:473, paras 95-6.
700. T-216/06 *Lucite International & Lucite International UK v Commission* ECLI:EU:T:2011:475, paras 95-102.
701. T-338/94 *Finnboard v Commission* ECLI:EU:T:1998:99, paras 120-132.

469 Recent case law nevertheless seems to have opened a few cracks in the principled position of the European Courts in *Musique Diffusion Française*. This is probably due to the increasing number of cases in which undertakings contest the attribution of liability for actions of their officers or employees in the last decades (which in turn may be the consequence of the increasing level of fines).

470 The *Slovak Banks* judgment, for example, suggests that an undertaking that discovers the inappropriate conduct of an employee could escape liability by publicly distancing itself from the infringement.[702] However, if this is meant not only to end the undertaking's participation in the infringement but also to escape liability for the past, this case law seems hard to reconcile with the even more recent *VM Remonts* judgment where the CJEU seems to have only foreseen such possibility in respect of the actions of independent service providers, not employees (*see* further below at paragraph 476).

471 In a number of judgments, the General Court has also seemed to allow for a defence against attributions of infringements by *rogue employees*. In the *Finnboard* judgment referred to above, it suggested that an express limitation in the representative powers of a person could be used as evidence against attribution.[703] In *Villeroy & Boch*, the General Court suggested that an undertaking can try to show that the employee participated in the meetings without the knowledge and against the will of the undertaking in question or for the account of another undertaking.[704] In these cases, these were subsidiary arguments, however, which are not easy to reconcile with other case law.

472 Despite this handful of ambiguous statements, the principled position still seems to be that employees perform their work for and under the direction of their employer and are therefore incorporated into the undertaking and form part of its economic unit.[705] The liability of undertakings for the actions of their officers or employees is therefore vicarious (*see* paragraph 86 above) and not contributory: no fault by the undertaking needs to be demonstrated (beyond the fault of the officer or employee) for that liability to arise.

473 Despite this, the liability of undertakings under EU competition law is also said to be 'personal'.[706] This is because of the fiction that 'an employee operating within the scope of his or her employment *is* the undertaking and therefore anti-competitive acts by an employee are the acts of the legal person who operates the undertaking (the employer)'.[707] But this fiction itself is based on the presumption that the undertaking

702. C-68/12 *Slovenská sporiteľňa* ECLI:EU:C:2013:71, para. 27.
703. T-338/94 *Finnboard v Commission* ECLI:EU:T:1998:99, paras 120-132. This seems hard to reconcile with the *Slovak Banks* judgment though.
704. Joined cases T-373, 374, 382 and 402/10 *Villeroy & Boch et al. v Commission* ECLI:EU:T:2013:455, para. 243. As pointed out above, this part of the General Court's reasoning was not confirmed by the CJEU.
705. C-22/98 *Becu et al.* ECLI:EU:C:1999:419, para. 26; C-542/14 *VM Remonts et al.* ECLI:EU:C:2016:578, para. 23.
706. *See* already C-49/92 P *Commission v Anic Partecipazioni* ECLI:EU:C:1999:356, para. 78.
707. O Odudu and D Bailey, 'The single economic entity doctrine in EU competition law' (2014) Common Market Law Review 1721, 1744 (emphasis in original).

controls its employees and is therefore able to stop them (or the undertaking through them) from engaging in anticompetitive conduct – which suggests that liability is nevertheless somehow based on fault.[708] At the very least there is a tension between the statement that liability is personal and the fact that, since the undertaking cannot act without representatives, its liability must somehow be based on the actions of its representatives.

474 Moving then beyond the direct representatives of an undertaking (its employees and officers), the case law has also stated that external representatives (agents) of an undertaking can implicate the latter's liability. If these agents do not bear any or only a negligible share of the commercial risks of their business, they will be viewed as part of the undertaking of their principal. However, if they assume (a significant part of) that risk themselves, they will be viewed as separate undertakings.[709] It will also be relevant whether the principal determines the time, place and content of the agent's work.[710]

475 An example of this is *voestalpine* which concerned a cartel in prestressed steel products. Voestalpine, an Austrian producer of such products, used an agent for its sales in Italy, the company Studio Crema CAP Srl, managed and represented by Mr G. The latter did not have the power to conclude contracts with customers: these were concluded directly by voestalpine. The Commission did not have evidence that voestalpine itself had participated in any cartel meetings in Italy (the so-called Club Italia), but it did have evidence of the regular participation of Mr G in these meetings. Because Mr G did not bear any commercial risks when selling the products, both the Commission and the General Court considered that he was not an independent agent of voestalpine and that his participation in the Club Italia could be attributed to his principal. Of note is that Mr G did not have an exclusivity contract with voestalpine and also acted as the agent for another producer of prestressed steel products (which also participated in the cartel): this did not prevent his qualification as representative of voestalpine.[711]

476 However, there is no vicarious liability for truly independent agents, as confirmed in the recent *VM Remonts* judgment. While much of the case law on agency has been devoted to the question of when a representative of an undertaking can be viewed as truly independent and when not (implying that its actions can be directly attributed to

708. O Odudu and D Bailey, 'The single economic entity doctrine in EU competition law' (2014) Common Market Law Review 1721, 1744-1745.
709. C-266/93 *Bundeskartellamt v Volkswagen & VAG Leasing* ECLI:EU:C:1995:345, para. 19. *See also* C-217/05 *Confederación Española de Empresarios de Estaciones de Servicio* ECLI:EU:C:2006:784, paras 51-58; C-279/06 *CEPSA* ECLI:EU:C:2008:485, paras 33-44; and C-542/14 *VM Remonts et al.* ECLI:EU:C:2016:578, para. 27. *See also* the Commission Guidelines on vertical restraints [2010] OJ C130/1, para. 13.
710. C-413/13 *FNV Kunsten Informatie en Media* ECLI:EU:C:2014:2411, para. 36.
711. Commission decision of 30 June 2010 in case 38.344 *Prestressed Steel*, recitals 769-789 and case T-418/10 *voestalpine & voestalpine Wire Rod Austria v Commission* ECLI:EU:T:2015:516, paras 130-179.

the undertaking),[712] in *VM Remonts* the CJEU went beyond this and clarified under which circumstances an undertaking can be liable for the conduct of a truly independent agent. To answer this question, the CJEU has recourse to principles of the *Anic* case law discussed in Chapter 2. It stated that liability for actions of a true agent can arise (i) 'if the undertaking was aware of the anti-competitive objectives pursued by its competitors and the service provider and intended to contribute to them by its own conduct' or (ii) 'if the [undertaking] could reasonably have foreseen that the service provider retained by it [would engage in anticompetitive conduct] and if it was prepared to accept the risk which that entailed'.[713] In the case of a truly independent agent, therefore, liability is similar to the liability for actions of other third parties as discussed in paragraphs 194ff. above.

477 Finally, a few words should be said about the role of *mens rea* in parental liability. Indeed, European antitrust law does not merely attribute conduct of individuals to corporations in a way that comes close to vicarious liability. The same could also be said about the attribution of conduct of corporations to their parent companies.

478 The question of parental liability has been the subject of an abundance of case law and literature. I certainly do not want to enter into the minute details of this topic here and will therefore merely summarize the main principles from the case law.

479 Already according to the *Dyestuffs* judgment of 1972, '[t]he fact that a subsidiary has separate legal personality is not sufficient to exclude the possibility of imputing its conduct to the parent company': the parent will (also) be liable for the conduct 'where the subsidiary, although having separate legal personality, does not decide independently upon its own conduct on the market, but carries out, in all material respects, the instructions given to it by the parent company'.[714] To determine whether this is the case, the case law developed a two-stage test: first, it needs to be determined whether the parent was able to exercise decisive influence over the subsidiary and, second, whether the parent did in fact exercise such decisive influence. In the case of a (quasi) 100% subsidiary, there is a rebuttable presumption that the parent did exercise such influence.[715]

480 In the literature, this approach has been criticized as being contrary to the principle of personal liability and the principle of innocence: the parent company

712. *See*, for example, cases C-217/05 *Confederación Espanola de Empresarios de Estaciones de Servicio* ECLI:EU:C:2006:784; C-279/06 *CEPSA* ECLI:EU:C:2008:485; and C-413/13 *FNV Kunsten Informatie en Media* ECLI:EU:C:2014:2411.

713. C-542/14 *VM Remonts and others* ECLI:EU:C:2016:578, paras 30-31. The CJEU did not take up the suggestions from AG Wathelet to create a presumption in this respect (*see* C-542/14 *VM Remonts and others* ECLI:EU:C:2015:797).

714. C-48/69 *ICI v Commission* ECLI:EU:C:1972:70, paras 132-133.

715. The test was first put explicitly in C-97/08 P *Akzo Nobel and Others v Commission* ECLI:EU:C:2009:536, para. 60 but there in relation to a 100% shareholding. However, the two-stage test also applies in other circumstances; only the presumption is limited to a quasi-100% shareholding.

would be held (jointly) liable for a fault it did not itself commit.[716] In *Schindler*, this criticism of parental liability was made explicit in similar terms as the criticism of corporate liability, namely that the parent could only be blamed for 'a fault of its own, which may result from its own participation in an infringement or from breach of certain organisational obligations existing within the group'.[717] AG Kokott rejected this argument pointing out that '[t]he connecting factor for the liability of the parent company is not deficient organisation or monitoring of operations within the group, but rather the fact that at the time of the cartel offence the parent company exercised decisive influence over the commercial policy of its subsidiary'.[718] She continued that in those circumstances, the behaviour of the subsidiary is ascribed to the parent as well. The presumption which exists in this respect is not a presumption of fault by the parent, but simply a presumption that the subsidiary and its parent make up one undertaking.[719] The CJEU also rejected this argument by reference to the notion of undertaking,[720] as it has done many times before.

481 Nevertheless, the noted tension in corporate liability between personal liability and liability derived from the actions of others (vicarious or contributory) which I referred to in paragraph 473 above also exists here, in respect of parental liability. Although this tension is less problematic here (the parent and the subsidiary are at least similar entities – namely corporations – contrary to the corporation and its representatives), there are circumstances where it can lead to paradoxes. An example of this is that, although the liability of a parent company cannot exceed that of its subsidiary, the former may nevertheless be fined even though action against the latter is time-barred.[721]

§4.03 FINES

482 Apart from civil law consequences (e.g. nullity of agreements which breach competition law and the possibility to obtain damages for such breaches),

716. *See*, for example, A Riesenkampff and U Krauthausen, 'Liability of parent companies for antitrust violations of their subsidiaries' (2010) European Competition Law Review 38; S Thomas, 'Guilty of a fault that one has not committed. The limits of the group-based sanction policy carried out by the Commission and the European Courts in EU-antitrust law' (2012) Journal of European Competition Law & Practice 11; B Leupold, 'Effective enforcement of EU competition law gone too far? Recent case law on the presumption of parental liability' (2013) European Competition Law Review 570, in particular 579; A-M Van den Bossche, 'Niet schuldig, wel verantwoordelijk. De toerekenbaarheid van inbreuken op het mededingingsrecht binnen groepen' in A Van Hoe en M Vanmeenen (eds) *De vennootschapsgroep in de greep van het recht* (Intersentia 2013) 23.
717. C-501/11 P *Schindler Holding and Others v Commission* ECLI:EU:C:2013:522, para. 90.
718. AG opinion in C-501/11 P *Schindler Holding and others v Commission* ECLI:EU:C:2013:248, para. 95.
719. *See* in particular AG opinion in C-501/11 P *Schindler Holding and others v Commission* ECLI:EU:C:2013:248, para. 118.
720. C-501/11 P *Schindler Holding and Others v Commission* ECLI:EU:C:2013:522, paras 101-116.
721. Compare C-597/13 P *Total v Commission* ECLI:EU:C:2015:613 and C-516/15 P *Akzo Nobel and others v Commission* ECLI:EU:C:2017:314. *See also* the opinion of AG Wahl in the latter case pointing out the tension between personal and derived liability in this respect (C-516/15 P *Akzo Nobel and others v Commission* ECLI:EU:C:2016:1004, in particular paras 61-63).

infringements of competition law can also result in fines. Indeed, the Commission's (and since Regulation 1/2003, NCA's) ability to impose fines for breaches of Article 101 and 102 TFEU is one of the most visible ways in which EU antitrust rules are enforced.

483 Article 23(2)(a) of Regulation 1/2003, like its predecessor Article 15(2)(a) of Regulation 17/62, specifically provides that fines may be imposed by the Commission on undertakings which 'either intentionally or negligently' infringe Articles 101 and 102 TFEU.[722] However, what this means is far from clear. One of the most extensive discussions on this topic in the literature has therefore pointed out that there are 'little developed dogmatics' in this field.[723] The confusion that reigns in this sphere led the European Parliament in 2010 to request that the Commission 'define specific criteria pursuant to which undertakings should be considered to have acted intentionally or negligently'.[724]

484 The case law is unclear in terms of both what 'intentionally or negligently' entails as a minimum to impose a fine (which I will discuss in section [A][1] below) and what the difference is between intentional and negligent infringements (section [A][2]). As pointed out in section [B] below, much of the confusion in this area is due to a mix-up between *mens rea* and ignorance/awareness of illegality. Finally, I will discuss in section [C] how, perhaps as a consequence of the confusion in this area, the impact on fine calculation of the intensity of the *mens rea* is also unclear.

[A] The Meaning of Intention and Negligence

[1] Minimal Mens Rea *Requirement*

485 The maxim *actus non facit reum nisi mens sit rea* is a principle of criminal law. However, Article 23(5) of Regulation 1/2003,[725] like its predecessor Article 15(4) of Regulation 17/62,[726] specifically provides that Commission fining decisions 'shall not

722. Note that pursuant to Article 23(1) of Regulation 1/2003 (and its predecessor Article 15(1) of Regulation 17/62) fines may also be imposed for procedural infringements (e.g. providing incorrect information to the Commission, obstructing a dawn raid, etc.) if undertakings commit these infringements 'intentionally or negligently'. The discussion below focuses on substantive infringements but on occasion I will also refer to case law on procedural infringements.
723. U Kindhäuser and F Meyer, 'Bussgeldrechtliche Folgen des Art. 101 AEUV' in *Frankfurter Kommentar zum Kartellrecht* (Otto Schmidt, 2012) 57 and 68.
724. European Parliament resolution of 9 March 2010 on the Report on Competition Policy 2008, para. 49. It is then quite ironic that recital 42 of Directive 2019/1/EU to empower the competition authorities of the Member States to be more effective enforcers and to ensure the proper functioning of the internal market [2019] OJ L11/3 provides 'The notions of intent and negligence should be interpreted in line with the case law of the Court of Justice of the European Union on the application of Articles 101 and 102 TFEU and not in line with the notions of intent and negligence in proceedings conducted by criminal authorities relating to criminal matters.'
725. Regulation 1/2003 of 16 December 2002 on the implementation of the rules on competition laid down in Articles 81 and 82 of the Treaty [2013] OJ L1/1.
726. Regulation 17 of 6 February 1962: First Regulation implementing Articles 85 and 86 of the Treaty [1962] OJ 13/204.

be of a criminal law nature'.[727] AG Gand stated in his opinion in *ACF Chemiefarma* – putting the cart somewhat before the horse – that this was necessarily so 'since the Member States have not delegated to the Community any powers of a criminal law nature, properly so-called'.[728]

486 Despite this, several Advocates General have opined that the fines imposed by the Commission (and NCAs) are at least of a quasi-criminal nature. AG Vesterdorf pointed out in *Rhône-Poulenc* that, while competition law procedure in the EU is administrative, this is not true of the 'substance of the cases, which all broadly exhibit the characteristics of a criminal law case'.[729] AG Darmon similarly opined in *Wood Pulp II* that '[a] Commission decision in the field of competition ..., particularly where it orders a trader to pay a fine ... is therefore manifestly of a penal nature'.[730] In her opinions in *Schenker* and *Dole Food*, AG Kokott stated that at least cartel penalties and proceedings are, in her view, of a 'quasi-criminal' nature.[731]

487 These opinions reflect the case law of the ECtHR. Although the ECtHR is currently not able to pronounce itself on the compatibility of European law with the European Convention of Human Rights, in the *Menarini* judgment it held that, because of the nature of the offence and the nature and the severity of the penalties imposed, cartel infringement proceedings by NCAs leading to fines constitute a 'criminal charge' in the sense of Article 6 of the ECHR.[732] In *M. & Co.*, which concerned Germany's actions (including the issuing of a writ of execution) in consequence of the Commission decision (substantially confirmed by the CJEU) fining Melchers for concluding agreements restricting parallel trade,[733] the European Commission of Human Rights even went as far as to state that 'the anti-trust proceedings in question would fall under Article 6 (Art. 6) had they been conducted by Germany and not by European judicial authorities'.[734] In her opinion in *KME Germany*, AG Sharpston also considers that a cartel procedure leading to the imposition of a fine 'falls under the "criminal head" of Article 6 ECHR as progressively defined by the European Court of Human Rights'.[735]

488 The CJEU has never explicitly accepted the criminal character of competition proceedings, which is obviously difficult considering the explicit wording of the implementing regulations that the fines are not of a criminal nature.[736] Nevertheless,

727. *See also* C-338/00 P *Volkswagen v Commission* ECLI:EU:C:2003:473, para. 96.
728. AG opinion in C-41/69 *Chemiefarma v Commission* ECLI:EU:C:1970:51, at [1970] ECR 722. *See also* the opinion of AG Mayras in C-7/72 *Boehringer Mannheim v Commission* ECLI:EU:C:1972:107, at [1972] ECR 1300.
729. AG opinion in joined cases T-1/89 to T-4/89 and T-6/89 to T-15/89 *Rhône-Poulenc et al v Commission* ECLI:EU:T:1991:38, at [1991] ECR II 885.
730. AG opinion in joined cases C-89, 104, 114, 116, 117 and 125 to 129/85 *Ahlström Osakeyhtiö and Others v Commission* ECLI:EU:C:1992:293, at [1994] ECR I 1551.
731. AG opinion in C-681/11 *Schenker & Co. and Others* ECLI:EU:C:2013:126, para. 59; AG opinion in C-286/13 P *Dole Food and Dole Fresh Fruit Europe v Commission* ECLI:EU:C:2014:2437, para. 26.
732. *A. Menarini Diagnostics S.R.L. v Italy* App No 43509/08 (ECtHR, 27 September 2011).
733. Commission decision of 14 December 1979 in case 29.595 *Pioneer*.
734. *M. & Co. v Germany* App No 13258/87 (Commission Decision, 9 February 1990).
735. AG opinion in C-272/09 P *KME Germany v Commission* ECLI:EU:C:2011:63, para. 64.
736. *See* C-338/00 P *Volkswagen v Commission* ECLI:EU:C:2003:473, para. 96.

the CJEU has in antitrust cases taken on board the case law of the ECtHR referred to above, 'given the nature of the infringements in question and the nature and degree of severity of the ensuing penalties',[737] also after the *Menarini* judgment.[738] At least implicitly the Court therefore accepts the quasi-criminal nature of antitrust proceedings leading to fines.[739]

489 Regardless of how one qualifies fines for antitrust infringements, in the case of fines imposed by the European Commission, there is an explicit legislative reason to consider that there is a *mens rea* requirement.[740] Indeed, Article 23(2)(a) of Regulation 1/2003, like its predecessor Article 15(2)(a) of Regulation 17/62, provides that fines may (only) be imposed by the Commission on undertakings which 'either intentionally or negligently' infringe Articles 101 and 102 TFEU. In *SPO*, the CJEU confirmed that these constitute 'the conditions which must be fulfilled to enable the Commission to impose fines'.[741]

490 AG Kokott has viewed this provision as the reflection of the principle *nulla poena sine culpa* (no punishment without fault).[742] For this reason, the Commission is required, before imposing a fine in a decision, to already indicate in the statement of objections that it considers that the infringement has been committed 'intentionally or negligently'.[743]

491 What does this entail? As already indicated in Chapter 1 (and as will be discussed in more detail in paragraphs 495ff. below), intentionality is a more stringent form of

737. C-199/92 P *Hüls v Commission* ECLI:EU:C:1999:358, para. 150.
738. C-501/11 P *Schindler Holding and Others v Commission* ECLI:EU:C:2013:522, paras 32-38.
739. W Wils, 'Is criminalization of EU competition law the answer?' in KJ Cseres, MP Schinkel and FOW Vogelaar (eds), *Criminalization of competition law enforcement: economic and legal implications for the EU Member States* (Edward Elgar 2006) 60 has pointed out that the notion of 'criminal charge' in the ECHR has a broader meaning than how criminal law is generally understood and that therefore the provision in Article 23(5) of Regulation 1/2003 is not contradictory to the case law of the ECtHR discussed above (*see* in particular 63-64).
740. *See also* R Bouscant, 'La faute dans les infractions aux règles de concurrence en droit européen' (2000) 36 (1) Revue trimesterielle de droit européen 67, 81-86.
741. C-137/95 P *SPO and Others v Commission* ECLI:EU:C:1996:130, para. 53. *See also* T-271/03 *Deutsche Telekom v Commission* ECLI:EU:T:2008:101, para. 276. Note that Article 5 of Regulation 1/2003 does not contain such a condition for fines imposed by NCAs (although such a condition may of course exist under national legislation), as confirmed by the CJEU in C-681/11 *Schenker & Co. and Others* ECLI:EU:C:2013:404, para. 35. However, Article 13 of Directive 2019/1/EU states that NCAs must be able to impose fines if undertakings intentionally or negligently infringe Article 101 and/or 102 TFEU.
742. *See* AG opinion in C-681/11 *Schenker & Co. and Others* ECLI:EU:C:2013:126, para. 42 and the AG opinion in C-501/11 P *Schindler Holding and others v Commission* ECLI:EU:C:2013:248, paras 114-116. This principle has been found to exist in European law by the opinions of AG verLoren van Themaat and AG Slynn in C-188/82 *Thyassen AG v Commission* ECLI:EU:C:1983:194, at [1983] ECR 3740 and C-270/84 *Estel v Commission* ECLI:EU:C:1983:357, at [1984] ECR 1225 respectively (both cases under the ECSC), but has not been confirmed by the CJEU. *See also* R Bouscant, 'La faute dans les infractions aux règles de concurrence en droit européen' (2000) 36 (1) Revue trimesterielle de droit européen 67, 84.
743. Joined cases C-189, 202, 205 to 208 and 213/02 P *Dansk Rørindustri v Commission* ECLI:EU:C:2005:408, para. 428. *See* already joined cases C-100 to 103/80 *Musique Diffusion Française v Commission* ECLI:EU:C:1983:158, para. 21.

mens rea than negligence. This implies that the minimum requirement in order to impose a fine on an undertaking is negligence. What does negligence mean?

492 Outside of the field of antitrust law, the CJEU has defined negligence 'as entailing an unintentional act or omission by which the person responsible commits a patent breach of the duty of care which he should have and could have complied with in view of his attributes, knowledge, abilities and individual situation'.[744] What such a duty of care entails in the context of competition law has not been clearly defined, however. According to the case law, the condition of Article 23(2)(a) of Regulation 1/2003, like its predecessor Article 15(2)(a) of Regulation 17/62, is 'satisfied where the undertaking concerned cannot be unaware of the anti-competitive nature of its conduct'.[745] This suggests that the duty of care of an undertaking entails that it considers the anticompetitive nature of its conduct.

493 The Commission and the European Courts rarely make explicit what this means in a specific case.[746] The General Court has stated on a number of occasions that 'an undertaking is aware of the anti-competitive nature of its conduct where it is aware of the essential facts' pertaining to that conduct, for example those 'justifying both the finding of a dominant position on the relevant market and the finding by the Commission of an abuse of that position' in the case of abuse of dominance[747] or those 'giving rise … to an effect on trade between Member States' if that is what is in dispute.[748] If the same logic would be followed, an undertaking which 'cannot be unaware' of such essential facts could be found to infringe competition law negligently. Reversely, an undertaking could not be said to be negligent if it could be unaware of such essential facts. The circumstances which would warrant an undertaking being ignorant in this way have not been defined in the case law.

494 As will be discussed in more detail in section [B][1]) below, a mix-up between the notion of negligence and mistake of law has caused an erosion of the notion of negligence to practically result in strict liability.

---

744. In a case concerning negligence under a contract which was part of a community assistance programme: C-47/07 P *Masdar (UK) v Commission* ECLI:EU:C:2008:726, para. 90. The definition comes from C-308/06 *Intertanko* ECLI:EU:C:2008:312, para. 77 where this was used to define 'serious negligence' in Article 4 of Directive 2005/35/EC on ship-source pollution and on the introduction of penalties for infringements [2005] OJ L255/11.
745. C-280/08 P *Deutsche Telekom v Commission* ECLI:EU:C:2010:603, para. 124; C-681/11 *Schenker & Co. and Others* ECLI:EU:C:2013:404, para. 37; C-295/12 P *Telefónica and Telefónica de España v Commission* ECLI:EU:C:2014:2062, para. 156. *See* already the opinion of AG Mayras in C-26/75 *General Motors v Commission* ECLI:EU:C:1975:141, at [1975] ECR 1388-9.
746. AG Mazák even recognized as much in his opinion in C-280/08 P *Deutsche Telekom v Commission* ECLI:EU:C:2010:212, para. 39, but the Court avoided the issue by stating in C-280/08 P *Deutsche Telekom v Commission* ECLI:EU:C:2010:603, para. 134 that it was beyond its jurisdiction to re-examine pleas made before the CFI.
747. T-336/07 *Telefónica and Telefónica de España v Commission* ECLI:EU:T:2012:172, para. 320 with reference to C-322/81 *Nederlandsche Banden-Industrie Michelin* ECLI:EU:C:1983:313, para. 107 and the opinion of AG Mazák in C-280/08 P *Deutsche Telekom v Commission* ECLI:EU:C:2010:212, para. 39.
748. Joined cases T-259 to 264 and 271/02 *Raiffeisen Zentralbank Österreich and Others v Commission* ECLI:EU:T:2006:396, para. 207.

[2] Difference Between Intention and Negligence

495 In the previous section, I have tried to sketch what the minimum requirement of *mens rea* as foreseen in Article 23(2)(a) of Regulation 1/2003 (and Article 15(2)(a) of Regulation 17/62), namely negligence, could entail. This section examines what the difference is between this minimum requirement and the other *mens rea* state mentioned in Article 23(2)(a) of Regulation 1/2003 (and Article 15(2)(a) of Regulation 17/62), namely 'intention'. When can an undertaking be said to have not merely been negligent in infringing Articles 101 and 102 TFEU, but instead to have intended such an infringement?

496 In its early decisional practice, the Commission regularly distinguished between intentional and negligent infringements, and the CJEU and its Advocates General therefore had occasions to pronounce themselves on what the difference was between these two notions.

497 In *Suiker Unie*, AG Mayras defined the intentionally committed infringement as 'to mean that undertakings and their agents were aware that the concerted practices implemented between them or the abuse which they made of their dominant position restricted competition and therefore fell within Article 85 (1) or of Article 86'.[749] Although the Advocate General also seems to imply that there is in these circumstances an awareness of the illegal character of the practices and not just of their objective, his view that the parties committed the infringement intentionally was only based on the latter: 'Among the documents produced for the Court file we have found that a great many of them not only prove the substance of the infringements but throw light on the intentions of the applicants and their common intention to eliminate competition between producers on their respective markets and share out between them exports to third countries.'[750]

498 AG Mayras followed the same logic in his opinion in *General Motors*. With explicit reference to the notions 'commonly accepted in the penal legislation of the Member States' he stated that the concept of intention 'can only be applied where the consequences of the action which gives rise to a claim for damages are intended, or are at least accepted as necessary by the undertaking against which the action is brought. On the other hand the concept of negligence must be applied where the author of the infringement, although acting without any intention to perform an unlawful act, has not foreseen the consequences of his action in circumstances where a person who is normally informed and sufficiently attentive could not have failed to foresee them'.[751] The Advocate General concluded on the facts of the case that General Motors had not

749. AG opinion in joined cases C-40 to 48, 50, 54 to 56, 111, 113 and 114/73 *Suiker Unie and Others v Commission* ECLI:EU:C:1975:78, at [1975] ECR 2120.
750. AG opinion in joined cases C-40 to 48, 50, 54 to 56, 111, 113 and 114/73 *Suiker Unie and Others v Commission* ECLI:EU:C:1975:78, at [1975] ECR 2120.
751. AG opinion in C-26/75 *General Motors v Commission* ECLI:EU:C:1975:141, at [1975] ECR 1388-9.

committed the infringement intentionally,[752] but the CJEU used these same facts to conclude that no abuse had been committed at all.[753]

499 Although the Commission did not distinguish between intention or negligence in its decision in *Hoffmann-La Roche* and the latter also contested that it had even negligently committed an abuse of dominance, the CJEU nevertheless provided some clarification as to what is meant by intentionality in its judgment in this case: 'The suggestions and instructions contained in Management Information and the other internal documents relating to the importance and the anticipated effects of entering into contracts, which provide for the purchaser obtaining his requirements exclusively from Roche and for a system of fidelity rebates, in relation to the retention by Roche of its market shares prove that the applicant intentionally pursued a commercial policy designed to bar the access to the market of new competitors.'[754]

500 In *BMW Belgium*, the Commission made a distinction between BMW Belgium and eight members of its dealers network that were part of the Belgian Dealers' Advisory Committee, on the one hand, and the other Belgian BMW dealers, on the other. The former, according to the Commission, 'intentionally' participated in the infringement because, in light of the case law and earlier Commission decisions, they 'were aware that in agreeing a general export prohibition they were infringing Article 85 (1) of the EEC Treaty [because] in their circular letter they subscribed to formulations of the general export prohibition which are not necessary for and go beyond a selective distribution system'.[755] The latter, on the other hand, 'were at least negligent by being unaware, when signing the agreement, that they were engaging in a prohibited restrictive practice. On reasonable reflection, they should have realized without difficulty that in signing the circular letter they agreed to a general export prohibition which went beyond the needs of a selective distribution system and thereby infringed the competitive rules of the EEC Treaty'.[756] Note that the Commission here again seems to confuse awareness of the consequences of the agreement and awareness of its illegality. On appeal BMW Belgium and the dealers of the Advisory Committee contested that they committed the infringement intentionally and claimed that – although this was contrary to the explicit wording of the circular letter – they had not intended to restrict parallel trade. The Court dismissed this argument, pointing precisely to the explicit terms of the letter.[757]

752. AG opinion in C-26/75 *General Motors v Commission* ECLI:EU:C:1975:141, at [1975] ECR 1389: according to AG Mayras, General Motors 'had failed to foresee that Opel cars which were the subject of parallel imports would be submitted to it for approval, and as it had also failed to carry out in advance a proper study of the real costs involved in such procedures, the department responsible for them applied, no doubt wrongly but as a result of what must merely be regarded as an error, the rate which was then in force'.
753. C-26/75 *General Motors v Commission* ECLI:EU:C:1975:150, paras 11-24.
754. C-85/76 *Hoffmann-La Roche v Commission* ECLI:EU:C:1979:36, para. 139. For the existence of a dominant position, the CJEU seems to limit its analysis to negligence (*ibid.*).
755. Commission decision of 23 December 1977 in case 29.146 *BMW Belgium NV and Belgian BMW dealers*, recital 26.
756. Commission decision of 23 December 1977 in case 29.146 *BMW Belgium NV and Belgian BMW dealers*, recital 27.
757. Joined cases C-32 and 36 to 82/78 *BMW Belgium v Commission* ECLI:EU:C:1979:191, para. 44.

501 In *IAZ*, the CJEU defined the notion of intention as follows: 'all the parties which took part in the drawing-up of the Agreement were aware that the Agreement [...] had as its purpose to restrict parallel imports and that it was capable of affecting trade between Member States, inasmuch as it was actually capable of making parallel imports more difficult, if not impossible. By signing the Agreement in full knowledge of those circumstances, they therefore acted deliberately'.[758] 'Deliberately' is clearly the (too literal) translation of the term '*de propos délibéré*' in Regulation 17/62 (which is 'intentional' in the English language version).

502 The discussion of the early case law above already shows that in many cases, the notions of intention and negligence were confused with awareness or ignorance of illegality. Furthermore, as I will discuss in section [C] below, in most of their case law, the European Courts also did not seem to think that the difference between negligence and intention should have an impact on the level of the fine. It is then not surprising that the Commission in many of its decisions does not specify whether the infringement was committed intentionally or negligently and uses the generic statement that the undertaking simply 'intentionally or at least negligently'[759] or 'intentionally or, at the very least, negligently'[760] or 'at least negligently'[761] committed the infringement.[762]

503 The case law and the decisional practice has therefore not provided much clarity on the difference between these two notions. The only certainty I see in the case law is that concealment efforts are an indication of the intentional nature of the infringement. The Commission has taken this position in several decisions (*see* the discussion in paragraph 622 below). Indeed, as already indicated in Chapter 1, there are good reasons to believe that awareness of illegality is indicative of intention.

504 Given the opacity of the case law, what does the literature say? In *Faull and Nikpay*, the distinction between intention and negligence and the meaning of these terms in Article 23(2)(a) of Regulation 1/2003 (and Article 15(2)(a) of Regulation 17/62) is not discussed.[763] *Bellamy & Child*, however, includes a good summary of the distinction between intention and negligence in antitrust infringements, namely that 'an intentional infringement requires at least the deliberate commission of an act which is designed to achieve anti-competitive ends, or which is committed in the knowledge

758. Joined cases C-96 to 102, 104, 105, 108 and 110/82 *IAZ v Commission* ECLI:EU:C:1983:310, para. 45.
759. *See*, for example, Commission decision of 9 June 1976 in case 29.020 *Vitamins*, recital 28; Commission decision of 4 July 2007 in case 38.784 *Telefónica*, recital 764.
760. *See*, for example, Commission decision of 5 February 1992 in case 31.572 and 32.571 *Building and construction industry in the Netherlands*, recital 140; Commission decision of 21 June 2017 in case 40.013 *Lightning Systems*, recital 73.
761. *See*, for example, Article 1 of Commission decision of 30 January 2008 in case 39.326 *E.ON Energie*; Commission decision of 2 October 2017 in case 39.813 *Baltic Rail*, recital 371.
762. Three decades ago, C Van Acker, *Communautaire sanctionering van ondernemingen* (Kluwer 1987) 330 already noted that the Commission at the time did not clearly distinguish between intention and negligence for fining purposes.
763. Fines are in fact only substantially discussed in the chapter on cartels and there only a short paragraph is devoted to the attenuating circumstance of negligence under the *2006 Fining Guidelines* (*see* A Colomabin, J Kloub and E Sakkers, 'Cartels' in J Faull and A Nikpay (eds), *The EU law of competition* (OUP 2014) 1023, 1308-1309).

that plainly anti-competitive effects would ensue' while '[a]n infringement is probably committed negligently when the undertaking concerned could reasonable foresee that its conduct would have anti-competitive effects'.[764] In the *Frankfurter Kommentar*, there is an extensive discussion of the case law on *mens rea* in fines, basically pointing out that the case law and decisional practice is very confused and mixes up intention and negligence.[765] The *Münchener Kommentar*, after a fairly brief discussion, concludes that 'intention in the sense of Art. 23 is however understood rather widely; it has - from the view of German criminal law - become a certain form of conscious negligence'.[766] It also sees as the only relevant indicator that, if there is an effort to keep the conduct secret, this points to intention.[767]

[B] *Mens Rea* and Ignorance/Awareness of Illegality

505 As is already apparent from the previous section, much of the case law on the relevance of *mens rea* in fines in fact (also) concerns ignorance or awareness of illegality of the infringement. The case law and literature on ignorance of illegality in particular is so substantial that I will devote most of §4.04 to this topic. But I already want to use the basis developed in the previous sections to discuss the relationship between *mens rea* and ignorance/awareness of illegality in the antitrust case law.

506 In Chapter 1, I pointed out that mistakes of law (contrary to mistakes of fact) are normally not considered to be an excuse for infringements. As I will discuss in more detail below in §4.04, this is also true in European antitrust law. Ignorance of the law is not an excuse for committing an infringement. This means that, even if an undertaking is unaware of the content of Article 101 and 102 TFEU and, consequently, of the application of these rules to its conduct, it can still commit an infringement (either intentionally or negligently). Awareness of the law is, in other words, not a *necessary* condition for either intentionality or negligence.

---

764. R Kreisberger and O Draper, 'Fines for substantive infringements' in V Rose and D Bailey (eds), *Bellamy & Child European Union law of competition* (OUP 2013) 1091, 1098 and 1099 respectively. Note that for negligence the text continues 'of the kind prohibited by Article 101(1) or Article 102'.
765. U Kindhäuser and F Meyer, 'Bussgeldrechtliche Folgen des Art. 101 AEUV' in *Frankfurter Kommentar zum Kartellrecht* (Otto Schmidt 2012), in particular 57-75 and 83-91. Much of the discussion of the case law prior to 2000 is based on H Engels, *Unternehmensvorsatz und Unternehmensfahrlässigkeit im Europäischen Kartellrecht* (Berlin Verlag Arno Spitz 2002): although this author points to an evolution in the early case law from a concept of intention that requires awareness of illegality to a concept of intention that does not, and from a concept of negligence that also concerns the normative awareness of law to one that is limited to a normative awareness of facts (*see* at 19-29), he also needs to admit that much of the case law does not fit into this mould (*see* at 30 and 34 in particular).
766. H-H Schneider, 'Art. 23 Geldbussen' in J Bornkamm, F Montag and FJ Säcker (eds), *Münchener Kommentar Europäisches und Deutsches Wettbewerbsrecht* (Beck 2015) 2241, 2252.
767. H-H Schneider, 'Art. 23 Geldbussen' in J Bornkamm, F Montag and FJ Säcker (eds), *Münchener Kommentar Europäisches und Deutsches Wettbewerbsrecht* (Beck 2015) 2241, 2253. There is also a suggestion that any factual mistakes may lead to the qualification of negligence but no practical examples of this are mentioned.

507 However, reversely, awareness of the law is a *sufficient* condition for intentionality. Indeed, if an undertaking is aware that Articles 101 and 102 TFEU prohibit certain conduct, the fact that it engages in this conduct will normally be indicative of intentionality.[768]

508 If *mens rea* is understood normatively (i.e. negligence), awareness of illegality does not come into the picture. Precisely because it is understood normatively, negligence does imply not only that the undertaking was unaware of the illegality of its conduct but also that it was unaware of the relevant facts that should have led it to conclude that what it was doing was wrong.

509 In some of the case law, the distinction (and relationship) between *mens rea* and ignorance/awareness of illegality is discussed according to this logic.

510 For Article 101 TFEU, *IAZ* is a good example. Although the Commission had found that one of the parties had merely acted negligently, the CJEU held that the parties had acted intentionally when signing the agreement in question because they were aware of its anticompetitive consequences and effect on trade. Whether or not they were also aware of the application of the antitrust rules in the Treaty was irrelevant: 'By signing the Agreement in full knowledge of those circumstances [i.e. the fact that the agreement restricted parallel trade], they therefore acted deliberately, whether or not they were aware that, in so doing, they were infringing the prohibition laid down by Article 85 (1) of the Treaty.'[769]

511 A clearly separate discussion dismissing ignorance of illegality as irrelevant for an assessment of intentionality can also be found in the CJEU Article 102 TFEU judgments *Hoffmann-La Roche*, *Michelin I* and *AstraZeneca*, for example, all of which will be discussed in §4.04 below.

512 The General Court has also regularly dismissed arguments as to ignorance of illegality on the basis that these do not demonstrate that an infringement was committed unintentionally. A good example is *Raiffeisen*, where some banks that were part of the Lombard Club cartel in Austria argued that they were not aware that their agreement affected trade between the Member States (and therefore that European antitrust rules were applicable to it). The CFI correctly pointed out that 'whether or not the applicants were aware of the interpretation of the cross-border criterion adopted by the Commission or the case-law is not decisive; what is important is whether they knew of the circumstances specifically giving rise to the capability of the cartel to affect trade between Member States'.[770] The Court concluded that the banks 'were ... aware of the essential facts giving rise in this case to an effect on trade between Member States' and that it was 'not ... appropriate in the present context to ascertain to what extent the

768. *See also* W Wils, 'The European Commission's 2006 guidelines on antitrust fines: a legal and economic analysis' (2007) World Competition 195, 223, footnote 152.
769. Joined cases C-96 to 102, 104, 105, 108 and 110/82 *IAZ v Commission* ECLI:EU:C:1983:310, para. 45.
770. Joined cases T-259 to 264 and 271/02 *Raiffeisen Zentralbank Österreich and Others v Commission* ECLI:EU:T:2006:396, para. 206.

applicants were aware of the incompatibility of their conduct with Article 81 EC' such that '[t]he applicants' arguments purporting to show the lack of any negligence are therefore irrelevant'.[771]

513 Despite the logic described above, on many occasions, the European Courts have mixed up the questions of *mens rea* and ignorance of illegality – often of course following a mix-up by the parties bringing applications for annulment. This has happened in essentially two ways. First of all, when enquiring whether an undertaking acted negligently, i.e. whether it was not but should have been aware of certain *facts*, the European Courts have instead discussed whether the undertaking was not but should have been aware of the *law*. Second, when enquiring whether an undertaking acted intentionally, i.e. whether it was aware of certain *facts*, the European Courts have instead discussed whether the undertaking was aware of the *law*. The first mix-up will be discussed in section [1], the second in section [2].

[1] Mix-Up of Mistake of Fact and Mistake of Law

514 As regards the first mix-up, the CJEU has stated multiple times that, for the minimum requirement to establish liability, namely *negligence*, i.e. that 'the undertaking concerned cannot be unaware of the anti-competitive nature of its conduct', it does not matter 'whether or not it is aware that it is infringing the competition rules of the Treaty'.[772] This statement is as such not wrong: it just confusingly discusses two different matters. It suggests that, because the undertaking has a duty to be aware of the competition rules of the Treaty (*nemo censetur ignorare legem – see* §4.04 below), it must also be aware of the anticompetitive nature of its conduct. But the latter does not follow from the former.

515 As stated above, awareness of illegality can be relevant in the context of intentional infringements, but in the case of allegedly negligent infringements, awareness of the law is simply not at stake: negligence assumes that the undertaking was even unaware of the relevant facts (e.g. the effect of its conduct) so that it could certainly not have been aware of the illegality of those facts (except in the rare case of conscious negligence).

516 Despite this, ignorance or awareness of illegality is often discussed, not only for intentional infringements but also for infringements for which merely negligence is alleged. A good example of this is *Windsurfing*, where the applicant contested a Commission decision finding that the agreements it concluded with licensees infringed

771. Joined cases T-259 to 264 and 271/02 *Raiffeisen Zentralbank Österreich and Others v Commission* ECLI:EU:T:2006:396, paras 207, 209 and 211. Other cases where ignorance of illegality is dismissed as a relevant argument for intentionality include T-15/89 *Chemie Linz v Commission* ECLI:EU:T:1992:37, para. 350; T-141/89 *Tréfileurope v Commission* ECLI:EU:T:1995:62, para. 176.

772. C-280/08 P *Deutsche Telekom v Commission* ECLI:EU:C:2010:603, para. 124; C-681/11 *Schenker & Co. and Others* ECLI:EU:C:2013:404, para. 37; C-295/12 P *Telefónica and Telefónica de España v Commission* ECLI:EU:C:2014:2062, para. 156.

(what was then) Article 85 EC. The applicant not only contested the infringement but also alleged that, if there had been an infringement, this was due to its misunderstanding the scope of a patent. It considered that its mistaken belief was 'in good faith' and that it could therefore not have been accused even of a negligent infringement. Rather than simply dismissing ignorance of the law as an excuse, both AG Lenz and the CJEU engaged with the argument, dismissing the good faith as not sufficiently substantiated.[773] This does not make sense: if a driver contests a speeding ticket because he claims he did not know that he was speeding, it suffices to tell him that he has a legal obligation to pay attention to the speed limit; there is no point in assessing whether he actually knew he was speeding or not.

517 A more recent example is *Deutsche Telekom*, where the dominant undertaking had been found guilty of margin squeeze and a fine had been imposed for 'intentionally or negligently' having committed this infringement. Deutsche Telekom contested this on the basis that because 'its wholesale and retail charges were all authorised by decisions of the [relevant telecom authorities, it] could thus legitimately assume that those charges were lawful'.[774] The General Court dismissed this argument by reference to the established case law,[775] but AG Mazák somewhat confusing only discussed the irrelevance of ignorance of illegality in relation to intentional infringements[776] – as if Deutsche Telekom had merely contested the intentional character. The CJEU followed its Advocate General with reference to *IAZ* (which concerned an intentional infringement) and *Michelin I* (where the CJEU merely stated that Michelin ought to have been aware of the application of the antitrust rules, without linking this to *mens rea*).[777]

518 The CFI has similarly discussed the irrelevance of ignorance of illegality for intentional infringements, even in cases where intentionality was not even claimed.[778]

[2] Mix-Up of Awareness of Facts with Awareness of the Law

519 As indicated above, a second mix-up concerns intentional infringements. Indeed, often undertakings contest the allegedly intentional nature of an infringement by claiming that they were unaware of the law. In response to this, the CJEU has pointed out that mistakes of law are no excuse, i.e. that everyone must be aware of the law (*see* §4.04 below). But it has on occasion gone further than this and deduced from this obligation to be aware of the law that an undertaking must also be aware of certain

773. *See* C-193/83 *Windsurfing International v Commission* ECLI:EU:C:1986:75, paras 104-107 and AG opinion in C-193/83 *Windsurfing International v Commission* ECLI:EU:C:1985:231, at [1986] ECR 639-640.
774. T-271/03 *Deutsche Telekom v Commission* ECLI:EU:T:2008:101, para. 291.
775. T-271/03 *Deutsche Telekom v Commission* ECLI:EU:T:2008:101, para. 295.
776. C-280/08 P *Deutsche Telekom v Commission* ECLI:EU:C:2010:212, para. 39.
777. C-280/08 P *Deutsche Telekom v Commission* ECLI:EU:C:2010:603, para. 124 with reference to joined cases C-96 to 102, 104, 105, 108 and 110/82 *IAZ v Commission* ECLI:EU:C:1983:310, para. 45 and C-322/81 *Nederlandsche Banden-Industrie Michelin v Commission* ECLI:EU:C:1983:313, para. 107.
778. *See*, for example, T-61/89 *Dansk Pelsdyravlerforening v Commission* ECLI:EU:T:1992:79, para. 157.

facts that are relevant for the infringement. However, such a normative awareness of facts is precisely what characterizes negligence, not intention.

520 In *Miller*, for example, the CJEU rejected Miller's argument that it had not committed the infringement intentionally because it was not aware that its conduct entailed a restriction of competition in the sense of Article 101 TFEU:

> the clauses in question were adopted or accepted by the applicant and the latter *could not have been unaware* that they had as their object the restriction of competition between its customers.
>
> Consequently, it is of little relevance to establish whether the applicant knew that it was infringing the prohibition contained in Article 85.[779]

521 Despite the 'consequently' in the last paragraph, it seems that the Court deduced from the irrelevance of Miller's ignorance of the illegality of its behaviour, that also the fact that it (allegedly) was not aware of the object of its conduct, was irrelevant to determine whether it acted intentionally.

522 Based on *Miller*, the CJEU took as confused a position in *Belasco*:

> As the Court has held (*inter alia* in Case 19/77 Miller International Schallplatten GmbH v Commission [1978] ECR 131), it is not necessary for an undertaking to have been aware that it was infringing Article 85 for an infringement to be regarded as having been committed intentionally; it is sufficient that it could not have been unaware that the contested conduct had as its object the restriction of competition.[780]

523 As discussed above, this does not make any sense: on this interpretation, there is no difference any more between intention and negligence.

524 Also in later case law, infringements were often found to have been committed 'intentionally' if the undertaking 'could not have been unaware' of the nature or effect of that behaviour. In *Dansk Pelsdyravlerforening*, for example, the CFI held that 'it is not necessary for an undertaking to have been aware that it was infringing the prohibition laid down by Article 85 of the Treaty for an infringement to be regarded as having been committed intentionally; it is sufficient that it could not have been unaware that the contested conduct had as its object or effect the restriction of competition in the common market'.[781] Similarly in *Raiffeisen*, even though the CFI distinguishes awareness of the law from awareness of facts (*see* paragraph 512 above), awareness of facts for intentional infringements is also interpreted normatively. Indeed, after distinguishing awareness of law from awareness of facts, the Court

779. C-19/77 *Miller International Schallplatten GmbH v Commission* ECLI:EU:C:1978:19, at [1978] ECR 148, para. 18 (emphasis added). *See also* already joined cases C-100 to 103/80 *Musique Diffusion Française v Commission* ECLI:EU:C:1983:158, paras 111-2.
780. C-246/86 *Belasco and Others v Commission* ECLI:EU:C:1989:301, para. 41.
781. T-61/89 *Dansk Pelsdyravlerforening v Commission* ECLI:EU:T:1992:79, para. 157. The CFI merely relied on the C-279/87 *Tipp-Ex v Commission* ECLI:EU:C:1990:57 in support of this ruling, even though this judgment was only published in summary form (*see* [1990] ECR I 261). *Tipp-Ex* refers to *Belasco*, however.

continues that, in order to determine intentionality, 'what is important is whether [the banks] knew of the circumstances specifically giving rise to the capability of the cartel to affect trade between Member States *or, at least, whether they could not have been unaware of them*'.[782]

525 The ambiguity of the normative wording becomes apparent in *Volkswagen*, where the CFI not only repeats this wording but also seems to conclude from the existence of legal rules that the eponymous undertaking 'could not have been unaware' of the effects of its conduct. Indeed, it follows the normative wording as to the constitutive elements of the infringement by saying: 'In view of the existence of settled case-law holding that actions partitioning markets are incompatible with the Community competition rules ..., the applicant could not have been unaware that its conduct hindered competition.'[783]

526 In all of the above examples, the European Courts too hastily conclude from the fact that the undertakings should have been aware of the law, that they also should be aware of certain facts and could be viewed as acting intentionally even if they are not aware of these facts.[784] It is not surprising, then, that the Commission has similarly found intentional infringements in some cases on the basis that the undertakings in question 'could not have been unaware' that their conduct was anticompetitive.[785]

[3] Conclusion

527 The explanations above have made apparent how the confusion between *mens rea* and ignorance of illegality has undermined the relevance of the *mens rea* criterion in sanctioning infringements. From the simple existence of legal rules and the principle that ignorance of the law is no excuse, the European Courts have concluded that infringements were committed negligently and even intentionally. In those circumstances, the difference between negligence and intention collapses and the entire concept of *mens rea* gives way. Contrary to the wording of Article 23(2)(a) of Regulation 1/2003 (and Article 15(2)(a) of Regulation 17/62), antitrust infringements then become strict liability offences and fines can be imposed absent any *mens rea* requirements.

782. Joined cases T-259 to 264 and 271/02 *Raiffeisen Zentralbank Österreich and Others v Commission* ECLI:EU:T:2006:396, para. 206 (emphasis added). *See also* T-399/09 *HSE v Commission* ECLI:EU:T:2013:647, para. 140.
783. T-62/98 *Volkswagen v Commission* ECLI:EU:T:2000:180, para. 334.
784. Note that there is also one instance of the opposite conclusion, namely that because an undertaking was aware of certain facts and therefore acted intentionally, it must have also been aware of the law. This is where Advocate General Mayras states in C-26/75 *General Motors v Commission* ECLI:EU:C:1975:141, at [1975] ECR 1388: 'The use of this term [intention] necessarily implies that the author of the infringement has acted intentionally with the will to commit an act which he knew was unlawful and prohibited by the Treaty and conscious of the unlawful consequences of his behaviour.'
785. *See*, for example, the Commission decision of 14 October 1998 in case 33.708 *British Sugar*, recital 191; Commission decision of 1 October 2003 in case 37.370 *Sorbates*, recital 316; Commission decision of 4 July 2007 in case 38.784 *Telefónica*, recital 725; Commission decision of 23 June 2010 in case 39.092 *Bathroom fittings and fixtures*, recital 1231.

[C] Relevance of the Difference Between Intention and Negligence

528 This section discusses the relevance of any gradation of *mens rea* for fining purposes. Given the confusion between the different levels of *mens rea* and between *mens rea* and ignorance of illegality discussed in the previous section, it can come as no surprise that gradations of *mens rea* have little relevance in fining.

[1] Prior to the 1998 Fining Guidelines

529 While in the old *Boehringer I* judgment, the CJEU still seemed to consider that intentionality (in that case evidenced by awareness of illegality) could be an aggravating factor,[786] most of the early case law seems to consider that whether an infringement has been committed intentionally or negligently does not matter for the level of the fine. Indeed, in *Suiker Unie*, despite the parties and the Advocate General's opinion arguing in that case about the presence of intent, the CJEU held that the infringements were committed 'intentionally or at least negligently, so that the undertakings concerned are liable to pay a fine'.[787]

530 Also in *United Brands*, the CJEU simply held that the infringements 'were at the very least negligent',[788] thereby dismissing arguments from United Brands that it was not aware of its dominant position or of the abusive nature of its practices. It should be noted, however, that the issue in this case was mainly as to the legal qualification of the position of United Brands and of the practices it engaged in, a matter that more concerns the awareness of illegality than the awareness of facts (*see* further below in §4.04).

531 In their opinions in *General Motors* and *BMW Belgium*, AG Mayras and AG Warner respectively disagreed about whether the qualification of negligence versus intention should make a difference in the amount of the fine.[789] But the CJEU did not pronounce itself on this, in the first case finding that there was no abuse and in the second agreeing with the Commission's assessment of the *mens rea* (*see* paragraphs 498 and 500 above).

786. C-45/69 *Boehringer v Commission* ECLI:EU:C:1970:73, para. 58.
787. Joined cases C-40 to 48, 50, 54 to 56, 111, 113 and 114/73 *Suiker Unie and Others v Commission* ECLI:EU:C:1975:174, para. 611.
788. C-27/76 *United Brands v Commission* ECLI:EU:C:1978:22, para. 301.
789. *See* AG opinion in C-26/75 *General Motors v Commission* ECLI:EU:C:1975:141, at [1975] ECR 1390 where AG Mayras states: 'The circumstances to which I have referred in order to find against the existence of "intention" would at least favour a substantial reduction in the amount of the fine, which should only constitute a nominal penalty.' In the AG opinion in joined cases C-32 and 36 to 82/78 *BMW Belgium v Commission* ECLI:EU:C:1979:149, at [1979] ECR 2497, AG Warner argued that 'even if their [i.e. the dealers that were part of the Advisory Committee] action is to be regarded as merely negligent, I do not see how the fines imposed on them could properly be reduced. Their role was a much more active one than that of the other 39, and their membership of the Committee imposed on them an added responsibility. What they did was designed to make their fellow BMW dealers fall into line. The circular they signed even contained a threat addressed to those who did not fall into line'.

532 The CJEU then explicitly stated in its order in *SPO* that, although a fine can only be imposed if an infringement is committed intentionally or negligently, whether it is intentional or merely negligent does not impact on the level of the fine: 'it is apparent from the clear and precise terms of Article 15(2) that it deals with two distinct matters. First, it lays down the conditions which must be fulfilled to enable the Commission to impose fines (initial conditions); these include the condition concerning the intentional or negligent nature of the infringement (first subparagraph). Secondly, it governs determination of the amount of the fine, which depends on the gravity and duration of the infringement (second subparagraph)'.[790] The Court also held in this case that 'infringements committed negligently are not, from the point of view of competition, less serious than those committed intentionally' and as a consequence, there is no need 'to verify, in order to determine the gravity of the infringement, whether it had been committed intentionally or negligently, still less to distinguish between the two cases'.[791] Despite the fact that this position was taken merely in an order (as opposed to a judgment) and that the discussion before the CFI mainly concerned the awareness of illegality, a significant part of the subsequent case law has followed this position. Indeed, the CJEU has repeated it in *Ferriere Nord*[792] and also the CFI has relied on it in later years.[793]

533 However, there is also another track in the case law. In *Thyssen Stahl*, which related to an infringement under the European Coal and Steel Community (ECSC), the CJEU held that, when assessing the seriousness of an infringement, 'the effect of an anti-competitive practice is not a conclusive criterion for assessing the proper amount of a fine. Factors relating to the intentional aspect may be more significant than those relating to the effects, particularly where they relate to infringements which are intrinsically serious, such as price fixing and market sharing'.[794] Based on this position, the CFI has in some subsequent judgments stated that intentional aspects can be taken into account in assessing the gravity in cartel cases.[795]

534 Although there are many instances in the earlier case law where the Commission took into account the intentional character of an infringement when determining its gravity for fine calculation,[796] as already pointed out above (*see* paragraph 502), other

790. C-137/95 P *SPO and Others v Commission* ECLI:EU:C:1996:130, para. 53.
791. C-137/95 P *SPO and Others v Commission* ECLI:EU:C:1996:130, paras 55 and 57.
792. C-219/95 P *Ferriere Nord v Commission* ECLI:EU:C:1997:375, para. 32.
793. T-271/03 *Deutsche Telekom v Commission* ECLI:EU:T:2008:101, para. 279 and (in the context of a procedural infringement) T-332/09 *Electrabel v Commission* ECLI:EU:T:2012:672, para. 237.
794. C-194/99 P *Thyssen Stahl v Commission* ECLI:EU:C:2003:527, para. 118.
795. T-279/02 *Degussa v Commission* ECLI:EU:T:2006:103, para. 251; T-54/03 *Lafarge v Commission* ECLI:EU:T:2008:255, para. 600.
796. *See* Commission decision of 23 April 1986 in case 31.149 *Polypropylene*, recital 107; Commission decision of 2 August 1989 in case 31.553 *Welded Steel Mesh*, recital 197; Commission decision of 19 December 1990 in case 33.133-C *Soda-ash – Solvay*, recital 70. For an example of a case where the Commission deduced intentionality from concealment efforts, *see* Commission decision of 10 January 1996 in case 34.279 *Adalat*, recital 235. A Ortega González, *The enforcement of EU competition law in cartel cases: seeking effectiveness in divergence* (PhD thesis Antwerp 2017) analysed thirty-seven Commission cartel decisions prior to the *1998*

Commission decisions do not specify whether the infringement was committed intentionally or negligently.

[2] *Since the* 1998 Fining Guidelines

535 The publication in 1998 of the first fining guidelines of the Commission could have provided some dogmatic clarity.[797] In these guidelines, the Commission made explicit different steps in the calculation of its fine for substantive infringements: first, it would assess the gravity of the infringement; second, it would calculate its duration; and, third, it would take into account any aggravating or mitigating circumstances.

536 The *1998 Fining Guidelines* pointed out that, to assess the gravity of the infringement, the Commission will look at the type of infringement committed: 'trade restrictions, usually of a vertical nature', were, depending on their market impact, 'minor' or 'serious' infringements, whereas 'price cartels and market-share quotas' were 'very serious' infringements.

537 Although this does not seem to leave any room for *mens rea* considerations, I already indicated in paragraph 533 above that some case law had affirmed that intentional aspects can play a role in assessing the gravity of infringements.[798] Furthermore, the fact that price cartels and market share quota are generally secret could suggest that the awareness of the illegality and the consequent necessary intentionality of the infringement is also relevant in assessing the gravity of the infringement (*see* further §4.04[B] below).

538 Nevertheless, drawing from the distinction between gravity of the infringement, on the one hand, and aggravating and attenuating circumstances, on the other, the CFI has in other case law relegated *mens rea* considerations to the latter. Indeed, it has clarified that, when assessing the gravity of the infringement, the Commission 'must consider the effects arising from the infringement as a whole', whereas 'the individual conduct of each undertaking' needs to be assessed to determine the presence of aggravating or attenuating circumstances.[799] In the literature this approach has (even before these judgments) been said to 'reveal... that market impact factors supply the

Fining Guidelines and found that in twenty-four decisions reference was made to the deliberate character of the infringement as a relevant factor for gravity and in seven decisions concealment efforts were mentioned.

797. Guidelines of 14 January 1998 on the method of setting fines imposed pursuant to Article 15 (2) of Regulation No 17 and Article 65 (5) of the ECSC Treaty [1998] OJ C9/3.

798. Also in the Commission decision of 20 September 2000 in case 36.653 *Opel*, recitals 193-194, to conclude to the 'very serious' character of the infringement, the Commission seems to have taken into account that the undertaking 'committed the infringement intentionally and in full knowledge of its illegality'. *See also* F Castillo de la Torre, 'The 2006 guidelines on fines: reflections on the Commission's practice' (2010) World Competition 359, 374-375 who suggests, based on case law discussed in para. 533 above, that intentional aspects may still play a role in assessing the gravity in cartel cases.

799. T-224/00 *Archer Daniels Midland and Archer Daniels Midland Ingredients v Commission* ECLI:EU:T:2003:195, para. 265; joined cases T-236, 239, 244 to 246, 251 and 252/01 *Tokai Carbon v Commission* ECLI:EU:T:2004:118, para. 203.

cardinal points on its sentencing tariff, while attitudinal factors (such as organized collusive activity, furtiveness and secrecy, antitrust awareness, recidivist behaviour) appear as aggravating factors, or ordinal points, moving up and down the tariff within a range founded upon a base gravity derived from market impact'.[800]

539 Since the intentional or negligent commission of an infringement is an attitudinal factor which is individual to an undertaking (the same infringement may be committed intentionally by one and negligently by another undertaking),[801] following this logic, it can only be taken into account as an aggravating or attenuating circumstance. And indeed, the *1998 Fining Guidelines* list as one of the attenuating circumstances: 'infringements committed as a result of negligence or unintentionally'.[802] Despite including this principle in the *1998 Fining Guidelines*, as far as I am aware, the Commission never actually found this mitigating circumstance present in the subsequent cases it dealt with under these guidelines.[803]

540 This has of course not stopped parties from (unsuccessfully) arguing before the European Courts that the Commission should have taken alleged negligence into account as a mitigating circumstance under the *1998 Fining Guidelines*.[804]

[3] Since the 2006 Fining Guidelines

541 The guidelines for fines for substantive infringements were replaced in 2006.[805] The *2006 Fining Guidelines* provide that the 'gravity' of an infringement is determined by 'the nature of the infringement, the combined market share of all the undertakings concerned, the geographic scope of the infringement and whether or not the

800. C Harding, 'Business cartels as a criminal activity: reconciling North American and European models of regulation' (2002) 9(4) Maastricht Journal of European and Comparative Law 393, 412.
801. *See*, for example, *BMW Belgium* and *IAZ*.
802. *See* section 3 of the Guidelines of 14 January 1998 on the method of setting fines imposed pursuant to Article 15 (2) of Regulation No 17 and Article 65 (5) of the ECSC Treaty [1998] OJ C9/3.
803. W Wils, 'The European Commission's 2006 guidelines on antitrust fines: a legal and economic analysis' (2007) World Competition 195, 223, footnote 151 also states that there have been no cases. *See also* F Engelsinn, 'Die Bussgeldleitlinien der Europäischen Kommission von 2006' (2007) Wirtschaft und Wettbewerb 470, 479.
804. *See* joined cases T-259 to 264 and 271/02 *Raiffeisen Zentralbank Österreich and Others v Commission* ECLI:EU:T:2006:396, para. 470.
805. Note that, although they only concern substantive infringements, that does not exclude that they also affect fine calculation for procedural infringements. AG Bot, for example, suggested in his opinion in C-89/11 P *E.ON Energie v Commission* ECLI:EU:C:2012:375, para. 130 that, since the *2006 Fining Guidelines* consider negligence an attenuating circumstances, this should also be the case in relation to procedural infringements. The CJEU did not follow this opinion, however (*see* C-89/11 P *E.ON Energie v Commission* ECLI:EU:C:2012:738). *See also* the Commission decision of 10 June 2009 in case M.4994 *Electrabel / Compagnie National du Rhône*, recitals 220-223 where the Commission rejected non-concealment as an attenuating circumstance although it did accept that this pointed to mere negligence (confirmed in T-332/09 *Electrabel v Commission* ECLI:EU:T:2012:672, para. 274).

infringement has been implemented'.[806] As the 'most harmful restrictions of competition' 'by their nature', these guidelines list '[h]orizontal price-fixing, market-sharing and output-limitation agreements'.[807]

542 Once again this suggests that *mens rea* factors do not play a role in assessing the gravity of an infringement. However, the *2006 Fining Guidelines* add, when determining that horizontal price-fixing, market-sharing and output-limitation agreements are the most serious infringements, that these are 'usually secret'. This suggests that awareness of illegality, which necessarily implies intentionality, is relevant for the gravity of the infringement. The Commission has taken this position not only in cartel cases but also, for example, in *Intel*, where it took into account, when assessing the gravity of the infringement, 'the fact that Intel took measures to conceal the conducts established in this Decision, which made it more difficult to detect and sanction them'.[808] Further case law and decisional practice will be discussed in paragraph 622 below.

543 Like their predecessor, the *2006 Fining Guidelines* explicitly state that *mens rea* can play a role in individualizing the fine. They provide in particular that a fine can be mitigated 'where the undertaking provides evidence that the infringement has been committed as a result of negligence'.[809] Instances where this attenuating circumstance has been found are rare.[810]

544 One instance in which the Commission granted a reduction for negligence was *Telefónica*. In this case the Commission found that the dominant Spanish telecom operator had abused its position by setting its national and regional wholesale broadband prices at a level which resulted in margin squeezes for downstream competitors. The Commission nevertheless, 'taking the view most favourable to the company', accepted that in respect of the *regional* broadband prices, Telefónica's conduct may have been merely negligent (albeit 'extremely serious' negligence) and therefore reduced the fine by 10%.[811] In fact, the Spanish telecom regulator had calculated maximum regional wholesale prices for Telefónica based on forecasted costs provided by Telefónica but 'it should have been clear to Telefónica that this forecast was unrealistic' as it had in fact exceeded the volume on which the forecast was based. As a consequence, 'a diligent economic operator, who is in possession of detailed information about its own actual cost and revenue data, must have realized that the

806. Paragraph 22 of the Guidelines of 1 September 2006 on the method of setting fines imposed pursuant to Article 23(2)(a) of Regulation No 1/2003 [2006] OJ C210/2.
807. Paragraph 23 of the Guidelines of 1 September 2006 on the method of setting fines imposed pursuant to Article 23(2)(a) of Regulation No 1/2003 [2006] OJ C210/2.
808. Commission decision of 13 May 2009 in case 37.990 *Intel*, recital 1785.
809. Paragraph 29, second indent of the Guidelines of 1 September 2006 on the method of setting fines imposed pursuant to Article 23(2)(a) of Regulation No 1/2003 [2006] OJ C210/2.
810. A Ortega González, *The enforcement of EU competition law in cartel cases: seeking effectiveness in divergence* (PhD thesis Antwerp 2017) 610 states that in no cartel cases under the *2006 Fining Guidelines* the argument that the infringement was committed out of negligence was accepted.
811. Commission decision of 4 July 2007 in case 38.784 *Telefónica*, recital 765.

actual data were quite different from the estimates used by the [regulator] during the relevant period'.[812]

545 Telefónica argued before the General Court that it should also have received a reduction for negligence in relation to the national wholesale prices, but this was rejected on the basis that national wholesale prices were never regulated by the national regulator. Also, the argument that the negligence was not 'extremely serious' was summarily rejected by the Court, as well as the argument that Telefónica should have benefited from a greater fine reduction than Deutsche Telekom which had received a 10% reduction because national authorities had permitted the wholesale prices in that case.[813]

546 The only other case where the undertakings appear to have substantially argued negligence on appeal is *ENI*, where the eponymous undertaking argued that the employee that attended the Candle Wax cartel meetings mistakenly believed that he attended meetings of a legitimate trade association. To substantiate this claim, it provided the CFI with a report prepared by this employee to its superior. The Court dismissed this argument pointing to the 'manifestly anticompetitive content' of the meetings, such that any appearance that they were organized by a legitimate trade association was irrelevant.[814]

[D] Conclusion

547 Article 23(2)(a) of Regulation 1/2003, like its predecessor Article 15(2)(a) of Regulation 17/62, specifically provides that fines may (only) be imposed by the Commission on undertakings which 'either intentionally or negligently' breach Article 101 or 102 TFEU. Negligence, which should be the minimum requirement for a fine, could be taken to mean that an undertaking could not be unaware of essential facts pertaining to its conduct (the conduct itself, its effects and its circumstances) which constitute the objective elements of the infringements. Intention, however, could refer to the actual awareness of the undertaking of these facts.

548 However, the discussion in the case law has mixed up these states of *mens rea* with awareness or ignorance of illegality. As a consequence, negligence has been found merely on the basis that an undertaking should have been aware of the relevant legal rules (suggesting that the fines could be imposed under strict liability) and intention has been found on the basis that the undertaking 'could not have been unaware' of the objective facts pertaining to the infringement (which uses an objective conception of intention akin to negligence).

812. Commission decision of 4 July 2007 in case 38.784 *Telefónica*, recitals 727-728.
813. T-336/07 *Telefónica and Telefónica de España v Commission* ECLI:EU:T:2012:172, paras 456-460. For the *Deutsche Telekom* case *see* paras 567 and 569 in §4.04 below.
814. T-558/08 *Eni v Commission* ECLI:EU:T:2014:1080, paras 264-272. *See also* T-332/09 *Electrabel v Commission* ECLI:EU:T:2012:672, para. 237 although this concerns a procedural infringement.

549 At the same time, although some case law suggests that evidence of intentionality (or the absence thereof) could be relevant for the calculation of the fine, either to assess the gravity of the infringement or as an individual aggravating or attenuating circumstance, in most of the case law, the impact of *mens rea* on the fine level is not explicitly discussed. Although the *1998 Fining Guidelines* (and the *2006 Fining Guidelines*) relegated *mens rea* to the individualizing factors for the calculation of the fine, some of the case law still discusses it in the context of gravity as well. In any event, also after the introduction of these guidelines, *mens rea* is rarely used to modulate the fine.

§4.04 KNOWLEDGE OR IGNORANCE OF ILLEGALITY

550 As we have seen in Chapter 1, the required *mens rea* for an offence can be absent in the case of a mistake of fact: if a gunman (wrongly) thinks that the target he is shooting is inanimate, he cannot have the intent to kill and therefore cannot be guilty of murder. Mistakes of law, however, generally do not exclude criminal liability.

551 The first part of this section describes how mistakes of law (and therefore an undertaking's ignorance of the illegality of its behaviour) are dealt with in EU antitrust law, in particular for the purpose of fines.

552 In the second part of this section, I will also consider the reverse situation, namely the situation where the undertaking is (or should be) acutely aware of the illegality of its behaviour.

[A] Ignorance of Illegality

553 Most competition law infringements are not *mala in se*, i.e. legal prohibitions that coincide with moral prohibitions. They are, *mala prohibita*, i.e. behaviour that is illegal simply because society has decided to prohibit it. Before the antitrust provisions were included in the ECSC and EEC treaties in the 1950s, the business world in Europe did not seem to consider that even cartels were somehow 'bad'. On the contrary, cartels were an economic institution before the Second World War.[815] The disbelief of the business world at the prohibition of cartels after the Second World War can be illustrated by the fact that certain cartels were even notified to the Commission for a negative clearance under Regulation 17/62.[816]

554 For example, a number of German, Belgian and Dutch cement producers notified the Commission on 30 October 1962 of a market-sharing agreement also containing price-fixing provisions and restrictions on the construction of new cement works.

815. *See* C Harding, 'Business cartels as a criminal activity: reconciling North American and European models of regulation' (2002) 4 Maastricht Journal of European and Comparative Law 393, in particular 407.

816. The fact that the Commission could not impose a fine for the cartel between notification and its decision on the notified agreement (*see* Article 15(5) of Regulation 17/62) certainly also encouraged notification. But cartelists who really wanted to continue their unlawful activities had better remained silent about them.

When the Commission in 1966 informed the parties to the agreement that it was incompatible with Article 101 TFEU, they brought an appeal (on procedural grounds) to the CJEU.[817]

555 The Dutch cement dealers' association also notified the Commission on 31 October 1962 of a number of agreements concluded between its members regarding the prices at which cement could be sold. The Commission's decision finding that these agreements were contrary to Article 101 TFEU was similarly appealed.[818]

556 'Even the most obstinate cartels have a learning curve'[819] though and, after these decisions and judgments made it clear that cartels were illegal, many businesses abolished cartels or concluded them in secret, hoping that the Commission would not detect them. But not everyone may have picked up the new law of the land, and there are still many areas of antitrust law where the rules are not 100% obvious. The question then arises as to whether it is relevant that undertakings know that what they are doing is illegal or not.

557 As I will discuss in more detail below, a number of Advocates General have argued that, under certain circumstances, mistakes of law should exclude liability of the undertaking concerned. In particular in the German literature, the same argument has been made.[820] The interest in this topic in Germany is probably due to the importance of the subjective element in the criminal law there and the scholarly debate between proponents of the *Schuldtheorie* and the *Vorsatztheorie* (*see* the discussion on this topic in paragraph 77 above).

558 Despite this, the Court of Justice has been fairly strict in absolving liability in the case of mistakes of law. In principle, the CJEU considers that, if the undertaking in question has the relevant factual information to assess its legal position, then it does not matter whether it is aware of the legal qualification of that position.

559 Undertakings have argued mistakes of law in respect of different material elements of the Article 101 and Article 102 TFEU infringements but mainly in relation to the existence of a restriction of competition (in Article 101 TFEU cases) and the existence of an abuse (in Article 102 cases).[821] In respect of both, the CJEU has held that a fine can be imposed 'where the undertaking concerned cannot be unaware of the

817. Joined cases C-8-11/66 *Cimenteries and Others v Commission* ECLI:EU:C:1967:7.
818. Case C-8/72 *Vereeniging van Cementhandelaren v Commission* ECLI:EU:C:1972:84.
819. JM Joshua and S Jordan, 'Combinations, concerted practices and cartels: adopting the concept of conspiracy in European community competition law' (2004) 24 Northwestern Journal of International Law & Business 647, 657.
820. Even more strongly since the modernization of EU antitrust law. *See* M Dreher and S Thomas, 'Rechts- und Tatsachenirrtümer unter der neuen VO 1/2003' (2004) Wirtschaft und Wettbewerb 8; F Dietrich, *Der Rechtsirrtum im Kartellrecht* (PhD thesis Bonn 2006) in particular 268-269; U Kindhäuser and F Meyer, 'Bußgeldrechtliche Folgen des Art. 101 AEUV' in *Frankfurter Kommentar zum Kartellrecht* (Otto Schmidt 2012).
821. But, for alleged mistakes of law as to the existence of a dominant position, *see* C-27/76 *United Brands v Commission* ECLI:EU:C:1978:22, para. 298; and for mistakes of law as to the effect on trade between Member States, *see* C-246/86 *Belasco and Others v Commission* ECLI:EU:C:1989:301, para. 41 and C-681/11 *Schenker & Co. and Others* ECLI:EU:C:2013:404.

anti-competitive nature of its conduct, whether or not it is aware that it is infringing the competition rules of the Treaty'.[822]

560 The position of the European Courts has basically been that, in case an undertaking entertains any doubts as to the application of the EU antitrust rules to an agreement or practice, it should notify the arrangement to the Commission to obtain legal certainty.[823] As discussed further on, the logic of this reasoning has been undermined by the modernization of EU antitrust law and the abolition of the negative clearance procedure, but the CJEU has nevertheless continued its strict interpretation.

561 There are, however, a few circumstances where the European Courts and the Commission have accepted that mistakes of law are excusable:

(a) This is first of all the case when the doctrine of legitimate expectations applies: if a mistake of law is the result of assurances given by an EU institution (such as the European Commission) on the legality of certain behaviour, an undertaking's mistake of law is not attributable to it.
(b) Second, the Commission sometimes foregoes fines in cases which raise novel legal questions, although the European Courts have rarely accepted such an argument by the undertakings concerned.
(c) Third, some of the literature suggests that the size of an undertaking should be a relevant consideration to determine whether a mistake of law is excusable. However, despite a number of *obiter* statements, the European Courts never seem to have accepted such an argument. The Commission's guidance, however, does allow for an argument based on size in limited circumstances.
(d) Finally, despite doctrinal arguments and AG opinions in this sense, erroneous legal advice has not been accepted as an excuse for a mistake of law.

562 Each of these elements will be discussed in more detail below.

[1] Mistakes of Law as a Result of Legitimate Expectations

563 The earliest antitrust judgment in which mistakes of law have been discussed appears to be *Suiker Unie*. This judgment is best known for its discussion of the notion of concerted practices, but the Commission decision to which it relates did not only allege a concerted practice between a number of sugar manufacturers. One of the manufacturers, Pfeifer & Langen, had also entered into a number of distribution agreements which required the distributors to exclusively procure sugar from Pfeifer & Langen: according to the Commission, this facilitated the market sharing between the

822. For the application of Article 101 TFEU, *see* C-681/11 *Schenker & Co. and Others* ECLI:EU:C:2013:404, para. 37; for Article 102 TFEU: C-280/08 P *Deutsche Telekom v Commission* ECLI:EU:C:2010:603, para. 124; C-295/12 P *Telefónica and Telefónica de España v Commission* ECLI:EU:C:2014:2062, para. 156.

823. C-85/76 *Hoffmann-La Roche v Commission* ECLI:EU:C:1979:36, para. 134; T-29/92 *SPO and Others v Commission* ECLI:EU:T:1995:34, para. 359.

different sugar producers. Pfeifer & Langen claimed that the distributors with which it had concluded the agreements were not actually independent dealers but should be viewed as commercial agents as described in the Commission Guidelines from 1962 on agency agreements applicable at the time.[824] The CJEU did not agree with Pfeifer & Langen's qualification of the distributors as agents. However, Pfeifer & Langen also argued that it should at least not be fined for entering into these distribution agreements, 'since the Commission's communication of 1962 misled it by giving the impression that the trade representatives contracts were in any case compatible with the provisions of [Article 101 TFEU]'.[825] Somewhat reluctantly, the CJEU followed Pfeifer & Langen's reasoning:

> Although the applicant must have known that the organization of its marketing network on the basis of agency agreements entered into by it with commercial undertakings which were not simply ordinary auxiliaries was likely to restrict competition, the possibility that the wording of the said communication could induce the belief that such a practice was accepted as being compatible with the Treaty cannot nevertheless be ruled out.
>
> Therefore this infringement cannot be taken into consideration for the purpose of fixing the amount of the fine.[826]

564 Another example where the defence of legitimate expectations was successfully made is in the *Far Eastern Freight Conference* judgment of the CFI. This case concerned the agreements by the Far Eastern Freight Conference to fix the tariffs for certain activities undertaken by its members. The fixing of the tariffs for maritime transport was at the time exempted from the application of Article 101 TFEU by Regulation 4056/86,[827] but the Conference had also fixed tariffs for certain inland transport services and cargo handling services, in particular in the context of intermodal transport. The Commission had found that there was no exemption for the fixing of tariffs of these services and had therefore found that the members of the Far Eastern Freight Conference had infringed Article 101 TFEU and had imposed fines of ECU 10,000 on each of the members.[828]

565 The CFI upheld the Commission's finding of an infringement but it annulled the fine imposed by the Commission. One of the grounds for this was that the Court considered that:

> numerous factors led the applicants to believe that the contested agreement was lawful. Besides the long-standing and public nature of the contested agreement, it should be stressed particularly that in a joint declaration annexed to the minutes of

824. Communication on exclusive dealing contracts with commercial agents [1962] OJ 139/2921.
825. Joined cases C-40 to 48, 50, 54 to 56, 111, 113 and 114/73 *Suiker Unie and Others v Commission* ECLI:EU:C:1975:174, paras 555.
826. Joined cases C-40 to 48, 50, 54 to 56, 111, 113 and 114/73 *Suiker Unie and Others v Commission* ECLI:EU:C:1975:174, paras 556-557.
827. Regulation 4056/86 laying down detailed rules for the application of Articles 85 and 86 of the Treaty to maritime transport [1986] OJ L378/4.
828. Commission decision of 21 December 1994 in case 33.218 *Far Eastern Freight Conference*.

> the Council meeting at which Regulation No 4056/86 was adopted, the Commission itself stated as follows: 'multimodal sea/land transport operations are subject to the rules of competition adopted for land transport and to those laid down for sea transport. In practice, non-application of Article 85(1) [of the EEC Treaty] will be the rule as regards the organisation and execution of successive or supplementary multimodal ... transport operations and the fixing or application of inclusive rates for such transport operations, since both Article 2 of Regulation No 4056/86 and Article 3 of Regulation No 1017/68 state that the prohibition laid down by Article 85(1) of the Treaty shall not apply to such practices'. Whilst there is no need in the context of the present plea to rule on the meaning and precise scope of that declaration, it suffices to point out that it at least gave rise to doubts on the part of the applicants and led them to believe that their agreement was not unlawful.[829]

566 Legitimate expectations can only arise as a result of assurances given by the EU institutions. While legal obligations imposed by national law can be the basis for the state compulsion defence,[830] mere assurances or permissions given by those authorities cannot absolve an undertaking from fines.

567 As a consequence, the setting of maximum prices by national legislation does not prevent companies from competing with lower prices and therefore an infringement of Article 101 TFEU can arise if they collude on these prices.[831] Similarly, the approval by the German telecoms regulator of the wholesale tariffs charged by Deutsche Telekom did not prevent the combination of those wholesale tariffs and Deutsche Telekom's retail tariffs from resulting in a margin squeeze: Deutsche Telekom 'could not be unaware that, notwithstanding the authorisation decisions of RegTP, it had genuine scope to fix its retail prices and, consequently, to reduce the margin squeeze by increasing those prices'.[832]

568 Authorizations granted by NCAs can also not absolve an undertaking from liability since national authorities and courts are not permitted to adopt decisions which prevent the application of EU competition law by the Commission and the European Courts.[833] Along the same lines, the General Court rejected the attempt of the undertaking in *Dansk Pelsdyravlerforening* to escape a fine by relying on the Danish Monopoltilsynet's opinion on the legality of its practices.[834]

569 Nevertheless, the Commission has accepted that the authorization or encouragement of an infringement by national authorities can be a mitigating circumstance in the

829. T-86/95 *Compagnie Générale Maritime and others v Commission* ECLI:EU:T:2002:50, para. 485.
830. *See* C-198/01 *CIF v AGCM* ECLI:EU:C:2003:430, para. 53. *See also* already joined cases C-40 to 48, 50, 54 to 56, 111, 113 and 114/73 *Suiker Unie and Others v Commission* ECLI:EU:C:1975:174, paras 36-73 where the CJEU held that Italian sugar regulations left too little space for competition for Article 101 TFEU to apply.
831. Joined cases C-240, 241, 242, 261, 262, 268 and 269/82 *Stichting Sigarettenindustrie v Commission* ECLI:EU:C:1985:488, paras 27-29.
832. T-271/03 *Deutsche Telekom v Commission* ECLI:EU:T:2008:101, para. 296, confirmed in C-280/08 P *Deutsche Telekom v Commission* ECLI:EU:C:2010:603, paras 125-126. *See also* T-336/07 *Telefónica and Telefónica de España v Commission* ECLI:EU:T:2012:172, paras 299-301.
833. C-375/09 *Tele2 Polska* ECLI:EU:C:2011:270, paras 19-30.
834. T-61/89 *Dansk Pelsdyravlerforening v Commission* ECLI:EU:T:1992:79, para. 156.

fine calculation. This practice developed by the European Commission several decades ago[835] was explicitly included in its *2006 Fining Guidelines*.[836] In *Deutsche Telekom*, the Commission granted a 10% reduction of the fine on this basis.[837] In *Bananas*, the Commission reduced the basic amount of the fine by 60% because of the 'specific regulatory regime relating to bananas' even though 'the regulatory regime cannot be regarded as having encouraged or condoned the infringing conduct'.[838]

570 The CFI has not granted fine reductions on this ground in any cases where the Commission did not do so.[839]

571 The question of legitimate expectations as a result of authorization by national authorities gained a particular poignancy after the entry into force of Regulation 1/2003. Would the increased role of NCAs in enforcing Articles 101 and 102 TFEU also affect their ability to create legitimate expectations? In the 2013 Grand Chamber *Schenker* judgment, the CJEU decided it did not.

572 As already indicated above in paragraphs 461 and 462, this case concerned a cartel between the Austrian freight forwarders which had been exempted from Austrian competition law as a minor cartel. The Austrian Cartel Court had also explicitly stated in response to the SSK's (earlier) request for approval of the conference and implicitly in response to the request for a declaration that the conference was a minor cartel that the cartel did not affect trade between the Member States. The question therefore arose as to what legitimate expectations the SSK could derive from this opinion of the Austrian Cartel Court.

573 AG Kokott referred to the doctrine of the excusable mistake of law under German law and expounded the view that, if certain conditions were fulfilled, the position taken by an NCA or court could create legitimate expectations. AG Kokott's opinion is to a significant extent informed by the changed institutional framework of EU antitrust enforcement under Regulation 1/2003. Indeed, since the entry into force of that Regulation, it is no longer possible to notify agreements to the European Commission to obtain a negative clearance, and it is therefore more difficult to obtain legal certainty as to the lawfulness of an agreement. Furthermore, Regulation 1/2003 decentralized

835. *See*, for example, the Commission decision of 19 April 1977 in case 28.841 *ABG/Oil companies*; Commission decision of 9 December 1998 in case 34.466 *Greek Ferries*, recital 163; Commission decision of 20 October 2005 in case 38.281 *Italian Raw Tobacco*, recitals 361-362.
836. Guidelines on the method of setting fines imposed pursuant to Article 23(2)(a) of Regulation No 1/2003 [2006] OJ C210/2, para. 29, last indent.
837. Commission decision of 21 May 2003 in cases 37.451, 37.578 and 37.579 *Deutsche Telekom AG*, recital 212.
838. Commission decision of 15 October 2008 in case 39.188 *Bananas*, recital 472.
839. *See* joined cases T-259 to 264 and 271/02 *Raiffeisen Zentralbank Österreich and Others v Commission* ECLI:EU:T:2006:396, paras 504-505. However, in joined cases T-217 and 245/03 *FNCBV and Others v Commission* ECLI:EU:T:2006:391, paras 355-361, the General Court increased the fine reduction granted by the Commission for the specific circumstances of the case (which included 'intervention measures taken by the Community and national authorities aimed at restoring balance in the beef market') from 60% to 70%, although this mainly seems to have been 'in consideration of the fact that this is the first time that the Commission has sanctioned this type of anti-competitive conduct'.

EU antitrust enforcement: although national authorities and courts cannot grant a negative clearance, in AG Kokott's view, if they find in a decision that certain behaviour does not infringe EU antitrust law (e.g. when a national court annuls a decision by a national authority to that effect), this can create legitimate expectations for the undertakings involved. The legitimacy of these conditions would be conditioned on (i) the undertakings having comprehensively and truthfully informed the authority/court of all relevant circumstances, (ii) express statements of the authority/court on the matter in relation to which an error of law is invoked, (iii) the statement by the authority/court not being manifestly incorrect and (iv) the undertaking in question acting in good faith. AG Kokott considered that these conditions were not fulfilled in this case.[840]

574 However, the CJEU did not follow its Advocate General. It simply held in a Grand Chamber judgment:

> As for the national competition authorities, since they do not have the power to adopt a negative decision, that is to say, a decision concluding that there is no infringement of Article 101 TFEU (Case C-375/09 *Tele2 Polska* [2011] ECR I-3055, paragraphs 19 to 30), they cannot cause undertakings to entertain a legitimate expectation that their conduct does not infringe that provision.[841]

575 Also after Regulation 1/2003, therefore, only mistakes of law induced by the European institutions can be excusable.

[2] Mistakes of Law Due to Novel Situations Excusable at the Commission's Discretion

576 An argument that is related to legitimate expectations and that has arisen several times before the Commission and the European Courts is the argument that no precedents existed in the specific field in which the Commission finds an infringement and that therefore no fine should be imposed – or that this should act as a mitigating factor. In the absence of clear precedents, the principle of legality (*nullum crimen sine lege, nulla poena sine lege*) may be breached: undertakings could not foresee that their practices would be illegal.[842] While the European Courts accept that this principle applies to sanctions in European competition law,[843] they have generally refused to absolve undertakings from liability entirely on this ground. However, the European Commission has on occasion granted fine reductions for this reason.

577 This issue was already raised in the Commission's 1975 decision in *Chiquita*, fining United Brands Company (UBC), the owner of the Chiquita brand, for four

840. Opinion of AG Kokott in C-681/11 *Schenker & Co. and Others* ECLI:EU:C:2013:126, paras 79-102.
841. C-681/11 *Schenker & Co. and Others* ECLI:EU:C:2013:404, para. 42.
842. *See* P Beauvais, 'Le droit à la prévisibilité en matière pénale dans la jurisprudence des cours européennes' (2007) 29 Archives de politique criminelle 3, in particular 11-18.
843. Joined cases C-189, 202, 205 to 208 and 213/02 P *Dansk Rørindustri v Commission* ECLI:EU:C:2005:408, para. 218.

different abuses of its dominant position on the Northern European banana market. These abuses included not only restrictive commercial conditions and a refusal to deal but also discriminatory and excessive pricing. In its decision, the Commission stated: 'With regard to UBC's pricing policy, account should also be taken of the fact that this Decision represents the first occasion on which such a policy has been fully considered in the light of Article 86 of the EEC Treaty. ... In all the circumstances the amount of the fine should be moderate in so far as it relates to infringements arising from UBC's pricing policy.'[844]

578 In its application to the CJEU, UBC raised the argument in a much broader manner, arguing that 'it did not know that it was in a dominant position, still less that it had abused it, especially as, according to the case-law of the Court to date, only undertakings which were pure monopolies or controlled an overwhelming share of the market have been held to be in a dominant position'.[845]

579 AG Mayras did not consider this issue in his opinion, but the CJEU rejected the argument on the facts:

> UBC is an undertaking which, having engaged for a very long time in international and national trade, has special knowledge of anti-trust laws and has already experienced their severity.
>
> UBC, by setting up a commercial system combining the prohibition of the sale of bananas while still green, discriminatory prices, deliveries less than the amounts ordered, all of which was to end in strict partitioning of national markets, adopted measures which it knew or ought to have known contravened the prohibition set out in Article 86 of the Treaty.
>
> The Commission therefore had good reason to find that UBC's infringements were at the very least negligent.[846]

580 This issue was again discussed shortly afterwards in the 1979 *Hoffmann-La Roche* judgment and the AG opinion in that case. The Commission had fined Hoffmann-La Roche for the abuse of a dominant position on a number of vitamin market through the use of exclusivity agreements and loyalty-inducing rebates. In respect of the fine, Hoffmann-La Roche argued that it had not acted 'intentionally or negligently': 'because of the uncertain interpretation of the concepts constituting the offence, [it] was so placed that its ignorance of the unlawful nature of its conduct was excusable'.[847]

581 AG Reischl followed the applicant's reasoning and opined that 'one should not hesitate to speak in terms of a mistake of law excluding liability' in this case. According to the Advocate General, '[i]t can at least be stated that the degree of guilt is so small that there was no ground for imposing a fine, especially on an undertaking which by common consent behaved in an extremely co-operative way during the administrative proceedings and was ready to discontinue the conduct complained of forthwith'.[848]

---

844. Commission decision of 17 December 1975 in case 26.699 *Chiquita*.
845. C-27/76 *United Brands v Commission* ECLI:EU:C:1978:22, para. 298.
846. C-27/76 *United Brands v Commission* ECLI:EU:C:1978:22, paras 299-301.
847. C-85/76 *Hoffmann-La Roche v Commission* ECLI:EU:C:1979:36, at [1979] ECR 501.
848. C-85/76 *Hoffmann-La Roche v Commission* ECLI:EU:C:1978:162, at [1979] ECR 597.

582 The CJEU did not approach Hoffmann-La Roche's objections from the perspective of the doctrine of the excusable error of law. It instead analysed the application of the antitrust provisions in the Treaty of Rome and pointed out that the relevant rules 'are not imprecise and impossible to foresee as Roche claims'.[849] According to the CJEU, 'at the very least the possibility, if not the probability of [a prohibitive] interpretation of the law had to be taken into consideration by a vigilant commercial operator', which furthermore could have requested a negative clearance from the Commission to obtain legal certainty.[850]

583 The Court took a similar position in its 1983 *Michelin I* judgment. The Commission had found that Michelin had abused its dominant position on the tyre market in the Netherlands through the use of a loyalty-inducing discount system. Michelin argued that the discount system it used was entirely based on quantitative factors and could therefore not be equated to the loyalty rebates described in the *Hoffmann-La Roche* judgment (and Michelin argued that the Commission's decision was even contrary to the *Hoffmann-La Roche* judgment). AG verLoren van Themaat tore Michelin's argument apart:

> I think that Michelin knowingly and successfully tried, by agreeing sales targets with the dealers, to bind them to itself and to maintain its production and sales at least at the level of previous years. ... It is therefore clear to me that, to refer again to paragraph 91 of the decision in Hoffmann-La Roche, Michelin NV knowingly sought through recourse to methods different from those which condition normal competition in products or services on the basis of the transactions of traders to ensure that its discount system should hinder 'the maintenance of the degree of competition still existing on the market or the growth of that competition'. I also share the Commission's view that the discount system applied by Michelin NV may from the economic point of view be considered a variant of 'fidelity rebate' ... and that Michelin NV did intend to bind dealers to itself and thereby restrict sales of its competitors' products. To that extent I agree with the Commission that at the least Michelin NV acted negligently and that the legal difference between its discount and the fidelity rebates at issue in the Hoffmann-La Roche case cannot diminish its degree of negligence. Personally I think that it may even be said that there was a clear intention on the part of Michelin NV to freeze the structure of the market for the purpose of maintaining its market share.[851]

584 The CJEU limited itself to: 'Michelin NV was aware of the factual elements justifying both the finding of the existence of a dominant position on the market and the assessment of the contested discount system as an abuse of that position. The discount system was set up deliberately. The fact that hitherto neither the Commission nor the Court has had to adjudicate on a discount system having the same features as the system in question does not exonerate Michelin NV. At all events, in view of the previous decisions of the Commission and judgments of the Court Michelin NV ought

849. C-85/76 *Hoffmann-La Roche v Commission* ECLI:EU:C:1979:36, para. 130.
850. C-85/76 *Hoffmann-La Roche v Commission* ECLI:EU:C:1979:36, para. 134.
851. C-322/81 *Nederlandsche Banden-Industrie Michelin v Commission* ECLI:EU:C:1983:168, at [1983] ECR 3546-7.

to have expected that such a system would fall within the sphere of application of Article 86 of the Treaty.'[852]

585 As far as I know, the only time the CJEU accepted that the absence of precedents could be a mitigating factor in determining the fine was in its 1991 *Akzo* judgment. In relation to the abusively low prices which Akzo was using, the CJEU held that 'it must be observed that abuses of this kind come within a field of law in which the rules of competition had never been determined precisely'.[853] This and other factors led the CJEU to reduce the fine imposed by the Commission by 25%.

586 In its 2010 *Deutsche Telekom* judgment, the CJEU again held that a lack of precedents for the specific abuse in the sector in question did not absolve the dominant undertaking from fines.[854] In the 2012 *AstraZeneca* judgment, the CJEU similarly held that the absence of precedents on the specific abuses practised by the dominant company in that case did not prevent the imposition of a fine. It took into account that AstraZeneca's practices 'had the deliberate aim of keeping competitors away from the market' and that 'AZ was aware of the highly anti-competitive nature of its conduct and should have expected it to be incompatible with competition rules under European Union law.'[855]

587 The General Court has also rejected the argument that the lack of precedents should absolve an undertaking from any fine.[856]

588 In any event, it seems that the argument that the case presents such novelty that fines should not be imposed or should be reduced cannot be relied on by the undertaking that was somehow aware that what it was doing was illegal. In *Lundbeck*, the General Court indeed rejected the argument that the case was unprecedented by reference to statements of some of the parties to the patent settlement agreements in that case which showed that they 'were aware of the infringing nature of agreements similar to the agreements at issue and refused to enter into such agreements precisely for that reason' and other evidence of awareness of antitrust rules.[857]

589 More generally, rejecting the argument of novelty fits well in the CJEU's position that if there were any doubts about the application of the law in the absence of

852. C-322/81 *Nederlandsche Banden-Industrie Michelin v Commission* ECLI:EU:C:1983:313, para. 107.
853. C-62/86 *Akzo v Commission* ECLI:EU:C:1991:286, para. 163.
854. C-280/08 P *Deutsche Telekom v Commission* ECLI:EU:C:2010:603, para. 127.
855. C-457/10 P *AstraZeneca v Commission* ECLI:EU:C:2012:770, para. 164.
856. *See*, for example, T-43/92 *Dunlop Slazenger v Commission* ECLI:EU:T:1994:79, para. 142-143; T-321/05 *AstraZeneca v Commission* ECLI:EU:T:2010:266, para. 901; T-472/13 *Lundbeck v Commission* ECLI:EU:T:2016:449, para. 831. However, in joined cases T-217 and 245/03 *FNCBV and Others v Commission* ECLI:EU:T:2006:391, paras 355-361, the General Court increased the fine reduction in light of the novelty of the case.
857. T-472/13 *Lundbeck v Commission* ECLI:EU:T:2016:449, paras 776 and 833. Para. 776 refers to three internal documents which are meant to show awareness that a patent settlement presents challenges from an antitrust perspective. The third document referred to by the General Court merely evidences awareness that resale price maintenance is illegal: it is unclear how this is meant to show awareness of the illegality of a patent settlement agreement.

precedents, undertakings had the possibility to obtain clarity on the law by requesting a negative clearance from the Commission.

590 Nevertheless, the Commission has granted fine reductions because its decision concerned a practice which it had not objected to before. We have already seen how this circumstance was relevant in the *Chiquita* decision (*see* paragraph 577 above) and also how in *Far Eastern Freight Conference*, the Commission had imposed fines of ECU 10,000, a level which can only be described as symbolic (*see* paragraph 564 above). It had already done so in other cases in the past. In *Fatty Acids*, for example, it imposed fines of only ECU 50,000 because it considered that this was 'the first case in which it has imposed a fine for a pure exchange of information agreement'.[858] In the *Eurocheque: Helsinki Agreement* decision, 'the first decision imposing fines in the banking sector', the Commission was similarly willing to apply 'a certain degree of clemency'.[859]

591 It seems that when the Commission included in its *1998 Fining Guidelines* the 'existence of reasonable doubt on the part of the undertaking as to whether the restrictive conduct does indeed constitute an infringement' as an attenuating circumstance, it was aiming to codify this practice.[860] This wording has disappeared in the *2006 Fining Guidelines*.

592 The Commission has also completely foregone the imposition of a fine, often in sectors which were in the process of liberalization or for practices that had not been considered problematic in the past.[861] A recent example is *Motorola Mobility*. This concerned Motorola seeking and enforcing an injunction against Apple for the latter's breach of one of the former's standard essential patents (SEPs). The Commission considered that in the specific circumstances of the case, this constituted an abuse of dominance because Apple was willing to license the SEP on fair, reasonable and non-discriminatory (so-called FRAND) terms. The Commission nevertheless forewent the imposition of a fine on Motorola because of the absence of EU decisional practice or case law on this matter and divergent positions of national courts on it.[862]

858. Commission decision of 2 December 1986 in case 31.128 *Fatty Acids*, recital 58. However, *see also* Commission decision of 23 December 1977 in case 29.176 *Vegetable Parchment*, recital 83 where no fine was imposed for the same reason.
859. Commission decision of 25 March 1992 in case 30.717-A *Eurocheque: Helsinki Agreement*, recital 90.
860. Guidelines on the method of setting fines imposed pursuant to Article 15 (2) of Regulation No 17 and Article 65 (5) of the ECSC Treaty [1998] OJ C9/3.
861. *See*, for example, the Commission decision of 23 December 1977 in case 29.176 *Vegetable Parchment*, recital 83; Commission decision of 23 December 1992 in cases 32.448 and 32.450 *Cewal, Cowac and Ukwal* and 32.448 and 32.450 *Cewal*, recital 100; Commission decision of 27 August 2003 in case 37.685 *GVG/FS*, recital 164; Commission decision of 2 June 2004 in case 38.096 *Clearstream*, recital 344; Commission decisions of 26 October 2004 in case 38.662 *GDF – decision GDF/ENI*, recital 133; decision GDF/ENEL, recital 163.
862. Commission decision of 29 April 2014 in case 39.985 *Motorola – Enforcement of GPRS standard essential patents*, recital 561.

[3] Size of the Undertaking and Market

593 On a number of occasions, the European Courts have rejected alleged mistakes of law based on the size of the undertakings in question. As we have seen, already in *United Brands*, the CJEU held that the eponymous dominant undertaking had 'engaged for a very long time in international and national trade' and had 'special knowledge of anti-trust laws and has already experienced their severity'.[863] Also in *Hoffmann-La Roche*, the CJEU referred to 'the experience which every undertaking of the size of the applicant operating throughout the Common Market ought to have of the practice of the authorities responsible in the Member States for applying competition law' to argue that Hoffmann-La Roche should have foreseen that fidelity rebates would not be compatible with European competition law.[864] The CFI in *Tate&Lyle* similarly took into account 'the fact that British Sugar is a large undertaking with the legal and economic knowledge necessary to enable it to recognise that its conduct constituted an infringement and to be aware of the consequences stemming from it under competition law'.[865]

594 This case law has led some authors to argue that the size of the undertaking is a relevant consideration in determining whether a mistake of law is excusable or not.[866] However, as far as I am aware, the European Courts have never accepted that the (small) size of an undertaking may excuse its ignorance of the law.

595 Nevertheless, in its *1998 Fining Guidelines*, the Commission has said that, when setting the basic amount of the fine, it would take into account the size of the undertaking, not only to reflect its capacity to cause damage and in order to ensure sufficient deterrent effect but also because 'of the fact that large undertakings usually have legal and economic knowledge and infrastructures which enable them more easily to recognize that their conduct constitutes an infringement and be aware of the consequences stemming from it under competition law'.[867] The *2006 Fining Guidelines* entail a completely different methodology to calculate the basic amount of the fine, largely based on turnover affected and the possible uplift related to the size of the

863. C-27/76 *United Brands v Commission* ECLI:EU:C:1978:22, para. 299.
864. C-85/76 *Hoffmann-La Roche v Commission* ECLI:EU:C:1979:36, para. 134.
865. Joined cases T-202, 204 and 207/98 *Tate & Lyle and Others v Commission* ECLI:EU:T:2001:185, para. 128. *See also* T-38/02 *Groupe Danone v Commission* ECLI:EU:T:2005:367, para. 175.
866. *See* M Dreher and S. Thomas, 'Rechts- und Tatsachenirrtümer unter der neuen VO 1/2003' (2004) Wirtschaft und Wettbewerb 8, 11; U Kindhäuser and F Meyer, 'Bußgeldrechtliche Folgen des Art. 101 AEUV' in *Frankfurter Kommentar zum Kartellrecht* (Otto Schmidt 2012) 86-87.
867. Guidelines on the method of setting fines imposed pursuant to Article 15 (2) of Regulation No 17 and Article 65 (5) of the ECSC Treaty [1998] OJ C9/3. *See* already the Commission decision of 10 July 1986 in case 31.371 *Roofing Felt*, recital 109 where the Commission conceded that 'the members [of trade association *Belasco*], particularly the smaller ones, may well not have fully appreciated that the cartel was prohibited by Article 85 (1)', although it does not seem to attach any consequences to this.

undertaking concerned is merely 'to ensure that fines have a sufficiently deterrent effect'.[868]

596 There are also two other notices in which the Commission takes into account size, not so much of the undertaking concerned but of the market share it holds or the market size of the products involved. It indicates there that the good faith assumption of undertakings that they do not meet certain *de minimis* market share thresholds or that the market for their products does not meet certain *de minimis* turnover thresholds can immunize them from fines. The fact that good faith assumptions suffice here shows that mistakes of law in this respect are not held against the companies involved.

597 This is first of all the case in the *De Minimis Notice*, where the Commission explains that, under certain circumstances, agreements between competitors with a market share of not more than 10%, and between non-competitors with a market share of not more than 15%, in principle do not appreciably restrict competition within the meaning of Article 101(1) TFEU.[869] In this notice, the Commission also points out that, even if it would come to a different conclusion in an individual case, if 'undertakings can demonstrate that they have assumed in good faith that the market shares ... were not exceeded, the Commission will not impose fines'.[870]

598 Similarly in its *Guidelines on the effect of trade concept*, the Commission establishes a presumption that trade is not affected by an agreement or practice, if the parties to it have a market share of not more than 5% and combined turnover in the EEA of not more than EUR 40 million.[871] In point 50 of these guidelines, the Commission explains:

> the Commission considers it appropriate to set out general principles indicating when trade is normally not capable of being appreciably affected, i.e. a standard defining the absence of an appreciable effect on trade between Member States (the NAAT-rule). When applying Article 81, the Commission will consider this standard as a negative rebuttable presumption applying to all agreements within the meaning of Article 81(1) irrespective of the nature of the restrictions contained in the agreement, including restrictions that have been identified as hardcore restrictions in Commission block exemption regulations and guidelines. In cases where this presumption applies the Commission will normally not institute proceedings either upon application or on its own initiative. Where the undertakings assume in good faith that an agreement is covered by this negative presumption, the Commission will not impose fines.

868. Guidelines on the method of setting fines imposed pursuant to Article 23(2)(a) of Regulation No 1/2003 [2006] OJ C210/2, para. 30.
869. Notice on agreements of minor importance which do not appreciably restrict competition under Article 101(1) of the Treaty on the Functioning of the European Union (De Minimis Notice) [2014] OJ C291/1.
870. Paragraph 5 of the Notice on agreements of minor importance which do not appreciably restrict competition under Article 101(1) of the Treaty on the Functioning of the European Union (De Minimis Notice) [2014] OJ C291/1.
871. Paragraph 52 of the Guidelines on the effect on trade concept contained in Articles 81 and 82 of the Treaty [2004] OJ C101/81. In case of vertical agreements, the EUR 40 million threshold concerns the turnover of the supplier.

599 While it is debatable whether undertakings can rely on these presumptions if they are simply ignorant of the law, these guidelines nevertheless imply that a mistake of law will not be held against an undertaking if it assumes in good faith that it fulfils the requirements of these exemptions.

[4] Erroneous Legal Advice

600 The fourth possible excuse for a mistake of law which I will discuss here is the reliance by an undertaking on erroneous legal advice. The CJEU dealt with this already in 1978 in *Miller*. When contesting the level of the fine, Miller had argued that it had not committed the infringement intentionally, as was demonstrated by the fact that it had requested an opinion from a legal adviser who had not mentioned that the clause prohibiting exports might be incompatible with Article 101 TFEU.

601 AG Warner was fairly sympathetic to the position of Miller and opined that 'whilst the fact that a layman has acted on the advice of a qualified lawyer is in general no defence either to a civil claim or to a criminal charge, it must, in the absence of bad faith, be a strong mitigating circumstance when it comes to the assessment of any penalty, even though expressed not to be "of a criminal law nature"'.[872] However, Miller had made its argument about the legal advice it obtained fairly late in the procedure, and AG Warner therefore thought it necessary to enquire into this matter further before the Court could deliver its ruling.

602 The CJEU did not consider this necessary and squarely rejected the argument of Miller that its legal adviser had not taken issue with the clause under Article 101 TFEU. According to the Court, Miller 'could not have been unaware' that the clause restricted competition between its customers and 'it is of little relevance to establish whether the applicant knew that it was infringing the prohibition contained in Article 85'.[873]

603 It has been argued that the rigidness of the CJEU in *Miller* may be explained by the fact – pointed out in the AG opinion – that Miller's legal adviser had been critical of the terms of sale of Miller more generally (although not specifically in relation to Article 101 TFEU) and that there was also evidence that Miller knew that Community law had something to say about export restrictions (but apparently failed to ask its legal adviser about this).[874] However, the CJEU has largely maintained its rigid stance in later cases.

604 Indeed, the position taken by the CJEU in *Miller* was reiterated a year later in *BMW Belgium*. In this case, BMW Belgium had requested advice from its lawyer as to the legality of the circulars it intended to send to its dealers to stop them from exporting vehicles. BMW Belgium's legal adviser had explicitly pointed out that the provisions as originally drafted infringed Article 101 TFEU and had suggested amendments to the

872. C-19/77 *Miller International Schallplatten GmbH v Commission* ECLI:EU:C:1978:1, at [1978] ECR 162.
873. C-19/77 *Miller International Schallplatten GmbH v Commission* ECLI:EU:C:1978:19, at [1978] ECR 148, para. 18.
874. *See* F Dietrich, *Der Rechtsirrtum im Kartellrecht* (PhD thesis Bonn 2006) 188-189, referring to C-19/77 *Miller International Schallplatten GmbH v Commission* ECLI:EU:C:1978:1, at [1978] ECR 162-3.

text – and pointed out that, even with these changes, they were at the limits of what was permissible. It is unclear whether BMW Belgium made the changes suggested by its adviser, but it did argue that the fact that it consulted a legal adviser showed that it had not committed the infringement intentionally.

605 AG Warner did not agree, arguing that the opinion of the legal adviser was, if anything, an aggravating factor. He pointed out that, in any event, the CJEU had held in *Miller* that a legal opinion could not be a mitigating factor.[875] In its judgment in *BMW Belgium*, the CJEU indeed closely followed *Miller*, stating that the letters sent by BMW Belgium 'clearly expresses an intention to stop all exports of new BMW vehicles from Belgium' and that, '[s]ince it cannot be denied that the terms of the circular in question were laid down by the applicant, it is irrelevant whether or not it was aware, in so doing, that it was at the same time infringing the prohibition contained in Article 85 (1) of the EEC Treaty'.[876]

606 A few years later, the CJEU once again reiterated this rigid position in a case concerning Article 101 TFEU in *IAZ*. Although at least one of the parties, ANSEAU, had obtained legal advice to the effect that the contested clauses in question should be amended, the Advocate General and the CJEU did not even take up this point when it came to assessing intent. The CJEU simply held that 'all the parties which took part in the drawing-up of the Agreement were aware that the Agreement [...] had as its purpose to restrict parallel imports and that it was capable of affecting trade between Member States, inasmuch as it was actually capable of making parallel imports more difficult, if not impossible'. It was irrelevant 'whether or not they were aware that, in so doing, they were infringing the prohibition laid down by Article 85 (1) of the Treaty'.[877]

607 The General Court has also rejected reliance on faulty legal advice.[878]

608 As discussed above, Regulation 1/2003 created important changes in the EU antitrust enforcement system, including the abolition of the possibility to request a negative clearance from the Commission.

609 Article 10 of Regulation 1/2003 still allows the Commission to find that Article 101 TFEU (or indeed Article 102 TFEU) is inapplicable to an agreement, a decision by an association of undertakings or concerted practice (a form of negative decision therefore). However, such a decision can only be adopted by the Commission, 'acting on its own initiative': while nothing prevents an undertaking or association of undertakings from requesting such a decision, the Commission is therefore not obliged to adopt such a decision, and no decisions on the basis of Article 10 have been adopted so far. This

875. Joined cases C-32 and 36 to 82/78 *BMW Belgium v Commission* ECLI:EU:C:1979:149, at [1979] ECR 2494-6.
876. Joined cases C-32 and 36 to 82/78 *BMW Belgium v Commission* ECLI:EU:C:1979:191, para. 44.
877. Joined cases C-96 to 102, 104, 105, 108 and 110/82 *IAZ v Commission* ECLI:EU:C:1983:310, at [1983] ECR 3398.
878. *See*, for example, T-175/95 *BASF v Commission* ECLI:EU:T:1999:99, para. 152; T-176/95 *Accinauto v Commission* ECLI:EU:T:1999:100, para. 119.

may also have to do with the additional condition contained in Article 10, namely that the Commission can only adopt such decisions 'where the Union public interest relating to the application of Articles 101 and 102 of the Treaty so requires'.

610 I am aware that the Commission has on occasion been willing to discuss the application of Article 101 TFEU to an agreement, decision of an association of undertakings or concerted practice in informal consultations. However, this has so far not resulted in any published guidance letters[879] and, in any event, such guidance letters are not meant to provide legal certainty to the undertakings involved.[880]

611 Undertakings are therefore almost entirely dependent on their own self-assessment of the compliance of their agreements and practices with European competition law. Naturally that means that their reliance on expert legal advice has increased. Mistakes of law arising from erroneous legal advice are therefore at risk of increasing, as there is no longer a possibility to obtain legal certainty by notifying the agreement to the Commission.[881] Despite this, the CJEU has been unwilling to be more lenient in this respect.

612 Indeed, in *Schenker*, the undertakings involved not only claimed that their error as regards the effect on trade of the conference they concluded was induced by the position of the Austrian Cartel Court (as discussed above in paragraphs 571ff.). They also referred to the advice they obtained from a reputable legal adviser. That adviser had assessed whether the SSK fulfilled the conditions for a minor cartel under Austrian law and continued to do so also in the years following the Austrian Cartel Court's declaration in this sense. The legal adviser never seemed to have questioned whether EU antitrust law could be applicable to the conference.

613 In her opinion, AG Kokott advised that, due to the systemic change brought about by Regulation 1/2003, the *Miller* case law could not be applied anymore: 'obtaining expert legal advice has a completely different importance in the system under Regulation No 1/2003 than was the case in the system under Regulation No 17. Consulting a legal adviser is now often the only way for undertakings to obtain detailed information about the legal situation under antitrust law'.[882] She therefore considered that 'any expectations on the part of an undertaking created by legal advice may be recognised as the basis for an error of law precluding liability' in case certain minimum requirements were met.[883]

879. To be issued in accordance with the Commission Notice on informal guidance relating to novel questions concerning Articles 81 and 82 of the EC Treaty that arise in individual cases (guidance letters) [2004] OJ C101/78, para. 21.
880. *See* Commission Notice on informal guidance relating to novel questions concerning Articles 81 and 82 of the EC Treaty that arise in individual cases (guidance letters) [2004] OJ C101/78, paras 22-25.
881. *See also* F Dietrich, *Der Rechtsirrtum im Kartellrecht* (PhD thesis Bonn 2006), in particular 262-270.
882. Opinion of AG Kokott in C-681/11 *Schenker & Co. and Others* ECLI:EU:C:2013:126, para. 57.
883. Opinion of AG Kokott in C-681/11 *Schenker & Co. and Others* ECLI:EU:C:2013:126, para. 61. These minimum conditions were (i) good faith reliance by the undertaking on the legal advice; (ii) that the advice is obtained from an independent external lawyer; (iii) that the lawyer was

614 The CJEU did not follow its Advocate General though. It continued to rely on the Miller case law, holding that '[u]ndertakings which directly coordinate their behaviour in respect of their selling prices quite evidently cannot be unaware of the anti-competitive nature of their conduct'.[884] It also held that 'legal advice given by a lawyer cannot, in any event, form the basis of a legitimate expectation on the part of an undertaking that its conduct does not infringe Article 101 TFEU or will not give rise to the imposition of a fine'.[885]

[5] Conclusion

615 Based on the *Suiker Unie* judgment, legitimate expectations induced by European institutions can exculpate an undertaking for a mistake of law. However, authorizations granted by national authorities do not give rise to legitimate expectations, although the Commission has on occasion been willing to reduce fines in those circumstances.

616 The lack of any precedents in a specific field has led the Commission to absolve undertakings from any liability for fines in a number of cases. On one occasion, the CJEU has also done so, but it has more often rejected such an argumentation.

617 The size of an undertaking and any legal advice it obtained have so far not been viewed as leading to an excusable mistake of law.

[B] Awareness of Illegality

618 So far, I have discussed the question of whether ignorance of the law (or a mistake of law) is relevant to exclude or reduce liability for sanctions. What about the reverse situation, i.e. where there is evidence that the undertaking is acutely aware of the illegality of its conduct? Or where there are other factors than merely the maxim *nemo censetur ignorare legem* that imply that the undertaking should have been aware of the law? This is a topic which is discussed much less in the literature, but it is no less relevant for the presence of *mens rea* than ignorance of the law, because awareness of illegality implies intent.

619 In the remainder of this chapter, I will discuss two instances where this is relevant:

---

specialized in competition law, including European antitrust law; (iv) that the advice is provided on the basis of full and accurate information provided by the undertaking; (v) that the advice deals comprehensively with the Commission's administrative practice and the case law of the European Courts; and (vi) that the advice is not manifestly incorrect. In addition, the due diligence expected by the undertaking concerned depends on its size and experience in competition matters and every undertaking must be aware that certain anticompetitive practices are, by their nature, prohibited. AG Kokott believed that, taking into account these conditions, no excusable error of law arose in this case. *See* paras 51-78.

884. C-681/11 *Schenker & Co. and Others* ECLI:EU:C:2013:404, para. 39.

885. C-681/11 *Schenker & Co. and Others* ECLI:EU:C:2013:404, para. 41.

(a) First of all, situations where the Commission has taken into account the belief of an undertaking that its behaviour was illegal (e.g. as demonstrated by concealment efforts) to increase the fine.
(b) Second, instances where increased awareness of the antitrust rules (due to the fact that the undertaking has already been found to have infringed competition law in the past or because of the existence of a compliance programme during the infringement) could imply increased awareness of the illegal nature of the conduct which the Commission investigates.

[1] Belief of Illegality and Concealment

620 There are several instances where the Commission has considered that the fact that an undertaking believes that what it was doing was illegal, for example because of the secrecy the undertaking practised, warranted an increase in the fine.

621 While in the past the Commission seems to have accepted that the fact that an infringement 'has not been one of a hidden, clandestine nature' could be an attenuating circumstance,[886] this is no longer considered to be a mitigating factor in setting the fine. One of the reasons may well be that, even if some aspects of an infringement may be public, usually not all aspects will be. It may therefore not be apparent to victims of the infringement and to enforcers that an infringement is being committed.[887]

622 Reversely, as already indicated in paragraphs 503 and 542 above, the Commission has on several occasions stated that secrecy is indicative of intentionality and therefore increases the gravity of the infringement.[888] Already in *Boehringer I*, the CJEU held that awareness of illegality constitutes an aggravating factor. Indeed, the CJEU pointed out that the minutes of the meetings of the quinine cartel in that case showed that the members of the cartel 'were aware of the incompatibility of their actions with the prohibitions in Community law. The serious and conscious nature of the infringements therefore justifies a larger fine'.[889] The CFI has also stated in *Finnboard* that the Commission was 'fully entitled' to take into account as 'aggravating circumstances when assessing the gravity of the infringement' the fact that 'the undertakings which

886. Commission decision of 5 February 1992 in cases 31.572 and 32.571 *Building and construction industry in the Netherlands*, recital 141.
887. *See*, on this point, joined cases T-259 to 264 and 271/02 *Raiffeisen Zentralbank Österreich and Others v Commission* ECLI:EU:T:2006:396, para. 506.
888. *See*, for example, Commission decision of 23 April 1986 in case 31.149 *Polypropylene*, recital 107; Commission decision of 2 August 1989 in case 31.553 *Welded Steel Mesh*, recital 197; Commission decision of 13 July 1994 in case 33.833 *Cartonboard*, recital 167; Commission decision of 2 April 2004 in case 39.610 *Power Cables*, recital 959; Commission decision of 11 March 2008 in case 38.543 *International Removal Services*, recital 565; Commission decision of 16 October 2009 in case 39.401 *E.On – GdF collusion*, recital 388; Commission decision of 21 October 2015 in case 39.639 *Optical Disc Drives*, recital 524; Commission decision of 8 February 2017 in case 40.018 *Car battery recycling*, recital 291 and 293; and, in a different context (gun jumping in merger control), T-332/09 *Electrabel v Commission* ECLI:EU:T:2012:672, para. 277.
889. C-45/69 *Boehringer v Commission* ECLI:EU:C:1970:73, para. 58.

participated in the meetings of [cartel] bodies were not only aware of the unlawfulness of their conduct but also took steps to conceal the collusion'.[890]

623 But the simple awareness of illegality may be indicative of intentionality. For example, in *Telekomunikacja Polska*, the Commission pointed in this context to the fact that its 'investigation file contains *inter alia* internal documents of TP showing that TP was aware of the illegality of its refusal to supply and was fully conscious that its behaviour could have the effect of distorting competition in the internal market'.[891]

624 The Commission decisional practice and the case law even suggests that an undertaking's belief as to the illegality of its behaviour (or secrecy practised by it) could be relevant to establish that its behaviour was illegal. In *LCD*, for example, the Commission stated that '[t]he anti-competitive object of the parties is also confirmed by the fact that they took deliberate action to conceal their meetings and to avoid detection of their arrangements'.[892] Also in *Wanadoo*, the Commission referred in its discussion of the existence of an abuse to internal documents expressing concerns over the lawfulness of the pricing practices.[893] In *Irish Sugar*, the CFI similarly pointed out that the undertaking was aware that its commercial policy was dangerous 'legally on the basis of selective pricing' when discussing the existence of an abuse.[894] And in *AstraZeneca*, the General Court referred to several documents showing that the dominant undertaking was aware of the incorrect information it was providing to the patent offices.[895]

625 Furthermore, certain defences may not be available for secret practices. This seems to be first and foremost the case for the defence of the mistake of law: the existence of concealment efforts has been used to show that the undertakings involved were aware of the illegal nature of their conduct and that the (limited) mistake of law defence was therefore not available to them.[896]

626 Secrecy also bars the undertaking from arguing early termination as a mitigating circumstance. Indeed, the *1998 Fining Guidelines* provided that 'termination of the infringement as soon as the Commission intervenes (in particular when it carries out checks)'[897] could be a mitigating factor when calculating the fine. On this basis, Archer Daniels Midland argued before both the CFI and the CJEU that the fine which the Commission imposed on it for the Citric Acid cartel should be reduced.[898] Both the CFI

890. T-338/94 *Finnboard v Commission* ECLI:EU:T:1998:99, para. 335.
891. Commission decision of 22 July 2011 in case 39.525 *Telekomunikacja Polska*, recital 892.
892. Commission decision of 8 December 2010 in case 39.309 *LCD*, recital 302.
893. Commission decision of 16 July 2003 in case 38.233 *Wanadoo Interactive*, title G3.
894. T-228/97 *Irish Sugar v Commission* ECLI:EU:T:1999:246, para. 183. *See also* para. 362 above.
895. T-321/05 *AstraZeneca v Commission* ECLI:EU:T:2010:266, para. 594.
896. *See* T-472/13 *Lundbeck v Commission* ECLI:EU:T:2016:449, paras 776 and 833, but also the Commission decision of 24 January 2007 in case 38.899 *Gas insulated switchgear*, recitals 171 and 476.
897. Guidelines on the method of setting fines imposed pursuant to Article 15 (2) of Regulation No 17 and Article 65 (5) of the ECSC Treaty [1998] OJ C9/3.
898. And in fact the Commission had granted Archer Daniels Midland a fine reduction on this basis in the previous *Amino Acid* case: *see* Commission decision of 7 June 2000 in case 36.545 *Amino Acids*, recitals 381-384.

and the CJEU rejected this pointing out that '[t]he secret nature of the cartel confirms the fact that the parties were aware of the unlawful nature of their actions'[899] and that '[t]o recognise an attenuating circumstance in situations where an undertaking is party to a manifestly unlawful agreement which it knew or could not be unaware constituted an infringement could encourage undertakings to continue a secret agreement as long as possible, in the hope that their conduct would never be discovered, while knowing that if their conduct were discovered they could expect, by then curtailing the infringement, their fine to be reduced'.[900] The *2006 Fining Guidelines* therefore clarify that a mitigating factor only arises 'where the undertaking concerned provides evidence that it terminated the infringement as soon as the Commission intervened: this will not apply to secret agreements or practices (in particular, cartels)'.[901]

[2] Increased Awareness of Antitrust Laws

627 In *United Brands*, the CJEU already held that the fact that a company has experienced the severity of antitrust laws in the past makes it more difficult for it to argue that it was ignorant of the law.[902] But in the decades afterwards, the Commission has become stricter with repeat offenders and has regularly increased their fines. This practice has been endorsed by the European Courts[903] and was codified in the *1998 Fining Guidelines* and further developed in the *2006 Fining Guidelines*.[904] The main purpose of this is obviously deterrence: if despite a previous finding (possibly including a fine), an undertaking reoffends, this suggests that that previous finding (and sanction) was not sufficiently deterrent.[905]

628 There are a number of reasons why deterrence may be increased by an uplift of fines for recidivism,[906] but it is submitted that this is also so because the previous finding must increase an undertaking's awareness of antitrust law. Recidivism therefore suggests increased turpitude which in turn increases the risk of repetition and reduces the chance of detection, thus justifying a higher fine.

899. T-59/02 *Archer Daniels Midland v Commission* ECLI:EU:T:2006:272, para. 340.
900. C-511/06 P *Archer Daniels Midland v Commission* ECLI:EU:C:2009:433, para. 105.
901. Guidelines on the method of setting fines imposed pursuant to Article 23(2)(a) of Regulation No 1/2003 [2006] OJ C210/2, para. 29, first indent. For an application, *see* T-199/08 *Ziegler v Commission* ECLI:EU:T:2011:285, paras 151-152; T-211/08 *Putters International v Commission* ECLI:EU:T:2011:289, para. 82.
902. C-27/76 *United Brands v Commission* ECLI:EU:C:1978:22, para. 299.
903. Joined cases C-204, 205, 211, 213, 217 and 219/00 P *Aalborg Portland v Commission* ECLI:EU:C:2004:6, para. 91; C-3/06 P *Groupe Danone v Commission* ECLI:EU:C:2007:88, para. 26; C-413/08 P *Lafarge v Commission* ECLI:EU:C:2010:346, para. 63.
904. Guidelines on the method of setting fines imposed pursuant to Article 15 (2) of Regulation No 17 and Article 65 (5) of the ECSC Treaty [1998] OJ C9/3; Guidelines on the method of setting fines imposed pursuant to Article 23(2)(a) of Regulation No 1/2003 [2006] OJ C210/2, para. 28, first indent.
905. *See* T-203/01 *Michelin v Commission* ECLI:EU:T:2003:250, para. 293.
906. For a discussion of four of these reasons, *see* W Wils, 'Recidivism in EU antitrust enforcement: a legal and economic analysis' (2012) 35 World Competition 5, 13-15.

629 Other factors that contribute to an increased awareness of the antitrust rules or simply evidence that the undertaking was aware of the illegality of its conduct have also been taken into account as an aggravating factor[907] and (particularly in older cases) in assessing the gravity of the infringement.[908]

630 The European Commission encourages undertakings to introduce antitrust compliance programmes. There was even a time when the Commission took the introduction of a compliance programme into account when setting the fines for infringements.[909] In the meantime, the Commission's policy is not to grant any fine reductions for compliance programmes: compliance should be its own reward.[910]

631 However, a company which introduces an antitrust compliance programme (possibly as a result of an antitrust investigation) can be expected to become more aware of competition law. If it commits an infringement after the introduction of such a programme, this could arguably be viewed as an aggravating circumstance. In the *British Sugar* decision, the Commission indeed increased the fine of British Sugar by 75% because it 'acted in a manner contrary to the clear wording contained in its compliance programme'[911] although the fact that the introduction of the compliance programme had been taken into account when British Sugar was fined for an infringement a decade earlier probably added to the Commission's outrage.[912] In other cases, the Commission has however not considered the existence of a compliance programme to be an aggravating factor in assessing the undertaking's behaviour.

632 In *Irish Sugar*, the Commission nevertheless pointed to the existence of 'a Competition Law compliance manual for [Irish Sugar's] employees in which the potential illegality of certain practices, such as discriminatory pricing and payment of fidelity rebates "or the like" by a firm in a dominant position' to conclude that the undertaking infringed the antitrust rules intentionally or at least negligently.[913] The Commission and the CFI also pointed to a document in which the undertaking's

---

907. In Commission decision of 23 July 2014 in case M.7184 *Marine Harvest/Morpol*, recital 148 (a gun jumping case under the Merger Regulation), the Commission took into account that Marine Harvest had already been fined for gun jumping by an NCA to conclude that it was negligent (although it did not take this into account as the aggravating circumstance of recidivism): 'A high level of diligence has to be expected from a company which has already been fined for negligent conduct in the context of merger control proceedings at national level in a Member State of the EEA.' Confirmed in case T-704/14 *Marine Harvest v Commission* ECLI:EU:T:2017:753, paras 258 and 538.
908. Commission decision of 19 December 1990 in case 33.133-C *Soda-ash – Solvay*, recital 70; Commission decision of 20 September 2000 in case 36.653 *Opel*, recitals 193-194, specifically accepted by the CFI in T-368/00 *General Motors Nederland and Opel Nederland v Commission* ECLI:EU:T:2003:275, para. 198.
909. *See*, for example, the Commission decision of 7 December 1982 in case 30.070 *National Panasonic*, recitals 67-68.
910. *See*, on this, the Note of the delegation of the European Union to the OECD Roundtable on promoting compliance with competition law of 7 June 2010 <http://ec.europa.eu/competition/international/multilateral/2011_jun_compliance.pdf> accessed 17 July 2017.
911. Commission decision of 14 October 1998 in case 33.708 *British Sugar*, recital 208.
912. Commission decision of 18 July 1988 in case 30.178 *Napier Brown - British Sugar*, recital 86.
913. Commission decision of 14 May 1997 in case 34.621 and 35.059 *Irish Sugar*, recital 167.

possible strategies were discussed and the legal concerns over selective pricing were enunciated.[914]

[C] Conclusion

633 So far, an undertaking's awareness or ignorance of the illegality of its conduct in light of EU antitrust law has played only a limited role.

634 The maxim *ignorantia iuris non excusat* is generally applicable in EU antitrust: an undertaking makes a mistake of law at its own peril. Only if the mistake of law is induced by assurances given by the European Commission which can give rise to legitimate expectations, the mistake of law will not be held against it. In exceptional circumstances, the European Commission has also foregone the imposition of a fine in case it proceeded against practices which it had not found to be illegal in the past. There are a number of other circumstances where a mistake of law can lead to a reduction of a fine, in particular when the mistake is induced by authorizations or encouragement by NCAs. Other circumstances such as the existence of (erroneous) advice by a lawyer or the limited size of the undertaking are in principle not relevant.

635 The fact that an undertaking is (more strongly) aware of the antitrust rules and/or the illegality of its own conduct has been taken into account as indicating intentionality of the conduct. That awareness will also estop an undertaking from claiming ignorance of the law or plead certain other attenuating circumstances.

914. Commission decision of 14 May 1997 in case 34.621 and 35.059 *Irish Sugar*, recital 58 and T-228/97 *Irish Sugar v Commission* ECLI:EU:T:1999:246, para. 183.

CHAPTER 5

Evaluation of the Role of *Mens Rea* in EU Antitrust Law

6.4321 Die Tatsachen gehören alle nur zur Aufgabe, nicht zur Lösung.

Wittgenstein, *Tractatus Logico-Philosophicus*

§5.01 SUMMARY OF CHAPTERS 2-4

636 In Chapter 2, I have discussed the role of *mens rea* in the different material elements of Article 101 TFEU. For the criterion of 'agreement' or 'concerted practice', the case law uses a psychological terminology but nevertheless exclusively focuses on the expressions exchanged between the parties. Also to determine the participation in an infringement, because of the '*Anic* presumption', it is the other parties' interpretation of an undertaking's alleged distancing from an infringement which determines whether the distancing was effective.

637 As to the second criterion of Article 101 TFEU, the case law clearly states that it is not necessary to establish that undertakings had anticompetitive intentions in order to establish that their agreement or concerted practice had the restriction of competition as its object. The intentions which the parties had when entering into an agreement or concerted practice are, however, relevant to the assessment of the object of the agreement or practice. Anticompetitive intentions are probably not sufficient to conclude that an agreement restricts competition.

638 Under Article 101(3) TFEU, *mens rea* evidence can be a tool to verify the credibility of the claims which undertakings make in respect of the conditions for the application of this exception. Contemporaneous documents which discredit the parties' claims (and the absence of any contemporaneous documents validating the parties' claims) are in that respect relevant.

639 In Chapter 3, the relevance of *mens rea* elements in the case law on Article 102 TFEU was analysed. It appeared that *mens rea* is not required to establish dominance, although an undertaking's views of its position in the market can be relevant (as is a joint intention of two or more companies to establish collective dominance). In order to establish an abuse, *mens rea* considerations appear to have a more significant place. Although such evidence is not always necessary and its relevance is even contested in some case law, other judgments state that, in some circumstances, such evidence is at the very least relevant and possibly even determinative to find an abuse.

640 Exclusionary intentions play a particularly decisive role in predatory pricing abuses and are even required (in the earlier case law more in the objective sense, in the later more in the subjective sense) to establish predation in case pricing is between average total cost and average variable cost. The relevance of *mens rea* in exclusionary price discrimination is not settled in the case law. In the case of explicit exclusivity agreements or loyalty rebates, evidence of exclusionary intentions does not seem to play a role (except in that it explains why such practices are illegal). When the exclusivity is not explicit, however, the case law suggests that in particular subjective intentions can help to interpret the behaviour.

641 In multimarket abuse cases, *mens rea* plays no significant role (except as an explanation of the conduct). However, internal documents evidencing subjective intentions can be used to assess objective justifications put forward by the dominant undertaking. In cases of abuse of regulatory process, however, the case law has very much relied on objective and subjective intentions of the dominant undertaking, although these concern the abuse of the regulatory process (rather than the abuse of the dominant position). The role of intentions in non-exclusionary abuses is not clear from the case law.

642 In Chapter 4, I considered the relevance of *mens rea* in the enforcement of the EU antitrust rules. There does not appear to be any case law on mistakes of fact (indicating the absence of intent) as regards effects on trade between the Member States, although there is case law on mistakes of law. The notion of undertaking under EU antitrust law implies that liability of undertakings for the actions of their officers and employees (and indeed of parent undertakings for their subsidiaries) is vicarious (strict); only for acts by truly independent agents an awareness requirement exists.

643 Although the implementing regulations provide that fines can only be imposed if the Articles 101 and 102 TFEU are 'intentionally or negligently' breached, this requirement has little relevance in the case law. Because of the confusion between mistakes of fact and mistakes of law, the case law has interpreted the minimum requirement of negligence as akin to strict liability. By objectivising intention, this notion has in turn been assimilated to negligence. Given that the *mens rea* requirement of the implementing regulation is therefore interpreted in such a shallow way, it has also played little role in determining the amount of the fine, with only few exceptions.

644 The case law on mistakes of law is quite clear, however. The CJEU has only accepted mistakes of law if these are based on legitimate expectations created by the

European institutions themselves. Authorizations by national authorities do not exculpate an undertaking, although the Commission has on occasion reduced the fine in these circumstances. The Commission has, however, decided to forego the imposition of fines in a few cases where clear precedents were missing. The size of the undertaking and the fact that it received erroneous legal advice do not create an excusable mistake of law or even a reason to reduce the fine. Reversely, an explicit awareness by the undertaking (as evidenced, for example, by concealment efforts) can constitute an aggravating factor in fine calculations.

§5.02 DOCTRINAL VIEWS ON THE RELEVANCE OF *MENS REA*

645 Within the literature, there are voices that are very critical of the use of *mens rea* (and in particular intent) evidence in antitrust law and voices that are more favourable to it.

646 I will start with a discussion of some views in the US. The author whose positive views on intent evidence in monopolization cases is most often cited is Marina Lao. The title of her 2004 article *Reclaiming a role for intent evidence in monopolization analysis* says it all. She argues that 'intent evidence remains (or should remain) very relevant because it informs economic analysis and can add to its functionality'.[915] According to her, 'empirical data and economic theory alone are sometimes inadequate for evaluating whether an allegedly exclusionary practice has anticompetitive effects' and therefore 'monopolization analysis will be well served by according more respect to intent evidence'.[916]

647 Chicago School scholars are more critical of the role of intent, but when push comes to shove, they seem to find it difficult to avoid reference to it. In their leading handbook, Areeda and Hovenkamp consider that 'the terms "purpose" and "intent" have been particularly slippery, ambiguous and unsatisfactory in the antitrust world' and 'bad intent is easily proven but seldom serves to distinguish situations where the defendant's conduct deserves condemnation from those in which it should be left alone'.[917] Richard Posner similarly said that '[a]ny doctrine that relies upon proof of intent is going to be applied erratically at best',[918] but he also had to admit that sometimes competitive and anticompetitive actions can only be distinguished by reference to their author's intent.[919] Manne and Williamson are openly critical:

915. M Lao, 'Reclaiming a role for intent evidence in monopolization analysis' (2004) American University Law Review 151, 155.
916. M Lao, 'Reclaiming a role for intent evidence in monopolization analysis' (2004) American University Law Review 151, 212.
917. PE Areeda and H Hovenkamp, *Antitrust law - An analysis of antitrust principles and their application* (Wolters Kluwer 1978, Supp May 2018) ¶ 601.
918. R Posner, *Antitrust law* (The University of Chicago Press 2001) 214.
919. R Posner, *Antitrust law* (The University of Chicago Press 2001) 216. JF Brodley and CA Ma, 'Contract penalties, monopolizing strategies, and antitrust policy' (1993) 45 Stanford Law Review 1161, 1201 also argue that '[e]vidence of intent becomes relevant when objective evidence is not decisive' although they seem to equate 'intent' with the objective purpose of an agreement or clause.

'motivations, intentions and rhetoric simply do not render economic activity anticompetitive (or procompetitive) or otherwise socially detrimental (or beneficial)'.[920]

648 Among European authors, Odudu is one of the few authors that has discussed the role of intentions in Article 101 TFEU in some detail. In relation to behaviour that has as its object (as opposed to its effect) to restrict competition, he argues that this 'object condition can be satisfied by subjective intention'; in other words, he considers that a subjective intention to restrict competition is sufficient to conclude that this condition is met.[921]

649 In relation to Article 102 TFEU, O'Grady does not go this far and believes that '[i]ntent is never sufficient by itself'.[922] He nevertheless argues that 'intent evidence plays a vital and irreplaceable role in disambiguating ambiguous practices which may, by their nature, constitute pro or anti-competitive behaviour depending upon the intent motivating the dominant undertaking so acting'.[923] Using intent evidence is then not anathema to an effect-based approach but 'may complement' it.[924]

650 Parcu and Stasi similarly see a role for intent evidence 'as a useful instrument to interpret complex companies' strategies', especially 'in new or complex markets ... that might create additional challenges in the analysis of a conduct and its effects on competitive dynamics in the market'.[925]

651 The position of Bavasso, still in the context of Article 102 TFEU, is more ambivalent. He argues that 'evidence of intent should not be part of a substantive test of exclusionary abuses under Art. 82 [since] [t]his may induce errors and would move the focus of enforcement away from an effects-based policy approach driven by the overriding consideration of consumer welfare'.[926] He nevertheless accepts that evidence of intent can be helpful to interpret allegedly abusive practices, including 'the

920. GA Manne and EM Williamson, 'Hot docs vs. cold economics' (2005) 47 Arizona Law Review 609, 619.
921. O Odudu, 'Interpreting Article 81(1): object as subjective intention' (2001) 26 European Law Review 60, 60.
922. C O'Grady, 'The role of exclusionary intent in the enforcement of Article 102 TFEU' (2014) World Competition 459, 464.
923. C O'Grady, 'The role of exclusionary intent in the enforcement of Article 102 TFEU' (2014) World Competition 459, 459.
924. C O'Grady, 'The role of exclusionary intent in the enforcement of Article 102 TFEU' (2014) World Competition 459, 459.
925. PL Parcu and ML Stasi, 'The role of intent in the assessment of conduct under Article 102 TFEU' in PL Parcu, G Monti and M Botta (eds), *Abuse of dominance in EU competition law. Emerging trends* (Edward Elgar 2017) 12, 32 and 21. These authors also briefly discuss the role of intent evidence in markets driven by artificial intelligence. This is a topic beyond the scope of my current enquiry but which I have discussed at length in J Blockx, 'Antitrust in digital markets in the EU: policing price bots' in M Veenbrink, A Looijestijn-Clearie and CS Rusu (eds), *Digital markets in the EU* (Wolf Legal 2018) 75.
926. A Bavasso, 'The role of intent under Article 82 EC: from "flushing the turkeys" to "spotting lionesses in Regent's Park"' (2005) European Competition Law Review 616, 623.

likely consequences of the behaviour of the dominant players' and that it is relevant 'to determine the gravity of such an infringement'.[927]

652 More critical is Akman who argues that 'the thus-far developed use of intent within the substantive assessment under art. 102 TFEU reduces legal certainty and increases the risk of decisional errors with negative welfare implications' and that therefore 'intent should not be used as part of the substantive legal test for establishing abuse'.[928] She nevertheless accepts that it is relevant when setting the fine.[929]

653 Melícias considers that *mens rea* is wholly irrelevant in the context of Article 102 TFEU: 'an abuse can be found independently of any element of fault or guilt on the part of the dominant undertaking, so long as the *effect* of its behaviour is to hinder "the maintenance of the degree of competition still existing in the market or the growth of that competition"'.[930] Along the same lines, O'Donoghue and Padilla argue that 'exclusionary intent is not relevant to the determination of whether conduct is abusive'.[931]

654 The latter position is echoed by AG Wahl in relation to Article 101 TFEU where he considers that 'identification of an "anticompetitive object" requires a properly objective examination, irrespective of the will of the parties. I therefore consider that any intentions expressed by the participants in a supposed restrictive agreement, decision or concerted practice, like any legitimate objectives pursued by them, are not directly relevant in examining whether the agreement, decision or practice has an anticompetitive "object"'.[932]

§5.03 ARGUMENTS AGAINST THE USE OF *MENS REA*

655 In what follows, I will discuss the different arguments made against the use of *mens rea* evidence in antitrust infringements. First of all, given the different meanings that 'intent' has in the case law and the literature, there is a risk of the fallacy of *petitio principi* when relying on intent: such a risk can only be avoided if it is made clear when

---

927. A Bavasso, 'The role of intent under Article 82 EC: from "flushing the turkeys" to "spotting lionesses in Regent's Park"' (2005) European Competition Law Review 616, 623.
928. P Akman, 'The role of intent in the EU case law on abuse of dominance' (2014) European Law Review 316, 316.
929. P Akman, 'The role of intent in the EU case law on abuse of dominance' (2014) European Law Review 316, 337.
930. MJ Melícias, 'The use and abuse of intent evidence in antitrust analysis' (2010) World Competition 569, 579 (emphasis in original). *See also* T Eilmansberger and F Bien, 'Art. 102 AEUV Missbrauch einer marktbeherrschenden Stellung' in J Bornkamm, F Montag and FJ Säcker (eds), *Münchener Kommentar Europäisches und Deutsches Wettbewerbsrecht* (Beck, 2015) 1519, 1573-1574.
931. R O'Donoghue and AJ Padilla, *The law and economics of Article 82 EC* (Hart 2006) 225-226.
932. C-67/13 P *Cartes Bancaires v Commission* ECLI:EU:C:2014:1958, para. 110. A similar critical stance seems to inspire P Ibáñez Colomo, 'The hard questions in the Lundbeck appeals: will Article 101 TFEU radically change' (*Chillin'Competition*, 18 January 2019) <https://chillingcompetition.com/2019/01/18/the-hard-questions-in-the-lundbeck-appeals-will-article-101-tfeu-radically-change/> accessed 12 February 2019, but then specifically in relation to potential competition.

intent evidence is useful and when it is not. The remainder of the arguments against the use of *mens rea* (in sections [B] to [E] below) will focus on evidence of *subjective* intentions in the form of documents expressing the thoughts, knowledge, intentions and motives of the individuals within the undertaking in relation to a certain commercial action.

[A] Risk of Circularity

656 A first objection to taking into account culpability is that this results in what the French call a '*procès d'intention*', i.e. the risk that rather than using evidence of culpability the blameworthiness of the actor is deduced from its actions. As already indicated in Chapter 1, also in the criminal law, an actor's intent to achieve a certain result is sometimes deduced from his actions, if that result is the natural consequence of his actions: in those cases it is claimed that the actor 'must have foreseen' the result. However, such an 'objective intention' is difficult to distinguish from negligence where the actor 'should have foreseen' the result. In those circumstances, referring to 'objective intentions' does not add anything to the facts themselves.

657 In the field of EU antitrust, this objection is probably most clearly voiced by Akman who, in the context of predatory pricing, has pointed out that, if the facts themselves demonstrate exclusion, 'then there should be no need to prove separate intent since the "fact" of exclusion will have been established'. References to the intention of the dominant company are then 'circular' and 'superfluous'.[933] In the US, the First Circuit summarized this objection nicely by pointing out that if intent 'is meant to refer to a set of objective economic conditions that allow the court to "infer" improper intent, ..., then, using Occam's razor, we can slice "intent" away'.[934]

658 What is the merit of this objection? Circularity is a real problem when it comes to references to intent as an aid to interpret the behaviour of undertakings. For example, as we have seen (*see* paragraph 341 above), the CFI was guilty of this in *Tetra Pak II* where it derived the predatory intent of the dominant undertaking from the prices it practised and then proceeded to use that intent to qualify these prices as predatory.[935] The CFI stated in other words: 'with such prices, Tetra Pak *must have* intended to exclude competitors' and this was considered sufficient intention to satisfy the second leg of the *Akzo* test of predatory pricing.

---

933. P Akman, 'The role of intent in the EU case law on abuse of dominance' (2014) European Law Review 316, 323. Akman refers specifically to the reasoning of the General Court in T-83/91 *Tetra Pak v Commission* ECLI:EU:T:1994:246. *See also* PE Areeda and H Hovenkamp, *Antitrust law - An analysis of antitrust principles and their application* (Wolters Kluwer 1978, Supp May 2018) ¶ 805b.
934. *Barry Wright Corp v ITT Grinnell Corp*, 724 F.2D 227, 232 (1st Cir. 1983).
935. The appellants in C-551/03 P *General Motors* ECLI:EU:C:2006:229, para. 48 also accused the General Court of using a 'circular' reasoning in T-368/00 *General Motors Nederland and Opel Nederland v Commission* ECLI:EU:T:2003:275, stating 'The Court first used the bonus policy to conclude that there was a general strategy to restrict all exports, and then uses that alleged general strategy to conclude that that bonus policy had a restrictive object.' The CJEU did not deal with this point, declaring the plea partly inadmissible.

659 References to 'objective intentions' are therefore indeed suspicious and, as already indicated, in the remainder of this chapter I will therefore focus on subjective intentions. Nevertheless, I think it worthwhile to point out here that referring to 'objective intentions' does not always need to result in circularity. Circularity only arises if two conditions are fulfilled, namely: (i) a specific act is interpreted as demonstrating improper intent and (ii) that improper intent is used to interpret that same act as improper.

660 But objective intentions can play a role in other circumstances. First of all, if (the objective intentions evidenced by) one act or type of acts of an undertaking is used to interpret another act or type of acts, no circularity arises.[936] This could, for example, be the case if a dominant undertaking uses prices below variable costs as well as prices below total but above variable costs: the fact that the first are in principle predatory, also casts doubts on the second. Another example could be the deduction of an exclusionary intention from the practice of predatory pricing to interpret discriminatory pricing as exclusionary as well (*see* the discussion on *Akzo* in paragraph 357 above). A third example is the deduction of exclusionary intent from the use of exclusivity agreements to interpret certain pricing practices (*see* the example of *Napier Brown* discussed in paragraph 411 above). Of course, care should be taken to interpret one act by way of another act: not all an undertaking's business practices should become suspect simply because it engaged in one anticompetitive act.[937] Nevertheless, in the right circumstances (e.g. if the two acts take place contemporaneously and are directed at the same customer or competitor), one act can help to interpret another act.

661 Second, intent can be demonstrated objectively in a negative manner. This is the case when it is not possible to come up with a legitimate business reason for a certain type of behaviour such that, by exclusion, the only explanation is the anticompetitive intention of the undertaking engaging in it. We presume that a dominant undertaking that prices below average variable cost must intend to exclude competitors because it is hard to find any other purpose in such actions (*see* the discussion on *Akzo* in paragraph 332 above).[938] The same applies in case of margin squeezes as the CFI indicated in *Teliasonera* (*see* paragraph 414 above). Once again, care should be taken in excluding legitimate business reasons and usually the alleged perpetrators of the

936. The possibility to interpret one practice in light of another was also suggested by then Director General P Lowe, 'EU competition practice on predatory pricing: Introductory address to the seminar 'Pros and cons of low prices' (5 December 2003) <http://ec.europa.eu/competition/speeches/text/sp2003_066_en.pdf> accessed 26 September 2018, 3-4.
937. As pointed out by the General Court in T-691/14 *Servier and Others v Commission* ECLI:EU:T:2018:922, paras 195-196.
938. This is the so-called no economic sense or profit sacrifice test to predatory pricing. In European competition law, the 'as efficient competitor' test is more common though: *see*, for example, the discussion in M Mandorff and J Sahl, 'The role of the 'equally efficient competitor' in the assessment of abuse of dominance' (2013) Konkurrensverket Working Paper Series in Law and Economics 2013-1 <http://www.konkurrensverket.se/globalassets/english/publications-and-decisions/the-role-of-the-equally-efficient-competitor-in-the-assessment-of-abuse-of-dominance.pdf> accessed 11 September 2017.

anticompetitive act will also advance such business reasons. But if a detailed assessment is made of possible business reasons to engage in the behaviour and none are found, an anticompetitive intent may be deduced. One could of course dispute that this really can be called intent. As Akman puts it: 'once the assessment is based on deciding what the rational explanation of the conduct in question is, there is no longer an inquiry into "intent" but into the possible economic and business rationales underlying the conduct regardless of the intent of the undertaking'.[939] However one wants to name it, though, I think this way of determining the (objective) purpose of conduct does not suffer from circularity.

662 I will leave these examples of objective intentions aside going forward and will focus instead on subjective intentions. When using internal documents reflecting subjective intentions to interpret an undertaking's conduct, there is no risk of circularity: words are then used to interpret behaviour.

[B] Difficulty to Distinguish Good and Bad Subjective Intentions

663 A first objection specifically levelled against the use of subjective intentions is: how to distinguish an anticompetitive intention from a procompetitive (or competitively neutral) intention? As Melícias puts it: 'there is no practical distinction between a desire to *compete* with a rival and a desire to *outcompete* him'[940] and 'intent to compete inherently entails the desire to *outcompete*, to defeat rivals. Therefore, in this sense, aggressive commercial practices will usually constitute normal competition on the merits'.[941] Also, Akman points out that 'it may be impossible to distinguish the intention to restrict competition from the intention to compete vigorously'.[942]

664 Judge Easterbrook's statement in the US appellate judgment in *A.A. Poultry Farms* is often quoted approvingly in the literature in this respect: 'price reductions are carried out in pursuit of sales, at others' expense ... a desire to extinguish one's rivals is entirely consistent with, often is the motive behind, competition'.[943] Or again: 'the fundamental goal underlying any player's actions is, as a rule, ultimately the same: the

939. P Akman, 'The role of intent in the EU case law on abuse of dominance' (2014) European Law Review 316, 317.
940. MJ Melícias, 'The use and abuse of intent evidence in antitrust analysis' (2010) World Competition 569, 592 (emphasis in original). *See also* GA Manne and EM Williamson, 'Hot docs vs. cold economics' (2005) 47 Arizona Law Review 609, 652: 'attempts to compete are operationally similar to attempts to monopolize'; and PE Areeda and H Hovenkamp, *Antitrust law - An analysis of antitrust principles and their application* (Wolters Kluwer 1978, Supp May 2018) ¶ 738c: 'The intention to prevail, even to gain a monopoly by lawful means, is lawful.' *See also* ¶¶ 601 and 1506.
941. MJ Melícias, 'The use and abuse of intent evidence in antitrust analysis' (2010) World Competition 569, 574-575 (emphasis in original). *See*, however, the discussion on the 'special responsibility' of dominant undertakings in paras 309-312 above.
942. P Akman, 'The role of intent in the EU case law on abuse of dominance' (2014) European Law Review 316, 318.
943. *A.A. Poultry Farms, Inc. v Rose Acre Farms, Inc.*, 881 F.2d 1396, 1402 (7th Cir. 1989).

promise of profit, and often, greed'.[944] To somehow think that market players should not act selfishly or that they should act altruistically would be contrary to the principles of the free market economy itself. Manne and Williamson therefore consider that the confusion that reigns in this respect 'stems from the broader conceptual ambivalence surrounding the propriety of business behaviour'.[945]

665 It is also said that, in the business world, there is a 'common practice of speaking in the language of war or of sport contests'[946] and an 'inveterate tendency of sales executives to brag to their superiors about their competitive prowess, often using metaphors of coercion that are compelling evidence of predatory intent to the naïve'.[947] Such metaphors suggesting subjective exclusionary intentions should not be taken at face value, the argument goes.

666 The risk of confusing vigorous competition with anticompetitive behaviour is particularly high in concentrated markets. While undertakings in atomized markets do not need to pay much attention to what their competitors do, in concentrated markets the opposite is true: what one undertaking does has a direct effect on the commercial conditions of others. As Hovenkamp says, 'in the concentrated markets in which plausible monopolization claims are made, firms cannot act rationally without considering the effects on and responses of particular rivals'. In those markets, 'the intent to increase one's own sales invariably reduces to the "intent" to take sales from rivals'.[948] Melícias similarly points out that in cases of alleged exclusionary abuses, 'a single firm's eliminatory intent is consistent with competitive behaviour and practical experience does *not* demonstrate that anticompetitive effects will necessarily ensue from a predatory intention' so 'the concern about false positives might be stronger in this area of the law'.[949]

667 The use of *mens rea* evidence may then lead to over-enforcement: since the intention to compete vigorously is mistakenly understood as an intention to predate or to exclude, an undertaking is ascribed an anticompetitive intention even though it is simply behaving competitively. It has been said that this leads to an 'inherent asymmetry' in that 'courts use intent evidence selectively only to condemn – never to exculpate – behaviour'.[950]

668 In the US literature, this worry is particularly framed in terms of the limits of the understanding of the laymen that populate juries. Indeed, while judges under the

944. MJ Melícias, 'The use and abuse of intent evidence in antitrust analysis' (2010) World Competition 569, 576.
945. GA Manne and EM Williamson, 'Hot docs vs. cold economics' (2005) 47 Arizona Law Review 609, 648.
946. RA Cass and KN Hylton, 'Antitrust intent' (2001) 74 Southern California Law Review 657, 676.
947. R Posner, *Antitrust law* (The University of Chicago Press 2001), 214-215.
948. H Hovenkamp, 'The monopolization offense' (2000) 61 Ohio State Law Journal 1035, 1039-1040.
949. MJ Melícias, 'The use and abuse of intent evidence in antitrust analysis' (2010) World Competition 569, 592 (emphasis in original).
950. GA Manne and EM Williamson, 'Hot docs vs. cold economics' (2005) 47 Arizona Law Review 609, 650.

common law determine questions of law, in jury trials, juries determine questions of fact. Since the presence of a particular intention is a question of fact, it is in principle left to the jury to determine whether such an intention was present.[951]

669 I agree that it is indeed not always easy, for example, to distinguish the intention to compete from the intention to exclude. Caution should therefore be exercised when interpreting evidence of subjective intentions in the form of the words or expressions of representatives of undertakings. An intention to win business often implies an intention to take business away from others. For example, whether a strategy of 'pre-emption', as in *Wanadoo* (*see* in particular paragraph 345 above), is really exclusionary is questionable: it could be interpreted as a willingness to be ahead of the curve, which should not be problematic as such.

670 However, any difficulty that may exist to distinguish procompetitive from anticompetitive *intentions* merely mirrors the difficulty that exists to distinguish procompetitive from anticompetitive *actions*. Practising low prices, for example, can be both pro- and anticompetitive: consumers in the short run will benefit from low prices but, if these low prices mean that competitors are driven out of the market, consumers may suffer from this in the long run (assuming of course that re-entry is difficult).[952]

671 In those circumstances, evidence of subjective intentions may provide an extra clue to interpret the actions. If a dominant undertaking sacrifices short-term profitability (*see* the discussion of *Wanadoo* in paragraphs 343ff. above) because it believes that it will be able to recover the losses it makes (by practising low prices) after the exit of its competitors, then this will be an indication that its low prices are probably anticompetitive.[953] Or, if there is evidence that an undertaking with proprietary technology believes that another undertaking will enter the market with a non-infringing competing product (as in *Lundbeck* discussed in paragraph 265 above), this is an indication that the possible entrant is a potential competitor.

672 Of course, evidence of subjective intentions will not always be clear and may sometimes be just as ambiguous as the undertaking's actions. Even a smoking gun may not contain a silver bullet to solve a case. Evidence of subjective intentions also requires interpretation; it needs to be analysed in the context in which it is created, and undertakings should obviously have the chance to provide an alternative reading of it. But it can provide additional clues to understanding the likely purpose (and therefore effect) of the conduct, as will be discussed in more detail in paragraphs 721ff. below.

673 As to the risk of over-enforcement: this assumes that there are more bad intentions than bad actions. In any event, the risk of over-enforcement is counterbalanced by a

951. *See* for the US: R Posner, *Antitrust law* (The University of Chicago Press 2001) 214 and M Lao, 'Reclaiming a role for intent evidence in monopolization analysis' (2004) American University Law Review 151, 207-208; and, for criminal trials in the UK: A MacCulloch, 'Honesty, morality and the cartel offence' (2007) European Competition Law Review 355, 359.
952. *See* the discussion on predatory pricing in paras 325ff. above.
953. At least assuming the market is not a natural monopoly, since in that case competition within the market is always excluded.

risk of under-enforcement if *mens rea* evidence is not taken into account. There is no doubt that procompetitive justifications can be invoked by defendants to escape antitrust liability: under Article 101 TFEU such justifications are explicitly mentioned in paragraph 3, and under Article 102 TFEU the case law has accepted objective justifications (*see* the discussion in Chapter 3). A similar position has been taken in US law.[954] Obviously, suitable evidence must be adduced by the defendant to support this justification: this can include not only economic analysis but also internal documents attesting to the undertaking's intentions. In the same way, a competition authority should be allowed to adduce evidence of the anticompetitive effects of an undertaking's conduct, again using either economic analysis or internal documents (or both) attesting to the undertaking's intended effects.

674 Any impression that courts or competition authorities rely more on evidence of anticompetitive intent than procompetitive intent may be due to the fact that cases where procompetitive intentions are apparent are unlikely to reach the decision stage and may simply be dropped during the investigation. Both the US Department of Justice[955] and the European Commission[956] have pointed out that intent evidence is relevant in prioritization.

[C] Possibility to Hide Intentions

675 A second, related objection was formulated by Posner in the context of predatory pricing: 'Judges and juries don't always understand that the availability of evidence of improper intent is often a function of luck and of the defendant's legal sophistication, not of underlying reality.'[957] Cass and Hylton also point out that '[w]here there is real intent to do something illegal, well-advised firms are unlikely to provide much in the way of helpful evidence. Lawyers will routinely advise clients not to leave in their files any memoranda or statements suggesting a desire to eliminate competitors'.[958] Melícias similarly argues that, in the context of predatory pricing, 'sophisticated firms would obviously go to great lengths not to leave behind any paper trail of their secret predatory aims, thus easily escaping liability'.[959] Akman develops that 'if internal documents are used to establish "intent", these can always be fabricated/

954. *See*, for example, *Aspen Skiing Co v Aspen Highlands Skiing Corp*, 472 U.S. 585, 597 (1985) where the Supreme Court states that a company with monopoly power who refuses to supply a competitor 'does not violate Section 2 if valid business reasons exist for that refusal'.
955. At least to determine whether to criminally prosecute: *see* Department of Justice, *Antitrust Division Manual* (5th edition, 2015) III-12.
956. At least in relation to the enforcement of Article 102 TFEU: *see* the Commission Guidance on the Commission's enforcement priorities in applying Article 82 of the EC Treaty to abusive exclusionary conduct by dominant undertakings [2009] OJ C45/7, para. 20.
957. *See* R Posner, *Antitrust law* (The University of Chicago Press 2001) 214.
958. RA Cass and KN Hylton, 'Antitrust intent' (2001) 74 Southern California Law Review 657, 676. *See also* 732.
959. MJ Melícias, 'The use and abuse of intent evidence in antitrust analysis' (2010) World Competition 569, 577.

avoided/discarded' and 'undertakings will learn not to leave any intent evidence behind'.[960]

676 Because of the risk of hiding intentions, scholars in particular in the US also fear that taking into account evidence of subjective intentions will greatly increase the cost of litigation. As Chicago School scholar and judge Frank Easterbrook said in the US 7th Circuit predatory pricing case of *A.A. Poultry Farms*: 'Lawyers rummage through business records seeking to discover tidbits that will sound impressive (or aggressive) when read to a jury. Traipsing through the warehouses of businesses in search of misleading evidence both increases the cost of litigation and reduces the accuracy of decisions.'[961]

677 I agree that there is indeed a risk that the most devious infringers will be able to hide their anticompetitive intentions best. But this does not pose different evidentiary problems than in the case of anticompetitive conduct: sophisticated cartelists are probably better at hiding their meetings than SMEs or one-time offenders as well. As O'Grady puts it: '[w]hile it is true that the detection and evaluation of intent evidence raises particular issues, the same could be said of many other forms of evidence'.[962]

678 Furthermore, if there is evidence of concealment, that in itself can be an important indicator of awareness of illegality and therefore of intent. As we have seen in paragraph 622, the European Commission has often pointed to such evidence of concealment to conclude that the infringement was committed intentionally. As any antitrust enforcer knows, when you are reviewing the contents of an email account of a suspect employee, you start with the deleted items.

679 With increased data retention it becomes increasingly difficult, even for sophisticated firms, to avoid creating any traces of anticompetitive intentions. More and more data is being created every day,[963] also by undertakings, and competition authorities therefore routinely review large quantities of digital information during inspections. These cover not only documents which also exist in hardcopy but also documents which never existed or no longer exist in hardcopy, as well as meta-information pertaining to documents such as who created it, when, etc.[964]

960. P Akman, 'The role of intent in the EU case law on abuse of dominance' (2014) European Law Review 316, 336.
961. *A.A. Poultry Farms, Inc. v Rose Acre Farms, Inc.*, 881 F.2d 1396, 1402 (7th Cir. 1989).
962. C O'Grady, 'The role of exclusionary intent in the enforcement of Article 102 TFEU' (2014) World Competition 459, 467. *See also* PL Parcu and ML Stasi, 'The role of intent in the assessment of conduct under Article 102 TFEU' in PL Parcu, G Monti and M Botta (Eds), *Abuse of dominance in EU competition law. Emerging trends* (Edward Elgar 2017) 12, 27.
963. According to an IBM 2017 marketing report, 90% of the data in the world was created in the last two years alone. *See* IBM, '10 key marketing trends for 2017' < https://comsenseconsulting.com/wp-content/uploads/2017/03/10_Key_Marketing_Trends_for_2017_and_Ideas_for_Exceeding_Customer_Expectations.pdf > accessed 17 May 2020.
964. *See* on this: ICN Cartels Working Group, 'Chapter on digital evidence gathering' in ICN Cartels Working Group, *Anti-Cartel Enforcement Manual* (2014) <https://www.internationalcompetitionnetwork.org/wp-content/uploads/2018/05/CWG_ACEMDigitalEvidence.pdf> accessed 24 January 2019, in particular 7-8.

680 That sophisticated firms would be successful in not creating evidence is not borne out by the enforcement track record so far. Of course, we do not know how much evidence was not created because of sophistication (the counterfactual), but the European Commission has in recent years fined very sophisticated undertakings in a variety of sophisticated sectors (tech, banking, pharmaceuticals). It could thereby rely on evidence of illegal conduct as well as of illicit intentions.[965]

681 Finally, although it is true that finding evidence of intentions may require additional efforts, the same applies to using extensive economic analysis for ambiguous practices.[966] Indeed, as will be discussed in more detail in §5.04 below, it is precisely because the economic analysis of the actual or likely effect of commercial practices is so arduous that *mens rea* evidence can provide a useful shortcut to an assessment of those effects.

[D] Difficulty of Ascribing Intentions of Individuals to Businesses

682 A third objection that is commonly raised against using internal documents as evidence of the subjective intentions of an undertaking relates to the fact that most businesses are comprised of multiple individuals. As a consequence, there may be different intentions and opinions within the same undertaking such that it is difficult to ascribe these to that undertaking as a whole. As we already saw in Chapter 1, it is indeed difficult to determine a corporation's 'state of mind'. As Melícias puts it:

> a legal entity is obviously a mere *fiction*, which only exists, desires, or *intends* through the acts of its owners or employees. If proving a natural person's mental state can cause its own set of intricacies, these are multiplied exponentially when trying to devise the true reason for a company's behaviour within a complex organizational setting. An *undertaking's* decision can be the ultimate result of a wide array of contributions from a variety of employees. Their views as to the appropriateness of a business decision can be driven by a range of varied motivations: in relation to the same action, some employees may be inspired by the goal of improving a product's brand value, while others may be just encouraged by a short-term objective of increasing market shares and 'squashing' rivals. Certain expressions may be too spontaneous and unconsidered, they may be the

---

965. In the tech sector, an obvious example is *Microsoft I*. *See*, for example, the Commission decision of 21 April 2004 in case 37.792 Microsoft, recital 463 and T-201/04 *Microsoft v Commission* ECLI:EU:T:2007:289, para. 1136. In the banking sector, the Commission has concluded a series of investigations on interest rate manipulation in recent years. Most of these cases were settled so little information is publicly available on the evidence used by the Commission. However, when the Commission adopted a fine on three banks for the EIRD cartel (case 39.914), the Commission's press release (IP/16/4304) noted that '[t]he participating traders of the banks were in regular contact through corporate chat-rooms or instant messaging services'. In the pharmaceutical sector, evidence of anticompetitive intentions played a key role in the assessment of the Commission and the General Court. *See* Commission decision of 19 June 2013 in case 39.226 *Lundbeck*, in particular recitals 803-816; 858-866; 950-954; 1000-1005; 1075-1079; 1161-1166 and T-472/13 *Lundbeck v Commission* ECLI:EU:T:2016:449, in particular paras 517-533.

966. *See* on this also AC Witt, 'The enforcement of Article 101 TFEU: what has happened to the effects analysis?' (2018) 55 Common Market Law Review 417, 436-437.

> result of mere wishful thinking, or done strictly to impress an audience, with little preparation and forethought. Accordingly, imputing a manager's reflections to his corporation can be an arbitrary exercise.[967]

683 Akman is similarly critical that 'in the case of undertakings that have no thoughts of their own but have agents acting on their behalf, one would have to decide on a case-by-case basis whose intent is the relevant intent'.[968]

684 Is this objection to the use of *mens rea* evidence insurmountable? In my view, these problems of attribution are not so different from those encountered in criminal corporate liability which we discussed in Chapter 1. Authorities should obviously be careful in attributing intentions and opinions of officers and employees to undertakings. The extent to which they can do so will depend on the prevalence of certain intentions and opinions within the undertaking, including at the highest levels. The 'tough talk' of one aggressive salesperson cannot suffice to attribute bad intentions to an undertaking, but if anticompetitive intentions are ubiquitous among the most senior management, such attribution should not be controversial. As Lao puts it: 'It should be entirely safe to attribute to the corporation, as an expression of its intent, statements made by its chief executive officer or its senior executives because these executives constitute the firm's top management and act on its behalf.'[969]

685 For less senior employees, the sphere in which they can make relevant statements is more limited, and it makes a lot of sense to determine whether the person who expresses the thought or intention is also the person that engaged in the conduct that is potentially problematic. In other words, the views of the person or group of persons (department of the undertaking) that took the potentially problematic decision are more likely relevant to interpret that conduct than those responsible for entirely different businesses within the undertaking. For example, if an undertaking drops its prices for product A, the views of the salespeople in charge of product A are more relevant than the views of the salespeople in charge of product B.[970]

686 Apart from the seniority and field of competence of the employees, other simple principles can be used to determine whether what they are saying should be given a lot of weight or not, such as (i) the context in which the expression is made (is it done in the formal setting of giving instructions, for example, or just an isolated comment); (ii) the prevalence of the expression of the intent and presence or lack of contradictory

967. MJ Melícias, 'The use and abuse of intent evidence in antitrust analysis' (2010) World Competition 569, 576-577 (emphasis in original).
968. P Akman, 'The role of intent in the EU case law on abuse of dominance' (2014) European Law Review 316, 336.
969. M Lao, 'Reclaiming a role for intent evidence in monopolization analysis' (2004) American University Law Review 151, 206.
970. *See* H Engels, *Unternehmensvorsatz und Unternehmensfahrlässigkeit im Europäischen Kartellrecht* (Berlin Verlag Arno Spitz 2002) 139 who also refers to the 'awareness relevant for the conduct in the entity that makes the relevant decisions' ['*die Verfügbarkeit des tatbestandsrelevanten Wissens in der jeweiligen entscheidungstreffenden Einheit*'].

statements; and (iii) whether the statement is made contemporaneous with the allegedly problematic conduct.[971]

687 An example where the CFI has taken into account such criteria is *Wanadoo* (*see* paragraph 345 above).

[E] Risk of Relying on the Perpetrator's View of Antitrust Rules

688 A final objection to using evidence of subjective intentions, in the sense of awareness, relates specifically to awareness of illegality. It asks: if an authority is meant to take into account the offender's own belief as to the illegality of its conduct, does that not mean that legality is merely in the eye of the offender? In those circumstances, the more warped an offender's understanding is of the rules, the more innocent he appears to become. This is a problem even in the core of the criminal law,[972] but it seems to be more acute in the sphere of economic regulation, which often concerns behaviour which is merely prohibited by convention.

689 In the literature on criminal law and on regulation, a distinction is often made in this context between *mala in se* and *mala prohibita*.[973] The former is the subject of the core of the criminal law: acts (or consequences of conduct) that humans apparently naturally believe to be bad (because contrary to morality), such as murder, rape and theft. *Mala prohibita*, however, are acts (or consequences of conduct) that are conventionally prohibited because they are believed to be an obstacle to the functioning of our society.

971. *See* M Lao, 'Reclaiming a role for intent evidence in monopolization analysis' (2004) American University Law Review 151, 207 and 210. *See also* M Lao, 'Aspen Skiing and Trinko: antitrust intent and sacrifice' (2005) 73 Antitrust Law Journal 171, 205-206.
972. It seems that, for this reason, the UK Supreme Court recently amended the test for dishonesty as a criterion to determine cheating in gambling in *Ivey v Genting Casinos* [2017] UKSC 67 (*see* in particular paras 57-59 and 72). In this judgment, the classic authority of *R v Ghosh* [1982] QB 1053 was overthrown which required for a finding of dishonesty that (i) the conduct was dishonest by the lay objective standards of ordinary reasonable and honest people and (ii) that the defendant must have realized that ordinary honest people would so regard his conduct. The second part of the test was dismissed in *Ivey* because it could allow defendants with an alternative morality to be acquitted. Interestingly, in *R v Ghosh* reference was made to Robin Hood, whose perception of the morality of theft was clearly different from the law enforcer's perception of the law of theft, but who, according to the Court of Appeal in that case, was nevertheless aware that his conduct was considered dishonest by ordinary people.
973. *See*, for example, RA Kagan, 'On regulatory inspectorates and police' in K Hawkins and JM Thomas (eds), *Enforcing regulation* (Kluwer 1984) 37, 53: D Nelken, 'White-collar crime' in M Maguire, R Morgan and R Reiner, *The Oxford handbook of criminology* (OUP 1997) 891, 913; A MacCulloch, 'Honesty, morality and the cartel offence' (2007) European Competition Law Review 355, 360; RA Robson, 'Crime and punishment: rehabilitating retribution as a justification for organizational criminal liability' (2010) American Business Journal 109, 138; ME Stucke, 'Morality and antitrust' (2006) Columbia Business Law Review 443, 489-490.

690 *Mala prohibita* concern behaviour which does not have any moral connotation at all or is morally ambiguous.[974] Society has decided that driving through a red light as well as crossing a continuous white line in the middle of the road is, by convention, prohibited and has even foreseen criminal sanctions for this kind of behaviour. Nevertheless, we would not find it immoral if someone on a deserted road with no other cars or pedestrians in sight would cross a white line or a red light. In the case of *mala prohibita*, the role of the law is obviously much more educational. If society agrees that certain conduct should be prohibited, even if only by way of convention (say, crossing a red light, as opposed to a green light) in order to allow certain activities to function, this can only work if everyone is aware of the rules.

691 That the antitrust rules (mostly) concern *mala prohibita* is often used to argue against the criminalization of antitrust law.[975] In fact, the trials and tribulations of the criminalization of cartels in the UK seem to be partially due to a decision by the House of Lord prior to the introduction of the 'cartel offence' in UK law[976] that entering into a cartel was not necessarily 'dishonest' according to the ordinary standards of reasonable and honest people.[977] It has been argued that the dishonesty requirement contained in the definition of the cartel offence subsequently impeded many prosecutions,[978] and when the UK competition regime was overhauled through the Enterprise and Regulatory Reform Act 2013, the dishonesty requirement was simply removed from the cartel offence. The offence became one of strict liability but, as a defence against liability, the alleged cartelist could demonstrate that he or she had made the existence of the cartel agreement public or at least known to his or her customers.[979]

692 *Mala prohibita* are thus not 'naturally' seen as bad and this means that ignorance of law is more likely. It is argued that, when dealing with *mala prohibita*, 'it is difficult to distinguish malevolence from incompetence' and 'we are often more concerned about the harmful effect of the latter'.[980] Regulated subjects (undertakings in the case

974. *See* RA Kagan, 'On regulatory inspectorates and police' in K Hawkins and JM Thomas (eds), *Enforcing regulation* (Kluwer 1984) 37, 53 and K Hawkins and JM Thomas, 'The enforcement process in regulatory bureaucracies' in K Hawkins and JM Thomas (eds), *Enforcing regulation* (Kluwer 1984) 3, 8.
975. *See*, for example, A Jones and R Williams, 'The UK response to the global effort against cartels: is criminalization really the solution?' (2014) 2 (1) Journal of Antitrust Enforcement 100, 102.
976. S. 188 Enterprise Act 2002 provided that a person was guilty of such an offence if he or she 'dishonestly agrees with one or more other persons to make or implement, or to cause to be made or implemented' specifically listed agreement between two undertakings, namely price-fixing, supply or production limitations, market or customer sharing, and bid rigging.
977. *Norris v United States* [2008] UKHL 16. Note that this ruling was based on the interpretation of 'dishonesty' in *R v Ghosh* [1982] QB 1053 which was overruled in *Ivey v Genting Casinos* [2017] UKSC 67.
978. *See* C Beaton-Wells, 'The politics of cartel criminalisation: a pessimistic view from Australia' (2008) 29 (3) European Competition Law Review 185, 191-192; A Stephan, 'How dishonesty killed the cartel offence' (2011) Criminal law review 446 and A Stephan, 'An empirical evaluation of the normative justifications for cartel criminalisation' (2017) 37(4) Legal Studies 621, 629.
979. S. 47 Enterprise and Regulatory Reform Act 2013.
980. *See* D Nelken, 'White-collar crime' in M Maguire, R Morgan and R Reiner, *The Oxford handbook of criminology* (OUP 1997) 891, 908, referring to M Clarke, *Business Crime: its nature and*

of antitrust law) need first to be aware of the rules before they can be expected to comply with them and, since the rules are not coincidental with morality, awareness of the rules does not come naturally. Ignorance, in the sense of error of law, may then indeed be worse than deviousness, and we should be as much concerned by negligent as intentional breaches of the law.

693 Incompetence becomes an even more important issue if regulations are exceedingly complex and the responsibility for complying with them is not always clear, e.g. when regulations apply to organizations (such as undertakings) or even organizations of organizations (such as markets). In those circumstances, the persons which are being investigated for a possible breach of the regulations (or, in the case of legal persons, their officers or employees) may feel that they acted in good faith and that they should not be subjected to the stigma of condemnation. Repression may then be counterproductive: in the case of undertakings, 'corporate officers may react by being less cooperative with regulatory agencies'.[981]

694 Beyond the difficulties with the defence of ignorance of law, relying on the private view of the antitrust rules also poses the reverse problem of erroneous beliefs of illegality. As we have seen, the European Commission and the European Courts regularly refer to evidence that an undertaking believed that it was breaching the antitrust rules to punish the undertaking more severely or even to establish the infringement in the first place (*see* paragraphs 622-624 above). Does that mean that a mere belief by an undertaking that it is breaching the rules should be sufficient to establish that it did break the rules?

695 I agree that the illegality of conduct cannot depend entirely on the views of the person that engages in it. Everyone that engages in the complex societies of today has to inform him or herself of the regulations that are applicable to the conduct he or she engages in, be it driving a car, hiring an employee or selling products. Sometimes the rules may be too complex, but the law also aims to instil a certain morality in its subjects, a second nature to abide by certain principles. In countries where cars are meant to drive on the right side of the road, drivers do not (need to) think each time they start driving that they need to drive on the right side. Drivers have internalized the convention and to start off on the right side of the road comes natural to them.

696 *Mala in se* and *mala prohibita* are therefore not impermeable categories (*see also* paragraph 66 above). The criminal law is meant to reflect the moral values of a society, but this is by no means a one-way process: the criminalization or decriminalization of behaviour also changes what society perceives as morally permissible or not through

---

control (Polity Press 1990) and M Clarke, 'The control of insurance fraud: a comparative view' (1990) British journal of criminology 30.

981. S Shapiro and R Rabinowitz, 'Punishment versus cooperation in regulatory enforcement: a case study of OSHA' (1997) 49(4) Administrative Law Review 713, 718. *See also* R Bouscant, 'La faute dans les infractions aux règles de concurrence en droit européen' (2000) 36 (1) Revue trimesterielle de droit européen 67, 97 and C Parker, 'The "compliance" trap: the moral message in responsive regulatory enforcement' (2006) 40 (3) Law & Society Review 591, 603.

the stigmatization that punishment entails. This process may of course tempt regulators to over-criminalize conduct in order to increase compliance. On the other hand, decriminalization of certain conduct may also contribute to removing moral stigma previously attached to that conduct.

697 I believe this also applies to competition law. The objective of antitrust enforcement is to make the antitrust rules a second nature of businesses. It is not obvious what this second nature would entail, but tentatively I would suggest that it at least entails 'competition as an ethics', i.e. that undertakings understand that, unless the law requires otherwise, they should strive for more competition in a market, not less, and also perhaps (but more difficult to determine) something like 'ethics in competition', in the sense of 'fair play'. This may sound very vague but if one thinks of business as a game or a sport,[982] it may make more sense. In many games, the aim is to win by competing with other players. If the players agree beforehand who is going to win, the game is rigged. At the same time, a game has a number of rules to ensure that there is a level playing field and that everyone in principle has a chance of winning (usually based on a combination of skill, effort and luck),[983] so that the game is 'fair'. Players that participate in the game are understood to sign up to these principles and cannot plead ignorance as an excuse for not complying with these rules – even though games are obviously based on conventions.

698 The same could be said of undertakings active on the market. If someone wants to participate in the market, he needs to sign up to the rules and cannot plead ignorance of the rules as an excuse. With many decades of antitrust enforcement, undertakings today will find it difficult to plead ignorance of the law. There is indeed empirical evidence that public opinion of anticompetitive conduct has shifted over recent decades and, for example, that cartels are currently viewed as worthy of punishment.[984] This appears to be a consequence of the educational effect of the punishment of cartels. That cartels were not viewed as 'dishonest' two centuries ago then does not imply that they are not viewed as 'dishonest' today. Even absent evidence of awareness of its illegality, the intention to fix prices or share markets with competitors, as a

982. My inspiration for this discussion is F Knight, 'The ethics of competition' in M Casson (ed.), *Culture, social norms and economics. Volume I: economic behaviour* (Edward Elgar 1997) 84, in particular 89, although he mainly discusses reasons why the principle of competition does not accord with our ethical understanding.

983. F Knight, 'The ethics of competition' in M Casson (ed.), *Culture, social norms and economics. Volume I: economic behaviour* (Edward Elgar 1997) 84, 63.

984. *See* A Stephan, 'An empirical evaluation of the normative justifications for cartel criminalisation' (2017) 37(4) Legal Studies 621, 640 who conducted a survey in the US, the UK, Germany and Italy which showed that in those countries 66%, 79%, 75% and 73% of respondents considered that a cartel should be punished (although only a minority in each of these countries considered that imprisonment was a suitable sanction). *See also* C Parker, 'The "compliance" trap: the moral message in responsive regulatory enforcement' (2006) 40 (3) Law & Society Review 591, 598 who points to interviews with managers in Australia which 'made it very clear that over the last 20 years they had seen a significant "generational" change in management attitudes to competition law compliance'.

'frontal assault' on the fundamental principle of competition underpinning the free market,[985] may then give rise to repressive action.

699 Reversely, if an undertaking is actually aware of the illegality of its conduct and nevertheless proceeds with it, this should allow for additional repression: it shows a disrespect to the law which could warrant a more severe penalty. An undertaking's awareness of the illegal nature of its conduct can, for example, be apparent from attempts at concealing the conduct (as in the case of secret cartels)[986] or be more likely in case of recidivism. This will be discussed in more detail below.

§5.04 ARGUMENTS IN FAVOUR OF TAKING INTO ACCOUNT *MENS REA*

[A] The Relevance of *Mens Rea* in Establishing Antitrust Infringements

700 After having dismissed or at least shown the limited application of the criticism that is commonly voiced against the use of *mens rea* evidence in antitrust investigations, I will now turn to the arguments as to why such evidence should be relevant.

701 My focus is on the use of evidence of the intentions of the undertaking that their conduct has as its object the restriction of competition or the exclusion of competitors (under Articles 101 and 102 TFEU respectively), both substantively and for enforcement purposes. This is not meant to imply that an undertaking's *mens rea* in respect of other material elements of the infringements is irrelevant, as I will briefly point out now.

702 First, as to the existence of an agreement or concerted practice, the case law described in §2.01 has largely rejected the relevance of subjective intentions. If such intentions would nevertheless be deemed relevant, I believe this will only make a difference in a small number of cases, where I would propose to take into account this factor (if it is established) in the sanctioning of the behaviour. As discussed in §2.01, the main instance where case law has accepted a role for *mens rea* is when it comes to attributing liability for participation in an infringement. In those circumstances, the question is whether the undertaking intended to contribute to the anticompetitive

985. GJ Werden, 'Sanctioning cartel activity: let the punishment fit the crime' (2009) European Competition Journal 19, 24.
986. In *Norris v United States* [2008] UKHL 16, the House of Lords considered that mere secrecy did not suffice to conclude that the cartel agreement was aggravated by misrepresentation and deception such that it could be viewed as 'dishonest' unless 'there is some sort of implied representation that the price at which goods are offered has been arrived at on a certain basis'. P Whelan, 'Cartel criminalization and the challenge of moral wrongfulness' (2013) 33 (3) Oxford Journal of Legal Studies 535, 553 has argued that there is always an implied representation that prices were set by market forces absent collusion, and A Stephan, 'An empirical evaluation of the normative justifications for cartel criminalisation' (2017) 37(4) Legal Studies 621 has empirically demonstrated that there is among consumers an expectation that prices were indeed set absent collusion. Even regardless of these general arguments, it seems quite likely that the tender documents filled in by the participants to the carbon products cartel contained terms and conditions to the effect that the participants attested that they were submitting competitive bids, but this matter was not discussed by the House of Lords.

objectives pursued by other undertakings. The question of *mens rea* is then very similar to the question of whether the undertaking had an anticompetitive intention.

703 Second, most of the case law under Article 102 TFEU concerns the question of abuse, rather than the question of dominance. This may be because the Commission prefers to take cases where the dominant position is fairly obvious. When dominance is disputed, *mens rea* could certainly play a role, but, again, this is probably only in a small number of cases.

704 Third, in respect of the criterion of the effect on trade: as pointed out in §4.01, this is mainly a jurisdictional criterion and mistakes of law are therefore going to play a more important role than mistakes of fact or other *mens rea* considerations.

705 Finally, the relevance of *mens rea* in ascribing corporate liability has been discussed at some length in paragraphs 682-687 above.

706 In what follows I will argue (in section [1]) that the analysis of the economic effects of conduct has its limits and that therefore, as explained in section [2], evidence of anticompetitive (including exclusionary) or procompetitive intent can play an important role in interpreting ambiguous conduct. In my view, evidence of intent also has an important role to play in the punishment of infringements (no matter whether they are established by purely economic analysis or otherwise), but this is a topic I will reserve for section [B].

[1] The Limits of Economics[987]

707 Economics is key to competition policy and enforcement. Not involving economists in a field of economic law would be like developing a climate policy without involving climatologists or writing rules on medical liability without understanding the trials and perils of medicine. Regulating markets and business without involving economists is bound to be counterproductive. But that does not mean that economic law, such as competition law, can limit itself to economics.

708 First of all, economics has its limits. Many economic theories are simply not empirically tested, either because the data to verify them are not available at this moment, or more fundamentally because they are based on non-economic values which simply cannot be confirmed empirically.[988]

987. *See also* J Blockx, 'The limits of the "more economic" approach to antitrust' (2019) World Competition 475.

988. *See* on the 'empirical stalemate in antitrust economics', MS Jacobs, 'An essay on the normative foundations of antitrust economics' (1995) 74 North Carolina Law Review 219, 250-258. But also FH Easterbrook, 'The limits of antitrust' (1984) Texas Law Review 1, 11: 'The economists might be able to reach agreement, though not on the basis of exhaustive empirical inquiry. They would resort to clues and shortcuts.'

709 Economics presents an interpretation of human behaviour within a certain school of thought alongside other disciplines such as sociology and psychology.[989] In the field of antitrust this means that 'beyond the simplest cases, economics seldom allows straightforward conclusions about the anticompetitive character of business practices'.[990] Indeed, even Frank Easterbrook, one of the most prominent Chicago School scholars, had to admit that '[t]he welfare implications of most forms of business conduct are beyond our ken. If we assembled twelve economists and gave them all the available data about a business practice, plus an unlimited computer budget, we would not get agreement about whether the practice promoted consumers' welfare or economic efficiency more broadly defined'.[991] He also pointed out that it is 'fantastic to suppose that judges and juries' could 'conduct a full inquiry into the economic costs and benefits of a particular practice in the setting in which it has been used'.[992]

710 The 'more economic' approach to competition law which has risen in prominence in Europe since the end of the 1990s argues for antitrust enforcement on the basis of an analysis of the economic effects of commercial practices. Mario Monti, the European Commissioner for Competition, who has been credited with introducing this approach in EU competition law, indeed said that under the 'more economic' approach, competition authorities 'look at the effects on the market rather than the legal form of the agreement'.[993] In its Communication following the 1997 *Green Paper on vertical restraints* (often viewed as the first reform to implement the 'more economic' approach), the Commission similarly argues that 'a more economics based approach is required. Such an approach should be based on the effects on the market ... This should facilitate a relaxation of the form-based requirements'.[994] The Economic Advisory Group on Competition Policy also listed as first principle in its report *An economic approach to Article 82* that 'the competition authority should adopt an effects-based rather than a form-based approach to competition policy'. It continues that 'a form-based approach is problematic' because '[i]n many instances alternative practices can serve the same purpose'.[995]

---

989. *See* W Wils, 'The judgment of the EU General Court in *Intel* and the so-called more economic approach to abuse of dominance' (2014) World Competition 405, 412.
990. N Giocoli, 'Old lady charm: explaining the persistent appeal of Chicago antitrust' (2015) Journal of Economic Methodology 96, 110.
991. FH Easterbrook, 'The limits of antitrust' (1984) Texas Law Review 1, 11.
992. FH Easterbrook, 'The limits of antitrust' (1984) Texas Law Review 1, 17. *See also* FH Easterbrook, 'Allocating antitrust decisionmaking tasks' (1987) Georgetown Law Journal 305, 306.
993. M Monti, 'Speech given at the formal introduction ceremony of the new President of the Bundeskartellamt' (Speech/00/6), Bonn, 13 January 2000 <http://europa.eu/rapid/press-release_SPEECH-00-6_en.htm?locale=en> accessed 18 July 2018.
994. Commission Communication on the application of the Community competition rules to vertical restraints - Follow-up to the Green Paper on vertical restraints [1998] OJ C365/3.
995. J Gual, M Hellwig *et al.* 'An economic approach to Article 82' (Report by the Economic Advisory Group on Competition Policy) (July 2005) <http://ec.europa.eu/dgs/competition/economist/eagcp_july_21_05.pdf> accessed 5 March 2018, 5.

711 However, in practice, it is very difficult to assess the welfare effects of business conduct, certainly in live cases before the courts.[996] Easterbrook therefore proposed to work with 'filters', the 'principal purpose' of which was 'to change the focus of antitrust from ascertaining the actual effects of practices (which leads the courts to condemn what they do not understand) to ascertaining whether practices harmed competition and consumers'.[997] As a result, the 'more economic' approach to competition law developed its own formalism and an obsession with quantification. This is simply the consequence of the influence of the Chicago School and its focus on price theory.[998]

712 The Article 82 EC review process provides a clear example of this. The discussion paper which the Commission published in 2005 describes in its 'Framework for analysis of exclusionary abuses' the difference between price-based and non-price based exclusionary conduct. Only a single short paragraph (basically two sentences) discusses foreclosure through non-price based conduct.[999] The rest of this section (seven long paragraphs) is devoted to price conduct. The Commission there discusses the need to apply the 'as-efficient-competitor' test and the various cost benchmarks that need to be taken into account (marginal cost, average variable cost, average avoidable cost, long-run average incremental cost and average total cost).[1000]

713 Cost measurements became the benchmark for all competition concerns in the field of abuse of dominance, and this not only in relation to pricing abuses such as predatory pricing. Even in relation to straightforward exclusivity agreements, the Commission proposes in the *Guidance Paper* to determine whether price (in that case the total price paid under the agreement) is below cost (*see* paragraph 373 above).

714 The use of mathematical models gives this approach an 'illusion of certainty', to use the words of a former Chairman of the US Federal Trade Commission.[1001] Many economists themselves have criticized the 'immoderate use of mathematical models, which are frequently no more than an excuse for occupying the terrain and masking the vacuity of the content'[1002] and the reduction of economics to 'a branch of applied mathematics'.[1003] Ronald Coase, winner of the Nobel Memorial Prize in Economic

996. *See* FH Easterbrook, 'The limits of antitrust' (1984) Texas Law Review 1,
997. *See* FH Easterbrook, 'The limits of antitrust' (1984) Texas Law Review 1, 17. *See also* at 11: 'A court could try to conduct a full inquiry into the economic costs and benefits of a particular practice in the setting in which it has been used. But it is fantastic to suppose that judges and juries could make such an evaluation.'
998. *See* MS Jacobs, 'An essay on the normative foundations of antitrust economics' (1995) 74 North Carolina Law Review 219, 230; N Giocoli, 'Old lady charm: explaining the persistent appeal of Chicago antitrust' (2015) Journal of Economic Methodology 96, 100.
999. DG Competition discussion paper on the application of Article 82 of the Treaty to exclusionary abuses, December 2005, para. 61.
1000. DG Competition discussion paper on the application of Article 82 of the Treaty to exclusionary abuses, December 2005, paras 62-68.
1001. R Pitofsky, 'The political content of antitrust' (1979) 127 University of Pennsylvania Law Review 1051, 1065. *See also* M Lao, 'Reclaiming a role for intent evidence in monopolization analysis' (2004) American University Law Review 151, 179.
1002. T Piketty, *Capital in the twenty-first century* (Harvard University Press 2014) 574.
1003. R Skidelsky, *Keynes. The return of the master* (Penguin 2010) 150.

Sciences in 1991, even said: 'In my youth it was said that what was too silly to be said may be sung. In modern economics it may be put in mathematics.'[1004] Also in Europe, Simon Bishop, for example, has expressed scepticism at over-reliance on mathematics: 'if the insights provided by the mathematic approach cannot be explained in an intuitive manner then there is something wrong with the mathematics'.[1005]

715 In any event, such an approach does not look at the economic effects, but is a complete a priori exercise, deducing presumed effects from a certain relation between numerical factors (cost and price).

716 The inherent difficulty in determining the effects of a practice, in particular if these need to be quantifiable, led to the laissez-faire approach to competition law (or 'non-intervention bias')[1006] that is typical of the Chicago School. According to these scholars 'monopoly is self-destructive'[1007] and the risks of allegedly anticompetitive practices are therefore small – especially compared with the risks of over-enforcement. The greatest danger, in their view, is 'false positives' (Type I errors), i.e. situations where antitrust enforcers erroneously prohibit (and punish) practices that are not restrictive of competition. 'False negatives' (Type II errors), where anticompetitive practices are not prohibited or punished because the perpetrators get the benefit of the doubt, are less problematic because the market will correct these errors: 'Letting the guilty go free in antitrust is generally a self-correcting problem.'[1008] For false positives, there is no market correction, these scholars argue, and any correction therefore depends on subsequent legislation or case law reversing the earlier error.[1009]

717 However, the Chicago School premise that Type II errors are self-correcting is dependent on the idea that barriers to entry are small. If they are small, exclusionary conduct by dominant undertakings, for example, will only have a short-lived effect: the competitor of the dominant company may exit the market because of it but will soon return once the exclusionary conduct (which is normally costly to the dominant undertaking) ends. Similarly, assuming that barriers to entry are low, cartels must be

1004. RH Coase, 'Notes on the problem of social cost' in RH Coase, *The firm, the market and the law* (University of Chicago Press 1988) 157, 185. *See also* W Wils, 'The judgment of the EU General Court in *Intel* and the so-called more economic approach to abuse of dominance' (2014) World Competition 405, 412.
1005. S Bishop, 'Expert economic evidence in European competition law cases: some personal views' in J Derenne and M Merola (eds), *The Role of the Court of Justice of the European Union in Competition Law Cases* (Larcier 2012) 293, 297. I honestly think that this is going a little bit far: part of the value of good research consists in it challenging our intuitions; hence the fact that something is not intuitive should not be sufficient to dismiss it, but merely to enquire in it further.
1006. M Lao, 'Reclaiming a role for intent evidence in monopolization analysis' (2004) American University Law Review 151, 192.
1007. FH Easterbrook, 'The limits of antitrust' (1984) Texas Law Review 1, 2.
1008. FS McChesney, 'Talking 'bout my antitrust generation: competition for and in the field of competition law' (2003) Emory Law Journal 1401, 1412.
1009. *See also* FH Easterbrook, 'Allocating antitrust decisionmaking tasks' (1987) Georgetown Law Journal 305, 307-312.

short-lived[1010] since any supra-competitive price which the cartel charges would attract entry. The idea that entry barriers generally do not play an important role in competition is one of the premises of the Chicago School that received much criticism in later years.[1011]

718 Furthermore, even very basic notions in competition law are uncertain, such as which behaviour is anticompetitive, and even more fundamental, which behaviour is competitive.[1012] The OECD put it this way in a policy brief of over ten years ago:

> There is broad agreement among competition agencies from OECD countries that the purpose of competition policy is to protect competition, not competitors. In pursuing that objective, many agencies and courts have repeatedly used the phrase 'competition on the merits' to explain and justify their views on how to distinguish conduct that harms competition from conduct that advances it. Yet that phrase has never been satisfactorily defined.[1013]

719 The limits of economics mentioned above obviously lead to a great deal of uncertainty, and this has been the traditional criticism of the excessive use of economics in competition law: that it is hard to reconcile with the requirement of legal certainty.[1014] But the problem of the indeterminacy of economics is much more fundamental: the use of economics does not only make it difficult for undertakings to determine whether their conduct is lawful or not but also make it difficult for enforcers or courts to make this determination.

720 The laissez-faire approach that assumes that conduct is procompetitive until the opposite is shown merely confirms the limits of economics in this respect.

[2] **Mens Rea *as an Addition to Economics***

721 What is the solution to this? Obviously, the best solution is to obtain better and clearer economic insights; to test hypotheses, to collect empirical data on the impact of

1010. FH Easterbrook, 'The limits of antitrust' (1984) Texas Law Review 1, 33 even claimed that '[c]artels themselves rarely last five years'. An analysis of the European Commission's cartel decisions between 2001 and 2015 shows that the cartel described in these decisions lasted an *average* of eighty-seven months (more than seven years) – and in half of these cases the cartel only terminated because of the intervention of the European Commission. *See* M Hellwig and K Hüschelrath, 'Cartel cases and the cartel enforcement process in the European Union 2001 – 2015: a quantitative assessment' (2017) 62(2) The Antitrust Bulletin 400.
1011. *See*, for example, SC Salop, 'Strategic entry deterrence' (1979) The American economic review 335 and DJ Neven, 'Strategic entry deterrence: recent developments in the economics of industry' (1989) Journal of economic surveys 213.
1012. *See* already FH Easterbrook, 'The limits of antitrust' (1984) Texas Law Review 1, 13: 'Part of the difficulty in antitrust comes from ambiguity in what we mean by competition.'
1013. OECD Policy Brief, 'What is competition on the merits?' (June 2006) <http://www.oecd.org/competition/mergers/37082099.pdf> accessed 31 October 2017.
1014. *See* L Ortiz Blanco and A Lamadrid De Pablo, 'Expert economic evidence and effects-based assessments in competition law cases' in J Derenne and M Merola (eds), *The Role of the Court of Justice of the European Union in Competition Law Cases* (Larcier 2012) 308.

business practices, and so on.[1015] But, in the meantime, antitrust authorities cannot sit back and take their hands of the markets. Even though 'the welfare implications of most forms of business conduct are beyond our ken',[1016] the position an antitrust authority takes in respect of that business conduct still has an impact on the market. If one believes that false negatives are just as harmful as false positive, following a laissez-faire approach is not an option.

722 I believe that evidence of an undertaking's subjective intentions, i.e. of *mens rea*, can be a useful addition to or substitute for economics in the many instances where the latter cannot come to an unambiguous and conclusive analysis of the effects of a practice.

723 In my view, it is in this sense that the words of the CJEU need to be understood that 'even if the intention of the parties does not constitute a necessary factor in determining the restrictive character of an agreement, there is nothing to prohibit the Commission or the Community courts from taking that intention into account'.[1017] Intentions are relevant because they provide a guide to the interpretation of the behaviour.

724 A subjective intention to restrict competition is not a necessary condition for the finding of an antitrust infringement:[1018] a restriction of competition can arise in the absence of an undertaking being aware of this or even without it being able to be aware of this. This is not only because the undertaking could have difficulty understanding the legal qualification of its conduct (a mistake of law)[1019] but also because it may not be aware of the relevant facts to foresee the restriction of competition (a mistake of fact). An example of the latter situation is provided by the case law on parallel vertical agreements: an undertaking which concludes a vertical agreement may not be aware that its competitors have concluded parallel agreements and that the combined effect

---

1015. OW Holmes, *The Common Law*, Lecture I: Early forms of liability (first published 1881, Belknap 2009) 36 seemed to believe that scientific progress to improve the law in this sense was inevitable: 'while the law does still and always, in a certain sense, measure legal liability by moral standards, it nevertheless, by the very necessity of its nature, is continually transmuting those moral standards into external or objective ones, from which the actual guilt of the party concerned is wholly eliminated'.
1016. FH Easterbrook, 'The limits of antitrust' (1984) Texas Law Review 1, 11.
1017. C-551/03 P *General Motors v Commission* ECLI:EU:C:2006:229, para. 78 and almost identical wording in C-8/08 *T-Mobile Netherlands and Others* ECLI:EU:C:2009:343, para. 27; joined cases C-501, 513, 515 and 519/06 P *GlaxoSmithKline Services and Others v Commission and Others* ECLI:EU:C:2009:610, para. 58; C-32/11 *Allianz Hungaria Biztosito* ECLI:EU:C:2013:160, para. 37; C-67/13 P *Cartes Bancaires v Commission* ECLI:EU:C:2014:2204, para. 54 and C-286/13 P *Dole Food and Dole Fresh Fruit Europe v Commission* ECLI:EU:C:2015:184, para. 118.
1018. *See also*, in this sense, R Bouscant, 'La faute dans les infractions aux règles de concurrence en droit européen' (2000) 36 (1) Revue trimesterielle de droit européen 67, in particular 69-77.
1019. *See*, for example, the Commission decision of 29 April 2014 in case 39.985 *Motorola – Enforcement of GPRS standard essential patents*, in particular recitals 559-561 where the Commission found an infringement but decided not to impose a fine because it had not qualified the conduct as anticompetitive in the past.

of such agreements is anticompetitive. Such conduct may nevertheless restrict competition and therefore infringe Article 101 TFEU.[1020]

725 But such a subjective intention to restrict competition is eminently relevant to interpret an undertaking's conduct. Since it is often impossible to determine what the effects of a particular practice will be, evidence of the intentions of the undertakings involved can help to clarify its likely effects. Indeed, as Lao points out, '[i]ntent evidence is useful since no one is likely to know better the probable effects of a practice than the firm engaging in it'.[1021] The reason for this is that '[f]irms presumably understand the market in which they operate and know the likely effect of their actions'.[1022] Also Parcu and Stasi state that 'it is generally true that firms can predict their conduct's effects on competition better than courts or antitrust enforcers, who are less familiar with the industry and the market's competitive dynamics'.[1023] It is for this reason that 'whenever the economics tools used by the enforcers provide ambiguous or inconclusive results, recourse to intent evidence may constitute a helpful supplementary element'.[1024] Also, under Article 101 TFEU, subjective intentions serve such a 'clarificatory function'.[1025]

726 As I already indicated in paragraph 265 above, this seems to be the reason why the Commission, endorsed by the General Court, took into account subjective intentions in *Lundbeck* to determine whether a settlement agreement between an originator and a generic is likely to restrict competition. But also in other instances where agreements are ambiguous, the intentions of the party may provide an explanation. A good example is in the case of agreements between competitors to make a joint bid for a tender: internal emails of the managers of the bidders can demonstrate whether the cooperation is aimed at improving the offer that can be made to the tenderer or if it is aimed at reducing the alternatives available.[1026]

1020. *See* case C-23/67 *Brasserie De Haecht v Wilkin Janssen* ECLI:EU:C:1967:54, in particular [1967] ECR 415-416 and C-234/89 *Delimitis v Henninger Bräu* ECLI:EU:C:1991:91, in particular paras 14-15. *See also* the Commission Guidelines on vertical restraints [2010] OJ C130/1, paras 75-77 and the discussion in R Bouscant, 'La faute dans les infractions aux règles de concurrence en droit européen' (2000) 36 (1) Revue trimesterielle de droit européen 67, 72.
1021. M Lao, 'Reclaiming a role for intent evidence in monopolization analysis' (2004) American University Law Review 151, 157. *See also* 197.
1022. M Lao, 'Aspen Skiing and Trinko: antitrust intent and sacrifice' (2005) 73 Antitrust Law Journal 171, 193.
1023. PL Parcu and ML Stasi, 'The role of intent in the assessment of conduct under Article 102 TFEU' in PL Parcu, G Monti and M Botta (eds), *Abuse of dominance in EU competition law. Emerging trends* (Edward Elgar 2017) 12, 20.
1024. PL Parcu and ML Stasi, 'The role of intent in the assessment of conduct under Article 102 TFEU' in PL Parcu, G Monti and M Botta (Eds), *Abuse of dominance in EU competition law. Emerging trends* (Edward Elgar 2017) 12, 21.
1025. KHF Kwok, 'Object and intention under Article 101 TFEU: lessons from Australia, New Zealand and analytical jurisprudence' (2019) Common Law World Review 114
1026. *See* C Thomas, 'Two bids or not to bid? An exploration of the legality of joint bidding and subcontracting under EU competition law' (2015) 6(9) Journal of European Competition Law & Practice 629, 634. Of course this means that well-advised firms may avoid intervention because they avoid creating the wrong type of emails but, as pointed out earlier, this should not stop intervention when the wrong type of emails is present.

727 In the field of Article 102 TFEU, evidence of the intentions of the dominant undertaking is, as we have seen, useful to disambiguate conduct that could (objectively speaking) be exclusionary or merely procompetitive. The obvious example is in predatory pricing with the *Akzo* case law requiring an assessment of the intentions of the dominant undertaking in case pricing is below average total but above average variable cost (*see* paragraphs 331ff.).

728 The idea that undertakings themselves are in the best position to assess the likely effects of their business conduct has been contested. Manne and Williamson argue: 'Even where business people perform their own competitive analyses and express not only their aspirations but also their reasoned expectations of economic effect, these analyses are still at a disadvantage compared to the analyses performed by government agencies or litigants. No matter how well-performed, the business analysis is always at an informational disadvantage because, with few exceptions, business analyses must be performed solely on the basis of a firm's own information and publicly-available information. Business do not have access to highly-relevant economic data internal to other companies.'[1027] AG Wahl similarly considered in his opinion in *Intel* that '[w]hile a strategy of foreclosure may certainly provide an indication of a subjective intent to foreclose competitors, the mere will to do so does not translate into capability to restrict competition'.[1028]

729 I agree that an undertaking may be wrong, but if it indeed has the subjective intention to foreclose competitors, this at least creates a prima facie case that its conduct will have that effect. Undertakings, whose entire existence is focused on running their business, must indeed be in the best position to assess the probable effects of their practices. If they are not capable of doing that, then presumably they will not be able to survive in the marketplace. So, when undertakings discuss the probable effect of their practices in internal documents, it makes sense to give credence to this.

730 If the analysis of Manne and Williamson is followed, it would appear that competition analyses need to be done independently of the information the firm had at the moment of engaging in the practice. Firms would then not be able to know whether they are engaging in an anticompetitive practice, which would fly in the face of the predictability of the law. And to take this one step further: if authorities are better able than firms to predict the effect of a firm's behaviour, this could be an argument for more state intervention in the economy, which presumably is not what Manne and Williamson have in mind.

731 Even authors who are sceptical about the use of intent evidence accept that it can sometimes *preclude* antitrust liability for behaviour that on its face appears anticompetitive. Hovenkamp, for example, states that in order to determine whether a technological modification by a monopolist is exclusionary (so-called predatory innovation), the Court should first of all assess whether the modification is actually an

1027. *See* GA Manne and EM Williamson, 'Hot docs vs. cold economics' (2005) 47 Arizona Law Review 609, 620.
1028. AG opinion in case C-413/14 P *Intel v Commission* ECLI:EU:C:2016:788, para. 128.

improvement; when this is not the case, second, 'then it becomes proper to probe the defendant's pre-innovation intentions: did it really set out to build a better product, or did it redesign only in order to exclude a rival?'[1029] Posner, as already pointed out, even goes further: although he is sceptical about the use of evidence of intentions, he accepts that to establish predatory pricing in the case of pricing below long-run but above short-run marginal costs, 'proof of intent to exclude is required'. He realizes that this is hard to reconcile with his scepticism of intent evidence but admits: 'I see no alternative.'[1030]

732 The extent to which evidence of subjective intentions will be relevant in a specific case should of course be related to the uncertainties of the economic analysis. Evidence of subjective intentions and economic analysis are communicating vessels: in the rare instances where the economic analysis is adamant that a particular practice is problematic (the example which readily springs to mind is: price-fixing cartels) or not problematic at all, anticompetitive intent or the absence thereof will be of little relevance. However, the greater the uncertainty of the economic analysis, the more helpful evidence of intent can be.[1031]

733 Intentions of the undertakings involved will be particularly relevant in case antitrust offences are inchoate, as they often are, i.e. when the effects of the allegedly anticompetitive conduct have not been (fully) realized yet. In respect of what is now Article 101 TFEU, AG Trstenjak, for example, has argued that the dichotomy between object and effect in what is now Article 101 TFEU militates for an interpretation 'that Article 81(1) EC, as regards the alternative of restriction of competition by object, is designed as a form of inchoate offence'.[1032]

734 The same applies in relation to Article 102 TFEU where the CJEU has made it clear that an exclusionary abuse can be found even before the competitors suffering from the allegedly exclusionary practice have left the market entirely.[1033] In relation to monopolization cases in the US, Lao has argued that '[t]o wait for definitive evidence of anticompetitive harm to become available before taking any action will mean that

1029. H Hovenkamp, 'The monopolization offense' (2000) 61 Ohio State Law Journal 1035, 1046. *See also* PE Areeda and H Hovenkamp, *Antitrust law - An analysis of antitrust principles and their application* (Wolters Kluwer 1978, Supp May 2018) ¶ 738c. Also scholars who favour a role of intent obviously consider exculpatory intent relevant: *see* M Lao, 'Reclaiming a role for intent evidence in monopolization analysis' (2004) American University Law Review 151, 198.

1030. R Posner, *Antitrust law* (The University of Chicago Press 2001) 216.

1031. *See also* ME Stucke, 'Is intent relevant?' (2012) 8 Journal of Law, Economics & Policy 801, 855-856.

1032. AG opinion in C-209/07 *Beef Industry Development and Barry Brothers* ECLI:EU:C:2008:467, para. 46 and footnote 23. AG Trstenjak finds support for this interpretation in the opinion of Advocate General Vesterdorf in his opinion in joined cases T-1/89 to T-4/89 and T-6/89 to T-15/89 *Rhône-Poulenc et al v Commission* ECLI:EU:T:1991:38, in particular at [1991] ECR II 945-6 who argues that Article 101 TFEU may prohibit inchoate offences (in particular agreements which have as their object the restriction of competition, regardless of any effect) but at the same time rejects the idea that an attempt at breaching Article 101 TFEU would be punishable.

1033. C-333/94 P *Tetra Pak v Commission* ECLI:EU:C:1996:436, para. 44.

antitrust intervention will rarely occur in time to make any difference'.[1034] Behavioural economics has shown that exclusionary abuses can have effects on competition even if they never lead to exclusion because they signal to competitors or potential entrants that the dominant undertaking could crush them if it wanted and therefore have a chilling effect on competition.[1035] In those circumstances, evidence of intentions will be particularly relevant to interpret conduct.

735 I think that situations where economic analysis reaches its limits arise quite regularly such that evidence of subjective intentions will often be relevant. To clarify this, it is worthwhile to return to the examples discussed in paragraph 731 above where even Hovenkamp and Posner accept that evidence of intentions can be relevant. Hovenkamp states that this is the case if a technological modification is not actually an improvement. But how are we meant to determine whether a technological modification is an improvement? Is it an improvement merely because there is demand for it, i.e. it increases sales? And should we then only look at in-market sales or also sales in related markets? Many factors need to be considered here and it may be very difficult to determine whether a modification is an improvement without considering the intentions of the undertaking from the very beginning.

736 Posner's example of predatory pricing is just as problematic. Whether marginal costs are short-run or long-run depends on what one considers short and long, and, as Bishop and Walker have pointed out, '[t]here is no widespread agreement over the relevant time period'.[1036] Any perceived reduction in profitability will reduce the incentives of (actual or potential) competitors to sell on the market: whether this is enough to exclude them will depend on a number of hypothetical (and future) factors (such as financing risks, market projections and the like) which are hard to determine. What the future gain is for the dominant undertaking and for which period of time it is worth sacrificing profits to achieve this is itself therefore an open question. A dominant undertaking's own perception can also be relevant to understand this.

737 In conclusion, antitrust authorities who do not take into account evidence of subjective intentions and merely look at established economic effects alone are often forced to abstain from intervention. My proposal to take evidence of subjective intentions more seriously would change this and is therefore likely to result in a more interventionist attitude in some cases. However, to the extent that evidence of such intentions may also be relevant to dismiss concerns of anticompetitive conduct, it may occasionally stop intervention as well - and, as we will see now, also mitigate punishment.

1034. M Lao, 'Reclaiming a role for intent evidence in monopolization analysis' (2004) American University Law Review 151, 196.
1035. *See* JB Baker, 'Recent developments in economics that challenge Chicago School views' (1989) Antitrust Law Journal 645, 648-649; C O'Grady, 'The role of exclusionary intent in the enforcement of Article 102 TFEU' (2014) World Competition 459, 478.
1036. S Bishop and M Walker, *The economics of EC competition law* (Sweet & Maxwell 2010) 304.

[B] The Relevance of *Mens Rea* in Punishing Infringements

738 Beyond its role in the interpretation of conduct, I believe *mens rea*, in the sense of subjective intention, can also play a role in determining the punishment of infringements.

739 My discussion of the role of *mens rea* in the punishment of offences will focus on two of the main justifications usually given for the use of punishment: retribution (the more primitive 'getting even') and deterrence (the more enlighted preventive function).[1037] I believe that *mens rea* can play a role for both these functions of punishment, which are together relevant in a 'mixed' justification of punishment.[1038]

740 Often a third function of punishment is cited: reparation/restitution, i.e. to return, as much as possible, to the situation that existed prior to the breach of the law or that would have existed absent the breach of law.[1039] There are indeed arguments to view sanctions under EU competition law as also having a reparatory function, namely that of disgorging the excess profits which the infringing undertaking obtained through the breach of EU antitrust law (and transferring them to the public coffers).[1040] However, the CJEU case law has made it clear that victims of antitrust infringement can also directly claim damages for the losses which they suffered,[1041] for both any actual loss and any loss of profit and interest.[1042] The reparatory function of public enforcement has accordingly diminished and the focus has been on facilitating private enforcement.[1043]

741 Furthermore, any function of restitution which sanctions have is not unique to them: it is the essence of (compensatory) damages for torts (and for breach of contract). It is only to the extent that the law goes beyond such a reparatory function that one can speak of sanctions (as in 'punitive damages'). If they do not go beyond

1037. G Becker, 'Crime and punishment: an economic approach' (1968) Journal of Political Economy 169, 198; C Roxin, *Strafrecht Algemeiner Teil* (Beck 2006) 64-104; J Pradel, *Droit penal general* (Cujas 2016) 521. *See also* the literature in the next footnote.
1038. The debate on the relationship between these two justifications is a particularly thorny issue in ethics which extends beyond the framework of this treatise and I will only touch upon some aspects of this here. *See*, for example, J Rawls, 'Two concepts of rules' (1955) 64 (1) The Philosophical Review 3; EW Strong, 'Justification of juridical punishment' (1969) 79 (3) Ethics 187; HLA Hart, 'Prolegomenon to the principles of punishment' in HLA Hart, *Punishment and responsibility: essays in the philosophy of law* (OUP 1970) 1; AH Goodman, 'The paradox of punishment' (1979) 9 (1) Philosophy & public affairs 42; MN Berman, 'Punishment and justification' (2008) 118 Ethics 258; J Claessen, 'Theories of punishment' in J Keiler and D Roef, *Comparative concepts of criminal law* (Intersentia 2019) 11.
1039. *See*, for example, G Becker, 'Crime and punishment: an economic approach' (1968) Journal of Political Economy 169, 198; J Pradel, *Droit penal general* (Cujas 2016) 521.
1040. *See*, for example, M Merola, J Derenne and J Rivas (eds), *Competition law in times of economic crisis: in need of adjustment* (Bruylant 2013) 124-125.
1041. C-453/99 *Courage and Crehan* ECLI:EU:C:2001:465.
1042. Joined cases C-295 to 298/04 *Manfredi* ECLI:EU:C:2006:461, para. 95.
1043. *See* in particular Directive 2014/104/EU on certain rules governing actions for damages under national law for infringements of the competition law provisions of the Member States and of the European Union [2014] OJ L349/1.

their reparatory function, they merely create a 'price' for certain behaviour[1044] and it becomes difficult to distinguish between crimes and transactions.[1045]

742 Finally, the role of *mens rea* in reparation is clearly more limited. National tort laws usually do not distinguish between intentional and negligent breaches of the rules (and regularly allow for claims based on strict liability). Although there is a distinction in the French *Code civil* between intentionally and negligently causing damage (Article 1382 and 1383 respectively), the two are largely assimilated.[1046] German law even has a single provision, § 276 of the *Bürgerliches Gesetzbuch*, that provides for liability for intentional and negligent acts, with only a limited amount of exceptions.[1047] Under English law, finally, the intention to cause harm is irrelevant for most types of tort and tort liability most commonly arises out of negligence.[1048]

[1] Punishment for Deterrence

743 Before discussing deterrence, I should spend some time considering the question of whether punishment is in fact the best way to deter offences. This is a debate which has a long history, but I will focus here on the debate in regulatory theory on the choice between deterrence (or repression) and compliance (or persuasion). Deterrence is achieved through the classical criminal law approach: law enforcement is aimed at 'detecting violations of law, determining who is responsible for their violation, and penalizing violators to deter violations in the future'.[1049] Compliance strategies, on the other hand, try to prevent violations in the first place by 'attending to conditions that induce conformity or to foreboding of harm'.[1050] While deterrence strategies are 'confrontational' and focus on 'establishing guilt', compliance strategies are characterized by '[b]argaining and negotiation'.[1051] A compliance strategy stresses that the person who is subject to regulation should also be seen as a partner to implement the regulation and not merely as its object.

1044. J Coffee, 'Paradigms lost: the blurring of the criminal and civil models – and what can be done about it' (1992) 101 Yale Law Journal 1875, 1882-1884.
1045. G Becker, 'Crime and punishment: an economic approach' (1968) Journal of Political Economy 169, 197 gives an example of how the two can be equated (although he gives it to demonstrate that fines can be a suitable punishment): 'If a rich man purchases a car and a poor man steals one, the former is congratulated, while the latter is often sent to prison when apprehended. Yet the rich man's purchase is equivalent to a "theft" subsequently compensated by a fine equal to the price of the car, while the poor man, in effect, goes to prison because he cannot pay this "fine".'
1046. *See* F Terré, P Simler and Y Lequette (eds), *Droit Civil. Les Obligations* (Dalloz 2005) 710.
1047. *See* P Schlechtriem and M Schmidt-Kessel, *Schuldrecht Algemeiner Teil* (Mohr Siebeck 2005) 264.
1048. *See* MA Jones, 'Principles of liability in tort' in MA Jones (ed.), *Clerk & Lindsell on torts* (Thomson Reuters 2018) 1, 37-41.
1049. AJ Reiss, 'Selecting strategies of social control over organizational life' in K Hawkins and JM Thomas (eds), *Enforcing regulation* (Kluwer 1984) 23, 23-24.
1050. AJ Reiss, 'Selecting strategies of social control over organizational life' in K Hawkins and JM Thomas (eds), *Enforcing regulation* (Kluwer 1984) 23, 24.
1051. N Gunningham, 'Enforcement and compliance strategies' in R Baldwin, M Cave and M Lodge (eds), *The Oxford handbook of regulation* (OUP 2010) 120, 120-121.

744 In practice, many regulations combine aspects of persuasion and repression since both have their upsides and downsides. Compliance strategies are less costly for regulators to implement and limited efforts to persuade regulated subjects to comply may achieve instant results. However, in the absence of (at least the threat of) repression, regulated subjects (who bear the cost of compliance) will often only take compliance as far as it is in line with their own interests. Compliance strategies without the possibility to move to deterrence strategies then risk being toothless.

745 For this reason, then, in order to achieve compliance, using repression in the sense of punishment is an important tool. This is certainly true of the system of punishment as a whole: it is only because sanctions are sometimes imposed that the threat of sanctions works. But also punishment in individual cases is meant to have a deterrent effect, both for the specific perpetrator who is being punished (specific deterrence) and for other actors who may contemplate engaging in the same behaviour (general deterrence).[1052]

746 I do not mean to call here for a specific enforcement style in antitrust enforcement. EU antitrust law today uses strategies all over the compliance and deterrence spectrum. On the one extreme, the European Commission and NCAs engage in antitrust advocacy. They furthermore can persuade undertakings to change commercial conduct, informally or formally through the use of commitments (in the sense of Article 9 of Regulation 1/2003). At the more deterrent side of the spectrum, there are antitrust fines, based on either settlements agreed with the undertakings involved or imposed unilaterally by an NCA or the Commission (under Article 23 of Regulation 1/2003). In several EU Member States, criminal sanctions (including imprisonment) are also available for the punishment of certain antitrust violations.

747 I do not mean to argue that the range of these enforcement strategies should be changed. My discussion will merely focus on the field where I believe *mens rea* considerations are more important, i.e. on the deterrent side of the spectrum. They are, of course, particularly important in criminal enforcement (*mens rea* being a typical condition for imprisonment)[1053] but, I would argue, also when fines are imposed unilaterally by the Commission or an NCA for breach of the EU antitrust laws. In the

1052. *See also* para. 4 of the Guidelines of 1 September 2006 on the method of setting fines imposed pursuant to Article 23(2)(a) of Regulation No 1/2003 [2006] OJ C210/2.

1053. Certainly in the US: *see* the discussion in paras 125ff. above. As indicated in para. 691 above, since 2013, the UK has a strict liability regime for criminal cartel offences sanctionable with imprisonment, although a defence of publicity is available. It is at least questionable, however, whether the 'dishonesty' requirement that was removed from the law in 2013, as interpreted in *Norris v United States* [2008] UKHL 16, was actually a *mens rea* requirement (as assumed by, for example, A MacCulloch, 'Honesty, morality and the cartel offence' (2007) European Competition Law Review 355, 356 and C Beaton-Wells, 'The politics of cartel criminalisation: a pessimistic view from Australia' (2008) 29 (3) European Competition Law Review 185, 191). Indeed, in *Norris v United States* [2008] UKHL 16, the House of Lords only looked at the first leg of the test described in *R v Ghosh* [1982] QB 1053, assessing the dishonesty requirement in light of the 'ordinary standards of reasonable and honest people' (a negligence standard), not in light of the awareness of the cartelists themselves (intention in its cognitive sense).

increasingly used settlement decisions in cartel cases, *mens rea* is likely to be of less importance than in ordinary fining decisions: while undertakings need to admit that they infringed the cartel prohibition, the decisions are usually short so there is little room for a discussion of *mens rea*. Furthermore, undertakings are likely to resist a detailed discussion of *mens rea* in light of the risk of damage actions.[1054]

[2] Deterrence and Retribution

748 The deterrent effect (D) of punishment for an individual offence is sometimes analysed as the product of the severity of the punishment (P) and the risk of detection (R): D = R x P. This principle can also be expressed more broadly as follows: the number of offences depends on a number of factors, including the chance of detection and the punishment.[1055] The deterrent effect of an antitrust fine can then be determined by multiplying the profit of the antitrust infringement by the likelihood of detection.[1056]

749 This approach to punishment of individual offences has a number of drawbacks, however. In particular, the formula described in paragraph 748 assumes that the chance of detection and the severity of the punishment are communicating vessels, so if the chance of detection is low, the penalty needs to become extremely severe. If the sanction of choice is a monetary penalty, the amount of such penalties needs to be extremely high to compensate for a low chance of detection. In those circumstances, deterrent fines may actually result in the insolvency of the person on which they are imposed. In the field of antitrust in particular, this may result in that person exiting the market, thereby reducing competition. This paradoxical result of sufficiently deterrent

1054. The greater role for *mens rea* in more repressive enforcement strategies is also reflected in the investigative measures usually available in such cases. Indeed, *mens rea* evidence is unlikely to be available when antitrust law is enforced only through private actions (unless there are very effective discovery rules). But even in case of the public enforcement of the antitrust rules – still very much the paradigm in Europe – *mens rea* evidence is only going to be available in case investigative techniques are used that allow for the uncovering of internal documents of the undertakings concerned, either requiring undertakings to hand over internal documents (such as inspections or compulsory information requests under Articles 18 and 20 of Regulation 1/2003 respectively) or at least incentivizing them to do so (such as leniency programmes). One can wonder whether it would not be helpful for this purpose to reinforce the ability of the Commission to take statements from officers and employees under Article 19 of Regulation 1/2003 (a technique currently rarely used) although this would require a balance to be struck with individual (criminal) liability for these individuals (which can invoke the right not to incriminate themselves).

1055. Other factors of course include the illicit gain that can be made. *See* G Becker, 'Crime and punishment: an economic approach' (1968) Journal of Political Economy 169, 177. For a more complete model, *see also* R Galbiati and N Garoupa, 'Keeping stigma out of administrative law: an explanation of consistent beliefs' (2007) 15 Supreme Court Economic Review 273.

1056. Such that deterrence can be achieved if the benefit of the crime is less than the product of the severity of the sanction and the risk of detection, *i.e.* D = B < R × P. *See also* W Wils, 'Optimal antitrust fines: theory and practice' (2006) 29(2) World Competition 183, 190; GJ Werden, 'Sanctioning cartel activity: let the punishment fit the crime' (2009) European Competition Journal 19, 28.

fines is one of the major reasons invoked to justify the imposition of custodial sentences for breaches of antitrust rules.[1057]

750 Furthermore, imposing an extreme penalty on an offender because he is caught for an offence which has a low likelihood of detection does not accord at all with our moral feelings, which are 'indifferent to ... the probability of detection'.[1058] Indeed, imposing a high penalty to compensate for a low risk of detection gives the impression of scapegoating, a well-known problem of all utilitarian theories of punishment.[1059] The impression of scapegoating will be even stronger in case of behaviour which is ambiguous, i.e. if the person that was punished would have had difficulty determining the likely benefits of its conduct and such benefits are only taken into account as effects to set the appropriate level of punishment. If the undertakings did not want or did not expect the practices in question to have a certain effect (but indeed pursued or expected another effect), then punishment (or non-punishment) of the practice could not have been avoided (or obtained) by the undertaking. From the perspective of the undertaking planning its conduct, enforcement will appear entirely arbitrary.

751 It is here that the notion of retribution comes in. The retributive aspect of sanctions distinguishes them from civil damages which, at least in principle, can also have a deterrent effect (namely when the damage caused by the tort to others is greater than the gain obtained by the tortfeasor).

752 Contrary to deterrence which is inherently a forward-looking, consequentialist (and utilitarian) approach to sanctions, retribution looks back at the offence and the person who committed it. When doing so, it 'imports a feeling of blame, and an opinion, however distorted by passion that a wrong has been done'.[1060] I agree with Oliver Wendell Holmes that retribution is the original function of sanctions: 'vengeance, not compensation, and vengeance on the offending thing, was the original object'.[1061] Such vengeance could even be directed at objects: 'The ox in Exodus was to

1057. *See*, for example, C Parker, 'The "compliance" trap: the moral message in responsive regulatory enforcement' (2006) 40 (3) Law & Society Review 591, 596-597; W Wils, 'Is criminalization of EU competition law the answer?' in KJ Cseres, MP Schinkel and FOW Vogelaar (eds), *Criminalization of competition law enforcement: economic and legal implications for the EU Member States* (Edward Elgar 2006) 60, 78-81; GJ Werden, 'Sanctioning cartel activity: let the punishment fit the crime' (2009) European Competition Journal 19, 30.

1058. CR Sunstein, 'On the psychology of punishment' (2004) 11 Supreme Court Economic Review 171, 174 bases this on social experiments where respondents were asked to sanction identical offences with different probabilities of detection and to approve or disapprove of judicial decisions taking into account the probability of detection in the severity of the sanction.

1059. *See* HJ McCloskey, 'A non-utilitarian approach to punishment' (1965) 8 Inquiry: An Interdisciplinary Journal of Philosophy 249. Because of this objection, J Rawls, 'Two concepts of rules' (1955) 64 (1) The Philosophical Review 3, in particular 5-6 has argued that the utilitarian view of punishment is more fundamental to punishment as an institution, whereas for punishment in individual instances, the retributive view is more suitable. *See also* HLA Hart, 'Prolegomenon to the principles of punishment' in HLA Hart, *Punishment and responsibility: essays in the philosophy of law* (OUP 1970) 1.

1060. OW Holmes, *The Common Law*, Lecture I: Early forms of liability (first published 1881, Belknap 2009) 5.

1061. OW Holmes, *The Common Law*, Lecture I: Early forms of liability (first published 1881, Belknap 2009) 33.

be stoned. The axe in the Athenian law was to be banished.'[1062] Although contemporary theories of punishment focus more on its objective of deterrence, at its origin punishment may just have been retribution.[1063] Even today, humans appear to be 'intuitive retributivists'.[1064]

753 The retributive aspect of sanctions for antitrust infringement is probably the most neglected in the case law and the literature,[1065] which may in a large part be due to the dominant economic approach to penalties in general and antitrust penalties in particular, which focuses on the deterrent function of sanctions.

[3] The Role of Mens Rea *in Retribution*

754 It is the retributive aspect of punishment that most obviously warrants taking into account *mens rea*: taking into account the intentions and knowledge of the person who is punished can counteract the feeling of being scapegoated. Persons can expect that if they have innocent intentions, they will be dealt with clemently by enforcers, while if they have sinister motives, the law will fall hard on them. The retributive aspects of punishment then imply that blameless offenders are dealt with clemently and that intentional offenders are punished more severely.

755 Our sense of natural justice seems to imply that intentionally caused harm deserves greater punishment. As already discussed in Chapter 1, there is empirical evidence that human beings judge the actions of others by reference to their intentions and are willing to punish intentional harm more severely than accidental harm (even if the extent of the harm caused accidentally is greater than the extent of the harm caused intentionally).

756 I would therefore argue that it is innate in humans to connect human action with the volitional and cognitive elements of the persons engaging in them – which in the criminal law means connecting *actus reus* with *mens rea*. Punishing the blameworthy (more severely) and being lenient with the innocent therefore corresponds to our natural sense of justice.[1066]

757 Also in the field of antitrust law this is relevant. If antitrust enforcement is based purely on economic policy, it 'could be widely perceived as unfair and wrong unless

1062. OW Holmes, *The Common Law*, Lecture I: Early forms of liability (first published 1881, Belknap 2009) 33.
1063. RA Robson, 'Crime and punishment: rehabilitating retribution as a justification for organizational criminal liability' (2010) American Business Journal 109, 110, footnote 7 distinguishes between vengeance and retribution where the first is unconstrained by the blameworthiness of the object of the vengeance and the latter is proportionate to the magnitude of the offence.
1064. CR Sunstein, 'On the psychology of punishment' (2004) 11 Supreme Court Economic Review 171, 175.
1065. Even the author of these words did not mention it when contributing to M Merola, J Derenne and J Rivas (eds), *Competition law in times of economic crisis: in need of adjustment* (Bruylant 2013): *see* in particular 120-125.
1066. W Chan and AP Simester, 'Four functions of mens rea' (2011) Cambridge Law Journal 381 consider that this is implied in the 'fair warning' function of *mens rea*.

the government can frame the policy so as to fit most comfortably with society's moral intuitions'.[1067] The limited empirical research that has been done into people's perceptions towards antitrust infringements similarly suggests that they believe that punishment for such infringements is justified more because of the dishonest character of such conduct than because of its adverse economic effects.[1068]

758 Second, beyond reflecting our natural sense of justice, *mens rea* is also relevant because of the stigma that punishment entails. Punishment indeed entails a sign of disapproval which is most obvious in the case of the criminal law.[1069] Contrary to an (unfavourable) tort judgment which carries 'no corresponding stigma',[1070] a sanction, certainly under the criminal law, expresses moral opprobrium about the transgression of the law. In the case of administrative or civil sanctions (e.g. punitive damages), there will be some expression of moral condemnation as well, although it may not be as serious as in the case of a criminal conviction.[1071]

759 This is also true in antitrust law. The stigma of punishment most obviously attaches to criminal prosecution, as in the US.[1072] But also in EU antitrust law, where fines are not part of the core of the criminal law but nevertheless quasi-criminal, this mechanism is at play. Condemnation under the EU antitrust rules also stigmatizes the penalized undertaking,[1073] and it is no surprise that there is an increased awareness of this in Europe where, contrary to the US, the 'demonization' of antitrust infringement (and particularly cartels) is more recent.[1074]

760 Delivering the stigma of punishment in the absence of blameworthiness undermines society's trust in the legal system. Punishment for guiltless behaviour just

1067. ME Stucke, 'Morality and antitrust' (2006) Columbia Business Law Review 443, 488.
1068. *See* C Beaton-Wells, 'Justifying criminal sanctions for cartel conduct: a hard case' (2012) Journal of Antitrust Enforcement 1, 16.
1069. *See* HM Hart, 'The aims of the criminal law' (1958) Law and Contemporary Problems 401, throughout but in particular 405, 409 and 424. *See also* RA Posner, 'An economic theory of the criminal law' (1985) 85(6) Columbia Law Review 1193; W Wils, 'Is criminalization of EU competition law the answer?' in KJ Cseres, MP Schinkel and FOW Vogelaar (eds), *Criminalization of competition law enforcement: economic and legal implications for the EU Member States* (Edward Elgar 2006) 60, 62-63 and W Wils, 'Optimal antitrust fines: theory and practice' (2006) 29(2) World Competition 183, 189.
1070. RA Posner, 'An economic theory of the criminal law' (1985) 85(6) Columbia Law Review 1193, 1205. R Bouscant, 'La faute dans les infractions aux règles de concurrence en droit européen' (2000) 36 (1) Revue trimesterielle de droit européen 67, 82-83 nevertheless sees a '*coloration punitive*' in damage awards.
1071. *See* CR Sunstein, 'On the psychology of punishment' (2004) 11 Supreme Court Economic Review 171; R Galbiati and N Garoupa, 'Keeping stigma out of administrative law: an explanation of consistent beliefs' (2007) 15 Supreme Court Economic Review 273.
1072. *See* R Hofstadter, 'What happened to the antitrust movement?' in *The paranoid style in American politics* (first published 1965, Vintage 2008) 188, 234-235.
1073. As pointed out by the General Court in T-442/08 *CISAC v Commission* ECLI:EU:T:2013:188, para. 95 and T-691/14 *Servier and Others v Commission* ECLI:EU:T:2018:922, para. 792 and by AG Kokott in her opinion in C-681/11 *Schenker & Co. and Others* ECLI:EU:C:2013:126, para. 59.
1074. *See* C Harding, 'Business cartels as a criminal activity: reconciling North American and European models of regulation' (2002) 9(4) Maastricht Journal of European and Comparative Law 393, in particular 413-415.

because such behaviour is 'undesirable' will appear arbitrary and such over-criminalization diminishes the moral stigma that attaches to a criminal conviction.[1075] For example, if an undertaking did not or could not and should not have foreseen that its conduct would result in a restriction of competition, it could not be blamed for such a restriction of competition. Such behaviour is morally neutral and any punishment for it will not accord with our moral understanding. Disjoining punishment from morality undermines moral support for punishment. Sanctions for corporate misconduct then simply become 'a cost of doing business'.[1076]

761 It is indeed precisely because of this moral opprobrium that the axiom *actus non facit reum nisi mens sit rea* was introduced: one should not be punished for a harmful act unless one has committed it with a blameworthy mind (intentionally, recklessly, etc.). It may well be that in the past even objects could suffer the stigma of punishment (as in the ox and the axe in Holmes' example discussed above). But these days everyone agrees that it is pretty pointless to ascribe blame to objects and vengeance is rarely a good guide to policy. As indicated earlier, it is important that the circularity of a *procès d'intentions* is avoided: blame should not be assigned because of punishment but punishment should be administered because of blame. Hence, any relevance that intent may have in qualifying or punishing conduct should be based on *other* evidence of intent than the conduct itself, and not be a mere attribution of blame based on the conduct.

[4] The Role of Mens Rea *in Deterrence*

762 But I would argue that taking into account *mens rea* also makes sense for the deterrent function of punishment, in terms of both general and specific deterrence.

763 As already indicated in paragraph 750, if undertakings did not want or did not expect their practices to have a certain effect (but indeed pursued or expected another effect), then punishment (or non-punishment) of the practice could not have been avoided (or obtained) by the undertaking. In those circumstances, it is questionable whether any deterrent effect will have been achieved through punishment since it will be similarly unclear for future offenders that they are engaging in the prohibited conduct. On the contrary, it is only because the offenders knew that what they were doing had certain consequences (and therefore could expect it to result in punishment) that they could choose to avoid engaging in the conduct.

764 Furthermore, the stigmatizing function of punishment provides a feedback effect to deterrence, through the internalization of the stigma. This internalization does not just affect the perpetrator or potential perpetrators – on the contrary, it may well be most important for the spontaneous law-abiding citizen whose commitment to the law

1075. ME Stucke, 'Morality and antitrust' (2006) Columbia Business Law Review 443, 536. *See also* HM Hart, 'The aims of the criminal law' (1958) Law and Contemporary Problems 401, throughout but in particular 405, 421.

1076. RA Robson, 'Crime and punishment: rehabilitating retribution as a justification for organizational criminal liability' (2010) American Business Journal 109, 135.

is reinforced by the moral opprobrium that attaches to its transgression.[1077] The stigma therefore serves general deterrence.

765 In the case of economic offences such as antitrust violations this is also the case. Indeed, corporate managers are not merely profit maximizers: they are also moral beings and as such will have a tendency to obey the law and not to infringe it.[1078] If managers perceive that others intentionally infringe the antitrust rules, this will diminish the social stigma that comes with infringing those rules: higher fines express higher moral condemnation to counter this effect.[1079]

766 It is this aspect of *mens rea* which has made several scholars argue for the punishment of inchoate offences under antitrust law (*see also* paragraphs 733-734 above). Odudu has argued that a subjective intention to enter into anticompetitive agreements or concerted practices should be punishable. He argues that in those cases a subjective intention to restrict competition is present and this should be sufficient to find an infringement of Article 101 TFEU: 'The rationale for intervention when there is a subjective intention to restrict competition is that without such intervention, the parties will eventually succeed in their attempts.'[1080] Odudu and others with him argue that equating object restrictions with subjective intentions allows for the punishment of attempt – in Wendt's words: 'The punitive rationale behind the prohibition of "object restrictions" is the classical justification in criminal law for punishing attempts.'[1081]

767 Regardless of how far one believes EU antitrust law does or should go to prohibit or punish inchoate offences (e.g. attempt), the logic of deterrence still holds: undertakings, which actually want or expect anticompetitive consequences from their actions, are more likely to engage in anticompetitive agreements or conduct in the future. Odudu therefore claims that Article 101 TFEU 'should prevent future misconduct where the parties to the agreement have demonstrated it is likely to occur, particularly since the line between success and failure may be slight'.[1082] This principle also holds if it is applied only in the cases where the infringement has been brought to its final conclusion and has produced its anticompetitive effects and *mens rea* is therefore only considered to be relevant for sanctioning. This is indeed the view

1077. *See* W Wils, 'The European Commission's 2006 guidelines on antitrust fines: a legal and economic analysis' (2007) World Competition 195, 201. *See also* ME Stucke, 'Morality and antitrust' (2006) Columbia Business Law Review 443, 511 and HM Hart, 'The aims of the criminal law' (1958) Law and Contemporary Problems 401, throughout but in particular 405, 409.

1078. W Wils, 'Is criminalization of EU competition law the answer?' in KJ Cseres, MP Schinkel and FOW Vogelaar (eds), *Criminalization of competition law enforcement: economic and legal implications for the EU Member States* (Edward Elgar 2006) 60, 84.

1079. W Wils, 'The European Commission's 2006 guidelines on antitrust fines: a legal and economic analysis' (2007) World Competition 195, 223.

1080. O Odudu, 'Interpreting Article 81(1): the object requirement revisited' (2001) European Law Review 379, 388.

1081. IF Wendt, *EU competition law and liberal professions: an uneasy relationship?* (Martinus Nijhoff, 2012), 259-260.

1082. O Odudu, 'Interpreting Article 81(1): object as subjective intention' (2001) European Law Review 60, 70.

adopted by Akman in relation to Article 102 TFEU: even though she believes intent should not be material for the determination of the offence, she accepts that '[f]or the purposes of deterrence, it is indeed important to distinguish between infringements committed intentionally, negligently or innocently' and to take this into account for the purpose of setting fines.[1083]

768 In case intentionality is combined with awareness of the illegality of the conduct, there is an additional reason to increase fines: undertakings that are aware that what they are doing is illegal are more likely to conceal their behaviour and therefore face a lower risk of detection. As Wils points out 'those who deliberately infringe the law generally have more opportunity to hide their tracks. They thus face a lower probability of detection and should therefore be fined more heavily for deterrence to occur'.[1084]

769 Both the retributive and the deterrent aspects of punishments then militate for taking into account *mens rea* in punishment. Under European competition law, as it stands, this would mean modulating the fine to reflect the presence or absence of subjective intention (i.e. awareness of the anticompetitive effects of the practice) and of awareness of illegality.

770 In principle, such awareness is a factor which is individual to an offender and should therefore be taken into account as an attenuating or aggravating factor under the Commission's *2006 Fining Guidelines*. Negligence is already listed there as a mitigating factor but, as discussed earlier, it is rarely used. I believe that it may be worthwhile to add intentionality as an aggravating factor for the fine. If there is evidence of anticompetitive intentions, the fine can then be increased. If there is evidence of procompetitive intentions (or of the complete lack of any anticompetitive intentions), the fine can be reduced. If the evidence does not point either way, no aggravating or mitigating factor should be used.

771 In terms of the level of the possible increase or reduction of the fine, I think the complete lack of anticompetitive intentions (i.e. the good faith of the undertaking concerned) should possibly lead to a full exemption from fines. For example, if an undertaking engages in a practice which it apparently believes to be procompetitive but which, after the fact, turns out to be anticompetitive (e.g. on the basis of an economic analysis of the effects), then such an exemption from fines could be justified, from both a preventive and retributive perspective. Reversely, an undertaking which evidently engaged in a practice with anticompetitive intentions should be punished significantly more severely than an undertaking for which the intentions are unclear or ambiguous.

1083. P Akman, 'The role of intent in the EU case law on abuse of dominance' (2014) European Law Review 316, 337.
1084. W Wils, 'The European Commission's 2006 guidelines on antitrust fines: a legal and economic analysis' (2007) World Competition 195, 223.

§5.05 CONCLUSION

772 The diversity of opinions in the case law of the European Courts about the relevance of *mens rea*, in the sense of intention, for the establishment and punishment of antitrust offences, is matched by the diversity of opinions in the literature on the subject.

773 Although critics of the use of *mens rea* evidence point to some serious risks and shortcomings when so-called intent evidence is relied upon in antitrust cases, I believe these risks and shortcomings are limited or at least manageable.

774 First of all, although there may be a risk of circularity in reliance on alleged intent evidence, this is only the case if the intent is directly derived from the conduct and the conduct subsequently interpreted in light of the intent. However, if the intention is derived from other conduct or is deduced from the absence of legitimate explanations for the conduct, the charge of circularity does not arise. In any event, circularity is not an issue when evidence of subjective intentions, in the sense of internal documents, is used.

775 Second, although it is not always easy to distinguish between good and bad subjective intentions, it is similarly difficult to distinguish between good and bad commercial conduct. Caution should therefore be exercised when relying on evidence of subjective intentions, but such evidence can be an additional piece in the puzzle of assessing conduct in light of the antitrust rules.

776 Third, although it is possible that evidence of bad intentions is concealed or that sophisticated firms avoid creating it, this is also true of the actions of firms. The more sophisticated a firm is, the more difficult it may be to obtain evidence of unlawful actions and evidence of unlawful intentions, but that should not stop authorities from considering either of these when they are available.

777 Fourth, although care should be taken when ascribing subjective intentions of individual employees or corporate officers to the undertaking as a whole, it is possible to come up with criteria to determine the reliability of individual subjective intentions for the policy of the firm. These include the seniority of the person, her field of responsibility, the pervasiveness of the views and the existence or absence of contradictory views, etc.

778 Finally, although the lawfulness or illegality of conduct cannot depend entirely on the undertaking's opinion of it, that does not mean that such an opinion should not be relevant at all in the assessment. Especially after several decades of antitrust enforcement, also in Europe, the opinions of undertakings may well reflect society's understanding of what is lawful and what is not.

779 I think there are strong arguments that militate for taking into account *mens rea* evidence in antitrust investigations, both to determine whether an infringement took place and to determine the sanction for such an infringement.

780 For the first of these uses of *mens rea* evidence, it is worth considering that the economic analysis of the effects of commercial conduct often does not suffice to conclude whether the conduct is anticompetitive or not. There are simply too many empirical uncertainties and, in addition, it is preferable that antitrust enforcement intervenes before any anticompetitive effects arise.

781 Evidence of subjective intentions can be helpful to interpret commercial behaviour since no one is better positioned to predict the likely consequences of an undertaking's conduct than that undertaking itself. *Mens rea* evidence can then be used to interpret the many types of commercial behaviour which economic analysis does not conclusively categorize as procompetitive or anticompetitive.

782 *Mens rea* evidence is also relevant for the punishment of antitrust offences. Without pronouncing myself on the necessity to always proceed to punishment in the case of a breach of the antitrust rules (sometimes other measures may be more suitable to ensure compliance), if sanctions are being considered, *mens rea* should be taken into account.

783 Indeed, in order to avoid the problem of scapegoating when determining sanctions, authorities should take into account whether the violator knew that the conduct he engaged in violated the antitrust laws or at least harmed competition. This fits with our natural sense of justice and the stigma that comes with condemnation should only be administered to those that are sufficiently blameworthy.

784 Furthermore, also for the deterrent aspects of punishment, it makes sense to consider whether the infringer was aware that what he was doing was wrong since otherwise it would have been difficult for him to avoid it and little deterrence can be achieved. From the perspective of general deterrence, the stigma of punishment only works if the stigma can be internalized and in that way ensure compliance. And from the perspective of specific deterrence, punishing intentional offenders more severely makes sense since they are more likely to reoffend.

Table of Judgments, Opinions and Decisions

European Court of Justice

Court of First Instance / General Court

Advocate General Opinions

Commission Decisions

US Case Law

UK Case Law

Australian Case Law

European Court and Commission of Human Rights

Table of Legislation

European Union

Legislation

Policy documents

International treaties

US legislation

French legislation

German legislation

UK legislation

Index

F

G

H

I

L

M

N

INTERNATIONAL COMPETITION LAW SERIES

1. Ignacio De Leon, *Latin American Competition Law and Policy: A Policy in Search of Identity*, 2001 (ISBN 90-411-1542-0).
2. Wim Dejonghe & Wouter Van de Voorde (eds), *M & A in Belgium*, 2001 (ISBN 90-411-1594-3).
3. Yang-Ching Chao, Gee San, Changfa Lo & Jiming Ho (eds), *International and Comparative Competition Law and Policies*, 2001 (ISBN 90-411-1643-5).
4. Martin Mendelsohn & Stephen Rose, *Guide to the EC Block Exemption for Vertical Agreements*, 2002 (ISBN 90-411-9813-X).
5. Clifford A. Jones & Mitsuo Matsushita (eds), *Competition Policy in the Global Trading System: Perspectives from the EU, Japan and the USA*, 2002 (ISBN 90-411-1758-X).
6. Christian Koenig, Andreas Bartosch, Jens-Daniel Braun & Marion Romes (eds), *EC Competition and Telecommunications Law*. Second Edition, 2009 (ISBN 978-90-411-2564-4).
7. Jürgen Basedow (ed.), *Limits and Control of Competition with a View to International Harmonization*, 2002 (ISBN 90-411-1967-1).
8. Maureen Brunt, Economic Essays on Australian and New Zealand Competition Law, 2003 (ISBN 90-411-1991-4).
9. Ky P. Ewing, Jr., *Competition Rules for the 21st Century: Principles from America's Experience*, Second Edition, 2006 (ISBN 90-411-2477-2).
10. Joseph Wilson, *Globalization and the Limits of National Merger Control Laws*, 2003 (ISBN 90-411-1996-5).
11. Peter Verloop & Valérie Landes (eds), *Merger Control in Europe: EU, Member States and Accession States*, Fourth Edition, 2003 (ISBN 90-411-2056-4).
12. Themistoklis K. Giannakopoulos, *Safeguarding Companies' Rights in Competition and Anti-dumping/Anti-subsidies Proceedings*, Second Edition, 2011 (ISBN 978-90-411-3404-2).
13. Marjorie Holmes & Lesley Davey (eds), *A Practical Guide to National Competition Rules across Europe*, Second Edition, 2007 (ISBN 978-90- 411-2607-8).
14. Sigrid Stroux, *US and EU Oligopoly Control*, 2004 (ISBN 90-411-2296-6).
15. Tzong-Leh Hwang and Chiyuan Chen (eds), *The Future Development of Competition Framework*, 2004 (ISBN 90-411-2305-9).

16. Phedon Nicolaides, Mihalis Kekelekis and Maria Kleis, *State Aid Policy in the European Community: Principles and Practice,* Second Edition, 2008 (ISBN 978-90-411-2754-9).
17. Doris Hildebrand, *Economic Analyses of Vertical Agreements: A Self- Assessment*, 2005 (ISBN 90-411-2328-8).
18. Frauke Henning-Bodewig, *Unfair Competition Law: European Union and Member States*, 2005 (ISBN 90-411-2329-6).
19. Duarte Brito & Margarida Catalão-Lopes, *Mergers and Acquisitions: The Industrial Organization Perspective,* 2006 (ISBN 90-411-2451-9).
20. Nikos Th. Nikolinakos, *EU Competition Law and Regulation in the Converging Telecommunications, Media and IT Sectors*, 2006 (ISBN 90-411- 2469-1).
21. Mihalis Kekelekis, *The EC Merger Control Regulation: Rights of Defence. A Critical Analysis of DG COMP Practice and Community Courts' Jurisprudence*, 2006 (ISBN 90-411-2553-1).
22. Mark R. Joelson, *An International Antitrust Primer: A Guide to the Operation of United States, European Union and Other Key Competition Laws in the Global Economy*, Third Edition, 2006 (ISBN 90-411-2468-3).
23. Themistoklis K. Giannakopoulos, *A Concise Guide to the EU Anti-dumping/ Anti-subsidies Procedures*, 2006 (ISBN 90-411-2464-0).
24. George Cumming, Brad Spitz & Ruth Janal, *Civil Procedure Used for Enforcement of EC Competition Law by the English, French and German Civil Courts*, 2007 (ISBN 978-90-411-2471-5).
25. Jürgen Basedow (ed.), *Private Enforcement of EC Competition Law,* 2007 (ISBN 978-90-411-2613-9).
26. Jung Wook Cho, *Innovation and Competition in the Digital Network Economy: A Legal and Economic Assessment on Multi-tying Practices and Network Effects*, 2007 (ISBN 978-90-411-2574-3).
27. Akira Inoue, *Japanese Antitrust Law Manual: Law, Cases and Interpretation of the Japanese Antimonopoly Act*, 2007 (ISBN 978-90-411-2627-6).
28. René Barents, *Directory of EC Case Law on Competition,* 2007 (ISBN 978-90-411-2656-6).
29. Paul F. Nemitz (ed.), *The Effective Application of EU State Aid Procedures: The Role of National Law and Practice*, 2007 (ISBN 978-90-411-2657-3).
30. Jurian Langer, *Tying and Bundling as a Leveraging Concern under EC Competition Law,* 2007 (ISBN 978-90-411-2575-0).
31. Abel M. Mateus & Teresa Moreira (eds), *Competition Law and Economics – Advances in Competition Policy and Antitrust Enforcement,* 2007 (ISBN 978-90-411-2632-0).
32. Alberto Santa Maria, *Competition and State Aid: An Analysis of the EC Practice*, 2007 (ISBN 978-90-411-2617-7).
33. Barry J. Rodger (ed.), *Article 234 and Competition Law: An Analysis,* 2007 (ISBN 978-90-411-2605-4).

34. Alla Pozdnakova, *Liner Shipping and EU Competition Law,* 2008 (ISBN 978-90-411-2717-4).
35. Milena Stoyanova, *Competition Problems in Liberalized Telecommunications: Regulatory Solutions to Promote Effective Competition*, 2008 (ISBN 978-90-411-2736-5).
36. *EC State Aid Law/Le Droit des Aides d'Etat dans la CE. Liber Amicorum Francisco Santaolalla Gadea*, 2008 (ISBN 978-90-411-2774-7).
37. René Barents, *Directory of EU Case Law on State Aids,* Third Edition, 2019 (ISBN 978-94-035-1101-6).
38. Ignacio De Leon, *An Institutional Assessment of Antitrust Policy: The Latin American Experience*, 2009 (ISBN 978-90-411-2478-4).
39. Doris Hildebrand, *The Role of Economic Analysis in EU Competition Law: The European School*, Fourth Edition, 2016 (ISBN 978-90-411-6245-8).
40. Eugène Buttigieg, *Competition Law: Safeguarding the Consumer Interest. A Comparative Analysis of US Antitrust Law and EC Competition Law*, 2009 (ISBN 978-90-411-3119-5).
41. Ioannis Lianos & Ioannis Kokkoris (eds), *The Reform of EC Competition Law: New Challenges,* 2010 (ISBN 978-90-411-2692-4).
42. George Cumming & Mirjam Freudenthal, *Civil Procedure in EU Competition Cases before the English and Dutch Courts*, 2010 (ISBN 978-90-411-3192-8).
43. A.E. Rodriguez & Ashok Menon, *The Limits of Competition Policy: The Shortcomings of Antitrust in Developing and Reforming Economies*, 2010 (ISBN 978-90-411-3177-5).
44. Mika Oinonen, *Does EU Merger Control Discriminate against Small Market Companies? Diagnosing the Argument with Conclusions*, 2010 (ISBN 978-90-411-3261-1).
45. Eirik Østerud, *Identifying Exclusionary Abuses by Dominant Undertakings under EU Competition Law: The Spectrum of Tests*, 2010 (ISBN 978-90-411-3271-0).
46. Marco Botta, *Merger Control Regimes in Emerging Economies: A Case Study on Brazil and Argentina*, 2011 (ISBN 978-90-411-3402-8).
47. Jürgen Basedow & Wolfgang Wurmnest (eds), *Structure and Effects in EU Competition Law: Studies on Exclusionary Conduct and State Aid*, 2011 (ISBN 978-90-411-3174-4).
48. George Cumming (ed.), *Merger Decisions and the Rules of Procedure of the European Community Courts*, 2012 (ISBN 978-90-411-3671-8).
49. Eduardo Molan Gaban & Juliana Oliveira Domingues (eds), *Antitrust Law in Brazil: Fighting Cartels,* 2012 (ISBN 978-90-411-3670-1).
50. Giandonato Caggiano, Gabriella Muscolo & Marina Tavassi (eds), *Competition Law and Intellectual Property: A European Perspective,* 2012 (ISBN 978-90-411-3447-9).
51. Ben Van Rompuy, *Economic Efficiency: The Sole Concern of Modern Antitrust Policy? Non-efficiency Considerations under Article 101 TFEU*, 2012 (ISBN 978-90-411-3870-5).

52. Liyang Hou, *Competition Law and Regulation of the EU Electronic Communications Sector: A Comparative Legal Approach*, 2012 (ISBN 978-90-411-4047-0).
53. Barry Rodger, *Landmark Cases in Competition Law: Around the World in Fourteen Stories*, 2012 (ISBN 978-90-411-3843-9).
54. Andreas Scordamaglia-Tousis, *EU Cartel Enforcement: Reconciling Effective Public Enforcement with Fundamental Rights*, 2013 (ISBN 978-90-411-4758-5).
55. Bernardo Cortese (ed.), *EU Competition Law: Between Public and Private Enforcement*, 2014 (ISBN 978-90-411-4677-9).
56. Barry Rodger (ed.), *Competition Law: Comparative Private Enforcement and Collective Redress across the EU*, 2014 (ISBN 978-90-411-4559-8).
57. Nada Ina Pauer, *The Single Economic Entity Doctrine and Corporate Group Responsibility in European Antitrust Law*, 2014 (ISBN 978-90-411-5262-6).
58. Urška Petrovčič, *Competition Law and Standard Essential Patents: A Transatlantic Perspective*, 2014 (ISBN 978-90-411-4960-2).
59. David Telyas, *The Interface between Competition Law, Patents and Technical Standards*, 2014 (ISBN 978-90-411-5418-7).
60. Katerina Maniadaki, *EU Competition Law, Regulation and the Internet: The Case of Net Neutrality*, 2014 (ISBN 978-90-411-4140-8).
61. Horacio Vedia Jerez, *Competition Law Enforcement and Compliance across the World: A Comparative Review*, 2015 (ISBN 978-90-411-5815-4).
62. Kadir Ba, *The Substantive Appraisal of Joint Ventures under the EU Merger Control Regime*, 2015 (ISBN 978-90-411-5816-1).
63. Alberto Santa Maria, *Competition and State Aid: An Analysis of the EU Practice*, Second Edition, 2015 (ISBN 978-90-411-5818-5).
64. Lúcio Tomé Feteira, *The Interplay between European and National Competition Law after Regulation 1/2003: "United (Should) We Stand?"*, 2016 (ISBN 978-90-411-5663-1).
65. Giovanni Pitruzzella & Gabriella Muscolo (eds), *Competition and Patent Law in the Pharmaceutical Sector: An International Perspective*, 2016 (ISBN 978-90-411-5927-4).
66. Małgorzata Cyndecka, *The Market Economy Investor Test in EU State Aid Law: Applicability and Application*, 2016 (ISBN 978-90-411-6102-4).
67. Damiano Canapa, *Trademarks and Brands in Merger Control: An Analysis of the European and Swiss Legal Orders*, 2016 (ISBN 978-90-411-6717-0).
68. Inge Graef, *EU Competition Law, Data Protection and Online Platforms: Data as Essential Facility*, 2016 (ISBN 978-90-411-8324-8).
69. Anders Jessen, *Exclusionary Abuse after the* Post Danmark I *Case: The Role of the Effects-Based Approach under Article 102 TFEU*, 2017 (ISBN 978-90-411-8996-7).
70. Baskaran Balasingham, *The EU Leniency Policy: Reconciling Effectiveness and Fairness*, 2017 (ISBN 978-90-411-8479-5).
71. Eugene Stuart & Iana Roginska-Green, *Sixty Years of EU State Aid Law and Policy: Analysis and Assessment*, 2018 (ISBN 978-90-411-8869-4).

72. Anna Renata Pisarkiewicz, *Margin Squeeze in the Electronic Communications Sector: Critical Analysis of the Decisional Practice and Case Law*, 2018 (ISBN 978-90-411-6246-5).
73. Ploykaew Porananond, *Competition Law in the ASEAN Countries: Regional Law and National Systems*, 2018 (ISBN 978-90-411-9102-1).
74. Corinne Ruechardt, *EU State Aid Control of Infrastructure Funding*, 2018 (ISBN 978-90-411-9099-4).
75. Amalia Athanasiadou, *Patent Settlements in the Pharmaceutical Industry under US Antitrust and EU Competition Law*, 2018 (ISBN 978-94-035-0113-0).
76. Miroslava Marinova, *Fidelity Rebates in Competition Law: Application of the 'As Efficient Competitor' Test*, 2018 (ISBN 978-94-035-0570-1).
77. Gabriella Muscolo & Marina Tavassi, *The Interplay Between Competition Law and Intellectual Property: An International Perspective*, 2019 (ISBN 978-90-411-8687-4).
78. Fevzi Toksoy, Bahadir Balki & Hanna Stakheyeva, *Merger Control in the EU and Turkey: A Comparative Guide*, 2019 (ISBN 978-94-035-0934-1).
79. Paulo Burnier da Silveira & William Evan Kovacic (eds), *Global Competition Enforcement: New Players, New Challenges*, 2019 (ISBN 978-94-035-0283-0).
80. Giovanna Massarotto, *Antitrust Settlements: How a Simple Agreement Can Drive the Economy*, 2019 (ISBN 978-94-035-1133-7).
81. Marc Veenbrink, *Criminal Law Principles and the Enforcement of EU and National Competition Law: A Silent Takeover?*, 2020 (ISBN 978-94-035-1434-5).
82. Ferdinand Wollenschläger, Wolfgang Wurmnest & Thomas M.J. Möllers (eds), *Private Enforcement of European Competition and State Aid Law: Current Challenges and the Way Forward*, 2020 (ISBN 978-94-035-0281-6).
83. Jorge Marcos Ramos, *Firm Dominance in EU Competition Law: The Competitive Process and the Origins of Market Power*, 2020 (ISBN 978-94-035-2030-8).
84. Ingrid Margrethe Halvorsen Barlund, *Leniency in EU Competition Law*, 2020 (ISBN 978-94-035-1722-3).
85. Jan Blockx, Mens Rea *in EU Antitrust Law: When Intentions Matter*, 2020 (ISBN 978-94-035-2353-8).

www.ingramcontent.com/pod-product-compliance
Ingram Content Group UK Ltd.
Pitfield, Milton Keynes, MK11 3LW, UK
UKHW020800290926
15470UKWH00003B/875

9 789403 523538